EAGLE VALLEY LIBRARY DISTRICT
P.O. BOX 240   600 BROADWAY
EAGLE, CO 81631   (970) 328-8800

Business
Plans
Handbook

Business Plans

A COMPILATION OF BUSINESS PLANS DEVELOPED BY INDIVIDUALS THROUGHOUT NORTH AMERICA

Handbook

VOLUME

34

**Kristin B. Mallegg,
Project Editor**

GALE
CENGAGE Learning·

Farmington Hills, Mich • San Francisco • New York • Waterville, Maine
Meriden, Conn • Mason, Ohio • Chicago

Business Plans Handbook, Volume 34

Project Editor: Kristin B. Mallegg

Content Developer: Michele P. LaMeau

Product Design: Jennifer Wahi

Composition and Electronic Prepress: Evi Seoud

Manufacturing: Rita Wimberley

For product information and technology assistance, contact us at
Gale Customer Support, 1-800-877-4253.
For permission to use material from this text or product,
submit all requests online at **www.cengage.com/permissions.**
Further permissions questions can be emailed to
permissionrequest@cengage.com

While every effort has been made to ensure the reliability of the information presented in this publication, Gale, a part of Cengage Learning, does not guarantee the accuracy of the data contained herein. Gale accepts no payment for listing; and inclusion in the publication of any organization, agency, institution, publication, service, or individual does not imply endorsement of the editors or publisher. Errors brought to the attention of the publisher and verified to the satisfaction of the publisher will be corrected in future editions.

Gale, a part of Cengage Learning
27500 Drake Rd.
Farmington Hills, MI 48331-3535

ISBN-13: 978-1-4103-1106-1
1084-4473

Printed in Mexico
1 2 3 4 5 6 7 19 18 17 16 15

Contents

CONTENTS

Highlights

Business Plans Handbook, Volume 34 (BPH-34) is a collection of business plans compiled by entrepreneurs seeking funding for small businesses throughout North America. For those looking for examples of how to approach, structure, and compose their own business plans, *BPH-34* presents 20 sample plans, including plans for the following businesses:

- Bartending Service
- Bed and Breakfast
- Chauffeur Service
- Counseling Practice
- Diner
- Drive-Through Coffee Business
- Dry Cleaner
- Engraving and Personalization Services
- Fitness Center
- Home Inventory Business
- Home Staging Business
- Men's Salon & Spa
- Mobile Hair Salon
- Mobile Petting Zoo
- Mural Painting Business
- Outdoor Equipment Rental Business
- Outdoor Sports Instruction Business
- Pet Daycare and Boarding Services
- Pipeline Fracture Testing Service
- Web Development Business

FEATURES AND BENEFITS

BPH-34 offers many features not provided by other business planning references including:

- Twenty business plans, each of which represent an attempt at clarifying (for themselves and others) the reasons that the business should exist or expand and why a lender should fund the enterprise.
- Two fictional plans that are used by business counselors at a prominent small business development organization as examples for their clients. (You will find these in the Business Plan Template Appendix.)

- A directory section that includes listings for venture capital and finance companies, which specialize in funding start-up and second-stage small business ventures, and a comprehensive listing of Service Corps of Retired Executives (SCORE) offices. In addition, the Appendix also contains updated listings of all Small Business Development Centers (SBDCs); associations of interest to entrepreneurs; Small Business Administration (SBA) Regional Offices; and consultants specializing in small business planning and advice. It is strongly advised that you consult supporting organizations while planning your business, as they can provide a wealth of useful information.

- A Small Business Term Glossary to help you decipher the sometimes confusing terminology used by lenders and others in the financial and small business communities.

- A cumulative index, outlining each plan profiled in the complete Business Plans Handbook series.

- A Business Plan Template which serves as a model to help you construct your own business plan. This generic outline lists all the essential elements of a complete business plan and their components, including the Summary, Business History and Industry Outlook, Market Examination, Competition, Marketing, Administration and Management, Financial Information, and other key sections. Use this guide as a starting point for compiling your plan.

- Extensive financial documentation required to solicit funding from small business lenders. You will find examples of Cash Flows, Balance Sheets, Income Projections, and other financial information included with the textual portions of the plan.

Introduction

Perhaps the most important aspect of business planning is simply doing it. More and more business owners are beginning to compile business plans even if they don't need a bank loan. Others discover the value of planning when they must provide a business plan for the bank. The sheer act of putting thoughts on paper seems to clarify priorities and provide focus. Sometimes business owners completely change strategies when compiling their plan, deciding on a different product mix or advertising scheme after finding that their assumptions were incorrect. This kind of healthy thinking and re-thinking via business planning is becoming the norm. The editors of *Business Plans Handbook, Volume 34 (BPH-34)* sincerely hope that this latest addition to the series is a helpful tool in the successful completion of your business plan, no matter what the reason for creating it.

This thirty-fourth volume, like each volume in the series, offers business plans created by real people. *BPH-34* provides 20 business plans. The business and personal names and addresses and general locations have been changed to protect the privacy of the plan authors.

NEW BUSINESS OPPORTUNITIES

As in other volumes in the series, *BPH-34* finds entrepreneurs engaged in a wide variety of creative endeavors. Examples include a bartending service, chauffeur service, drive-through coffee business, and an engraving and personalization service. In addition, several other plans are provided, including a fitness center, a men's salon, and a mobile petting zoo, among others.

Comprehensive financial documentation has become increasingly important as today's entrepreneurs compete for the finite resources of business lenders. Our plans illustrate the financial data generally required of loan applicants, including Income Statements, Financial Projections, Cash Flows, and Balance Sheets.

ENHANCED APPENDIXES

In an effort to provide the most relevant and valuable information for our readers, we have updated the coverage of small business resources. For instance, you will find a directory section, which includes listings of all of the Service Corps of Retired Executives (SCORE) offices; an informative glossary, which includes small business terms; and a cumulative index, outlining each plan profiled in the complete *Business Plans Handbook* series. In addition we have updated the list of Small Business Development Centers (SBDCs); Small Business Administration Regional Offices; venture capital and finance companies, which specialize in funding start-up and second-stage small business enterprises; associations of interest to entrepreneurs; and consultants, specializing in small business advice and planning. For your reference, we have also reprinted the business plan template, which provides a comprehensive overview of the essential components of a business plan and two fictional plans used by small business counselors.

SERIES INFORMATION

If you already have the first thirty-three volumes of *BPH*, with this thirty-fourth volume, you will now have a collection of over 620 business plans (not including the updated plans); contact information for hundreds of organizations and agencies offering business expertise; a helpful business plan template; more than 1,500 citations to valuable small business development material; and a comprehensive glossary of terms to help the business planner navigate the sometimes confusing language of entrepreneurship.

ACKNOWLEDGEMENTS

The Editors wish to sincerely thank the contributors to *BPH-34*, including:

- Fran Fletcher
- Paul Greenland
- Claire Moore
- Zuzu Enterprises

COMMENTS WELCOME

Your comments on *Business Plans Handbook* are appreciated. Please direct all correspondence, suggestions for future volumes of *BPH*, and other recommendations to the following:

Managing Editor, Business Product
Business Plans Handbook
Gale, a part of Cengage Learning
27500 Drake Rd.
Farmington Hills, MI 48331-3535
Phone: (248)699-4253
Fax: (248)699-8052
Toll-Free: 800-347-GALE
E-mail: BusinessProducts@gale.com

Bartending Service
Delta Breeze Bartending Services LLC

321 T Street
Sacramento, CA 95834

Claire Moore

Delta Breeze Bartending Services LLC will be a mobile bartending service established as a limited liability company as of May 2015. The business location will be in Sacramento, California.

EXECUTIVE SUMMARY

Delta Breeze Bartending Services LLC will be formed to bring its customers an entertaining service that will make organizing an event much easier. We will take the stress out of serving beer, wine and spirits by providing tools and equipment, set up and clean up, ice and glassware.

Our bartenders are professional mixologists with a passion for combining elixirs and creating extraordinary cocktails rather than merely mixing great drinks.

Delta Breeze Bartending Services LLC will be a mobile bartending service established as a limited liability company as of May 2015. The business location will be in Sacramento, California.

The head of the Delta Breeze Bartending Services LLC team will be CEO and professional mixologist Jared Wilson. Jared is a graduate of the National Bartenders School in Costa Mesa, California. Jared has fifteen year experience at such venues as Atlantis Casino Resort Spa and Harrah's Reno Hotel and Casino in Reno, Nevada.

The team also includes mixologist Tom Pollock who has twenty year experience tending bar at hotels and upscale restaurants and clubs in Europe and in the U.S. For the past eight years Tom has been teaching high-end bartending, layering techniques, impressive garnishing and cocktail presentation at the ABC Bartending School in Sacramento. Aiding the team will be the firm's accountant, bookkeeper and Michael Brewer of the California Alcoholic Beverage Consulting Service.

The greater Sacramento area includes the cities of El Dorado Hills, Folsom, Granite Bay, Roseville, Rocklin, Elk Grove and Lincoln. Sacramento County alone includes a population of over 1.4 million according the Census Bureau's 2014 estimate.

Delta Breeze Bartending Services LLC services will include standard service fee packages for events with hosted bars where the client is responsible for all alcohols, mixers, beer and wine purchases. We will assist with creating the purchase list.

There are fewer than ten viable mobile bartending services within the greater Sacramento area. The marketing strategy for Delta Breeze Bartending Services LLC will be a combination of networking, newspaper ads, promotion at local events and online publicity including social media.

Delta Breeze Bartending Services LLC is not seeking investment at this time but may wish to pursue additional investment for growth within the next five years.

Mission

Vision: To bring professional high-end mobile bartending service to private events in the greater Sacramento area by providing layered drinks, exotic creations and impeccable customer service.

Mission: Delta Breeze Bartending Services LLC is dedicated to providing a high-end bartending service that ensures a worry-free, entertaining and safe environment for private events.

Organization

Company Name
The legal name is: Delta Breeze Bartending Services LLC.

Legal Form of Business
Delta Breeze Bartending Services LLC is incorporated as an LLC located at the address: 321 T Street, Sacramento, CA 95834.

MANAGEMENT SUMMARY

Delta Breeze Bartending Services LLC will be administered by Jared Wilson as CEO with the aid of Tom Pollock and experienced business professionals: Jacob Northup, CPA, Marilyn Klemp and Michael Brewer. Advisor to the management team will be James Elmhurst, expert mixologist and Head Instructor at the ABC Bartending School of Sacramento.

Jared Wilson, CEO, certified bartender and expert mixologist; graduate of the National Bartending School in Costa Mesa, California, 1999.

Jared is from Los Angeles, California. He worked as a bartender part-time to support himself while attending Los Angeles City College and learned the basics of bartending on the job. Jared earned his certification in bartending in 1999 from the National Bartending School in Costa Mesa, California after graduating from LACC with an associates' degree in business administration.

Jared's bartending experience includes years of experience at venues such as Atlantis Casino Resort Spa and Harrah's Reno Hotel and Casino in Reno, Nevada. Jared currently works for a local casino as a bartender.

Tom Pollock has twenty years' experience tending bar at hotels and upscale restaurants and clubs in Europe and in the U.S. For the past eight years Tom has been teaching high end bartending, layering techniques, impressive garnishing and cocktail presentation at the ABC Bartending School in Sacramento.

Both Jared and Tom have TIPS Certification. TIPS (Training for Intervention Procedures) is the global leader in education and training for the responsible service, sale and consumption of alcohol. TIPS is a skills-based program that is designed to prevent intoxication, underage drinking, and driving drunk.

Advisory Committee

Michael Brewer of the California Alcoholic Beverage Consulting Service has 25 years' experience helping clients obtain the appropriate license for operation within California. Michael is also the co-founder of License Locators, one of California's largest liquor license brokerage firms.

Jacob Northup, CPA has provided tax, accounting and management advisory services to individuals and businesses in the Sacramento area for the past 26 years.

AAA Bookkeeping Service: Marilyn Klemp is an independent bookkeeper with 15 years' experience in providing bookkeeping services to businesses in Sacramento. Marilyn will compile monthly accounting data and create information reports to management for review and preparation of required tax reports.

Location

Delta Breeze Bartending Services LLC is located and operated out of Jared Wilson's home at 321 T Street, Sacramento, CA 95834. Daily operations require a telephone, fax machine, copier, computer and printer. QuickBooks accounting software will be used to track the company's accounting. Mobile apps that integrate with the QuickBooks software will allow for billing in the field. We have signed up for Intuit's payroll service to allow for quick and easy payroll preparation, payroll tax filings and payment of payroll taxes.

AAA Bookkeeping Service has been contracted to compile monthly accounting data, create monthly financial statements, and review payroll tax filings. Jacob Northup, CPA will review accounting data on a quarterly basis and provide advice on income tax planning and tax compliance as well as oversight regarding maintenance of our LLC status.

PERSONNEL PLAN

Jared Wilson and Tom Pollock will manage the company. Jared's responsibilities will include: vendor relations, accounting and personnel management and bartending. Tom's responsibilities will include: marketing, client services and bartending.

Both Jared and Tom will continue to work in their day jobs for the first two years of operation while the company establishes its brand. They will gradually transition to at least half-time in year two and full time by year 5.

Because most events hosted by individuals take place on evenings and weekends, we expect that this strategy will work in the short term. However, Delta Breeze Bartending Services LLC plans to develop business and corporate clients as well. Tom's teaching schedule allows him the flexibility to meet with client prospects during the day and to network at business events.

During the first three years, bartenders and bar backs will be hired on an as-needed basis. We hope to convert these part-timers to full-time workers beginning in year three.

Delta Breeze Bartending Services LLC plans to gradually take on more bartenders and assistants as the business grows. All bartenders will be required to have TIPS training and will be covered under the firms' liability insurance policy.

Bartender: Bartenders will work with clients to create drink menus and shopping lists. Event services will include setup and cleanup of the bar and supervision of bartender assistants.

Bartender assistants: Assistants will work under the supervision of the bartender in setup, clean up, bussing tables and bar back activities.

SERVICES

Delta Breeze Bartending Services LLC will establish its beach head market with individuals who are hosting private events where alcohol is served in a host bar. A requirement of these venues is that the client purchases all of the alcohol. For this reason all of our packages include a 45 minute consultation and creation of the shopping list. Because sales of alcohol are not involved, Delta Breeze Bartending Services LLC will not be required to carry an ABC liquor license.

Retail liquor licenses in California can be obtained through a lengthy process. We are working with Michael Brewer of the California Alcoholic Beverage Consulting Service to eventually obtain the appropriate liquor license that will allow us to service events with no-host bars where alcohol is sold. We expect to obtain our liquor license by the third year of operation.

Standard service fee packages for events with hosted bar(s)—client is responsible for all alcohols, mixers, bar supplies, beer and wine. Consultation - 45 minute meeting with client to discuss cocktail menu, bar location and specific event requirements. All events are based on 6 hours bar service (includes: 1.5 hour set up time, 4 hours cocktails service during the event, 0.5 hour cleaning and tear apart time). Additional hours are billed at $80 each.

Each package includes preparation of the shopping list, decoration of the bar area, fruit preparation, design and preparation, color printing and lamination of bar menus.

Portable Bar Set Up—includes: 1 portable bar (6' front), 2 side tables, 2 back tables, black satin table skirts and cloths for all tables, 2 blenders, 1 drink mixer, set of bar utensils, serving tray, 4 juice bottles, 1 garnish tray, 1 napkin/straws holder, 1 salt/sugar rimmer, 6 beer and soda storage containers (for up to 20 beer bottles), 2 bar serving mats, and battery powered lighting for bar if event is outdoors at night.

Gold Package

- Events for 70 to 140 guests
- Consultation one hour to discuss cocktail menu, bar location and other event requirements
- One bartender, one bar back
- Portable bar set up
- $599

Platinum Package

- Events for 141 to 200 guests
- Consultation
- Two Bartenders
- Two Bar backs
- Portable bar set up
- $899

Menus

Sample Menu
New Year's Eve Party

- Grapefruit vodka, OJ, Grapefruit Juice, Campari, Champagne, Cherry
- Cosmopolitan: Vodka, Triple sec, Lime Juice, Cranberry Juice, Lime
- Lemon Drop: Vodka, Triple Sec, Sweet & Sour, Lemon
- Mojito: Rum, simple syrup, Mint Leaves, Soda Water, Lime
- Chocolate Martini: Vodka, Godiva, White Créme de Cocoa, cream, Chocolate Syrup
- Pink Squirrel: White Creme de Cocoa, Créme de Almond, Cream

- Blue Margarita: Tequila, Blue Curacao, Lime Juice, Sweet & Sour, Lime

- Pina Colada: Rum, Pina Colada Mix, Pineapple Juice, Cherry

- Cape Code: Vodka, Cranberry Juice, Grenadine, Lime

- Layered Shooters

MARKET ANALYSIS

Delta Breeze Bartending Services LLC has identified several target customers. Anyone who is hosting a private event where alcoholic beverages are being served to a guest list of 40 to 200 guests would be a prime candidate for the services provided by Delta Breeze Bartending Services LLC.

The prime targets for our services include individuals, corporate and nonprofit organizations hosting private events for up to 200 guests.

Events that would be appropriate venues for Delta Breeze's services include:

- Weddings

- New Year's Eve Parties

- Engagement Parties

- Bridal showers

- Christmas Parties

Other venues that we have serviced include:

- Spanish Night

- Halloween

- Indian Birthday

We are willing and able to customize our services to any venue and target audience, including non-alcoholic venues where our menu includes the following:

- Sunrise: Orange juice, Grenadine Tonic Water, Cherry

- Blue Fusion: Blue Curacao, Sweet & Sour, Pineapple Juice, Lime, Cherry

- Appletini: apple sour mix, Simple syrup, Triple Sec, Tonic Water, Apple

Those who wish to forego the bartender services may rent the portable bar. Services include:

- Portable bar

- Two side tables, 2 back tables with black satin cloths

- Two blenders

- Set of bar utensils

- Juice bottles, garnish tray, napkin/straw holder

- Beer and soda storage containers for up to 20 bottles

Glassware is available for $0.50 each per event and additional bar equipment can be rented as follows:

- Ice cooler (165 QT): $10 each

- Ice tea/lemonade jar (4 QT): $10

- Coffee urn (55 cups): $20

- Wine/Champagne cooler cart (20 QT): $15

- Bar floor mat (4' x 3', 1.5" thick): $15

We recommend one bartender and one bar-back per 100 people so that guests are served quickly with great tasting drinks. A $100 dollar non-refundable cash deposit is required at the time of the contract signing. This deposit will be applied to the final balance.

Drinks will never be served later than 12:30 AM to ensure the safety of the guests. A maximum of 6 hours of alcohol service will be provided at the event to ensure guest safety. Our bartenders are trained in alcohol awareness per California ABC requirements and we reserve the right to refuse service to any guest who in the judgment of our bartender has had too much to drink. We also reserve the right to ID anyone who appears to be under 35 years of age.

COMPETITION

Competition includes several mobile bartenders. Some of these competitors hold a liquor license that allows them to service both host and no host bars. Currently, Delta Breeze Bartending Services LLC does not possess a California liquor license that would permit us to service no host bars where drinks are sold. We can only provide service to private venues where the client purchases all of the alcohol and it is served free to guests.

We plan to obtain an ABC liquor license in the future that would allow us to sell alcohol on the premises of each venue. In California, such licenses are difficult to obtain. Our best chance for obtaining a license is to buy one from someone who currently possesses a license and wishes to sell it to a qualified vendor. To this end, we have engaged Michael Brewer of California Alcoholic Beverage Consulting Service to advise us and help us in obtaining the proper licenses as we expand our services.

Name	Type of service	Type of license
Cocktail coquettes	Flair bartender	Host bar
Primo bar	Mobile bartending	Host and no host bar
A perfect pour	Mobile bartending	Host and no host bar
Mix & mingle bartending	Mobile bartending	Host bar
Gigs bartender	Mobile bartending	Host bar

MARKETING

Marketing Objective

To establish ourselves as a premier mobile bartending service that offers outstanding signature drinks with professionalism and flair.

Delta Breeze Bartending Services LLC will use social media such as Twitter and Facebook to reach current and potential customers. Our Facebook page will be a meeting space where customers and potential customers can see menus, new items and print coupons.

We will also maintain a web site with information on our company, bartenders, menus and services. The web site will include a contact form that prospects can use to connect with us and place orders and inquiries. All communications will be followed up by 4 p.m. the next business day.

Delta Breeze Bartending Services LLC has contracted with a local web design firm that will create our web site and social media presence on Twitter and Facebook. This firm will also ensure that Delta

Breeze Bartending Services LLC has a presence on any listing sites for entertainment and event planning services on the web such as GigSalad.

Once established, Jared Wilson and his wife Tanya will take over the maintenance of the web presence until we can afford to hire a social media expert on a regular basis.

Through his contacts in the event planning industry, Tom Pollock has formed alliances with two event planners and three caterers in the Sacramento area. He is also close to completing agreements with several event venues including: Hawks Valley Restaurant in Folsom and Belle Winds Bed & Breakfast in Newcastle.

We believe that networking is one of the most important methods available to us as an emerging mobile bartender service. By working jointly with established event planners and the managers of event venues, we can expand our exposure to potential clients. These arrangements work to the benefit of both parties in creating the potential for increase in business.

RISK FACTORS

There are many risks involved in any business and mobile bartending is no exception. However, the risks are fewer than those encountered by a brick-and-mortar establishment. We have determined the following risks for Delta Breeze Bartending Services LLC .

Risks

Lack of business. If we are unable to schedule enough events during any fiscal period then we will not be able to cover fixed costs. In our favor, our fixed costs are low because auxiliary staff are hired on a "per event" basis. Moreover, the client is responsible for purchasing alcohol and mixers for each event based on the menu chosen.

Competitors. A major risk is posed by the presence of competitors who are able to provide additional services in the form of no host service related to the possession of a liquor license for the sale of liquor at events. Delta Breeze Bartending Services LLC is limited to providing services for hosted bars where alcohol sales do not occur. Eventually we plan on obtaining our own liquor license.

Liability issues. Because our clients are technically the ones providing the liquor our liability is somewhat limited. However, there is always the possibility that Delta Breeze Bartending Services LLC could be named as defendant in a legal dispute for liability. To limit our liability exposure, all of our staff will be trained and certified appropriately to determine when someone has had too much to drink. In California this includes the California Responsible Serving Course for bartenders (ServSafe Alcohol), sellers and servers governed by the California Department of Alcoholic Beverage Control, TIPS (Training for Intervention ProcedureS) and Professional Server Certification/Bartender Certification Training.

In addition Delta Breeze Bartending Services LLC will carry one million dollars' worth of general liability insurance including liquor liability coverage for all events.

Opportunities

Expansion. If we are successful, we plan to add more bartenders to our staff in order to be able to service more venues. We also plan to obtain the appropriate liquor licenses to sell liquor at events. This will allow us to provide services on our own at public venues.

Cost containment. The costs of labor and bar supplies are based on the number of people served and the number of hours of service provided at each event. The fee for each event includes the cost of labor and supplies. Therefore, if prices are set appropriately, Delta Breeze Bartending Services LLC will realize at least a 60 percent gross profit on each event.

Strategic alliances. We will engage in a continuous effort to align our interests with those in complementary service areas such as event planners, caterers and local hotels and conference centers as well as nonprofit groups that organize fundraising events.

FINANCIAL PLAN

First Year Capital Requirements

The total startup costs for working capital, supplies and equipment equals $50,000. These funds have been contributed equally by Jared Wilson and Tom Pollock.

While a mobile bartending service can be established with an investment of a few thousand dollars in bar supplies and equipment, Delta Breeze Bartending Services LLC has chosen to invest in its own mobile bar, tables and storage equipment. This has increased our startup costs but will allow us to immediately compete with many of our established competitors.

Our portable Flash Bar folds to 14 inches and includes three beer taps, a sunken speed well, two cutting boards and two ice bins. The bar has LED lighting and interchangeable panels that can be used to highlight either a product or event theme. The bar can plug directly into a wall or into an eight hour rechargeable battery.

If a larger bar is required for an event, we can rent additional bar sections that will easily connect to our basic bar unit. We have also invested in the Flash Bar road case that enables us to carry two Flash Bar segments and protect them during transport.

For the present we are using Jared Wilson's van to transport equipment and supplies to each event. In addition, both Jared and Tom are using their personal autos to meet with clients and to engage in networking activities. Delta Breeze Bartending Services LLC is reimbursing Jared and Tom on a per-mile basis. Eventually we would like purchase a van in the company name for use in the business.

Estimated startup costs and funding

Requirements	
Start-up expenses	
Licenses	$ 300
Bar supplies	$ 700
Office supplies	$ 300
Advertising	$ 1,200
Insurance	$ 1,000
Legal and professional fees	$ 2,000
Web site development	$ 1,500
Total start-up expenses	**$ 7,000**
Start-up assets	
Cash required	$ 25,000.00
Other current assets	$ 3,000.00
Long-term assets	$ 15,000.00
Total assets required	**$43,000.00**
Total start-up expenses	**$ 7,000.00**
Total requirements	**$50,000.00**
Start-up funding	
Start-up expenses	$ 7,000.00
Start-up assets	$ 43,000.00
Total funding required	**$50,000.00**

Projected Profit and Loss

Profit and loss

	Year 1	Year 2	Year 3
Sales	**$47,000**	**$85,000**	**$110,000**
Direct labor	$18,800	$34,000	$ 44,000
Gross margin	$28,200	$51,000	$ 66,000
Gross margin %	60.00%	60.00%	60.00%
Expenses:			
Administrative salaries	$12,000	$24,000	$ 36,000
Sales and marketing and other expenses	$ 1,200	$ 1,500	$ 1,700
Depreciation	$ 2,400	$ 2,400	$ 2,400
Insurance	$ 1,500	$ 1,500	$ 1,500
Auto/travel	$ 800	$ 1,200	$ 1,400
Payroll taxes	$ 3,080	$ 5,800	$ 8,000
Supplies	$ 400	$ 500	$ 700
Repairs & maintenance	$ 200	$ 300	$ 300
Telephone/Internet	$ 1,200	$ 1,200	$ 1,200
Professional fees	$ 2,400	$ 1,200	$ 1,600
Other	$ 1,000	$ 1,000	$ 1,000
Total operating expenses	**$26,180**	**$40,600**	**$ 55,800**
Profit before interest and taxes	$ 2,020	$10,400	$ 10,200
Net profit/sales	**4.3%**	**12.2%**	**9.3%**

Projected Balance Sheet

Pro forma balance sheet

Assets	Year 1	Year 2	Year 3
Current assets	$12,000	$23,175	$32,100
Cash			
Other current assets	$ 1,000	$ 1,200	$ 1,500
Total current assets	**$13,000**	**$24,375**	**$33,600**
Long-term assets			
Long-term assets	$15,000	$15,000	$15,000
Accumulated depreciation	($ 3,000)	($ 3,000)	($ 3,000)
Total long-term assets	**$12,000**	**$12,000**	**$12,000**
Total assets	**$25,000**	**$36,375**	**$45,600**
Liabilities and capital			
Current liabilities			
Accounts payable			
Other current liabilities: payroll tax	$ 1,800	$ 2,200	$ 2,000
Total current liabilities	**$ 1,800**	**$ 2,200**	**$ 2,000**
Long-term liabilities			
Total liabilities	**$ 1,800**	**$ 2,200**	**$ 2,000**
Paid-in capital	$15,000	$15,000	$15,000
Retained earnings	$ 6,180	$ 8,775	$18,400
Earnings	$ 2,020	$10,400	$10,200
Total capital	**$23,200**	**$34,175**	**$43,600**
Total liabilities and capital	**$25,000**	**$36,375**	**$45,600**

Bed and Breakfast

The Charleston Inn

42064 Ocean Ave.
Charleston, SC 29409

Fran Fletcher

A modern bed and breakfast with Southern hospitality and 21st century flair.

BUSINESS SUMMARY

The Charleston Inn is not your ordinary bed and breakfast. It includes all of the southern hospitality that you would expect but with modern amenities that guests need to stay connected to the outside world. Guests won't find outdated décor or have to share a bathroom with other guests. Each of its ten spacious rooms are equipped with a full entertainment center, featuring a flat screen TV, gaming system, and free on-demand programming. Additionally, each room has a private bath with garden tub and shower. All rooms either lead to a private balcony or patio. This Charleston, South Carolina home away from home specializes in providing a luxurious getaway for couples, families, or business travelers who want nice accommodations in a relaxing environment.

According to the Bureau of Labor Statistics, the demand for workers in the lodging industry will increase 25% over the next decade. These projections are likely even higher for a vacation destination like Charleston. According to tourism data, Charleston hosts over 4 million visitors each year.

The Mitchells are making their dreams come true by buying an established bed and breakfast. They will shut down for one month during the slow season while they make the necessary updates to the property.

There are several other bed and breakfasts in the historic district of Charleston, but the new owners are not worried. The inn already has an established list of repeat guests, and the Mitchells are confident that The Charleston Inn will become even more successful as they reach vacationers and business travelers who want a modernized bed and breakfast with amenities for the digital age. The Charleston Inn will set itself apart by offering:

- Free wifi

- Charging ports

- Gaming systems

- Free movies on demand

- Complimentary bicycles

- Concierge service

The Charleston Inn will obtain clients predominantly through referrals. The Mitchells will list their services at B&B.com They will also partner with area entertainment providers to better ensure their customers have a great overall experience while visiting Charleston.

The Mitchells are seeking a business loan in the amount of $549,000. Financing will cover start-up fees and personal expenses for one month. The inn is located on prime real estate so they will use the establishment as collateral for the loan. The Mitchells expect to make a profit from the beginning since the business is already established. They expect profits to increase over time and plan to repay the line of credit within ten years.

COMPANY DESCRIPTION

Location
The Charleston Inn is a 10-room bed and breakfast located in Charleston, South Carolina. It is conveniently located in the historic district, only a short walk from numerous restaurants and shops.

Hours of Operations
The Charleston Inn will be open 365 days a year.

Reservations can be made over the phone or through the website, charlestoninn.com.

Check-in time is between 4 p.m. and 9:00 p.m.

Checkout time is 12 p.m.

Personnel

Jeremy and Haley Mitchell (Owners)
The Mitchells will manage and provide services associated with the Charleston Inn. Owning a bed and breakfast has been a dream of the couple since staying at one in Maine on their honeymoon. They enjoyed it so much, that they decided to buy an inn in their hometown of Charleston. To make the bed and breakfast a little more appealing to younger guests, they have equipped all rooms with amenities to keep customers connected while traveling.

Hazel Hurst
Ms. Hurst has been working at the Charleston Inn for 10 years. She is well loved by the guests and the Mitchells are excited that she will help run the inn and provide continuity between the old and new management.

Products and Amenities

Products
The Charleston Inn will carry products made by local artisans, including soaps, jellies, and handcrafted items, which are all available for purchase.

Amenities
- Hot breakfast
- Fresh baked desserts
- Free drinks
- Afternoon wine and cheese reception
- Each room includes plush bath robes, soap, shampoo, toothbrush, toothpaste

- Each room equipped with flat screen TV, gaming system, free movies on demand, free wifi, and charging stations

- Each room leads to a private balcony or patio

- Each room has a private bathroom with garden tub and shower

- Concierge service (restaurant reservations, venue tickets, shuttle service)

- Peaceful garden area

- Convenient location and parking area

- Complimentary bicycles

MARKET ANALYSIS

Industry Overview

According to the Bureau of Labor Statistics, jobs in the lodging industry are expected to increase 25% over the next decade. These projections are expected to be even higher in Charleston since it is a tourist destination.

According to tourism data, over 4 million people visit Charleston, South Carolina each year. Due to the area's mild climate, visitors are steady all year long.

Target Market

The Charleston Inn will market its services to tech savvy young adults and families who do not want to be without Internet, games, and movies when traveling.

Competition

There are currently five bed and breakfasts in Charleston's historic district. However, the modern amenities offered at The Charleston Inn are unmatched by the competition.

1. King George Inn, 1600 Royal Street; 12 guest rooms; $325 per night

2. The Patterson House, 3855 Carriage Street; 9 guest rooms; $300 per night

3. Baybrook Inn, 6400 Baybrook Street; 8 guest rooms; $290 per night

4. The Bay Street Inn, 7509 Bay Street; 10 guest rooms; $295 per night

5. Becky's Bed and Breakfast, 6776 Willow Street; 10 guest rooms; $325 per night

GROWTH STRATEGY

The Charleston Inn is already established, but the new owners will use advertising sites and social media to introduce its new owners and showcase its improvements. The inn plans to make a name for itself as the most modern bed and breakfast in Charleston. The owners want to reach younger customers and families. The Mitchells will achieve this growth one guest at a time by providing unparalleled customer service. The owners will strive to provide old Southern hospitality mixed with 21st century conveniences.

Sales and Marketing

Referrals will continue to be the backbone of the inn's marketing strategy. The Charleston Inn will also attract business travelers by offering specials during business conferences.

The Charleston Inn will market the following:

- Southern hospitality with 21st century flare

- Reasonable rates

- Concierge service

- All the comforts and connections of home

- Complimentary bicycles

- Special packages available

- Discounts to many area attractions

Advertising

Advertising will include:

- Social media

- Local newspaper

- B&B.com

FINANCIAL ANALYSIS

Start-up costs

The Mitchells are updating an existing bed and breakfast. The couple plans to live in the inn-keeper's suite. The bed and breakfast will cost $500,000 and will be the largest expense. Mr. Mitchell has experience as a builder and will make any updates needed. The bed and breakfast has an updated kitchen and all of the mattresses are less than three years old. The Mitchells would like to decorate with a "less is more" approach, and want to buy or borrow pieces from local artisans. The Mitchells plan to have an antique sale, and hope to make about $10,000 to offset the cost of updating.

Estimated start-up costs

Property loan	$500,000
Updating	$ 20,000
Electronics	$ 10,000
Bedding	$ 5,000
Advertisement	$ 1,000
Legal fees (LLC)	$ 1,800
Insurance	$ 1,000
Total	**$538,800**

Estimated Monthly Income

Since The Charleston Inn is an established bed and breakfast, the owners expect that they will continue to book return customers. They plan to close for one month to update the property so they do not expect any income the first month. After the first month, monthly income will be determined by bookings. The previous owner was generally 50% booked, so the owners will use this as a starting point and work to achieve 100%.

The Mitchell's conservatively estimate that five rooms will be occupied each week, including one suite.

Available suites/rooms and features

The charleston suite	1 king bed/sitting room	Garden tub and walk-in shower	Private balcony
The south carolina suite	1 king bed/sitting room	Garden tub and walk-in shower	Private patio
The atlantic room	1 queen bed	Garden tub and shower	Private balcony
The southern comfort room	1 queen bed	Garden tub and shower	Private patio
The magnolia room	1 queen bed and 1 full bed	Garden tub and shower	Private balcony
Front garden room	2 queen beds	Garden tub and shower	Private patio
Back garden room	2 queen beds	Garden tub and shower	Private patio
The rose room	2 full beds	Garden tub and shower	Private balcony
The azalea room	2 full beds	Garden tub and shower	Private balcony
The pelican room	1 queen bed	Garden tub and shower	Private patio

Packages

The following packages are available upon request:

- The Honeymoon Package ($250)—a chilled bottle of champagne, two champagne flutes, a dozen red roses, a box of chocolate covered strawberries, a carriage ride for two through historic downtown Charleston, and reservations/$100 voucher to a local fine dining establishment.

- Romantic Getaway Package ($125)—a bottle of wine, two wine glasses, basket of seasonal flowers, box of chocolates, and a carriage ride for two through historic downtown Charleston.

- Family Package ($200)—a carriage ride for four through historic downtown Charleston, four tickets to the aquarium, and four day passes for the trolley.

Rates

Rates may be discounted at the innkeeper's discretion. Examples of discounts are single occupancy business customers and guests staying more than three nights. The owners may offer an off-season discount, but they must determine if that is necessary and will offer as an internet special to their email subscribers and/or social media followers.

	Mon/Tues	Wed/Thurs	Fri/Sat/Sun
The charleston suite	$180	$160	$200
The south carolina suite	$180	$160	$200
Back garden room	$130	$120	$150
The rose room	$130	$120	$150
The atlantic room	$130	$120	$150
The southern comfort room	$130	$120	$150
The magnolia room	$130	$120	$150
Front garden room	$130	$120	$150
The azalea room	$130	$120	$150
The pelican room	$130	$120	$150

Estimated Monthly Expenses

Expenses will be kept to a minimum. The Mitchells would like to earn $4,000 monthly. However, the number of guests will determine the couple's salary.

Monthly expenses

Loan payment	$ 2,000
Phone/Internet	$ 100
Ms. Hurst's salary	$ 2,880
Insurance	$ 250
Electricity	$ 1,000
Food/wine/cheese	$ 4,000
Wages for The Mitchells (est.)	$ 4,000
Total	**$14,230**

The first month's expenses will be $10,230 since no food will be bought during renovation.

Profit/Loss

Due to updating the inn, the first month will show no profit. The Mitchells conservatively estimate that in the second month of operation, the inn will be booked at 50% capacity and stay this way for 3 months. Then, the Mitchells expect that they will start gaining more and more guests each month until the inn is fully booked.

The Mitchells conservatively estimate that expenses will increase by approximately $2,000 a month if booked to capacity. The owners do not expect to raise service prices during the first year, so income is expected to plateau after Month 12. The Charleston Inn should realize a pre-tax profit of approximately $138,000 the first year and $317,000 the second and third years.

Estimated profits year 1

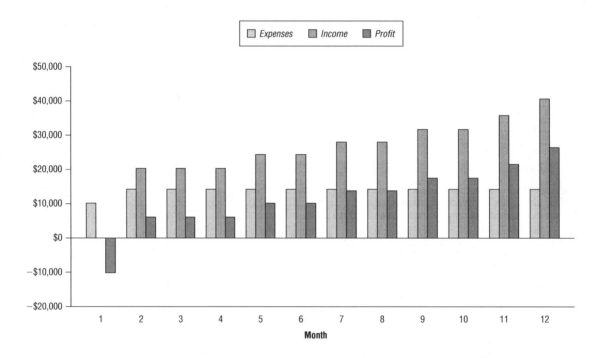

Estimated profits years 1–3

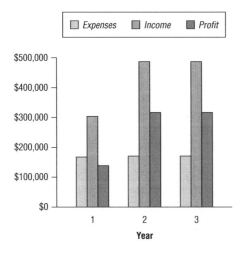

Financing

The Mitchells wish to obtain a loan for $549,000, which covers the start-up costs and one month of expenses. The Mitchells will use the inn as collateral for the loan and plan to repay the line of credit in the third year of operation. They have budgeted $2000 per month for loan repayment, but will pay additional principal if possible.

Repayment plan

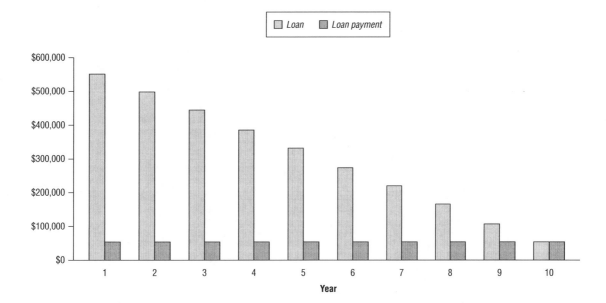

The Mitchells will pay $2,000 per month for a total of $24,000 per year. At the end of each year, they will make a lump sum payment toward the principle in the amount of 20% of the annual profit. The owners expect to have the loan paid off in approximately ten years.

Chauffeur Service

Pick Me Up

14487-D 42nd Street
New York, NY 10036

Fran Fletcher

BUSINESS SUMMARY

Pick Me Up is a New York City based ride share/tourist service operated by Ryder Wythme. Pick Me Up will pick up clients and drive them to destinations of their choice. Mr. Wythme will also offer City Tours and Night Tours since he enjoys sharing his knowledge of the city with others.

Mr. Wythme recently graduated from NYU and is taking a break before starting graduate school. Mr. Wythme has lived in the city for five years and during that time, he has worked part time as a private driver in various parts of Manhattan, including Midtown, the Upper East Side, the Upper West Side and SOHO.

According to the Bureau of Labor Statistics, the job outlook for taxi drivers and chauffeurs is favorable and is expected to increase by 16% over the next ten years. New York City welcomes 42.9 million domestic visitors and 11.4 million international visitors each year. Pick Me Up is partnering with the concierges of several large hotels to provide driving and tour services to hotel guests.

Of course there are other drivers in the city, but Mr. Wythme believes he has found a niche with Pick Me Up. He thinks that clients will want to use his services the whole time they are in the city and will enjoy the continuity of having the same driver throughout their stay, like a private tour guide. Mr. Wythme will use his knowledge of the city and attractions to help clients find places that are off the beaten path and give them a true taste of NYC life.

Marketing and advertising will focus on the following:

1. Pick Me Up offers both day and nighttime tours of the city.

2. Pick Me Up will offer a discount for repeat customers.

Pick Me Up will initially advertise through local hotels. Referrals are essential in this type of business, and Mr. Wythme has already gained rapport as a driver with several doormen in the Manhattan area. As the business grows, Mr. Wythme will consider adding additional cars and drivers.

Mr. Wythme is seeking a business line of credit for approximately $41,000 to finance this venture. Financing will cover start-up fees, including a minivan, and three months expenses. Mr. Wythme plans to repay the line of credit within five years.

COMPANY DESCRIPTION

Location

Pick Me Up is located in New York City. Mr. Wythme plans to work out of his home.

Hours of Operations

Monday-Sunday, 24/7. By reservations only.

Personnel

Ryder Wythme (Owner/Driver)

Mr. Wythme will provide all driving services. He has lived in NYC for five years and was employed as a private driver while in college.

Products and Services

Services

• Provide driving services for tourists.

• Provide tourist information to customers.

MARKET ANALYSIS

Industry Overview

According to the Bureau of Labor Statistics, the job outlook for taxi drivers and chauffeurs is favorable and is expected to increase by 16% over the next ten years.

According to the New York Visitor's Bureau, New York City welcomes 42.9 million domestic visitors and 11.4 million international visitors each year. Tourists spend an estimated 38.8 billion annually while visiting the city.

Mr. Wythme plans to work with the doormen and concierges at three popular midtown hotels and they are confident that they can supply a steady stream of customers.

Target Market

The target market of Pick Me Up will be visitors to NYC who want more than a taxi service or a chauffeur. Pick Me Up will offer a friendly knowledgeable driver that serves an extension of the concierge services offered by the hotel.

Competition

There are currently two other independent car services that work in conjunction with the hotels that Mr. Wythme will be working with.

1. Jones Driving Services, 43rd St., NYC

2. NYC Chauffeur Services, 1443-F Park Avenue, NYC

Mr. Wythme will set himself apart by being personable and by giving interesting facts while he is driving. His knowledge of the city will also allow him to suggest places of interest and to know the best days and times to go to tourist spots.

GROWTH STRATEGY

The overall strategy of the company is to give such great customer service that the concierges at the three hotels will always call Pick Me Up first. The company will mainly generate customers through referrals, both through the concierge services as well as from former customers. Pick Me Up will keep in touch with customers through social media.

As the business grows, Mr. Wythme will consider purchasing an additional van and hire a couple of drivers.

Sales and Marketing

Referrals from the hotel concierges will serve as the main advertising method for Pick Me Up. Mr. Wythme has identified key advertising avenues and tactics to bring in customers and build a reputation for quality.

Pick Me Up will market VIP pickups through the concierge services of local hotels.

Advertising

Advertising will include:

*   Hotel concierge

*   Business cards at the hotel

*   Social media

FINANCIAL ANALYSIS

Start-up costs

Estimated start-up costs

Van	$35,000
Business license	$ 400
Total	**$35,400**

Estimated Monthly Income

Mr. Wythme believes that his time will be split into the following service segments:

Service segments

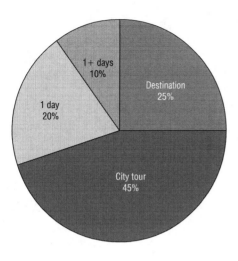

Prices for Services

The van can carry up to six passengers and has room for shopping bags, etc.

Service	Price
Driving to a destination	$40; add $1 per mile
Driving city tour	$50 per hour
Driving city night tour (8 p.m.–2 a.m.)	$70 per hour
Driving all day (12 hours)	$300
Driving multiple days	10% discount on each drive within 7 days of the first

Estimated Monthly Expenses

Loan payment	$ 700
Phone/Internet	$ 100
Advertising	$ 100
Insurance	$ 400
Gas	$ 600
Total	**$1,900**

Profit/Loss

Mr. Wythme will have the luxury of deciding how many hours he works each week. In the beginning, he will take on as many customers as he can, but wants to try to keep his hours at 40-60 per week. He conservatively estimates that in the first month of operation, he will book 3 night tours per week, 3 day tours per week, and 2 all day rentals per week for a total of $8,160 income the first month.

In the second month, it is estimated that Mr. Wythme will book 4 night tours, 4 day tours, and 1 day of destination driving each week for a total of $10,400 income.

In the third month and beyond, Mr. Wythme plans to be booked solid with 5 night tours, 5 day tours, and 2 days of destination driving each week for a total income of $14,200.

Estimated profits months 1–6

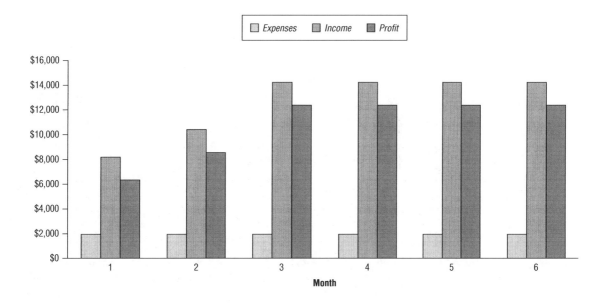

Estimated profits months 7–12

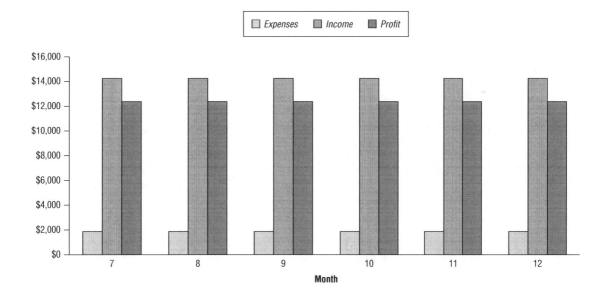

Mr. Wythme conservatively estimates that his expenses will increase about 3% a year and that his income will increase about 5% a year.

Estimated profits years 1–3

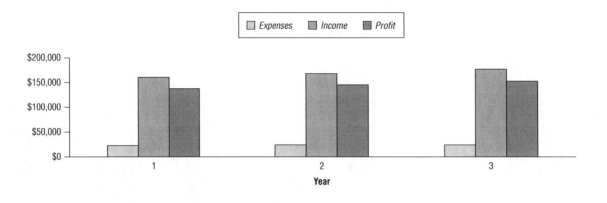

Financing

Mr. Wythme would like to take out a business line of credit for $41,100, the amount needed to cover the start-up costs and three months' expenses. Mr. Wythme plans to repay the line of credit at the end of the second year of operation. He has budgeted $700 per month for loan repayment, but will pay a lump sum on the loan (approximately 10% of annual profit) at the end of each year. Mr. Wythme will increase the end of year payments if necessary in order to meet his two-year repayment timeline.

Repayment plan

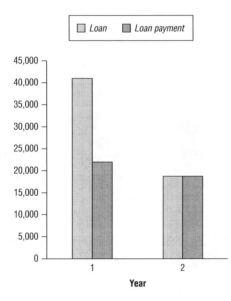

Counseling Practice

Roper Counseling Services Inc.

4302 Welty St.
Stonefield Building, Ste. 750
Chicopee Bend, Colorado 80500

Paul Greenland

Roper Counseling Services provides individuals, groups, and families with confidential and effective treatments for a wide range of emotional and behavioral difficulties.

*This plan appeared in a previous volume of **Business Plans Handbook**. It has been updated for this volume.*

EXECUTIVE SUMMARY

Roper Counseling Services offers confidential and effective treatments for a wide range of emotional and behavioral difficulties. Specifically, our practice provides individual counseling services for children, adolescents, and adults. Group therapy is offered for people dealing with similar issues, such as eating disorders. Finally, we also provide both marital and family therapy.

Business Overview

Over the course of one's life, challenges and difficulties are inevitable. Individuals are often able to overcome difficult times and deal with challenges in successful, optimal ways. However, sometimes even effective coping strategies and the support of family and friends is not enough. Situations resulting from abusive relationships, traumatic childhoods, addictions, loss, and chemical imbalances can spiral out of control, requiring assistance from trained professionals. With nearly 25 years of experience, Roper Counseling Services has a broad range of professional expertise, allowing us to help troubled individuals in almost any situation.

Organizational Structure

Our practice is incorporated in the state of Colorado and employs three licensed psychologists with doctorate degrees from programs approved by the American Psychological Association, as well as three licensed clinical social workers.

Company History

Roper Counseling Services was established in 1992, when President Dr. George Roper first established his independent practice. Since that time, the business has grown at a measured pace. Until 2008, Roper Counseling Services was a partnership comprised of Dr. Roper and Dr. Renée Coates. Our growth was such that, by 2008, we had identified the need to add another practitioner. At that time, Dr. Mary Anne Townsend joined the business, which continued to grow.

Our burgeoning patient base, which grew largely through word-of-mouth referrals, as well as exposure from local, regional, and national speaking commitments, required us to add additional capacity.

In 2015 we agreed to merge with an existing counseling practice named Evergreen Associates. This resulted in the addition of three licensed clinical social workers: Peter Mullen MSW, LCSW; Steven Vetro MSW, LCSW; and Halley Peterson MSW, LCSW. All three practitioners had established reputations in the community. By joining Roper Counseling Services, they enabled our practice to become the largest of its kind in the Chicopee Bend area.

MARKET ANALYSIS

Mental illnesses, as well as behavioral and emotional difficulties, are quite common throughout the population. For example, according to data issued by the American Psychiatric Association in 2013, each year approximately 20 percent of U.S. adults suffer from a diagnosable mental illness.

According to a national study conducted by PXPL Associates Inc. in April 2015, stress levels throughout the United States were at an all-time high. The research, which involved interviews with 2,347 people, revealed that 37 percent of individuals categorize their stress level as overwhelming. Sixty-four percent of respondents indicated that their stress levels were significantly higher compared to the same period the previous year. According to the study, overall economic uncertainty was the leading cause of stress (31%), followed by relationship problems (29%), and financial concerns (24%). Although most people have adequate support networks in place to deal with their stress, a significant portion of the population either lacks such support, or does not rely upon appropriate coping mechanisms.

Despite the fact that there is a strong market for the services offered by Roper Consulting Services, the partners realize that several barriers to our growth exist within the marketplace. These namely are a lack of awareness about mental illness, as well as a variety of misconceptions.

For example, according to a 2013 consumer survey on mental health conducted by the American Psychiatric Association, 44 percent of U.S. adults indicated that they know little or virtually nothing about mental illness. Furthermore, 33 percent believed that mental illnesses are caused by either personal or emotional weakness. Finally, some 24 percent of the population believed that, most of the time, personal or emotional strength is enough to overcome common mental illnesses.

INDUSTRY ANALYSIS

According to data from the Bureau of Labor Statistics, 160,200 psychologists were employed in 2012. By 2022, this number is projected to grow 12 percent, reaching 179,000. In addition, 607,300 social workers were employed 2012. That profession is projected to grow 19 percent by 2022, at which time the number of social workers will rise to 721,400. According to Colorado's Department of Regulatory Agencies, Division of Registrations, in 2015 the state was home to approximately 3,031 active licensed psychologists.

PERSONNEL

George M. Roper, Ph.D., President—Dr. Roper graduated in 1991 from the Massachusetts School of Professional Psychology, where he earned his doctorate degree in psychology. He earned a master's degree in psychology from South University in West Palm, Florida. Dr. Roper has been a mental health practitioner since 1985, providing services to individuals, couples, families, and groups. His special interests include stress management, co-dependent relationships, substance abuse, and marital therapy. Dr. Roper is a licensed psychologist and has been practicing in Colorado since 1992.

Renee Coates, Ph.D., Vice President—Dr. Coates earned Master's and Doctor of Psychology degrees from the University of the Rockies in Colorado Springs, graduating in 1997. Dr. Coates has worked in the counseling field since 1992, working mainly with individuals and couples. Her special interests include women's issues, depression, domestic violence, and marital therapy. Dr. Coates is a licensed psychologist and has been practicing in Colorado since 1992.

Mary Anne Townsend, Ph.D.—Dr. Townsend received her doctorate degree in 2004 from The Chicago School of Professional Psychology, as well as a master's degree in psychology from the University of Illinois in 1998, at which time she began working in the counseling field. A highly skilled practitioner, Dr. Townsend specializes in working with children and adolescents in both residential and outpatient settings. Dr. Townsend is especially interested in attention deficit hyperactivity disorder, grief-and-loss-related issues, and anxiety. She is a licensed psychologist and has been practicing in Colorado since 2008.

Peter Mullen MSW, LCSW—With more than 20 years of experience, Peter is a graduate of The School of Social Work at Colorado State University, where he received his undergraduate and graduate degrees. He provides both individual and group therapy in a wide range of settings. Peter is especially interested in men's issues, parent-child conflicts, anxiety, eating disorders, and depression. He has been a licensed clinical social worker since 1996.

Steven Vetro MSW, LCSW—Steven received his BSW degree from the Arizona State University School of Social Work, and his MSW degree from the School of Social Work at Colorado State University. He has been serving our community for 15 years, providing individual, family, and group therapies. His areas of interest include personal and occupational stress, life balance, creativity enhancement, anger management, divorce and divorce recovery, blended families, and life transition issues. He has been a licensed clinical social worker since 2001.

Halley Peterson MSW, LCSW—After receiving her BSW degree from Illinois State University, Halley earned an MSW degree from the School of Social Work at Colorado State University in 2006. She offers individual, family, and group therapies. Halley specializes in working with older adults and their families, and focuses on grief and loss, isolation and loneliness, life transition issues, end-of-life issues, anxiety, and depression. She has been a licensed clinical social worker since 2006.

Eric Simms, Practice Manager—Our practice is especially fortunate to have Eric on-board. With an undergraduate education that includes double majors in accounting and marketing, he has the necessary skills to handle accounting, bookkeeping, and payroll for the practice, and also develops and executes marketing strategies needed to help us grow. Additionally, Eric manages professional licensure for all the counselors, ensuring that we remain in compliance, and also negotiates fee schedules with insurance companies, as well as area hospitals and counseling centers where we provide services.

Mary Sidwell, Administrative Assistant—Mary is responsible for greeting clients and other professionals when they enter our practice. She often is the first impression that people have of our business, and we value her exceptional interpersonal skills. She is especially gifted at dealing with individuals who can be challenging in various ways. Mary books appointments for clients and maintains schedules for our therapists. In addition, she handles all travel arrangements, orders office supplies and other items, maintains patient records, takes care of inbound and outgoing U.S. mail and overnight packages, and performs a wide range of other duties as needed.

Professional & Advisory Support

Roper Counseling Services relies upon the firm of Willington, Bradfield & Terell for legal services. Tax services are provided by Rocky Mountain Professional Services. In addition, our firm has established checking accounts with the Bank of Colorado, which also provides us with merchant card services, allowing us to take credit card payments from clients.

GROWTH STRATEGY

Our practice will rely on word-of-mouth referrals, as well as the marketing tactics outlined in the Marketing & Sales section of this plan, to achieve meaningful growth over the next five years. Based upon the growth that both of our practices have experienced over the past five years (prior to merging), the Bureau of Labor Statistics projections for our professions referenced in the Industry Analysis section of this plan, and our professional observations of the local market, we anticipate our patient base will grow at a compound annual rate of 3.5 percent over the next five years.

SERVICES

Roper Counseling Services provides assessment and treatments for a wide range of mental health issues, drawing from nearly 25 years of experience. Our specialties include:

- ADD/ADHD
- Abuse
- Anxiety
- Bipolar Disorder
- Career Issues
- Conduct Disorder
- Couples/Marital
- Creativity Enhancement
- Cultural Issues
- Depression
- Divorce
- Eating Disorders
- Gender Identity
- Grief
- Impulse or Habit Control
- Interpersonal Conflict
- Intimacy
- Isolation or Loneliness
- Life Balance
- Life Transition
- Men's Issues
- Obsessive Compulsive Disorder
- Oppositional Defiant Behavior
- Parent-child Conflicts
- Women's Issues

MARKETING & SALES

Practice Manager Eric Simms has developed a detailed marketing plan for our practice that includes specific tactics for furthering our growth. These include:

- Printed materials describing our practice for prospective clients and referral sources.

- An ongoing, highly targeted direct mail campaign that promotes our capabilities to professional referral sources in a 20-mile radius surrounding our practice.

- An expanded Yellow Page advertisement with pictures of our counselors and a short list of common services offered.

- A professional networking strategy that involves membership in the local chamber of commerce and county medical society.

- Local, regional, and national public speaking engagements on a wide range of mental health topics.

- A regular presence on a weekly local radio program called On Your Mind, where callers can phone in and ask our counselors general questions on the air.

- A Web site with complete details about our practice, as well as a resource section where people can obtain general information about mental health issues. In addition, our site allows people to request their first appointment with us online.

OPERATIONS

Facility & Location

Following its merger with Evergreen Associates, Roper Counseling Services relocated its offices to the Stonefield Building. Located on the thriving east side of Chicopee Bend, with ample parking space and access to major highways and bus routes, this office complex is home to other professionals who may serve as new referral sources for us. These include several attorneys and physicians, as well as two social service agencies.

In addition to the benefits listed above, we chose to relocate to the Stonefield Building because the office space was already suitable for our specific needs. It previously was home to a burgeoning psychiatry practice that closed its doors when two of the partners retired, and another decided to relocate elsewhere. In addition to the main entrance accessible off the waiting area, a separate entrance is available for therapists and staff. In addition, the facility offers soundproof counseling rooms, as well as a large, secure space for records storage.

Billing & Payment

Roper Counseling Services accepts payments from private insurance plans, as well as self-payments from individuals. Unless clients make other arrangements with us ahead of time, we require payment at the time of service. In addition to personal checks, we also accept Visa, MasterCard, Discover, and American Express. We have an existing computerized billing system for mental health practitioners that tracks patient accounts and generates all necessary forms and statements.

Fees

The fees that we charge vary depending upon contracts negotiated with different insurance companies, hospitals, and other agencies. Due to the complexity associated with various contracts, this information is not normally included with our business plan. However, it can be provided upon request. Generally speaking, our fee schedule is comparable with other counseling practices in our market.

Hours of Operation

Regular appointments are offered by appointment only; walk-ins are not welcomed. However, we do leave several slots in our schedules open every day for clients with urgent needs. In addition, all of our counselors rotate on-call duty, so that one is always available at any time for emergencies. An answering service forwards relevant after-hours calls received via our main number to the counselor on-call's cell phone.

LEGAL

Colorado's Department of Regulatory Agencies, Division of Registrations, has minimum licensure requirements that must be met by both psychologists and social workers.

Our psychologists meet all necessary requirements, including:

- Doctoral degrees from American Psychological Association-approved programs.

- One year of supervised post-degree experience.

- Successfully passing an examination in psychology prescribed by the state's Board of Psychologist Examiners.

- Completion of a jurisprudence examination developed by the Board of Psychologist Examiners.

Our social workers also have met the minimum licensure requirements for their profession established by Colorado's Board of Social Work Examiners.

In addition to compliance with licensure requirements, our practice also has secured appropriate liability insurance coverage from Smithfield Insurance Associates.

FINANCIAL PROJECTIONS

In 2015, Roper Counseling Services and Evergreen Associates generated combined net income of approximately $104,830. A detailed breakdown can be seen in the following balance sheet, which covers the time period January 1, 2015 to December 31, 2015.

Income

Billings	$691,986
Consulting	$141,306
Public speaking	$ 18,524
Royalty income	$ 7,458
Total income	**$859,274**

Expenses

Salaries	$550,506
Utilities	$ 5,170
Rent	$ 30,360
Insurance	$ 23,694
401 K contributions	$ 35,782
Office supplies	$ 10,780
Marketing & advertising	$ 14,135
Telecommunications & Internet	$ 5,478
Professional development	$ 37,378
Travel & entertainment	$ 14,608
Subscriptions & dues	$ 5,720
Repairs & maintenance	$ 1,418
Taxes	$ 19,415
Total expenses	**$754,444**
Net income	**$104,830**

Based on our analysis of the market, and taking current economic conditions into consideration, we are forecasting that net income for our expanded practice will grow at a compound annual rate of 4 percent for the next five years.

2015	$104,830
2016	$109,023
2017	$113,385
2018	$117,920
2019	$122,637

Diner

The Diner Depot Inc.

3619 4th Ave.
Rochelle, IL 61068

Paul Greenland

The Diner Depot is a classic American railcar-style diner situated near a popular railroad park.

EXECUTIVE SUMMARY

The Diner Depot is a classic American railcar-style diner. It is located at 3619 4th Ave. in Rochelle, Illinois, near the Rochelle Railroad Park, a popular tourist destination for railroad enthusiasts and train watchers. The Diner Depot is similar in appearance to the shiny railcar diners of yesteryear, many of which have disappeared from the American landscape, but is of new construction. Serving classic fare, such as hamburgers, club sandwiches, soups, malts, milkshakes, and a full breakfast menu, the diner caters to local residents, as well as the thousands of tourists who travel from all corners of the country, and even other parts of the world, to visit the railroad park every year. There, they enjoy an observation pavilion that enables them to safely watch approximately 90 trains that pass through the area on a daily basis, as well as other amenities, such as displays of old locomotives and loudspeakers that broadcast radio transmissions between train crews and railroad dispatchers.

INDUSTRY ANALYSIS

The Diner Depot is part of the restaurant industry. According to the National Restaurant Association, industry revenues were expected to reach $683.4 billion in 2014, up significantly from $586.7 billion in 2010 and $379 million in 2000. The restaurant industry's share of the food dollar totals 47 percent, compared to only 25 percent in 1955. Eating places like The Diner Depot account for the majority ($455.9 billion) of industry sales. Employment at the industry's 990,000 locations also is increasing, rising from 11.9 million in 2004 to approximately 13.5 million in 2014. By 2024, the restaurant industry is projected to employ 14.8 million people.

MARKET ANALYSIS

The city of Rochelle is located 25 miles south of Rockford, one of the largest cities in Illinois, and 80 miles west of Chicago. Although it is a smaller community, Rochelle has emerged as a major logistics hub because of its location at the crossroads of two Class 1 railroads and two interstate highways. In addition, the city owns the short-line City of Rochelle Railroad, which provides a lead-track switching service to the Burlington-Northern/Santa Fe and Union Pacific Railroads. Area employers enjoy access to a pool of 300,000 skilled and unskilled workers from a three-county area.

According to the city's economic development developer, more than $1.2 billion in capital and $50 million in infrastructure investment has been made in the area over the past decade, resulting in 4.5 million square feet of industrial space and some 1,500 new jobs. The community also is home to the Rochelle Business and Technology Park, which offers companies access to a regional multi-gigabit fiber optic broadband network that enables the transmission of large amounts of data at high speeds.

According to demographic data obtained by the owners at their local public library, Rochelle was home to an estimated 9,336 people in 2014 (3,750 households). The city's average household income was $60,982. Between 2000 and 2010, residents experienced average income growth of 23.8 percent. This remarkable figure is projected to grow an additional 19.9 percent between 2014 and 2019. On average, consumers' annual expenditures on food and beverages away from home broke down as follows in 2014:

- Breakfast & Brunch ($256)
- Dinner ($1,126)
- Lunch ($633)
- Snacks & Non-Alcoholic Beverages ($160)

Steady growth in each of these categories was projected through 2019.

Rochelle's success as a logistics and business destination creates demand for services provided by other businesses, such as The Diner Depot. At present, there are no other eating and drinking places quite like The Diner Depot. The owners anticipate a favorable response and repeat business from local residents, area employees, and tourists alike.

The Diner Depot's main competitors will be:

- McDonald's
- Smith's Family Restaurant
- Ivan's Ice Cream

SERVICES

The Diner Depot will serve classic diner food to its customers, including these signature menu items:

Appetizers
- Cheddar Cheese Fries
- Chicken Tenders
- French Fries
- Mozzarella Sticks
- Onion Rings
- Sweet Potato Fries

Soups & Salads
- Chef Salad
- Homemade Soup of the Day
- Soup & Salad Combo

Hamburger Platters (served with french fries)

- Barbecue Burger
- Classic Cheeseburger
- Classic Hamburger
- Patty Melt
- Sourdough Swiss Burger
- Veggie Burger

Sandwiches

- BLT
- Double-Decker Club
- French Dip Sandwich
- Fried Chicken
- Grilled Chicken Wrap
- Grilled Ham & Cheese
- Meatloaf Sandwich
- Pork Tenderloin
- Veggie Melt

Dinner Platters

- Chicken Fried Steak
- Yankee Pot Roast
- Meatloaf
- Fried Catfish
- Fried Chicken
- Fish & Chips
- Chicken Tenders

Breakfast

- Bacon
- Biscuits & Gravy
- Cinnamon Rolls
- Country Scramble
- Denver Omelet
- Eggs, Hash Browns & Toast
- Four Cheese Omelet
- French Toast
- Garden Omelet
- Ham & Cheese Omelet

- Muffins
- Pancakes
- Sausage
- Waffles

Beverages
- Apple Juice
- Coffee
- Hot Chocolate
- Hot Tea
- Iced Tea
- Juice
- Lemonade
- Milk
- Orange Juice
- Soda (Pepsi, Diet Pepsi, Mountain Dew, Sierra Mist, Dr. Pepper, Mug Root Beer)
- Tomato Juice

Malts & Shakes
Various Flavors: Root Beer, Chocolate, Cherry, Banana, Brownie Fudge, Peanut Butter Cup, Oreo, M&M, Chocolate, Vanilla, Strawberry

Desserts
- Apple Pie
- Cherry Pie
- Chocolate Sundae
- Pumpkin Pie
- Strawberry Sundae

PERSONNEL

Owners

The Diner Depot is owned by brothers Rick and Larry Stanley. The Stanleys have extensive experience in the restaurant business. Their father, Richard Stanley, operated Stanleys Family Restaurant for 23 years in nearby Rockford, Illinois. There, Rick and Larry learned the ins and outs of the business from the ground up, beginning as busboys during high school. Inspired by their father's success, and with strong work ethics, the Stanley Brothers opened their own steakhouse, Rick & Larry's, with support from their father. In only seven years, this restaurant has become a tremendous success. As train enthusiasts, the Stanley family frequently visits nearby Rochelle to watch trains and spend time with other train watchers. Their appreciation for the Rochelle community in general, and the Rochelle Railroad Park in particular, played a key role in their decision to establish The Diner Depot. Rick and Larry Stanley will assume responsibility for daily management of The Diner Depot, including managing relations with all food suppliers and vendors and human resources management.

Support Staff

The Stanleys will employ a staff that includes the following positions:

(1) Waitstaff Lead (this position will serve in a supervisory capacity, providing the owners with some management assistance)

(1) Full-Time Waiter/Waitress

(2) Part-Time Waiters/Waitresses

(1) Full-Time Cook

(1) Part-Time Cook

(2) Part-time Dishwashers

The Stanleys will issue payroll checks to employees every other Friday. They have utilized a popular online legal document service to obtain basic policies and procedures for their business, ensuring compliance with all Illinois wage and hour laws.

Professional and Advisory Support

The owners will utilize their existing accounting firm, John Covey & Associates, to provide bookkeeping and tax advisory services for The Diner Depot. They have established commercial checking accounts with Central Community Bank, and will utilize a popular mobile point-of-sale service to accept credit card and debit card payments cost-effectively.

GROWTH STRATEGY

The Stanleys have established the following three-year growth strategy for The Diner Depot:

2015: Focus on establishing awareness about The Diner Depot in Rochelle and among railroad enthusiasts/train watchers planning to visit the Rochelle Railroad Park. Establish a reputation for excellent customer service and great food to encourage repeat business. Generate annual sales of $728,243 and net income (before taxes) of $167,885.

2016: Continue to increase awareness about the diner both locally and within the railroad enthusiast community. Maintain a reputation for great service and food to encourage ongoing word-of-mouth growth. Generate annual sales of $801,067 and net income (before taxes) of $184,245.

2017: Develop stronger ties with railroad enthusiasts by hosting railroad-related special events at The Diner Depot. Generate annual sales of $881,174 and net income (before taxes) of $202,670.

OPERATIONS

Location

Rick and Larry Stanley have identified an empty, one-acre commercial lot at 3619 4th Ave. in Rochelle, on which they will build their new diner. The cost of the lot, which is located close to the railroad park, is $150,000.

The owners have made arrangements with a specialty contractor to construct a 50-seat diner at a cost of $200,000. Featuring a stainless steel exterior, steel stud construction, and concrete floors, the diner has a railcar-like appearance. Inside, the structure will feature vinyl tile flooring, both table/chair and barstool/counter-style seating, decorative neon lighting, and two handicap-accessible bathrooms.

Equipment

Additionally, $75,000 in equipment purchases will be required to outfit the diner for operations. Among the equipment and furnishings that must be purchased are:

- Barstools
- Burners
- Chairs
- Countertops
- Dishes
- Equipment Stand
- Exhaust Hood
- Fire Suppression Equipment
- Freezer
- Fryer
- Griddle
- Icemaker
- Prep Sink
- Refrigerated Sandwich Unit
- Shelving
- Silverware
- Sink
- Storage Units
- Tables
- Toaster
- Worktable

Finally, the Stanleys have budgeted $15,000 to procure a selection of railroad memorabilia that they will use to decorate their new diner.

Hours

6 AM-2 PM, Monday-Sunday

MARKETING & SALES

The Diner Depot will use a variety of tactics to drive customer growth. The owners plan to commit considerable resources to promote the diner among local residents and employees, as well as railroad enthusiasts who visit the nearby railroad park.

1. Social Media: The Diner Depot will maintain a Facebook page and place targeted advertisements on this popular social media channel. Social media also will provide the owners with opportunities to reach niche markets, including train watchers and railroad enthusiasts planning to visit Rochelle, especially those from other cities and states.

2. Membership in the Rochelle Area Chamber of Commerce: This will provide the business with credibility and exposure, and provide the Stanleys with an opportunity to network with other business leaders throughout the community.

3. Newspaper Advertising: The Diner Depot will become a regular advertiser in *The Rochelle News Leader*, a newspaper serving the local community.

4. Radio Advertising: The Diner Depot also will become a regular advertiser on the local radio station, WRHL.

5. Coupons and Specials: The Stanleys will promote special offers in their newspaper advertising, and also via a coupon value pack that is distributed to Rochelle-area households every month.

6. Web Site: The Diner Depot will promote itself online as a unique railroad-themed destination. The business' Web site will include information about the diner's menu, location, hours, and owners, as well as a link to The Diner Depot's Facebook page.

7. E-mail Marketing: The Stanleys will develop a simple loyalty program, giving customers the ability to opt-in to a proprietary database so that they can receive information about breakfast and lunch specials.

8. Apparel: Customers, many of whom will be tourists, will be able to purchase Diner Depot T-shirts and hats, which will help spread word about the business.

9. Brand Identity: An eye-catching logo has been developed for The Diner Depot, in partnership with a local graphic designer. This will be utilized on signage, apparel, advertisements, etc.

FINANCIAL ANALYSIS

The Stanleys have been approved for a $350,000 commercial mortgage (terms 7%/15 years). They will put $35,000 down and finance $315,000. The owners will pay the $75,000 in equipment costs, and the $15,000 in railroad memorabilia decor, from their own personal savings, but anticipate recovering those costs during the first year of operations.

A complete set of pro forma financial statements have been prepared and are available upon request. The following table provides a monthly breakdown for The Diner Depot's first year of operations:

Projected income & expense (year one)

	Apr	May	Jun	Jul	Aug	Sep
	1	2	3	4	5	6
Income						
Total sales	$42,406	$44,566	$50,035	$58,327	$53,248	$53,821
Cost of goods sold	$13,570	$14,261	$16,011	$18,664	$18,202	$17,223
Labor cost	$ 7,750	$ 8,143	$ 9,144	$10,658	$10,394	$ 9,835
Total cost of goods sold	$21,320	$22,404	$25,155	$29,322	$28,596	$27,058
Gross profit	$21,085	$22,161	$24,880	$29,005	$24,653	$26,763
Expenses						
Advertising & marketing	$ 1,427	$ 1,427	$ 1,427	$ 1,427	$ 1,427	$ 1,427
Accounting & legal	$ 707	$ 707	$ 707	$ 707	$ 707	$ 707
Insurance	$ 423	$ 423	$ 423	$ 423	$ 423	$ 423
Mortgage	$ 2,831	$ 2,831	$ 2,831	$ 2,831	$ 2,831	$ 2,831
Sales tax	$ 345	$ 345	$ 345	$ 345	$ 345	$ 345
Telephone	$ 182	$ 182	$ 182	$ 182	$ 182	$ 182
Utilities	$ 1,331	$ 1,331	$ 1,331	$ 1,331	$ 1,331	$ 1,331
Owner draw	$ 3,630	$ 3,630	$ 3,630	$ 3,630	$ 3,630	$ 3,630
Total expenses	$10,876	$10,876	$10,876	$10,876	$10,876	$10,876
Net income before taxes	$ 5,133	$ 6,209	$ 8,928	$13,053	$ 8,701	$10,811

Projected income & expense (year one)—Cont.

	Oct	Nov	Dec	Jan	Feb	Mar	
	7	8	9	10	11	12	Total
Income							
Total sales	$43,729	$45,411	$74,004	$45,485	$43,729	$47,093	$728,243
Cost of goods sold	$13,994	$14,532	$23,681	$14,555	$14,498	$15,069	$235,055
Labor cost	$ 7,991	$ 8,298	$13,523	$ 8,311	$ 7,991	$ 8,606	$133,879
Total cost of goods sold	$21,984	$22,830	$37,204	$22,867	$22,489	$23,675	$368,934
Gross profit	$21,745	$22,581	$36,800	$22,619	$21,240	$23,418	$359,309
Expenses							
Advertising & marketing	$ 1,427	$ 1,427	$ 1,427	$ 1,427	$ 1,427	$ 1,427	$ 17,124
Accounting & legal	$ 707	$ 707	$ 707	$ 707	$ 707	$ 707	$ 8,484
Insurance	$ 423	$ 423	$ 423	$ 423	$ 423	$ 423	$ 5,076
Mortgage	$ 2,831	$ 2,831	$ 2,831	$ 2,831	$ 2,831	$ 2,831	$ 33,972
Sales tax	$ 345	$ 345	$ 345	$ 345	$ 345	$ 345	$ 4,140
Telephone	$ 182	$ 182	$ 182	$ 182	$ 182	$ 182	$ 2,184
Utilities	$ 1,331	$ 1,331	$ 1,331	$ 1,331	$ 1,331	$ 1,331	$ 15,972
Owner draw	$ 3,630	$ 3,630	$ 3,630	$ 3,630	$ 3,630	$ 3,630	$ 43,560
Total expenses	$10,876	$10,876	$10,876	$10,876	$10,876	$10,876	$130,512
Net income before taxes	$ 5,793	$ 6,629	$20,848	$ 6,667	$ 5,288	$ 7,466	$167,885

Drive-Through Coffee Business

College Bros. Coffee Inc.

285 Main St.
Cedar Mount, IN 46000

Paul Greenland

College Bros. Coffee Inc. is a drive-through coffee business, providing coffee lovers with the most popular coffee drinks fast!

EXECUTIVE SUMMARY

College Bros. Coffee Inc. is a drive-through coffee business, providing coffee lovers with the most popular coffee drinks fast! Part of the $30 billion coffee industry, the business is owned by brothers Pete and Jeremy Johnson, recent graduates of Central University's MBA program who both worked at leading coffee retailers while pursuing their graduate business degrees. This provided them with a first-hand opportunity to see the tremendous potential of a coffee-related business. College Bros. Coffee will maximize profits by adhering to a drive-through business model, keeping its real estate and overhead lower than a traditional coffee shop. To ensure fast service, the business will begin with a limited menu of the most popular coffee drinks. As operations are refined, additional beverage selections will be added. College Bros. Coffee also will offer seasonal coffee drinks.

INDUSTRY ANALYSIS

College Bros. Coffee is part of the coffee industry, which generated annual revenues of approximately $30 billion in 2013, according to *USA Today*. Industry estimates place the number of coffee shops between 20,000 and 24,000 nationwide, generating between $10 billion and $12 billion in sales annually. Industry leaders, which present the most significant competition, include Starbucks, Peet's Coffee, and Seattle's Best.

The industry is represented by two main trade organizations: the National Coffee Association of U.S.A, Inc. (NCA) and the Specialty Coffee Association of America (SCAA). The NCA's members account for more than 90 percent of coffee commerce in the United States, and include small and mid-sized companies, ranging from growers, roasters, and retailers to importer/exporters and wholesaler/suppliers. The NCA's focus is on providing the industry with "market and scientific research, domestic and international government relations, issues management and public relations, and education."

The SCAA provides its members, who hail from approximately 40 different countries and include both coffee roasters and retailers, with a number of benefits, including training, education, resources, and business services.

MARKET ANALYSIS

According to the NCA, 61 percent of U.S. adults drink coffee every day, compared to 41 percent for soft drinks. Those in the 25-39 age bracket are the strongest gourmet or specialty coffee consumers, with daily consumption rates of 42 percent. This compares to approximately 33 percent among those in the 18-24 and 40-59 age brackets, and 25 percent among those over age 60. Daily consumption of specialty coffees has been increasing steadily, climbing from 25 percent of adults in 2011 to 31 percent in 2012 and 2013, and reaching 34 percent in 2014. The number of adults consuming specialty coffees on a weekly basis also has been increasing, growing from 36 percent in 2011 to 44 percent in 2012, 47 percent in 2013, and 50 percent in 2014.

College Bros. Coffee is located in Cedar Mount, Indiana, a bedroom/commuter community with approximately 20,000 residents. The majority of the population works in Belton Center, Indiana, a larger city about 15 miles to the south. In recent years, downtown Cedar Mount has been experiencing revitalization as new businesses (including restaurants, art galleries, and a performing arts center) have opened in the town square area (especially on Main Street).

In 2014 the average household income in Cedar Mount was $60,005. This number is projected to increase 4.7 percent by 2014, reaching $71,213. The largest household income category consists of those earning between $50,000 and $74,999 (25.8%). The second-largest category includes those earning between $35,000 and $49,999 (19.6%).

PERSONNEL

College Bros. Coffee Inc. is owned by brothers Pete and Jeremy Johnson. Recent graduates of Central University's MBA program, Pete's degree concentrated on entrepreneurship, while Jeremy's emphasized finance. The brothers both worked at leading coffee retailers, including Starbucks, while pursuing their graduate business degrees. This provided them with a first-hand opportunity to see the tremendous potential of a coffee-related business.

Staff

Although the Johnsons will be hands-on owners, they will begin operations with a staff of two full-time and two part-time baristas. This will provide the brothers with flexible scheduling options and allow them to concentrate on administrative tasks, marketing initiatives, and growth strategies.

Professional and Advisory Support

The Johnsons have secured local accountant Paul Stanley to handle bookkeeping and provide tax advisory services. Additionally, commercial checking accounts have been established with Cedar Mount Community Bank, which also will provide merchant accounts needed for accepting credit card and debit card payments.

GROWTH STRATEGY

College Bros. Coffee has developed the following growth projections for its first three years of operations:

	2015	2016	2017
Units/year	172,993	207,592	298,932
Units/month	14,412	17,299	24,911
Units/day	480	576	830

Strong unit growth will support projected annual sales increases of 20 percent, with revenues reaching $518,980 in 2015, $622,776 in 2016, and $896,797 in 2017. By year three, the business is expected to generate a substantial net profit ($200,305), providing capital for further expansion.

Mobile Strategy

In addition to increasing unit sales at the business' physical location, Pete and Jeremy Johnson plan to expand operations via the addition of mobile coffee carts that will be utilized at special events in Cedar Mount, and also in nearby Belton Center, Indiana (as local Cedar Mount residents become loyal customers and desire the availability of College Bros. Coffee beyond the immediate local market). The owners plan to add one mobile coffee cart in 2016, followed by an additional cart in 2017.

SERVICES

College Bros. Coffee will begin operations with the following drink menu:

- Americano $2.50/$3.50
- Bottled Water $1.75
- Breve $3.25/$4.25
- Cafe Au Lait $3.25/$4.25
- Cafe Latte $3.25/$4.25
- Cappuccino $3.25/$4.25
- Chai Latte $3.25/$4.25
- Coffee $1.50/$1.75
- Espresso $2.50/$3.50
- Hot Chocolate $2.50/$3.50
- Iced Coffee $3.25
- Macchiatto $3.25/$4.25
- Mocha $3.25/$4.25

The company will differentiate itself by purchasing coffee beans from Romano's, a local coffee roaster.

Baked Goods

In addition to beverages, the business will offer a very limited selection of fresh-based cookies, muffins and scones from Britta's, a popular local bakery.

MARKETING & SALES

College Bros. Coffee has developed a marketing plan with the following tactics:

1. Exterior Signage: Eye-catching exterior signage, visible to pedestrian and vehicle traffic from both Main St. and Andrews Ave., has been developed.

2. Social Media: Consumers will be able to follow College Bros. Coffee on Instagram, Twitter, and Facebook, and access exclusive drink specials.

3. Mobile Marketing: The business will utilize a mobile marketing service, enabling consumers to receive text message alerts about special discounts and upcoming events.

4. Web Site: College Bros. Coffee has developed a Web site with information such as menu, location, hours, and details about special discounts.

5. Outdoor Advertising: College Bros. Coffee will use billboard advertising in two strategic locations to route traffic to the business. Additionally, the business will run regular print advertising in the *Cedar Mount Gazette,* a free community paper.

6. Incentives: Pete and Jeremy Johnson have hired local college students to distribute approximately 750 coupons for one free cup of College Bros. Coffee, as well as one half-price latte. The coupons will be distributed to mailboxes in residential neighborhoods in the Cedar Mount area the week before the business opens. The business also will promote specials and incentives in a coupon pack that is mailed to area households.

7. Community Outreach: College Bros. Coffee will sponsor local community events, including parades and festivals, in order to build goodwill with area residents.

OPERATIONS

Location

College Bros. Coffee's location is one of its most significant assets. The business is located at 285 Main St. in Cedar Mount, Indiana, a bedroom/commuter community with approximately 20,000 residents. The majority of the population works in Belton Center, Indiana, a larger city about 15 miles to the south. In recent years, downtown Cedar Mount has been experiencing revitalization as new businesses (including restaurants, art galleries, and a performing arts center) have opened in the town square area (especially on Main Street).

Situated at the intersection of Main St. and Andrews Ave., College Bros. Coffee is located in a long vacant drive-in, which the owners have renovated and converted into a drive-through operation at a cost of $40,000. The 30' x 15' (350 sq. ft.) structure is located on a rectangular lot, which allowed for the addition of a drive-through lane capable of accommodating a long, steady line of vehicles.

Features of the College Bros. Coffee structure include:

- 2 drive-up windows

- 1 60-foot drive-through lane

- 1 walk-up window

- Coffee condiment/beverage staging area

- 75-square-foot ingredient/paper product storage area

Hours

Catering primarily to the residents of Cedar Mount, College Bros. Coffee will operate from 6 AM-6 PM Monday through Friday, 6 AM-2 PM on Saturday, and 11 AM-2 PM on Sunday.

Suppliers

College Bros. Coffee has chosen several local, regional, and national food service distributors who will supply the business with food and beverage items. This list is available upon request. One of the business's differentiating factors will be its use of local suppliers whenever possible. These include the local coffee roaster, Romano's, as well as Britta's, a popular local bakery.

Start-up Costs

The following equipment will be required prior to start-up:

Equipment

Beverage dispensing equipment

Automatic coffee maker	$ 656
Coffee grinder	$ 742
Espresso machine 240v	$ 2,150
Commercial blender	$ 485
Medium capacity (1 phase-air cooled) ice machine	$ 1,874
Water purification system	$ 765
Cup dispensers (2)	$ 125
Carafes (6)	$ 150

Sales & display equipment

Cash register	$ 1,265
Menu board	$ 1,550
Daily special panel	$ 135

Miscellaneous equipment

Electric can opener	$ 55
Refrigerator	$ 1,750
Safe	$ 1,390
Dish sink with pre-wash sprayer	$ 275
Water heater	$ 600
Tackboard	$ 125
Mop & broom holder	$ 25
Tablet computer, printer and software	$ 1,425
Commercial microwave	$ 350
Total equipment costs	**$15,892**

LEGAL

College Bros. Coffee complies with all state and federal food laws and regulations, and is considered a retail food establishment per the Indiana Administrative Code (IAC) under 410 IAC 7-24-79. The business is registered through the Walton County Health Department, as required by the Indiana State Food Law. In addition, Pete and Jeremy Johnson have secured appropriate business and liability insurance (policies available upon request) for their coffee drive-through operation.

FINANCIAL ANALYSIS

The Johnsons have secured a $65,000 business loan (term 5 years, 6% interest) to cover facility renovations and initial operations. They will cover the $15,892 in start-up costs from personal savings.

A complete set of pro forma financial statements have been prepared and are available upon request. The following table provides an overview of key projections for years one through three:

	2015	2016	2017
Sales	**$518,980**	**$622,776**	**$896,797**
Direct cost of sales	($177,609)	($211,744)	($304,911)
Payroll (production)	($134,733)	($141,470)	($148,544)
Total cost of sales	**($312,341)**	**($353,214)**	**($453,455)**
Gross margin	$206,639	$269,562	$443,342
Gross margin percentage	39.80%	43.30%	49.40%
Expenses			
Advertising & marketing	$ 50,000	$ 60,000	$ 70,000
General/administrative	$ 1,500	$ 1,500	$ 1,500
Legal	$ 1,500	$ 750	$ 750
Coffee carts	$ 0	$ 15,000	$ 15,000
Accounting	$ 1,800	$ 2,000	$ 2,200
Office supplies	$ 1,500	$ 1,500	$ 1,500
Business insurance	$ 4,500	$ 5,000	$ 5,500
Payroll (administrative)	$ 60,000	$ 70,000	$ 80,000
Payroll taxes	$ 29,210	$ 31,721	$ 34,282
Mortgage	$ 9,900	$ 9,900	$ 9,900
Postage	$ 325	$ 325	$ 325
Utilities	$ 3,250	$ 3,500	$ 3,750
Startup loan	$ 15,080	$ 15,080	$ 15,080
Repairs & maintenance	$ 3,250	$ 3,250	$ 3,250
Total expenses	**$181,815**	**$219,526**	**$243,037**
Net income	**$ 24,824**	**$ 50,036**	**$200,305**

Dry Cleaner

Express Clean

3112 Stetson Hills Blvd.
Colorado Springs, CO 80923

Zuzu Enterprises

Express Clean is an established and profitable dry cleaner in the Black Forest neighborhood of Colorado Springs. Peter and Lynn Samuelson are purchasing the business from its original owner and have plans to add hours and services to increase its sales by 25% or more.

EXECUTIVE SUMMARY

Express Clean was established May, 2005 in Colorado Springs, Colorado. It has been owned and operated by the same owner and at the same location since that time. After working for 40 years, the owner is ready to retire and is looking to sell the business including all inventory, furnishings, and equipment.

Express Clean is located in the Black Forest neighborhood next to golfing, high scale residential neighborhoods, and schools. It is positioned in large shopping center with excellent traffic flow and features a drive-thru drop off and pickup window.

The business also features good repeat customers and goodwill. Express Clean is well known for their quality of work and service, and this solid customer base will ensure the business remains profitable for years to come.

INDUSTRY ANALYSIS

Laundry and dry cleaning services were a $9 billion dollar industry in the United States in 2014. This is expected to remain stable, with a very modest decline projected over the next 10 years (less than 0.1%).

Poor economic conditions over the past 7 years have led many consumers to reduce spending on discretionary services including laundry and dry cleaning. Consumer shifts to low-maintenance clothing has also dampened the market for dry cleaning services, as has the emergence of at-home dry cleaning products.

Most revenue (76.5%) in the laundry and dry cleaning industry is earned through standard dry cleaning services. Of this amount, retail dry cleaning make up 64.2% while commercial dry cleaning accounts for the remaining 12.3%.

As of 2014, 147,900 people were employed in the laundry and dry cleaning business. Employment of laundry and dry-cleaning workers is projected to grow 10 percent from 2012 to 2022, about as fast as the average for all occupations.

While economic concerns and a change in consumer clothing purchases have affected the dry cleaning industry, it still remains a significant business that isn't going away. Changes to the business in terms of new services and updating processes to be more environmentally friendly will only add to its appeal and relevance in people's lives.

MARKET ANALYSIS

Colorado Springs is the second-largest city in Colorado, after Denver. It is the seat of El Paso County, making up about three-quarters of the county's population. It is located on the edge of the Rocky Mountains, with Pikes Peak towering beside it to the west. To the east begin the Great Plains.

The city's economy is still based heavily on the military (with the US Air Force Academy, Fort Carson, etc.) and tourism, although in more recent years, Colorado Springs has gained a strong foothold in the electronics, high-technology, and manufacturing industries. The city is the headquarters of the U.S. Olympic Committee and Olympic Training Center facility.

The local economy has rebounded with significant increases in sales tax collections and home sales. The largest retail benefactors of increased sales are grocery stores and clothing stores, up 14.6 % and 9.8%, respectively, from the same time last year. As of May, 2015, home sales in Colorado Springs were up 24.3% with the average home price increasing by 13.9%. Additionally, the population of Colorado Springs (439,000 in 2014) has continued to grow at pre-recession levels. Between July 2012 and July 2013, Colorado Springs grew 1.5% keeping on the long term growth rate of 21% since 2000. All of these numbers are having and will continue to have a positive impact on retailers and service providers.

Competition

While there are other dry cleaners in Colorado Springs, none are within 5 miles of Black Forest. The closest dry cleaners include:

- Powers Center Cleaners, 5519 Powers Center Point. Powers Center is highly regarded and well-reviewed. They are located approximately 8 miles from the Black Forest neighborhood.

- Summit Cleaners, 8710 N Union Blvd. Summit is known for their high prices, as reflected in their numerous reviews on Yelp, Google, and other review sites. They are located approximately 6 miles from the Black Forest neighborhood.

- 189 Super Quality Dry Cleaners, 9475 Briar Park Point #160. 189 Super Quality has received many negative reviews on Yelp, Google, and other review sites for their poor customer service. They are located approximately 10 miles from the Black Forest neighborhood.

SERVICES

Express Clean offers a full line of services including:

- Laundry—wash and fold services

- Dry cleaning—clothes

- Dry cleaning—household items

- Alterations/Repairs

All services are available on either a retail or commercial basis.

Dry cleaning specialties include silk, leather, suede, area rugs, and wedding dresses.

Express Clean also offers same and next day service for an additional charge.

PRICING SCHEDULE

Pricing schedule

Laundry	Price
Shirt (men)	$ 1.85
Tuxedo shirt	$ 4.20
Shirt (women)	$ 5.00
Pants	$ 5.00
Shorts	$ 4.50
Golf shirt	$ 4.50
Sweater	$ 5.00
Lab coat	$ 7.00
Boxed shirts	$ 2.50

Dry cleaning—clothes

2 piece suit	$ 9.50
Tuxedo suit	$10.50
3 piece suit	$12.50
Blazer	$ 6.50
Dress	$ 9.50
Dress silk	$12.00
2 piece dress	$13.50
Vest	$ 4.50
Sweater—regular	$ 5.00
Sweater—cashmere	$ 6.00
Sweater—thick	$ 6.25
Tank top	$ 4.35
Robe	$12.00
Rain coat	$13.00
Rain coat with lining	$15.00
3/4 length coat	$12.00
Long coat	$15.00
Heavy jacket/short coat	$ 8.00
Skirt	$ 5.00
Skirt suit	$ 9.00
Evening dress	Varies
Tie	$ 4.00
Scarf	$ 6.00
Cap	$ 5.00
Glove	$ 6.00
Blouse (regular)	$ 5.00
Graduation gown/ Choir robe	$13.00
Thick gown/clergy robe	$18.00

Dry cleaning—household Items

Comforter full	$20.00
Comforter queen/kind	$25.00
Comforter (down)	$30.00
Blanket	$16.00
Quilt	$20.00
Pillow cover	$ 3/$7
Sheet (each)	$13.00
Table cloth, skirt	$18.00
Napkin	$ 1.80
Apron	$ 6.00
Curtain	$10.00
Curtain with lining	$15.00
Curtain with pleat (per pleat)	+ $ 2.50
Cushion	$12.00
Cushion cover	$ 6.00
Sofa cover	$ 8.00
Sleeping bag	$20.00

Alterations/repairs	Price
Hems	
Blindstitched pants	$ 8.00
Topstitched pants	$10.00
Cuffed pants	$14.00
Lined pants	$14.00
Lined & cuffed	$18.00
Cotton dress 1 layer	$15.00
Cotton dress 2 layers	$25.00
Lycra dress 1 layer	$20.00

Pants/skirt

Waist in/out	$15.00
Waist in/out, lined	$20.00
Waist in/out w/zipper	$25.00
Lined w/side zipper	$35.00
Take in hips only slacks/skirt	$10.00
Taper legs	$15.00
Stride in/out	$20.00
Replace zipper	$15.00 & up

Khaki type pants/skirts

Waist in (top stitching)	$20.00
Waist thru hips (top stitching)	$30.00
Hips in (top stitching)	$20.00
Taper legs	$20.00
Take in stride (without top stitching)	$20.00
Take in stride (top stitching)	$35.00

Jeans

Regular hem	$12.00
Original hem	$18.00
Take in back seam	$30.00
Taper legs non-welted seam	$30.00
Taper legs w/welted seam	$45.00
Take in stride	$45.00
Replace zipper	$25.00

Miscellaneous

Re-stitch seam	$ 5.00 each seam
Sew buttons	$ 0.50 each
Add hook/eye	$ 0.50 set
Patches	$ 5.00 + (vary depending on shape)

Men's/women's suits

Jackets	
Hem sleeves (vented)	$35.00 & up
Hem sleeves (lined/no vent)	$15.00
Shorten jacket	$25.00 & up
Reline	$50.00
Take in/let out	$20.00 & up
Shoulders	
Take up/redo	$75.00
Shirts/blouses	
Hem straight bottom	$10.00
Make curved hem straight	$15.00
Hem bottom w/slits or tails	$15.00
Lining additional	$10.00
Hem long sleeve w/cuff	$25.00
Hem short sleeve	$10.00
Take in sides w/top stitching	$25.00
Darts in back	$15.00
Embellishments	Prices vary per garment

Same day and next day service is available for an additional charge. Upcharges may also apply for the following reasons:

- Excessive Animal Hair Removal

- Top Brand Clothing (requires special handling)

- Removing Buttons (diamonds, delicate buttons like shells, etc.)

- Luxurious Accessories (fancy beads, sequins, etc.)

- Silk and Leather

- Coats/Scarves (length and weight of material)

- Antique Items

- Extra Sizing starting with 2XL

- Spotting

PERSONNEL

Owners

Peter and Lynn Samuelson will own and operate Express Clean. Peter worked in a dry cleaner's in college and has 10 years' experience working in a business environment. Lynn has worked in the upscale retail industry for 9 years. The Samuelsons are interested in owning their own business and the opportunity to own and operate Express Clean is a good fit for their experience and desires.

Support Staff

The three current employees will stay working for Express Clean when ownership transfers to the Samuelsons. All have five or more years' tenure with the company and have received favorable reviews from customers and coworkers alike. Their continuation with the company will ease the transition to the new owners and reinforce the commitment to quality service and customer care to our current clients.

Professional and Advisory Support

Express Clean will use the local accounting firm, Miller & Morrison, for assistance with tax preparation and bookkeeping. In addition, they have established a commercial checking account with First State Bank, and will utilize a popular mobile point-of-sale service to accept credit card and debit card payments from customers. Liability insurance has been obtained from a national provider.

GROWTH STRATEGY

Although Express Clean has remained profitable over the years, the Samuelsons will employ a multi-pronged growth strategy over the next five years. This strategy includes:

- Offer a pick up and drop off service

- Increase availability by offering Sunday business hours

- Explore the option of wholesale cleaning services to other dry cleaners

• Investigate and implement new greener dry cleaning options to limit worker exposure to harmful chemicals and be better for the environment. Heavily promote and advertise any green improvements.

We believe these tactics will increase revenue up to 25%.

ADVERTISING & MARKETING

Advertising and marketing have been almost nonexistent for the past several years, with business relying almost exclusively on repeat customers and word-of-mouth referrals. This is an area where Express Clean will improve. Specifically, we plan to:

• Advertise in local print and electronic media

• Develop a website and social media presence, including Facebook, Instagram, and Twitter

• Plan and advertise a grand re-opening/new owner party with daily specials

• Send mailers and coupons to current customer or include with their orders

• Approach large and mid-size local companies to explore the option of a corporate account

• Procure vibrant signage to advertise Sunday openings

• Approach other dry cleaning companies to explore wholesale options

• Heavily advertise and promote any advances in green technology and processes

OPERATIONS/COMPANY DESCRIPTION

Hours of Operation

Express Clean is currently open from 7:30 am until 7 pm, from Monday to Saturday. The new, expanded hours will include:

Monday to Saturday, 6:30am until 7:00pm

Sunday, 12:00pm until 5:00pm

Location

Express Clean is located in a large shopping center in Colorado Springs in the upscale neighborhood known as Black Forest. The site occupies approximately 1,900 square feet and features a drop off/pick up window and excellent traffic flow for easy in and out. There is excellent lighting and visibility as well as parking. The shopping area has a great mix of retail stores, markets and fantastic restaurants.

The property is leased with 5 years remaining and renewable for another 5 years. The lease is set at $1,715 per month.

Equipment

All necessary equipment comes with the sale of the store. This equipment includes:

• Full-service dry cleaning machines

• Industrial washing machines

• Industrial dryers

• Industrial sewing machine

- Automatic folding machines
- Clothing pressers (including shirt press, sleever, collar/cuffs, etc.)
- Clothing steamer
- 75 gallon recycled water tank
- 100 gallon water heater
- Compressors
- Markers—hand and machine
- Point of Sale (POS) system
- State-of-the-art computers
- Custom-made counters
- Double deck automatic conveyor system

All equipment is in impeccable condition, maintained throughout the years and made by top brands such as Unisec and Sankosha.

Payment Options

Customers have the option to pay with cash, check, Visa, Mastercard, Discover, or American Express at the time the service is rendered. Commercial accounts may be billed monthly.

SWOT ANALYSIS

Strengths

- Express Cleaners is located in large shopping center with excellent traffic flow.
- We have earned a great reputation for our excellent customer service and prices.
- There is no competition within 5 miles.
- We are surrounded by numerous upscale residential neighborhoods.
- The owner is willing to train/assist the new owner and current employees will stay to make the transition smoother.
- 1,900 square foot service hall allows for plenty of room to accommodate expanded services and increase in business.
- 5 year renewable lease ensures no increase in building costs.

Weaknesses

- There has been a lack of advertising and marketing in the past several years.
- Sales have remained steady, yet stagnant for the past 3 years.

Opportunities

- By adding pick-up and delivery service, being open on Sundays, and adding wholesale service to this existing retail store, we can see an increase in volume of 25% or more.
- Equipment in the plant is underutilized and has capability to handle larger volume. We could take advantage of the existing dry cleaning client base to cross sell its ancillary services.
- Aggressively seeking more corporate and business accounts could increase revenue by another 10%.

- We could increase worker satisfaction by rotating jobs and allowing for time to move around, change position, and sit.

- We can investigate and implement new greener dry cleaning options to limit worker exposure to harmful chemicals and be better for the environment. Any progress towards a green solution should be heavily advertised and promoted.

- Express Clean will seek membership in the Drycleaning & Laundry Institute for technical assistance, networking, customer service training, website development, and regulatory information.

- Membership will also be pursued in the National Cleaners Association, a valuable resource for training, webinars, trends, new products, and regulatory information.

Threats

- Sales may be slowed as consumers purchase clothing and other articles that can be cleaned at home.

- Consumers may choose to purchase at-home dry cleaning kits to avoid the cost of dry cleaning services.

FINANCIAL ANALYSIS

Express Clean is being offered for sale for $175,000. Tax returns and other financial information prove that Express Clean has always earned a profit. Cash flow is reported as $56,640 with $229,217 in revenue. Furniture, fixtures and equipment (FF&E) are estimated to be worth $120,750. It is estimated that $1,000 a month is currently invested in supplies.

Engraving and Personalization Services

Unique Laser Engraving & Keepsakes

405 North Riverside Avenue
St. Clair, MI 48079

Zuzu Enterprises

Unique Laser Engraving & Keepsakes has been in business since 2003. We started in a small home studio with one laser and showcased our products at various fairs and art festivals. We are currently looking to expand our storefront into a larger facility to accommodate our growing business.

EXECUTIVE SUMMARY

Unique Laser Engraving & Keepsakes has been in business since 2003. We started in a small home studio with one laser and showcased our products at various fairs and art festivals.

As the years have passed, we have grown from one laser in a small office to several lasers and a bricks and mortar storefront as well as an online store. We've traveled to New Mexico to learn glass etching and stone carving, added dye sublimation, porcelain memorials, and UV printing. There are so many beautiful things that can be made with all of the different processes that we do. From a simple metal tag to a beautiful photo lasered on wood, we can make a keepsake that lasts a lifetime.

We are currently looking to expand our storefront into a larger facility to accommodate our growing business.

INDUSTRY ANALYSIS

The Engraving Services industry experienced strong growth over the five years to 2015, largely recovering from a low base, and growing at an average annual rate of 6.9%. Because the bulk of services that this industry provides is largely discretionary, revenue experienced a substantial increase of 17.2% over 2011, thanks to rising disposable income and improved consumer confidence. No longer strapped for cash, many consumers have been increasingly willing to engage in the customization of certain products, such as trophies, plaques, jewelry, and other keepsakes.

MARKET ANALYSIS

St. Clair is a relatively small town, with a population of approximately 5,400 in early 2015. This number is expected to increase 5.5% between now and 2040. The senior (50+) population is significant and expected to grow the most during this time. The median household income and property values are slightly higher than the rest of the state, while the cost of living is slightly less. Most residents do not work in the city, but have a mean travel time to work of 27 minutes. People move here not for the jobs but because of its natural beauty on the St. Clair River overlooking Canada. Its many dedicated parks and small-town feel make it a perfect refuge from the big city.

St. Clair is also known as a town that appreciates and cultivates artists. The St. Clair Art Association boasts a retail outlet and renowned educational facility and is host to a large annual art show. The St. Clair Art Fair is one of the oldest art fairs in Eastern Michigan and features over 120 artists.

PROCESSES/SERVICES

- Dye Sublimation

- Glass Etching/Stone Carving

- Laser Engraving

- Specialty Engraving

- UV Printing

Dye Sublimation

Dye sublimation is the process of putting photos, text or artwork onto specially coated materials with special inks, paper and heat. From metals, glass, wood, porcelain, plastics to fabric, dye sublimation is a way to create some beautiful gifts and keepsakes.

Dye Sublimation as a process is really very simple. It is the method of applying an image to specially coated ceramics, metals and polyester cloth, using three main ingredients: sublimation ink, heat and pressure.

Sublimation ink is unique in its ability to convert from a solid to a gas without going through a liquid form. (Just like dry ice.) The conversion is initiated by heat and controlled with pressure and time. Hard items such as ceramic, fiber board, metals, etc. require a special coating to accept the sublimation inks.

Glass Etching/Stone Carving

Glass etching and stone carving are great ways to make beautiful gifts. For weddings and special occasions, wine glasses, serving pieces, and beer mugs make great gifts. Stones and bricks can also be used for memorials in the home and in gardens.

Laser Engraving

Unique Laser Engraving & Keepsakes can laser engrave on just about any type of material including wood, marble, acrylics, plastics, metals, and more. From text to photos, we can do your product marking or create a beautiful keepsake to last a lifetime.

Laser engraving has many advantages over traditional printing. Laser engraving is:

- Durable—Laser engraving markings stand up to years of use.

- Inexpensive—Laser engraving per piece costs are very low.

- Precise—Resolution and precision make laser engraving unique.

- Impressive—Laser engraving presents an exciting compliment to the item.

Specialty Photo Engraving

Specialty photo engraving can be done to almost any material, including acrylic, anodized aluminum, cloth, coated metals, Corian, cork, glass, some plastics, leather, marble, matte board, melamine, stainless steel, tile, wood, and more.

Products are made using customers' own photographs. We scan the photo and do any cropping or retouching that needs to be done and return the original photo intact.

UV Printing

Unique Laser Engraving & Keepsakes can put photos, designs or other artwork on to almost any surface with the UV digital print service. Our company offers a process that decorates products in full color with no special coating needed. UV Printing can be used for industrial applications, part marking, bar coding, Data Matrix codes, UID marking, decorative printing, small signage (indoor and outdoor), gifts and more.

Where conventional printing uses water-based ink, this new process uses UV ink that is not absorbed into the material. It is cured with a UV lamp as it is applied.

Why UV printing?

- It's green! Because the ink is dried immediately with UV lamps, there are virtually no chemicals (VOC's) released into the air.

- It's fast! Again, no waiting around for inks to dry. This means your printed piece can move along the production line without stopping to dry!

- It's cost effective! You save time in drying and in costly coatings. A costly aqueous coating is often applied when using traditional inks to promote faster drying times and to prevent smearing and smudging. UV printing does not require aqueous coating!

- It's more appealing! The UV inks are more vibrant since the ink does not have as much time to soak into the stock. It is also a harder surface with a lot more sheen!

PRODUCTS

- Glassware

- Brick and stone products

- Photo throw blankets

- Porcelain memorials & urns

- Signs

- Tile murals

- Wall tributes

- Miscellaneous

Glassware

Engraved glassware includes such items as personalized beer mugs and wine glasses as well as glass serving pieces like platters, bowls, casserole dishes, pie plates, and cakes stands. Just about anything can be personalized. Monogrammed pieces are an especially nice and thoughtful wedding present with having the added benefit of being easily identifiable at parties and pot luck dinners.

Brick and Stone Products

Brick and stone products are another specialty of Unique Laser Engraving & Keepsakes. From paving stones and garden stones to memorial bricks, we can design pieces with text and small pictures or logos.

Photo Throw Blankets

Photo Throws are either made with a knitting process or they are sublimated on to fleece. Either way they are an exquisite gift anyone would be proud to give and elated to receive. Photo Throws can be done in full color or in black and white.

Porcelain Memorials & Urns

Porcelain memorials have been around for over a century and have proven to be able to stand the test of time. They add a special character to a head stone, affording the present generation to be able to see the generations of the past. They are placed on headstones whether it is a grass flat marker or a vertical monument. They are a beautiful tribute to someone you love.

We also have Urns, including beautiful wood pieces for loved ones or special pets. A photo can be lasered on any of the pieces we carry.

Signs

Looking for a sign for your home, cabin or business? Unique Laser Engraving & Keepsakes can help you with that. We can make a wood or "Up North" sign for your cabin, your camper, home or garden. Small, full color signs can be made for indoors or out with our new UV print process. Indoor signage are also available for business, name plates, wall or door signs with two color laserable plastic, plates for gas and electrical panels, and more. Even larger, custom signs for business owners can be made with a great exterior material called HDU that doesn't absorb water from high humidity, rain, snow or ice so it does not expand or contract because of water. This means it doesn't warp or crack so the paint lasts longer and stays brighter than on wood.

Tile Murals

Tile has been around for years—you can put it in the kitchen, bathroom, on the floor or on the walls, even on a bar top. But you are regulated by what the box store has on the shelf.

Not anymore! We can customize tile just for you. Whether it be a high resolution photo that you have taken yourself or an idea that we can help you create, Unique Laser Engraving & Keepsakes has you covered! Both large and small tiles are available to help create the custom design you are looking for.

Wall Tributes

These beautiful wall tributes are different than any other plaque or trophy you have come across. They can be personalized to fit your needs, should you need a 6" ornament or a plaque up to 48" in diameter. These wood wall tributes are truly a stunning piece and can be customized with your design or logo. They can even be made into a clock!

Miscellaneous

Just about any product can be created using our various engraving and printing processes. From wall plates and knobs to wind spinners to home decor, Unique Laser Engraving & Keepsakes can make unique, personalized items to fit your any need.

PERSONNEL

Owners

Owners Paul and Peggy Roberts began their laser engraving business in 2003 in a small home studio with one laser and showcased their products at various fairs and art festivals. Since that time, business has grown substantially along with their product line and available services. In addition to building the business to the point of opening an online store, the Roberts were able to expand to the point of requiring and supporting a retail outlet. Business demand has increased still more, necessitating a move to a bigger facility.

Paul specializes in manning the machines and creating product, while Peggy runs the website and sees to the retail aspects of the online and bricks and mortar store.

Staff

There are four part-time staff in addition to Paul and Peggy. One staff member assists Peggy in retail duties, while the remaining three assist Paul with product creation. All staff have been with the company for 1 or more years.

COMPANY DESCRIPTION

Hours of Operation

Unique Laser Engraving & Keepsakes will be open Monday through Saturday, from 9am until 6pm. The online store is available 24/7.

Location

The new store will be located just down the street from the old store, but offers an additional 900 square feet. This space will be utilized to house raw materials and store orders for both the online and physical stores, while at the same time providing more work space for employees as they create the products. The front retail area will also have an additional 75 square feet to accommodate a new consultation/design area.

Equipment

Unique Laser Engraving & Keepsakes already owns all of the equipment necessary for operations. These include:

- Custom computer with graphics software and scanner
- Sublimation system with HD cartridges and multi-bypass tray
- Desktop engraver
- Glass Etching/Stone Carving system
- Laser engraver
- UV printer/cutter

The value of this equipment is estimated at $30,000.

Payment Options

We accept Visa, MasterCard, and PayPal for online sales. Cash, Visa, MasterCard, Discover or personal check with ID are the available payment options for those who are purchasing products in the bricks and mortar storefront.

Fitness Center

Fitness City

697 Lapeer Rd.
Lake Orion, MI 48360

Zuzu Enterprises

Laura Newton would like to assist people in meeting their fitness and weight loss goals. Having overcome obesity herself, she knows the importance of a good diet and hard work. She strives to be a motivational factor that will help people's lives for the better. She will utilize her knowledge and expertise garnered from personal experience and education to start Fitness City and do everything she can to help her clients realize their full potential.

EXECUTIVE SUMMARY

Around the world, scores of people participate in some sort of exercise, sports, or physical activity. They are overcoming excuses and realizing numerous benefits that one can achieve from undertaking physical activity on a regular basis. Exercise is important to keep both your body and mind in top condition.

With the obesity epidemic that is currently going on in the United States, fitness and weight loss have been growing in popularity, if not becoming an obsession, for Americans. The rate of obesity grew steadily from 1987 to 2007 and all states except Colorado consider at least one fifth of their population obese. Over 72 million Americans, or one third of the population of the United States, are considered clinically obese.

Fitness businesses offer individuals supervision, assistance, and motivation for all fitness levels. There are many reasons people choose to join a gym, rather than work out at home. Common reasons are equipment, programs, and socializing. Health clubs are providing specialized programming and trainers that are specifically trained and certified to work with older adults. There are also more youth programs as health club members younger than 18 grew from 6.1 million in 2010 to 8.9 million in 2015.

Gym-goers are staying motivated with the help of new technology. Interactive workout programs incorporated into gym equipment are helping exercisers track mileage, speed, number of workouts, calorie burn, and more. Technological advancements have allowed more people to take advantage of exercise options.

Laura Newton would like to assist people in meeting their fitness and weight loss goals. Having overcome obesity herself, she knows the importance of a good diet and hard work. She strives to be a motivational factor that will help people's lives for the better. She will utilize her knowledge and

61

expertise garnered from personal experience and education to start Fitness City and do everything she can to help her clients realize their full potential.

INDUSTRY ANALYSIS

Rising health consciousness has been an impetus in the fitness industry for the past several years, and it will continue driving growth in fitness club membership for the foreseeable future. Currently, fitness is a $33 billion industry with 2.2% growth projected for the next 10 years, partially due to demographic changes that are expected to expand the industry's potential market and partially because increased discretionary income will allow consumers to purchase higher-value services. As of 2015, there are 162,481 gyms, health, and fitness clubs in the United States.

Individuals working in the fitness industry will also see an increase. In 2012, there were 267,000 people employed in the fitness industry; this number is expected to grow at a rate of 13% so that, by 2022, and additional 33,500 jobs will have been created.

MARKET ANALYSIS

The city of Lake Orion had a population of 2,973 in the 2010 Census; this number increased 9.5% since that time to have a current population of 3,208. It is expected to continue to rise through 2040, when the population is predicted to be 3,881. The majority of this increase will be comprised of individuals aged 25-34, the prime age for those seeking to improve their health and fitness. Furthermore, these numbers only cover individuals residing in the village proper; many other smaller, rural communities nearby come to Lake Orion for shopping and other services.

The population of Lake Orion is also well educated, with nearly 65% having some college up to an advanced degree. These individuals earn more money and have more discretionary income than those will no completed college coursework.

January, February, and March are the biggest months in the fitness industry because of New Year's resolutions, and the winter weather in Michigan has people choosing to work out primarily indoors. The summer months are slower in our area because people are on vacation or outside participating in outdoor activities. Unpredictable weather including rain and extremely hot temperatures will have people return to the gym during the summer months, however.

Competition

Competition in the fitness industry is fierce with large, all-inclusive clubs vying against smaller independent gyms. There is also competition coming from other recreational activities and home fitness programs, such as the popular P90X. To stay strong in a competitive industry, health club operators must focus on what makes their club stand out from the crowd.

There are 3 gyms in the immediate area, all of which are chains. These include:

- Powerhouse Gym, Lake Orion
- Anytime Fitness, Oxford
- Snap Fitness, Oxford

While these clubs are nice, they lack the homey feel and personal attention we seek to provide at Fitness City. They tend to provide equipment and little else, preferring members to come and go as they like with little or no interaction with staff or other members. Fitness City will strive to have members feel like they are part of a community of people who care about them and their fitness goals; they are supported and encouraged every step of the way.

SERVICES

Fitness City will offer many different types of services including personal and group training, fitness classes, exercise machines, weight equipment, and community events. These are detailed below.

Training

Training will include the following activities:

- fitness assessments, consultations and introduction sessions for new clients

- creating personal exercise programs

- demonstrating activities for clients to follow

- showing clients how to use exercise machines and free weights properly

- supervising clients to make sure that they are exercising safely and effectively

- giving advice on healthy eating and lifestyle

This training can be done one-on-one or in group settings depending on client preference and budget. These available options include:

Personal Training
- One-on-One Training, $65 per hour (for one person)

Group Training
- Buddy Training (2 People), $45 per hour, per person

- Small Group Training (3-4 People), $25-33 per hour, per person

Fitness Classes

Several different fitness classes will also be offered. A detailed scheduled will be posted and followed for each quarter. The class will provide adequate warm-up, stretching, the specific class exercises, and cool down. All appropriate equipment, music, and handouts for each class are included. Clients can be assured that all classes will begin and end on time.

Classes include:

- Zumba

- Dance Fit

- Strength Training

- Active Aging

- Bowka

- Pilates

- Yoga

- Kick boxing

- Weight training

In addition to these, classes will be offered for specialist groups of people, such as older adults, children, people with disabilities, or people referred by doctors. These will be added to the regular schedule as interest dictates.

Exercise Machines/Weight Equipment

A wide variety of exercise machines and weight equipment will be made available to clients. While some people will be interested only in classes or training, having a variety of options available will help people to target different areas of their body and avoid boredom in their workout routines.

Gym machines and equipment include:

- four treadmills

- two elliptical machines

- two exercise cycles

- two stair climbers

- weight machines, including bicep/tricep component, vertical press, AB/back component, leg/calf press, inner/outer thigh component, and leg curl component

- free weights

Community Events

A unique offering for Fitness City will be the periodic community events. These will include things like teams that compete at local 5k/10k /half marathons/marathons, local bike rides, grocery store shopping excursions, recipe exchanges, and restaurant outings. We are open to any and all ideas to increase the feeling of community and support each other in our quest for health and fitness.

PRICING STRATEGY

Clients are highly encouraged to join Fitness City on a yearly basis with monthly membership fees automatically deducted from their checking account. This membership allows them unlimited access to the facilities as well as 4 class sessions per month at a cost of $75 per month. However, we realize that this level of commitment and cost will not work for everyone. To this end, clients are also offered the option of purchasing single use or multi-use packages for training or classes. The cost for these services is outlined below.

Pricing schedule

One-on-one training

Individual single session hourly rate: $65

Packages	Hourly rate		Savings	Prices
24 sessions	$ 50		$360	$1,200
12 sessions	$ 55		$120	$ 660
6 sessions	$ 60		$ 30	$ 360

Group training

Buddy training (2 people)

Two person single session hourly rate: $90

Packages	Hourly rate	Per person	Savings	Total price per person
12 sessions	$ 80	$40.00	$ 60ea	$ 480
6 sessions	$ 85	$42.50	$ 15ea	$ 255

Small group training (3–4 people)

Three person single session hourly rate: $100

Packages	Hourly rate	Per person	Savings	Total price per person
3 people–12 sessions	$ 90	$30.00	$240/$80ea	$ 360
3 people–6 sessions	$100	$33.34	$ 60/$20ea	$ 200

Fitness classes

Five or more people

Drop-in classes	$ 8
5 class punch card	$ 35
10 class punch card	$ 65
1 month unlimited class pass	$ 50

PERSONNEL

Fitness trainers and instructors lead, instruct, and motivate individuals or groups in exercise activities, including cardiovascular exercise (exercises for the heart and blood system), strength training, and stretching. They work with people of all ages and skill levels.

Fitness trainers must be outgoing and friendly. They are passionate about health, wellness and exercise and use their skills to help motivate and inspire others in reaching their fitness and weight goals. Fitness trainers, or personal trainers, work with people from many different backgrounds and abilities, from professional athletes to elderly people. A job as a fitness trainer can be rewarding and fulfilling as trainers help others to improve their health through exercise and nutrition.

Owner

Laura Newton will own Fitness City. Having overcome obesity herself, she knows the importance of a good diet and hard work. She strives to be a motivational factor that will help people's lives for the better. She will utilize her knowledge and expertise garnered from personal experience and education to do everything she can to help her clients realize their full potential.

Laura struggled with her weight all through school. In her senior year of high school, her weight topped out at 255, which put significant strain on her 5 foot 6 inch frame. Her doctor was increasingly concerned with her health and Laura knew she had to make a change. She sought nutritional advice from a certified nutritional counselor and joined the local gym. She was trying, but still struggling, when she met a personal trainer that changed her life. She was motivated and finally knew that she wasn't alone; this feeling of community and support helped her achieve her health and fitness goals and she decided that she wanted to have the same impact on other people's lives as well.

To that end, Laura earned a Bachelor's degree in Exercise Science from Lake Superior State University in May, 2010. While at Lake Superior State, Laura took classes in:

- Leadership/Recreation Leadership
- Health Fitness
- Athletic Injury and Illness Prevention
- Exercise Physiology
- Essentials of Strength Training and Conditioning
- Fitness Evaluation
- Nutrition for Sport and Exercise Performance
- Kinesiology
- Research Methods in Exercise Science
- Exercise Prescription
- Allied Health Administration
- Anatomy & Physiology
- Applied Chemistry
- Applied Organic Chemistry
- Applied Biochemistry
- Health Psychology
- Athletic Injury & Illness Recognition and Evaluation
- Therapeutic Modalities and Exercise
- Psychological Aspects of Exercise and Athletic Rehabilitation
- Neurological Basics of Motor Learning
- Exercise Prescription and Testing for Special Populations

Upon graduation, she earned certifications as a Personal Trainer from both the American College of Sports Medicine (ACSM) and the National Strength and Conditioning Association (NSCA).

With these credential to her name, Laura began her career as a personal trainer in June, 2010 with a large chain. While she loved her job, she longed for the more personal connections she herself experienced. Finally, in early 2015, Laura decided to start her own gym so that she could provide the level of service and type of experience she felt her clients deserved.

Support Staff

Laura will be hiring an additional two personal trainers to start. Like her, they will be responsible for carrying out routine tasks such as:

- assisting patrons
- answering questions
- answering the phone
- greeting clients
- performing health and safety checks
- demonstrating the correct way to use exercise equipment

- monitoring the misuse of equipment

- ensuring the gym is clean and free of health and safety hazards

- keeping management informed of customer and facility needs

Most importantly, all staff must do their best to maintain a positive exercise experience for all members and class participants.

The hired staff will be evaluated on the following important qualities:

Customer-service skills. Fitness trainers and instructors must sell their services, motivating clients to hire them as personal trainers or to sign up for the classes they lead. Fitness trainers and instructors must therefore be polite, friendly, and encouraging to maintain relationships with their clients.

Listening skills. Fitness trainers and instructors must be able to listen carefully to what clients tell them to determine the client's fitness levels and desired fitness goals.

Motivational skills. Getting fit and staying fit takes a lot of work for many clients. To keep clients coming back for more classes or to continue personal training, fitness trainers and instructors must keep their clients motivated.

Physical fitness. Fitness trainers and instructors need to be physically fit because their job requires a considerable amount of exercise. Group instructors often participate in classes, and personal trainers often need to show exercises to their clients.

Problem-solving skills. Fitness trainers and instructors must evaluate each client's level of fitness and create an appropriate fitness plan to meet the client's individual needs.

Speaking skills. Fitness trainers and instructors must be able to communicate well because they need to be able to explain exercises and movements to clients, as well as motivate them verbally during exercises.

Fitness instructors will work on a rotating basis to cover early mornings, evenings and weekends. They will be paid on an hourly basis as well as receive additional compensation for classes or training sessions that they lead.

Education and Certifications

All employees will be expected to have certification in CPR, First Aid, and AED. In addition, they should have certification as a personal trainer from a respected institution.

MARKETING AND SALES

The profitability of individual companies depends on good marketing. Large companies have economies of scale in advertising and in buying equipment. Small companies can compete effectively if they have favorable locations or meet customer demands for personalized service and friendly atmosphere.

OPERATIONS/COMPANY DESCRIPTION

Hours of Operation

Fitness City will be open from 6 am until 8 pm, Monday through Saturday.

Location

Fitness City is located in Lake Orion, Michigan in a commercial and shopping area that is easily accessible for customers.

Fitness City contains one large classroom where all classes will be held. The room features mirrors on all walls so that participants can check their form as they work out. There is a sizable closet in the classroom that will house equipment used in classes such as mats, stretch bands, stereo system, and kickboxing bags, among other equipment.

The gym area will house all machines and equipment as well as weights. Mirrors are also placed along walls in the weight area to encourage proper form as well.

Two private unisex bathrooms featuring showers are also available.

Payment Options

Customers are encouraged to pay for memberships with automatic monthly deductions from their checking account. Training sessions and classes can also be paid for using cash, check, Visa, Mastercard, and American Express.

Home Inventory Business

Eagle Eye Home Inventory Specialists, Inc.

2424 Folsom Blvd.
Folsom, CA 95630

Paul Greenland

Eagle Eye Home Inventory Specialists is organized as a corporation operating within California. We propose to offer home inventory services to residents and businesses located in the greater Sacramento area. We will use state-of-the-art High Definition video technology to document the inside and outside of homes, storage and business locations. All material will be stored digitally for security and easy access.

EXECUTIVE SUMMARY

According to the National Fire Protection Association (NFPA) in the year 2014 U.S. fire departments responded to an estimated 1,240,000 fires with an estimated $11.5 billion in direct property loss. The Insurance Information Institute found that in 2013 property damage and theft accounted for 97 percent of the claims filed by homeowners. The Institute added that on average, only half of homeowners said that they were able to provide an inventory of their possessions as part of their insurance claim.

When a loss occurs due to natural disaster, theft, fire or accident, the insured is required to provide prompt notice of the loss and details about the property that has been lost or damaged. By this time it is too late for the insured to document the existence and value of the insured property. Our mandate is to assist customers in creating the documentation that they will need should disaster strike.

As California enters its fourth year of drought, the threat of loss by fire increases. We accept the challenge of educating the public on the importance of preparing for the possibility of loss. And we will assist our customers by completing and maintaining a current inventory of their property.

Eagle Eye Home Inventory Specialists is organized as a corporation operating within California. We propose to offer home inventory services to residents and businesses located in the greater Sacramento area.

We will use state-of-the-art High Definition video technology to document the inside and outside of homes, storage and business locations. All material will be stored digitally for security and easy access.

Objectives

Eagle Eye Home Inventory Service, Inc. seeks to launch its line of home inventory services which will be offered to residents and businesses in the greater Sacramento area.

We have set the following objectives:

- To launch our service offerings over a six month period with one documenter

- To achieve annual revenues sufficient to allow our documenter to work full-time for the company by the end of three years

- To achieve net profit of $25,000 in three years

- To employ an additional documenters in five years

Mission

Eagle Eye Home Inventory Service, Inc. aims to provide comprehensive documentation of property through the most advanced technology to residents and businesses in the greater Sacramento area. Our services will ensure that, should losses occur, our clients will be able to easily comply with all insurance requirements to achieve the highest possible reimbursement for their losses.

Keys to Success

The home inventory business is one that is based on trust. Our clients trust us to create the required documentation of their possessions, to securely store the data and to maintain confidentiality.

Keys to success include:

- Establishing trust with clients

- Creating comprehensive inventories that are stored in a secure environment

- Maintaining confidentiality regarding clients and their possessions

- Adhering to legal and ethical business practices

Financing

Eagle Eye Home Inventory Service, Inc. is not seeking investment capital at this time.

COMPANY SUMMARY

Eagle Eye Home Inventory Service, Inc., Inc. is a corporation operated by John Colvin. We will provide home inventory services to the greater Sacramento area including Folsom, Elk Grove, Roseville, Lincoln, Rocklin, Citrus Heights and Newcastle.

Our clientele will include both residential and commercial customers who desire to document their possessions and property.

Eagle Eye Home Inventory Service, Inc. was founded in 2015 by John Colvin. John has 25 years experience in business. His experience includes working as a project manager for a major technology company where he played a major role in the roll out of several new products.

In 2009 John and his family were among the many families who experienced major losses when a wildfire ravaged their housing development. It was that experience and the stress of dealing with their home insurance company that inspired John to pursue the home inventory business.

When his employer offered John a golden parachute deal during a period of downsizing, John seized the opportunity to become his own boss and provide the public with a valuable service. He took the next six months to learn all he could about insurance and claims. At the same time he laid the groundwork for what would become Eagle Eye Home Inventory Service, Inc.

Working out of his home, John invested $18,000 start up capital in video equipment and other startup costs. Building on his contacts in the technology field, John oversaw the creation of proprietary software that could be used to facilitate the home inventory process.

Equipment needed for startup

Item	Estimated cost
Computer/printer/copier/scanner/fax	$1,700
Video camera/tripod/batteries	$2,500
Telephone/cell phone	$ 200
Storage/filing/shelving	$ 150
Adding machine	$ 25
Paper shredder	$ 50
Desk/table/chair	$ 375
	$5,000

ADDITIONAL STARTUP COSTS

Start-up expenses

Licenses	$ 150
Supplies	$ 150
Advertising	$ 250
Web site development	$ 850
Legal fees	$ 1,500
Magnetic truck signs	$ 100
Software development	$10,000
Total start-up expenses	**$13,000**

MANAGEMENT TEAM

John Colvin, Founder and CEO. John Colvin's extensive business experience includes over 20 years experience as a project manager for a major technology company. During his career John oversaw the creation and roll out of much of the software and hardware that is in use in homes and businesses today.

Born from his own experience of property loss, John Colvin concluded that the public needs to be better prepared to deal with required paperwork for filing insurance claims. Without proper documentation, a personal disaster can become even more stressful when a legitimate claim for damages is diminished due to lack of proof.

John's proprietary software solution to home inventory, DocuProof will be utilized to conduct a customized inventory for clients. Because the software is housed in the cloud, it can be accessed quickly and easily on the Internet 24/7/365. Clients can use the software to create customized reports and update the inventory as needed.

Advisory Committee

Jack Reynolds, software engineer. As creator of the DocuProof software, Jack continues to add value to Eagle Eye Home Inventory Service, Inc.. While ownership of the software code for DocuProof resides with Eagle Eye Home Inventory Service, Inc., Inc., Jack's design and maintenance of the software will ensure that clients will always have the most current inventory at their fingertips.

Sam Reynaldo, SPPA is a principal of Greenspan Claims Management, Inc. in Sacramento, California. As a Senior Professional Public Adjuster and Principal of The Greenspan Co./Adjusters International,

Sam Reynaldo brings 37 years of experience in the public adjusting field to the company. He is responsible for the company's adjusters, estimators and inventory staff, and promotes working together as a team in order to achieve excellent results for clients. Sam is licensed in 25 states and has represented victims of disasters across the United States and internationally.

SERVICES

Eagle Eye Home Inventory Service, Inc., Inc. will provide the following services.

- Detailed video and photos of the home or business and their contents

- Digital storage online with 24/7/365 access to edit and update with a secure username and password

- The ability to create custom reports

- Digital storage on a portable USB drive

- Storage of your inventory reports in a safe deposit box for an annual fee

Customized packages of services are available as follows:

- Home inventory: a narrated HD video of the inside and outside of the home, HD photography, digital storage on a flash drive. Billed by the square foot.

- Basic home inventory: includes appliances, electronics, furniture

- Complete home inventory: Includes the services of the Basic home inventory plus: pictures, collections, home decor, artwork, pictures of items in cabinets, closets and drawers.

- Complete home inventory plus: Includes the services of the Complete home inventory plus: garage items, shed items, vehicles, trailers, boats and document scanning of important papers.

- Apartment inventory: Includes all of the services of the Home Inventory. Billed by the number of bedrooms up to 1,500 square feet.

- Small Business Inventory: furniture, equipment, electronics, office décor and artwork. Billed at $80 per hour.

- Self Storage Inventory: Estimate required.

- Collector's inventory: a focused inventory of artwork, stamps, coins, antiques and other items of value. Billed at $99 for the first hour and $30 for each additional hour.

- Business document archive: digital backup of important business documents such as Articles of Incorporation, contracts, employment records, tax returns, patent and trademark registration

Situations and circumstances that could call for the services of a home inventory specialist include:

- Vacation home or rental

- Estate planning

- Church

- Divorce settlement

- Home staging for sale

MARKET ANALYSIS

Eagle Eye Home Inventory Service, Inc. will provide inventory services to the following types of clients:

- Homeowners

- Renters

- Small businesses

We plan to target customers whose property values are in excess of $300,000. One of our main strategies to reach our target audience will be through bulk mailing of flyers to specific geographic areas based on zip code. In this way we can target the type of customer most likely to have sufficient property to benefit from and afford our services.

In Sacramento, these zip code areas include:

- 95811

- 95814

- 95839

Others areas that we will serve include :

- Auburn where estimated median house or condo value in 2012 was $338,193

- Rocklin where estimated median house or condo value in 2012 was $355,817

- Folsom where estimated median house or condo value in 2012 was $359,200

Other methods of reaching potential customers will include:

- Working with insurance agents and realtors

- Presentations at meetings of business and social groups such as Rotary

- A seminar through the Learning Exchange on how to protect your property from loss and deal with insurance recovery after a disaster or loss

One of our main marketing tools is a booklet that has tips and information on the importance of having proper insurance, maintaining records of ownership and values, and how to work with your insurance company after a disaster or loss. Each booklet has our business name and contact information. The booklets also have a space where the name of an insurance agent or realtor can be added. We will give the booklets to agents and realtors for their use as a gift to their customers.

Another major marketing tool will be our web site which will house useful information and resources for site visitors. Our web site will include a contact form that can be used to connect with us. All inquiries will receive a response on the next business day.

COMPETITION

Our research shows that there is only one other company in the Sacramento area that provides services similar to ours. However, we have found that there are several online tools and venues that offer home inventory software that customers can use themselves.

We believe that our personalized approach to home inventory will enable us to be successful despite the availability of online tools, many of which are free to use. We know from our own experience that even though there are free tools to help people complete their tax returns online, most consumers still prefer to deal with a professional. We can offer our clients both information and support that is not possible with these online tools.

Knowing what to do is one thing but then actually doing it is something else. We believe that most consumers who are inclined to complete a home inventory would rather hire a professional to do the job. A professional service that specializes in home inventory has the tools and experience to complete a thorough inventory in the shortest amount of time.

MARKETING PLAN

Marketing Objectives

•   Establish relationships with insurance providers and realtors within our targeted market.

•   Create an online presence that provides exposure for our brand, educates the public and allows for contact from the public.

Eagle Eye Home Inventory Service, Inc. is a member of The Inventory Institute™ and is listed in their directory of inventory service providers. Membership affords credibility, referrals, education and support.

Other marketing strategies will include maintenance of an informational web site that contains articles on the importance of the home inventory. Our site will include a contact form that can be used to send us inquiries. All contact submissions will receive a response on the next business day.

Our site will gather information from other sources as well in order to educate the public on the subject of keeping a home inventory. For example, a June 2009 article from AARP, "Take a Home Inventory," described how one could perform an inventory.

The list of steps included:

1. Gather all receipts

2. Open closets and drawers and photograph everything

3. Take pictures of every room

4. Guestimate the number of different clothing items

5. Photograph all artwork and furniture

6. Upload photos to a software tool and add information on purchase date and serial numbers

7. Count dishes and silverware

8. Itemize kitchen appliances and cookware

Although software tools exist to help consumers take their own home inventory, it is doubtful that most people will be able to complete an inventory on their own. As with tax preparation, software and tools exist to complete a tax return but still, thousands of people choose to have professional help. They find peace-of-mind in having someone with experience take over what can be a stressful task.

We believe that providing a referral to this article on our web site serves two purposes: it educates the public and it may drive the reader to seek professional assistance once they see how involved the inventory process can be.

Our marketing materials will stress our storage and update services because having a home inventory is only useful if it is current and accessible.

Much time will be devoted to networking with professionals in complementary service industries such as:

- Realtors

- Insurance providers

By establishing a network we can help each other to grow by providing referrals to each other. Sales leads will be generated in the following ways:

- Referrals from those in our network

- Personal appearances and courses taught

- Web site

We will provide information over the phone stating that our average fee runs about $375. However a personal meeting is the best way to arrive at the cost. All of our marketing efforts are designed to result in a personal meeting with a prospective client. We believe that once we meet face-to-face that we will have greater success in closing the sale.

MILESTONES

- Complete filing of paperwork for setting up the corporation

- Complete the business plan which will serve as a roadmap for the business. The business plan will continue to evolve as the business grows.

- Completion of proprietary software for maintaining inventories.

- Establish a network of contacts in the insurance and realty industries

FINANCIAL PLAN

We expect that sales will grow slowly but gradually in the first six months. We will stress the fact that after four years of drought, this fire season may be one of the worst on record. Property owners need to include home inventory in their preparations for this fire season.

John Colvin continues to use his golden parachute to cover his living expenses. He expects to begin drawing a salary in year two of the business.

Projected Profit and Loss

Pro forma profit and loss

	Year 1	Year 2	Year 3
Sales	**$25,000**	**$55,000**	**$72,000**
Expenses			
Payroll	$ 0	$18,000	$24,000
Depreciation	$ 100	$ 100	$ 100
Rent	$ 0	$ 0	$ 0
Phone/Internet	$ 640	$ 960	$ 960
Insurance: liability life/disability	$ 350	$ 350	$ 400
Payroll taxes	$ 0	$ 1,800	$ 2,400
Professional dues/memberships	$ 300	$ 300	$ 350
Advertising	$ 1,800	$ 1,800	$ 1,800
Office supplies	$ 200	$ 250	$ 300
Auto	$ 3,000	$ 3,400	$ 4,000
Software maintenance	$ 500	$ 2,500	$ 2,000
Other expenses	$ 400	$ 600	$ 800
Total operating expenses	**$ 7,290**	**$30,060**	**$37,110**
Profit before interest and taxes	$17,710	$24,940	$34,890
Taxes incurred	$ 2,657	$ 3,741	$ 5,234
Net profit	**$15,054**	**$21,199**	**$29,657**
Net profit/sales	**60%**	**39%**	**41%**

Projected Balance Sheet

Projected balance sheet

Assets	Year 1	Year 2	Year 3
Cash in bank	$ 5,000	$20,054	$41,253
Other current assets			
Total current assets	**$ 5,000**	**$20,054**	**$41,253**
Fixed assets			
Office furniture & equipment	$ 2,500	$ 2,500	$ 2,500
Video equipment	2,500	2,500	2,500
Software	10,000	10,000	10,000
Misc equipment			
Less: depreciation	($ 1,500)	($ 3,000)	($ 3,000)
Total assets	**$18,500**	**$32,054**	**$53,253**
Liabilities			
Current liabilities			
Accounts payable	$ –	$ –	
Current maturities loan			
Total current liabilities	**$ –**	**$ –**	
Long term liabilities loan	**0**		
Total liabilities	**$ –**	**$ –**	
John Colvin, capital	18,500	23,024	31,856
Total owner's equity	**18,500**	**23,024**	**31,856**
Total liabilities & equity	**$18,500**	**$32,054**	**$53,253**

Home Staging Business

Alex Adams Home Staging LLC

21 Laramie Ave.
Houston, TX 77001

Paul Greenland

Alex Adams Home Staging LLC maximizes the marketability and overall appeal of a home seller's property, helping them to achieve the highest possible selling price in the shortest amount of time.

EXECUTIVE SUMMARY

Alex Adams Home Staging LLC maximizes the marketability and overall appeal of a home seller's property, helping them to achieve the highest possible selling price in the shortest amount of time. The business is being established by Alexandra "Alex" Adams, a former furniture store manager/buyer with an entrepreneurial spirit. Adams will begin the business as a part-time endeavor, but anticipates full-time operations by the second year.

In 2009 (during the Great Recession) CNN placed "home stager" atop a list of seven jobs that were projected to experience the most growth in the coming years. Alex Adams Home Staging is fortunate to be located in one of the strongest real estate markets in the nation. More home sellers and realtors are realizing that, with a comparatively small investment, home staging can result in significantly higher selling prices.

INDUSTRY ANALYSIS

The home staging industry is represented by a number of different professional organizations and associations, including the International Association of Home Staging Professionals, the American Society of Home Stagers, and the Real Estate Staging Association. Although professional certification is not required to work in the staging field, industry organizations do offer educational programming and certification that provides professional distinction and can serve as a competitive differential. In addition, staging associations also provide benefits to their members, including networking opportunities, professional conferences, and continuing education. Some associations also offer assistance with activities such as marketing and insurance.

MARKET ANALYSIS

Alex Adams Home Staging is fortunate to be located in one of the strongest real estate markets in the nation. Supported by affordable land and building costs, Houston, Texas, enjoyed stability during the most difficult years of the Great Recession. Subsequently, real estate demand has increased thanks to a growing number of companies that are relocating and/or establishing operations in the area. This growth has led to an increase in real estate demand, as well as rising home prices. Alex Adams Home Staging is positioned to help homeowners achieve the very best return when they are ready to sell their homes.

According to demographic data that Alex Adams obtained at her local library, the Houston market was comprised of 300,976 homes in 2014. At that time the median home value was $126,458 (although other estimates placed this number much higher, at approximately $181,000). More than 69 percent of homes in the Houston area had a value between $100,000 and $399,999. Homes priced between $150,000 and $199,999 represented 24.8 percent of the overall total. About 60 percent of homes were owner-occupied. By 2019 the number of total housing units in Houston is projected to reach 329,359, and the median value is projected to reach $145,472.

SERVICES

Alex Adams will begin all projects with an initial consultation with the customer (homeowner or real estate agent). This will include a review of the property in need of staging, the establishment of specific goals, and finally a written estimate specifying the scope of services to be provided.

Alex Adams Home Staging provides a wide range of services to home sellers, ranging from brief consultations (providing do-it-yourself tips for staging one's own home) to professional staging projects that involve painting, decorating, and furnishing a vacant property. The majority of Alex Adams Home Staging's projects will fall somewhere in the middle of this range. The business' services include, but are not limited to:

"Do-It-Yourself" Consultations (in Person)

Some home sellers and realtors simply want some basic advice to help maximize the sales potential of a particular property. In this regard, Alex Adams will provide a one-hour, on-site consultation to them. This will involve a walk-through of the property and specific suggestions for staging different rooms using a customer's own furniture, or newly purchased items.

"Do-It-Yourself" Consultations (Virtual)

Alex Adams Home Staging also will offer conceptual or virtual staging services, where Alex Adams provides online staging advice to customers utilizing digital photography and video chat. This service may involve editing photos of empty rooms to demonstrate how a client might stage different rooms within a home using their own furniture or newly purchased items.

Professional Staging

When hired to professionally stage a home, Alex Adams generally will focus on several key rooms, rather than staging the entire home. Usually, this includes the front/living room to capture and hold a prospective buyer's attention. Other main focal points include the kitchen, downstairs bathroom, and master bedroom. Although the particular services provided will vary from situation to situation, Alex Adams Home Staging often will employ one or more of the following tactics:

- Adding new accessories
- Adding new furniture
- Addressing lighting problems
- Cleaning
- Color consultations (suggesting new paint colors to maximize appeal)

- Eliminating clutter or "editing" rooms

- Painting

- Rearranging existing accessories and artwork

- Rearranging furniture

- Styling bookshelves

- Styling fireplace mantels

PERSONNEL

Alex Adams has always had a knack for interior decorating. Although she has no formal training, friends and family members are always quick to take notice when she rearranges and decorates different areas of her home. In fact, when others feel the need to reinvigorate their home, Alex typically is the first person they call for advice. Her natural talent has been honed during a 15-year career in the furniture industry. After working as a sales associate at a local furniture store, the owners soon promoted her to manager. Ultimately, she transitioned to the role of furniture buyer for the owners' chain of five locations in three states.

With an entrepreneurial spirit and a burning desire to establish her own business, Alex was very receptive to the advice of her sister, a successful realtor, who urged her to explore a career as a home stager. After completing a short home staging training course, which resulted in professional certification, and earning a small business management certificate from a local community college, Alex is positioned for success in her new business.

Professional and Advisory Support

Alex Adams will use the local accounting firm, Tax Smart Inc., for assistance with tax preparation and bookkeeping. In addition, she has established a commercial checking account with Bennington Community Bank, and will utilize a popular mobile point-of-sale service to accept credit card and debit card payments from customers.

GROWTH STRATEGY

Alex Adams has established detailed growth projections for her business. The following tables provide projected contracts for Alex Adams Home Staging's three main service categories (professional staging, on-site consultations, and virtual consultations) for the first four years of operations.

Professional staging

	2016	2017	2018	2019
January	1	2	3	4
February	2	3	4	5
March	2	3	4	5
April	3	4	5	6
May	4	5	6	7
June	5	6	7	8
July	6	7	8	9
August	6	7	8	9
September	5	6	7	8
October	4	5	6	7
November	2	3	4	5
December	1	2	3	4

On-site consultations

	2016	2017	2018	2019
January	1	2	3	4
February	2	3	4	5
March	2	3	4	5
April	3	4	5	6
May	4	5	6	7
June	5	6	7	8
July	6	7	8	9
August	6	7	8	9
September	5	6	7	8
October	4	5	6	7
November	2	3	4	5
December	1	2	3	4

Virtual consultations

	2016	2017	2018	2019
January	1	1	2	3
February	1	2	3	4
March	1	2	3	4
April	2	3	4	5
May	2	4	5	6
June	3	5	6	7
July	3	6	7	8
August	3	6	7	8
September	2	5	6	7
October	1	4	5	6
November	1	2	3	4
December	1	1	2	3

OPERATIONS

Start-up Costs

Alex Adams will use $10,000 from her personal savings to establish the business. These funds will be used to cover the formation of her LLC (utilizing a popular legal document service), Web site and literature development, and the completion of a training course from an industry organization. Based on her net profit projections, Adams will recoup this investment during the first and second years of operations.

Location

Alex Adams initially will operate her business from a home office to keep expenses low. She has designated space within her home to be used exclusively for business purposes, and has subscribed to business class Internet service, allowing her to upload and download large files for clients. Through her cable provider, Adams has subscribed to an affordable Internet-based telephone service, allowing her to make cost-effective phone calls throughout the United States. She already has a Macintosh computer, desk, and filing cabinet that can be used for her business.

Inventory

Some home staging professionals purchase and maintain an extensive inventory of their own furniture and accessories (e.g., lamps, pillows, vases, etc.), which can be drawn from when needed. However, the cost to clean, transport, store, and insure a large inventory can be very expensive. Therefore, Alex Adams will limit her inventory to key accessories that can be stored in the basement of her home.

Alex Adams Home Staging's inventory will consist mainly of neutral items (e.g., not seasonal or tailored to very specific decorative tastes) that will appeal to the broadest possible number of homebuyers. In addition to purchasing new items from discount retailers, she will build and maintain her inventory with gently used/like new items from garage sales and resale shops.

MARKETING & SALES

Alex Adams Home Staging will limit its marketing budget to 5% of gross sales. Alex Adams has identified a number of tactics that she will use to promote her business, including:

1. **Portfolio:** One of Alex Adams Home Staging's key marketing tactics will be "before" and "after" photos of the properties that Alex Adams has staged. These can be displayed in a number of ways, including online, with a mobile device, in brochures, and in a three-ring binder.

2. **Web Site:** Alex Adams Home Staging will develop and maintain a basic Web site that provides key information about the business, including the range of services provided, links to an online portfolio, information about Alex Adams, and contact details. Many stagers consider their Web sites to be the most effective means of marketing.

3. **Stationery:** Business cards, letterhead, and envelopes will be produced for the business at a local office supply store.

4. **Blog:** Alex Adams will develop and maintain a blog about home staging.

5. **Media Relations:** Alex Adams will pursue opportunities to gain free media exposure from local network TV affiliates by serving as a guest on morning and noon shows. In addition, she will submit guest columns to local newspapers and industry trade publications, and also make herself available for radio interviews.

6. **Networking:** Alex Adams will attend open houses on Sunday afternoons to introduce herself to realtors. When doing this, she will offer one or two suggestions for maximizing the sales potential of that particular home. She will leave her business card with the realtor and suggest that they share it with their clients in need of professional staging services. Additionally, Alex will develop a relationship with her local Board of Realtors.

7. **Constant Contact:** Alex Adams Home Staging will utilize this e-mail marketing service to stay in touch with prospects and contacts in the company's database.

FINANCIAL ANALYSIS

On a percentage basis, Alex Adams anticipates that Alex Adams Home Staging's revenues will break down as follows during the business' first year of operations:

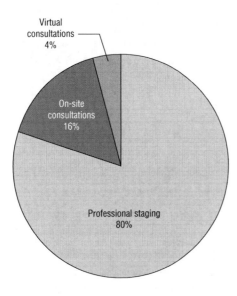

A complete set of pro forma financial statements have been prepared and are available upon request. The following table provides a breakdown of Alex Adams Home Staging's projected revenues and expenses during its first four years of operations:

	2016	2017	2018	2019
Sales				
Professional staging	$30,750	$39,750	$48,750	$57,750
On-site consultations	$ 6,150	$ 7,950	$ 9,750	$11,550
Virtual consultations	$ 1,575	$ 3,075	$ 3,975	$ 4,875
Total	**$38,475**	**$50,775**	**$62,475**	**$74,175**
Expenses				
Advertising & marketing	$ 1,900	$ 2,500	$ 3,000	$ 3,500
General/administrative	$ 350	$ 350	$ 350	$ 350
Legal	$ 750	$ 500	$ 500	$ 500
Accounting	$ 1,200	$ 1,200	$ 1,200	$ 1,200
Office supplies	$ 300	$ 300	$ 300	$ 300
Business insurance	$ 1,850	$ 1,850	$ 1,850	$ 1,850
Payroll	$20,000	$30,000	$40,000	$50,000
Payroll taxes	$ 3,000	$ 4,500	$ 6,000	$ 7,500
Postage	$ 450	$ 450	$ 450	$ 450
Business-class internet	$ 1,750	$ 1,850	$ 1,950	$ 2,050
Education & training	$ 750	$ 750	$ 750	$ 750
Total expenses	**$32,300**	**$44,250**	**$56,350**	**$68,450**
Net income	**$ 6,175**	**$ 6,525**	**$ 6,125**	**$ 5,725**

Men's Salon & Spa
The Clubhouse

301 Quay St.
Port Huron, MI 48060

Zuzu Enterprises

The Clubhouse is a men's salon and spa that will feature haircuts and tinting, waxing/trimming, shaving, airbrush tanning, massage, and manicure/pedicure services specifically tailored to the male customer. We make sure that we give everyone who steps through our door the time, attention, and courtesy that they deserve.

EXECUTIVE SUMMARY

The Clubhouse is located adjacent to the Port Huron Yacht Club in downtown Port Huron, Michigan. The yacht club features a hot tub, sauna, fitness center and sports courts, and a restaurant with bar. In the summer months, many members relocate and live on their boats docked at the PHYC.

The Clubhouse is aligned to perfectly fit with the services offered by the PHYC and pick up where they leave off. We will offer salon and spa services including haircuts and tinting, waxing/trimming, shaving, airbrush tanning, massage, and manicure/pedicure, all of which are specifically tailored to the male customer. We make sure that we give everyone who steps through our door the time, attention, and courtesy that they deserve.

INDUSTRY ANALYSIS

The U.S. hair care services industry includes about 86,000 establishments, of which 82,000 are beauty salons and the remaining 4,000 are barber shops. The combined revenue of these establishments is roughly $20 billion annually. Demand in the hair care industry is driven by demographics and population growth. The profitability of individual companies depends on technical expertise and marketing skills.

The Health and Wellness Spas industry has experienced steady growth during the five years to 2015. Revenue growth is expected to improve over the next five years, rising at an average annual rate of 3.2% to $58.7 billion by 2020. This will be driven by increases in per capita disposable income and declining unemployment over the five-year period, coupled with higher consumer confidence. Higher disposable incomes will also lead hair salon customers to spend more on higher-value services such as manicures, pedicures, facials, hair modification treatments, and massages.

Another service trend to generate growth is antiaging and medical treatments. The baby-boomer generation is expected to take advantage of expanding antiaging services over the next five years, making the demographic an especially important source of industry growth.

Personal Care Services

The largest households and older householders are the best customers of personal care services such as haircuts, massages, manicures, and facials. Householders aged 35 to 64 spend 8 to 14 percent more than average on this item. Married couples without children at home (most of them empty-nesters) spend 25 percent more than average on personal care services, while those with school-aged or older children at home (the largest households) spend 31 to 37 percent more than average.

Hair Care Products

Sales of hair care products are an important revenue source for many salons, providing from 5 to 15 percent of revenue. Gross margins are higher for hair care products than for services.

The best customers of hair care products are the largest households and households with the most women. Married couples with children at home spend 58 percent more than average on this item, the figure peaking at 65 percent more than average among couples with preschoolers.

Householders aged 35 to 54, many with children at home, spend 25 to 28 percent more than average on hair care products and control half the market.

MARKET ANALYSIS

The population of Port Huron is approximately 30,000 with the median age of 35.8 years. Approximately 38% of the population is white collar; this number is significantly more if one takes into account the neighboring communities of Marysville, Fort Gratiot, and Lakeport, all of which travel to Port Huron for all significant services including shopping, medical, and recreation.

Port Huron plays host to many festivals and events throughout the year including the Port Huron to Mackinac race; Men's Modified National Softball Championship tournament; Blue Water Sand Fest; Gus Macker basketball tournament; and other events that bring a significant amount of tourist traffic into the area, specifically of the male gender.

Competition

There are many salons within a 10 mile radius, but none cater specifically to men. The greatest competition comes from Spa 229, a high-end spa located less than a mile away in the downtown district area. While this spa is luxurious and is known for their excellent customer service and wide range of amenities, they do not offer hair service and the decor and services are decidedly feminine. We will set ourselves apart by tailoring our business especially to the needs of men and having a decidedly masculine vibe to our design scheme.

SERVICES

The Clubhouse will feature a wide range of services of interest to our male customers, from hair care to massage. We understand the specific genetic styling and grooming needs of a man, as well as his desire to never step foot in a salon filled with wall-to-wall estrogen, French fashion magazines, and gossip rags.

To that end, The Clubhouse specializes in delivering exemplary grooming and styling treatments for men who want to look their absolute best. Each and every one of our services is focused toward helping men look and feel better and gain more confidence in their overall appearance. Never underestimate what a pair of scissors, a razor, and quality professional grooming products can do when put in the right hands. We understand that men desire a salon that services their needs to look their very best so they can be their very best.

Each service we offer men to be their best is outlined in detail below.

Hair Care

Our primary service line is hair cutting and styling. Our stylists are knowledgeable in the latest trends and techniques and know how to bring out the best in each individual. Related services include neck and hairline cleanup and beard and mustache trim as well as grey blending and other color services.

Tinting

Tinting service is available on both eyebrows and lashes.

Shaving

Nothing feels as good as a hot shave. Our classic shave service features hot lather, straight or regular razor, and hot towel finish. Mini-facial treatments are also available.

Waxing/Trimming

All of our waxing and trimming services are offered in private treatment rooms and are performed by one of our experienced estheticians. Our estheticians have numerous years of experience and provide top-of-the-line men's waxing and trimming services in a professional and relaxing spa environment.

Waxing/trimming services available include:

- Brows
- Ears
- Neckline
- Back
- Man-kini
- Guy-zilian

Hands/Feet

Hands—Get your nails trimmed, detailed and massaged for that well-groomed and professional look of a power broker.

Feet—Kick back and sink your feet into comfort. Enjoy a relaxing, mineral-rich sea salt soak in a soothing jet bath while experiencing a marine therapy foot scrub and exfoliation, trimmed and detailed nails; the service includes our renowned foot massage. An organic option is also available.

Massage

A variety of massage services are offered at The Clubhouse. Each is offered in 30-, 60- or 90-minute increments. The types of massage we offer includes:

- Custom massage
- Hot stone massage—Feel your body melt as the warmth of heated, smooth basalt stones release the deepest tension in your muscles. Highly synchronized massage techniques with the stones stimulate your body muscles and help increase circulation.
- Reflexology—Ancient therapy founded on reflex & pressure points targeted on your hands and feet.
- Scalp massage—Invigorating, deep massage of your thinking cap. Warm oil with a stimulating aromatherapy blend, worked through your hair and scalp, takes all your stress away.

Airbrush Tan

This customized service provides the most natural-looking sunless tan that will last about 5-7 days. Each treatment is contoured to enhance your best assets leaving skin with a healthy and radiant glow.

Packages

Several different packages are available that combine the services offered to maximize time and savings. The different packages are detailed below.

The Marquis

Escape the stress of life with this spa package, designed just for you. Enjoy a 1 hour customized massage and a 1 hour customized mini-facial and shave/trim. This package will last 2 hours.

The Monarch

Get the full royal treatment. A 60-minute customized massage, followed by a mini-facial and shave/trim and relaxing hand a foot detail. This package will last 3 hours.

The Sovereign

It's the ultimate spa experience. A 90-minute customized massage, mini-facial and shave/trim, and relaxing hand a foot detail. This package will last 4 hours.

The Crown Jewels

The best of the best. Allow the spa to indulge you in a day of decadence. This package includes a 90 minute customized massage, mini-facial and shave/trim, specialized waxing service (Man-kini or Guy-zilian) and relaxing hand and foot detail. Lunch is included; the package will last 5 hours and 30 minutes.

PRODUCTS

Sales of hair care products are an important revenue source for many salons, providing from 5 to 15 percent of revenue. Gross margins are higher for hair care products than for services.

The Clubhouse will offer a full line of the latest hair care and styling products as well as shaving creams, lotions, scissors/trimmers, and the like for use during treatments as well as for sale to clients.

PRICING STRATEGY

Pricing schedule

Hair care

Men's cuts and style	Starting at $ 40
Gray blending	Starting at $ 45
Color services	Starting at $ 50
Neck & hairline cleanup	Starting at $ 20
Beard/stash trim	Starting at $ 20

Waxing/trimming

Brows	$ 24
Ears	$ 20
Neckline	$ 20
Back	$ 60
Man-kini	$ 50
Guy-zilian	$100

Other waxing services are available and priced upon request

Skin

Manscaping	$ 40
Anti-oxidant blast	$ 55
Self-healing	$ 85
Shave (hot towel/hot lather)	$ 29
Mini-facial	$ 19

Hands & feet

Spa pedicure	$ 70
Organic pedicure	$ 50
Manicure	$ 45

Tinting

Brow	$ 20
Lash	$ 20
Lash & brow	$ 30

Body massage

30 minutes	$ 45
60 minutes	$ 90
90 minutes	$120

Airbrush tanning

30 minutes	$ 40

Package deals

The marquis	$175
The monarch	$200
The sovereign	$275
The crown jewels	$600

Series

To get the most out of your spa experience, the Series is the perfect way for the frequent spa-goer to save! Our customizable series options make it easy to build your own package so that you can enjoy the ultimate spa experience during each visit.

Series of 6—6 pre-paid treatments of your choice at 12% off.

Series of 9—9 pre-paid treatments of your choice at 15% off.

Series of 12—12 pre-paid treatments of your choice at 20% off.

PERSONNEL

Owners

The Clubhouse is owned and operated by Miles Wehler and Simon Mullins. Both men have over 15 years' experience in the salon and spa industry with experiences ranging from hair stylist to receptionist to manager. They will utilize their knowledge and expertise to build The Clubhouse into the premier salon and spa for all men in the area who are interested in grooming to be the best they can be.

Support Staff

In addition to Miles and Simon, The Clubhouse will offer freelance positions to two stylists, two estheticians, two massage therapists, two nail specialists, and one airbrush tan operator. More freelance positions will be added on an as-needed basis. These individuals will rent space from The Clubhouse and pay for reception services and a small percentage of their sales.

A part-time receptionist will be hired as an employee of The Clubhouse.

Professional and Advisory Support

The Clubhouse will use the local accounting firm Stewart Beauvais & Whipple for assistance with tax preparation and bookkeeping. In addition, The Clubhouse has established a commercial checking account with Talmer Bank and Trust, and will utilize a popular mobile point-of-sale service to accept credit card and debit card payments from customers. Liability insurance has been obtained from State Farm.

ADVERTISING AND MARKETING

The Clubhouse will be aggressively marketed to members of the Port Huron Yacht Club as well as members of all local golf clubs (Black River Country Club, Port Huron Elks Golf Club, etc.) and members of the chamber of commerce. Advertisements will be placed in the *Times Herald* newspaper as well as local billboards, and specials will be run during a grand opening week. Other methods of marketing and advertising will be determined at a later date.

OPERATIONS/COMPANY DESCRIPTION

Hours of Operation

The Clubhouse will be open Tuesday through Saturday from 10am until 8pm. Times may be extended during special events.

Location

The atmosphere of The Clubhouse is reminiscent of a 1920's country club, featuring leather chairs, wood paneling, and sailing decor. Beverages will be provided as part of the service.

The business is located in downtown Port Huron adjacent to the Port Huron Yacht Club and within easy walking distance of the downtown shopping and entertainment district, featuring upscale retail establishments, bars/breweries, coffee shops, and restaurants.

Payment Options

Customers are able to choose from cash, Mastercard, Visa, American Express, and Discover. Payment is expected at the time services are rendered. Gift certificates are available for purchase.

FINANCIAL ANALYSIS

The total startup cost for The Clubhouse $100,000 and includes:

- rent
- building updates and decorating
- furniture and fixtures
- treatment chairs and tables
- mirrors
- sinks
- storage cabinets and counters
- display spaces
- towels and robes
- on-site laundry
- refrigerator and other small appliances
- product inventory
- reception area desk
- computer, printer, and office supplies
- brochures, marketing materials, and business cards
- magazine subscriptions and books (short stories, nonfiction, biographies, etc.)
- stereo system

Mobile Hair Salon Business

MostlyKids Hair Styles Inc.

5821 Cunningham Ave.
High Point, WI 53000

Paul Greenland

MostlyKids Hair Styles is a full-service mobile hair salon specializing in serving children and busy moms.

EXECUTIVE SUMMARY

MostlyKids Hair Styles is a full-service mobile hair salon specializing in serving children and busy moms. Owned by hairstylist Tina Parker, the business provides an innovative solution to busy families by bringing a regularly needed service directly to their homes. By taking a mobile approach and offering flexible hours, MostlyKids Hair Styles saves customers valuable time compared to traditional brick-and-mortar hair salons. Additionally, the business also is a helpful option for individuals with short-term or permanent disabilities, for whom traveling to a traditional hair salon is inconvenient, difficult, or impossible. By adhering to a mobile business model, Tina Parker is able to establish a new business without the overhead of a traditional salon, including mortgage/rent payments, utilities, and property taxes.

INDUSTRY ANALYSIS

According to the U.S. Bureau of Labor Statistics (BLS), 13 percent annual employment growth is projected for hairdressers, hairstylists, and cosmetologists from 2012 to 2022 (about as fast as the average for all occupations). Among the factors contributing to job growth is rising demand for services such as hair straightening and coloring, as well as other "deluxe" services. Nationwide, the BLS expects that employment will increase from 611,200 in 2012 to 688,700 in 2022. Many hairdressers and cosmetologists are self-employed and work irregular hours (e.g., evenings and weekends), when it is most convenient for their customers. The industry is represented by national associations, such as the National-Interstate Council of State Boards of Cosmetology and the Professional Beauty Association.

MARKET ANALYSIS

MostlyKids Hair Styles is located in the affluent Milwaukee suburb of High Point, Wisconsin. According to market data from LRC Research Associates, the community was home to 61,265 people in 2014. This figure essentially was expected to remain steady through 2019, with nominal growth projected. In 2014 approximately 20 percent of the population was under the age of 12 (the business' primary

91

target market). Specifically, individuals aged 0 to 4 accounted for 5.5 percent of the population, while those in the 5 to 14 age category accounted for 14.5 percent.

MostlyKids Hair Styles will target its marketing initiatives toward households with income of $50,000 or more. In 2014 the largest household income segment (19.6%) was the $50,000 to $74,999 category. Next were households with income between $75,000 and $99,999 (15.3%), $100,000 to $149,999 (12.7%), and more than $150,000 (6%).

SERVICES

MostlyKids Hair Styles will offer the following services:

- Hair Cut (children under 12) $20-$30

- Hair Cut (adult women) $35-$75

- Shampoo & Style $25

- Bang trim $15

- Event Styling $50

- Perms $70

- Dimensional Coloring $75

- Single Process Color $65

On a percentage basis, Tina Parker anticipates that sales will break down by category as follows:

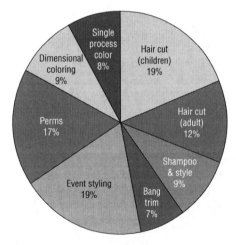

Service Area

Services typically will be provided in a 25-mile radius surrounding the community of High Point, although exceptions will be made in special cases.

Payment

Tina Parker will require customers to provide notice of any cancellations within two hours of their scheduled appointment time. Otherwise, they may be subject to a $15 cancellation fee (at her discretion). Acceptable payment methods will include cash, check, and debit/credit card. Tina Parker will utilize a service that enables her to swipe debit/credit cards using her mobile phone. She will track expenses and appointments utilizing a free mobile app that synchronizes with her accounting software.

PERSONNEL

Tina Parker (Owner)

MostlyKids Hair Styles is owned by Tina Parker, who holds an Associate of Cosmetology degree from High Point Community College. While pursuing her degree, Parker received intensive education and training pertaining to cutting and styling hair, as well as salon management, state regulations, and health and safety. Tina Parker's sister, Monica, was the inspiration for the establishment of MostlyKids Hair Styles. A busy stay-at-home mom with four children, Monica was constantly seeking ways to meet the needs of her large family. Balancing family commitments, school responsibilities, and sporting activities was challenging. Adding other appointments to the mix made things even more difficult. Understanding that other families faced similar challenges, Tina decided to establish a business that provides a regularly needed service in a convenient way.

Professional & Advisory Support

Tina Parker incorporated her business using a popular online legal document service, allowing her to save on attorney costs since her business needs were very straightforward. MostlyKids Hair Styles has established a commercial checking account with High Point Community Bank, along with a merchant account for accepting credit card payments. Tax advisory services are provided by High Point Accounting Services.

GROWTH STRATEGY

Tina Parker will begin her business on a part-time basis. She has established weekly targets for the first three years of operations, pertaining to each of the different services that MostlyKids Hair Styles will provide. These are outlined in the following tables:

Year one:

Service	Fee	Weekly volume	Annual volume	Weekly revenue	Annual revenue
Hair cut (children under 12)	$25	6	550	$150	$ 7,500
Hair cut (adult women)	$50	2	200	$100	$ 5,000
Shampoo & style	$25	3	250	$ 75	$ 3,750
Bang trim	$15	4	300	$ 60	$ 3,000
Event styling	$50	3	300	$150	$ 7,500
Perms	$70	2	200	$140	$ 7,000
Dimensional coloring	$75	1	100	$ 75	$ 3,750
Single process color	$65	1	100	$ 65	$ 3,250
				$815	**$40,750**

Year two:

Service	Fee	Weekly volume	Annual volume	Weekly revenue	Annual revenue
Hair cut (children under 12)	$25	10	950	$ 250	$12,500
Hair cut (adult women)	$50	4	400	$ 200	$10,000
Shampoo & style	$25	5	450	$ 125	$ 6,250
Bang trim	$15	6	500	$ 90	$ 4,500
Event styling	$50	4	400	$ 200	$10,000
Perms	$70	3	300	$ 210	$10,500
Dimensional coloring	$75	2	200	$ 150	$ 7,500
Single process color	$65	2	200	$ 130	$ 6,500
				$1,355	**$67,750**

Year three:

Service	Fee	Weekly volume	Annual volume	Weekly revenue	Annual revenue
Hair cut (children under 12)	$25	15	1,400	$ 375	$18,750
Hair cut (adult women)	$50	6	550	$ 300	$15,000
Shampoo & style	$25	7	600	$ 175	$ 8,750
Bang trim	$15	6	500	$ 90	$ 4,500
Event styling	$50	4	400	$ 200	$10,000
Perms	$70	5	450	$ 350	$17,500
Dimensional coloring	$75	3	300	$ 225	$11,250
Single process color	$65	3	250	$ 195	$ 9,750
				$1,910	**$95,500**

OPERATIONS

Equipment

Tina Parker will begin operations with most of the supplies that she will need, as they were obtained prior to her beginning cosmetology school. These items, which cost approximately $300 in all, include:

- 2000-Watt Professional Hair Dryer
- 3/4" Professional Curling Iron
- Professional Hair Straightening Iron
- Universal Hair Dryer Diffuser
- Stylist Apron
- Shampoo Cape
- Styling Cape
- 5 1/2" Cutting Shears
- 6" 28 Tooth Thinner
- 5 1/2" Hair Shaper
- Large Paddle Hair Brush
- Styling Brush
- Oval Paddle Brush
- Vented Round Brush
- Hair Combs (assorted types/sizes)
- Clips Assortment (e.g., bobby pins, gator clips, duck bill clips, butterfly clips, etc.)
- Perm Rods (assorted sizes)
- Rollers (assorted sizes)
- Spray Bottle

Tina will need to buy several items (from personal savings) before she can begin operations. These items include:

- Salon Stool $35
- Portable/Adjustable Shampoo Basin/Hair Treatment Bowl $60
- Portable Stylist Case (aluminum) $75 (features include wheels and telescoping handle, mirror, storage compartments, extendable trays, and tool pouches)

Inventory

Tina Parker will need to purchase an initial inventory of professional hair products (e.g., shampoo, conditioner, hair coloring, etc.). She has identified a supplier from which she can purchase the items at wholesale by providing her beautician's license. Parker will spend approximately $500 for her initial inventory, which will be stored in dedicated space within her home.

Location

As a mobile business, MostlyKids Hair Styles will conduct the majority of its operations in other peoples' homes. However, Tina Parker will maintain a home office at 5821 Cunningham Ave. in High Point, Wisconsin, along with dedicated space for inventory storage.

MARKETING & SALES

MostlyKids Hair Styles has developed a cost-effective marketing plan that includes the following primary tactics:

1. **Web Site:** MostlyKids Hair Styles has developed a basic Web site (using templates and e-commerce modules from a popular Web site service) that provides key information about the business, including services provided, rates, policies, and contact information. Additionally, customers have the ability to schedule services (using an online calendar that shows Tina Parker's availability), pre-pay for services if desired, and sign up for automated e-mail/SMS text appointment reminders. Links will be provided to the business' Facebook and Instagram pages, and the site also will include testimonials and a photo gallery showcasing examples of Tina Parker's work.

2. **Promotional Flier:** A four-color flier, targeted toward parents of young children, has been developed. This printed piece can be left behind or posted at various public places. A local copy center will design and print the fliers.

3. **Word-of-Mouth Marketing:** MostlyKids Hair Styles will rely heavily upon word-of-mouth to promote the business. To encourage referrals among family and friends, Tina Parker will provide customers with a 50 percent discount on their next haircut for every referral she receives.

4. **Vehicle Graphics:** Tina Parker has made arrangements to have magnetic vehicle graphics produced at a nominal cost, allowing her to promote MostlyKids Hair Styles while driving around town and providing a free source of mobile marketing.

5. **Magnetic Business Cards:** Affordable magnetic business cards have been ordered from a promotional products company, providing MostlyKids Hair Styles with an excellent "leave behind" for existing and prospective customers.

6. **Social Media:** A presence on Facebook and Instgram, to connect with prospective customers via social media and showcase (with clients' permission) examples of haircuts and hairstyling done by Tina Parker.

Tina Parker will evaluate this plan on a quarterly basis during her first year of operations and semi-annually thereafter.

LEGAL

Local & State Licensure

Tina Parker has met all of the Wisconsin Department of Safety and Professional Services' requirements for operating a cosmetology business in her home state, including graduation from both high school and a licensed cosmetology program involving at least 1,550 training hours. Additionally, she has registered her new business in Wakefield County, and also with the Wisconsin Department of Revenue.

Insurance Coverage

Tina Parker has secured both professional (errors and omissions) and general liability insurance for MostlyKids Hair Styles. This type of insurance provides her with protection in the event that she is sued for accidentally harming a customer or damaging their hair.

FINANCIAL ANALYSIS

MostlyKids Hair Styles has prepared a complete set of pro forma financial statements, which are available upon request. The following table provides an overview of key projections for years one through three:

	2015	2016	2017
Sales			
Hair care	$40,750	$67,750	$95,500
Retail	$ 5,000	$ 5,500	$ 6,000
Cost of goods sold	−$ 2,750	−$ 3,025	−$ 3,300
Net sales	$43,000	$70,225	$98,200
Expenses			
Salary	$25,375	$38,875	$52,750
Payroll taxes	$ 3,056	$ 5,081	$ 7,163
Supplies	$ 2,038	$ 3,388	$ 4,775
Gas	$ 3,000	$ 3,300	$ 3,600
Marketing	$ 2,446	$ 4,066	$ 5,730
Business insurance	$ 750	$ 850	$ 950
Equipment	$ 500	$ 500	$ 500
Mobile phone	$ 1,200	$ 1,200	$ 1,200
Miscellaneous	$ 250	$ 250	$ 250
Total operating costs	**$38,615**	**$57,510**	**$76,918**
Net profit/loss	**$ 4,385**	**$12,715**	**$21,282**

Mobile Petting Zoo Business

Zoo Go Round Inc.

5821 Cunningham Ave.
Mason Hill, TN 37000

Paul Greenland

Zoo Go Round Inc. is a mobile petting zoo which brings a variety of different animals to birthday parties, special events, groups, churches, and schools for education and entertainment purposes.

EXECUTIVE SUMMARY

Zoo Go Round Inc. is a mobile petting zoo, which brings a variety of different animals directly to birthday parties, special events, groups, churches, and schools, providing customers with a unique source of entertainment and education. The business is being established by John and Mary Richardson of Mason Hill, Tennessee, a small town located near I-24 between the communities of Lawrenceville and Easton. The Richardsons, who live on a small "farmette," have identified a lucrative part-time business opportunity with full-time potential, the foundation of which is a group of animals their family already owns and cares for.

INDUSTRY ANALYSIS

According to the Silver Spring, Maryland-based Association of Zoos and Aquariums (AZA), in 2014 there were 228 accredited zoos and aquariums in eight countries. Of these, 214 were located in the United States, contributing approximately $16 billion annually to the U.S. economy on the strength of 142,000 employees and 181 million visitors. In addition to zoos and aquariums, the organization's accredited members included science and nature centers, safari and theme parks, aviaries, and butterfly houses. Each year, AZA's members provide informal science education to about 12 million student learners on field trips, and 50 million children who visit locations with their families.

According to its mission statement, the AZA "provides its members the services, high standards and best practices needed to be leaders and innovators in animal care, wildlife conservation and science, conservation education, the guest experience, and community engagement." In addition to the AZA, the zoo keeping industry also is represented by the American Association of Zoo Keepers, whose mission is "to advance excellence in the animal keeping profession, foster effective communication beneficial to animal care, support deserving conservation projects, and promote the preservation of our natural resources and animal life."

MARKET ANALYSIS

Zoo Go Round is located in the small town of Mason Hill, Tennessee. The business is situated near I-24 between the larger cities of Lawrenceville and Easton, which will comprise its primary market area. The business' target market is children under the age of 14, as well as community organizations, companies, churches, and schools seeking education and/or entertainment options for special events. Using demographic information available at their public library, John and Mary Richardson have developed the following market profiles for Lawrenceville and Easton.

Lawrenceville

In 2014 Lawrenceville was home to 85,473 people, a total that was expected to remain relatively flat through 2019. That year, approximately 20 percent of the population was under the age of 14. Individuals aged 0 to 4 accounted for 6.5 percent of the population, while those in the 5 to 14 age category accounted for 13 percent.

Zoo Go Round will concentrate its marketing efforts on households with income of $40,000 or more. In 2014 approximately 15 percent of households had income between $35,000 and $49,999. The largest household income segment (19.6%) was the $50,000 to $74,999 category. Next were households with income between $75,000 and $99,999 (15.3%), $100,000 to $149,999 (12.7%), and more than $150,000 (6%).

Beyond the consumer market, services will be marketed to specific types of organizations. These include, but are not limited to:

- Entertainment & Recreation Services (50 establishments)

- Membership Organizations (106 establishments)

- Lawrenceville Area School District

- Churches & Religious Organizations (150 establishments)

Easton

Easton was home to 42,822 people in 2014. As with Lawrenceville, the community's population is projected to remain steady for the next five years. Approximately 15 percent of the population was under the age of 14 in 2014. Individuals aged 0 to 4 accounted for 6 percent of the population, while those in the 5 to 14 age category accounted for 9.3 percent.

In 2014 approximately 15 percent of households had income between $35,000 and $49,999. The largest household income segment (16.5%) was the $50,000 to $74,999 category. Next were households with income between $75,000 and $99,999 (10.5%), $100,000 to $149,999 (8.3%), and more than $150,000 (3.8%).

Organizational prospects include:

- Entertainment & Recreation Services (28 establishments)

- Membership Organizations (45 establishments)

- Easton Area School District

- Churches & Religious Organizations (115 establishments)

SERVICES

Zoo Go Round provides a unique source of entertainment and education for birthday parties, as well as special events. The business provides a mobile petting zoo where attendees have the opportunity to experience encounters with the following animals:

- Miniature Ponies

- Goats

- Rabbits

- Chickens

- Potbelly Pigs

- Ferrets

Rates

Zoo Go Round provides the following service packages:

- $265 (1.5 hours)

- $365 (1.5 hours/pony rides)

Guests who wish to enjoy the mobile petting zoo and/or pony rides for a longer time span can do so at a rate of $125 per additional hour.

Scope of Services

Zoo Go Round will arrive 45 minutes before the event begins to set up a 20 x 20 pen for the animals and review animal handling policies with the customer, in order to help ensure a safe and enjoyable experience. Customers are required to provide a flat, grassy area for setup, as well as access to electricity (for cooling fans during hot months) and running water for the animals during the time that services are being provided. Zoo Go Round will provide hand sanitizer for guests to use before and after handling the animals. Typically, 30 minutes is required to tear down and vacate a customer's property following the conclusion of an event.

PERSONNEL

Zoo Go Round is being established by John and Mary Richardson of Mason Hill, Tennessee.

John Richardson (co-owner)

John Richardson works as a biology teacher and has been seeking a second source of income (especially during the summer months), which will allow him to share his love of animals and science with others. John will concentrate on marketing Zoo Go Round in the Lawrenceville and Easton markets and building relationships with area organizations. Additionally, he will oversee the aspect of transporting animals to and from different events.

Mary Richardson (co-owner)

Mary Richardson has lived on farms most of her life and has extensive experience caring for animals on a daily basis. Before raising a family, Mary worked as a veterinary assistant for 10 years. Since that time, she has continued to care for various animals at the Richardson's small farmette. Mary primarily will concentrate on attending to the health and maintenance of Zoo Go Round's animals. She also will oversee booking and scheduling activities.

Staff

The Richardsons will be joined in the business by their children, Brent (age 18) and Samantha (age 20), who live at home and attend a nearby college. Brent and Samantha will provide assistance with event setup, operation, and tear-down activities, including guest relations.

Professional & Advisory Support

The Richardsons have incorporated their business using a popular online legal document service, allowing them to save money on attorney costs. Zoo Go Round has established a commercial checking account with Central Community Bank, along with a merchant account for accepting credit card payments. Tax advisory services are provided by Community Accounting Services. Veterinary care will be provided by Dr. Jonathan Myers.

GROWTH STRATEGY

The following strategy has been developed for Zoo Go Round's first three years of operations:

Year One: Begin operations on a limited/part-time basis with one goat, one miniature pony, five rabbits, one potbelly pig, 10 chickens, and one ferret. Generate net income of about $1,000 on sales of nearly $41,000.

Year Two: Continue to operate Zoo Go Round part-time, but with expanded availability. Add one additional goat, miniature pony, and ferret. Generate net income of about $6,000 on sales of approximately $81,750.

Year Three: Make Zoo Go Round a full-time business. Expand operations by adding two Nigerian dwarf goats, one potbelly pig, 10 chickens, and five English Lop Doe rabbits, providing enough animals to make two complete mobile zoo teams. Purchase additional fencing and a second trailer. Generate nearly $45,000 on sales of approximately $163,500.

The following graph provides a visual depiction of Zoo Go Round's sales and net income projections for years one through three:

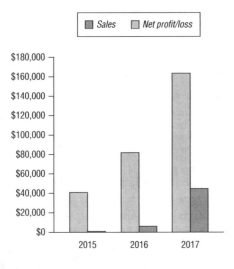

MARKETING & SALES

A marketing plan has been developed for Zoo Go Round with the following tactics:

1. **Web Site:** Zoo Go Round has created a site that lists information about its mobile petting zoo and pony ride services, including pictures and information about its animals, rates, policies, and contact details. The site will include an online form that customers can complete to book services, along with a calendar showing all available dates.

2. **Promotional Fliers:** Two separate color fliers have been developed. One is targeted toward parents of young children, while another is aimed at organizations interested in entertainment options for various functions. These printed pieces can be used for direct mailings, left behind, or posted at various public places. A local printer that can produce these in small quantities as needed has been identified.

3. **Print and Online Advertising:** A regular advertising presence will be established in *The Westchester County Gazette*, which serves residents in both Lawrenceville and Easton. In addition to print advertising, the Richardsons have negotiated an advertising package that also includes online advertising, including ads on the mobile version of *The Westchester County Gazette*.

4. **Social Media:** Zoo Go Round will maintain a Facebook page, and also explore keyword advertising on this popular social media site. In addition, the business will maintain an Instagram page to showcase photos of its animals and their appearance at various events (with customer permission).

5. **Sales Presentations/Incentives:** Each month, the Richardsons will make presentations to local community groups and organizations promoting their business. Following the presentation, they will distribute certificates that entitle the holder to a 15 percent discount off their first event. A schedule of planned presentations during the first year is available upon request.

6. **Word-of-Mouth Marketing:** Zoo Go Round will rely heavily upon word-of-mouth to promote the business. To encourage referrals among family and friends, the Richardsons will present the aforementioned 15 percent discount certificates to each new customer, entitling them to a discount off their next booking if they make a successful referral. In addition, the discount will apply to the referred customer as well.

The Richardsons will evaluate their marketing plan on a semi-annual basis during the first year of operations, and annually thereafter.

OPERATIONS

Payment

Customers are required to provide a major credit card to book Zoo Go Round for their event. A 50 percent deposit is required five days prior to the event.

Hours

Zoo Go Round will accept phone calls and/or e-mails during regular business hours (9 AM-5 PM) via a dedicated phone number at the Richardsons' home office. Typically, the Richardsons will respond to all inquiries within one business day. They will provide access to the mobile zoo during variable hours (e.g., weekends and evenings when needed).

Equipment & Supplies

Because the Richardsons live on a small farm and already care for animals, they have the facilities, equipment, and supplies needed to care for a wide range of animals, including a barn with cages, corrals, and pens; fenced areas of land for animals to roam and graze; and tools such as shovels, rakes, buckets, etc. In addition, they have a 16-foot trailer (value $12,000) capable of transporting the animals to and from different locations.

The Richardsons will purchase the following items (from personal savings) specifically for their mobile petting zoo:

- Trash Containers ($50)

- Portable Electric Fans ($200)

- First Aid Kit ($50)
- Portable Livestock Fencing ($1,500)

LEGAL

Zoo Go Round meets all requirements established by the United States Department of Agriculture, Marketing and Regulatory Programs, Animal and Plant Health Inspection Service for Animal Care, under the Animal Welfare Act, and is licensed as a Class C Exhibitor. Per the Tennessee Agritourism Liability Act, our business is not liable for injury or death resulting from participation in an agritourism activity. However, Zoo Go Round has obtained appropriate business and liability insurance through a local insurance broker.

FINANCIAL ANALYSIS

The Richardsons have prepared the following calculations to estimate ongoing expenses for both routine veterinary care and animal feed:

Projected annual feed costs

Animal	2015	2016	2017
Miniature ponies	$4,236	$ 8,472	$ 8,472
Goats	$ 330	$ 660	$ 1,320
Rabbits	$1,750	$ 1,750	$ 3,500
Chickens	$ 600	$ 600	$ 1,200
Potbelly pigs	$ 500	$ 500	$ 1,000
Ferrets	$ 200	$ 400	$ 400
Total	**$7,616**	**$12,382**	**$15,892**

Projected routine veterinary costs

Animal	2015	2016	2017
Miniature ponies	$ 350	$ 700	$ 700
Goats	$ 180	$ 360	$ 720
Rabbits	$ 375	$ 375	$ 750
Chickens	$ 300	$ 300	$ 600
Potbelly pigs	$ 500	$ 500	$1,000
Ferrets	$ 125	$ 250	$ 250
Total	**$1,830**	**$2,485**	**$4,020**

A complete set of pro forma financial statements have been prepared and are available upon request. The following table provides an overview of key projections for years one through three:

Pro forma profit and loss statement

	2015	2016	2017
Sales	**$40,876**	**$81,752**	**$163,504**
Expenses			
Salary	$18,000	$40,000	$ 60,000
Payroll taxes	$ 2,700	$ 6,000	$ 9,000
Accounting & legal	$ 1,500	$ 1,500	$ 1,500
Transportation	$ 1,000	$ 1,500	$ 2,000
Marketing	$ 4,000	$ 6,000	$ 8,000
Business insurance	$ 1,500	$ 1,750	$ 2,000
Animal feed	$ 7,616	$12,382	$ 15,892
Animal acquisitions	$ 0	$ 2,150	$ 1,625
Equipment	$ 500	$ 500	$ 13,500
Telecommunications	$ 750	$ 750	$ 750
Veterinary care	$ 1,830	$ 2,485	$ 4,020
Miscellaneous	$ 500	$ 500	$ 500
Total operating costs	**$39,896**	**$75,517**	**$118,787**
Net profit/loss	**$ 980**	**$ 6,235**	**$ 44,717**

Mural Painting Business

Murals by Mark & Misty

8775 Groovy Blvd.
Woodstock, GA 30189

Fran Fletcher

Murals by Mark & Misty is a Woodstock, Georgia home-based business owned and operated by Mark Stone and Misty Mason, artists who share a passion for painting. This talented duo will paint murals in both residential and business settings, including nurseries, kids rooms, hospitals, churches, schools, and daycare facilities.

EXECUTIVE SUMMARY

Murals by Mark & Misty is a Woodstock, Georgia home-based business owned and operated by Mark Stone and Misty Mason, artists who share a passion for painting. This talented duo will paint murals in both residential and business settings, including nurseries, kids rooms, hospitals, churches, schools, and daycare facilities.

The owners have 20 years combined art experience, and have painted murals for coworkers, family, and friends. The owners have decided to start painting murals part-time and hope to eventually paint full time.

According to the Bureau of Labor Statistics, jobs in the Craft and Fine Artists industry are dependent upon local economic conditions. Demographics in their area (including Alpharetta and Buckhead) reveal a majority of high-income households with expendable income. The owners are confident that there are plenty of homes and businesses in their area that will generate clients.

Murals by Mark & Misty will have two target markets.

- Residential—The owners expect 70% or more of their income to derive from private individuals.

- Businesses/Churches—The owners expects business clients to account for 30% of income, but expects these jobs to be larger and more time consuming.

There are several mural painting businesses in the area but only one other business that will provide services to both business and residential clients. The owners are confident that Murals by Mark & Misty will stand out from its competitors. Marketing and advertising will focus on the following customer service features:

- Custom one-of-a-kind murals

- Night and weekend hours

- No job too small

- You imagine it, we'll create it

Murals by Mark & Misty will initially advertise through baby and kids boutiques as well as through local contractors and interior design firms. They will also use mailers, the local Chamber of Commerce, newspaper ads, and radio ads. Referrals are essential to an artist's survival, and the owners will work hard to gain the respect of clients by providing superb customer service and one-of-a-kind murals.

The owners will cover start-up costs, so they will not be seeking additional financing at this time.

COMPANY DESCRIPTION

LOCATION

Murals by Mark & Misty is located in Woodstock, Georgia. This location is within thirty miles of Atlanta's wealthiest suburbs. They will travel and perform work at the client's location.

Hours of Operations

The owners will take calls and make appointments by phone or email. Work hours will be determined by the complexity of the job.

Personnel

Mark Stone (Owner/Painter)

Mark is a graduate of the Georgia Institute of Art. His work can be viewed at various locations around Atlanta, including Woodstock Women's Center, Children's Hospital of Atlanta, and Lollipop Daycare Center in Lilburn.

Misty Mason (Owner/Painter)

Misty is currently employed with the Woodstock City School System as an art teacher. She loves to paint in her spare time, and would like to eventually paint full time. Examples of her work are displayed at the New Hope Christian Church in Alpharetta and around Woodstock Primary School.

Products and Services

Services

The owners will create custom murals for both business and residential clients. Examples include:

- Custom murals for baby nurseries
- Baptistery murals
- Character murals for kids' rooms, and party rooms at local venues
- Custom murals for schools and daycare facilities
- Custom murals for hospitals and clinics
- Custom murals for restaurants
- Custom murals for libraries

MARKET ANALYSIS

Industry Overview

According to the Bureau of Labor Statistics, jobs in the Craft and Fine Artists industry are expected to increase 3% over the next ten years. Jobs and job growth in this industry are economy dependent since custom murals are considered luxury items.

According to demographic data, there were 7,900 households in Woodstock in 2010 and median household income is $71,722, which is above the state average. Within 30 miles are the areas of Alpharetta and Buckhead, which have 21,483 and 10,876 households with median household incomes of $97,825 and $131,138 respectively.

Target Market

Murals by Mark & Misty will have two target markets.

- Residential—The owners expect 70% or more of their income to derive from individual clients. They also expect clients to steadily increase over time due to referrals.

- Businesses/Churches—The owners expect business clients to account for 30% of income, but expect these jobs to be larger and more time consuming.

Market percentages

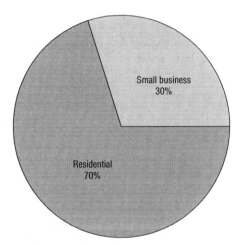

Competition

There are currently five businesses offering murals in the same area as Murals by Mark and Misty, but they plan to set themselves apart by offering beautiful, one-of-a-kind murals at an affordable price and by working with the client to meet any deadlines. Also, there is only one other local business offering mural services to both business and residential clients.

Competition includes:

1- Atlanta Murals, 1025 N. Third St., Atlanta, GA—offers mural services to business clients only

2- Mural Masters, 16754-G Ferry Rd., Atlanta, GA—offers mural services to business clients only

3- A Colorful Affair, 5392 Waldorf Way, Alpharetta, GA—offers mural services to both business and residential clients

4- Dalia's Designs, 4050 Glenwood Dr., Marietta, GA—offers mural services to residential clients only

5- Kidz Korner Kanvas, 7673 Shadow St., Atlanta, GA—offers mural services to residential clients only

GROWTH STRATEGY

The main growth strategy is to make Murals by Mark & Misty the premier place to get custom one-of-a-kind murals in Atlanta. This will be achieved by:

- Attracting residential customers by showcasing their work at several local children's boutiques.

- Obtaining referrals through satisfied clients as well as through local building contractors and interior design firms.

- Attracting business clients by offering customers the option of adding additional characters or scenes to their murals in phases. They will also work with businesses to diminish effects on the business's customers.

The owners are confident that they will be booked solid by the end of the first year. The owners plan to work alone initially, and will hire additional staff, such as art school interns, as needed.

Sales and Marketing

According to the Small Business Development Center, referrals serve as the main advertising method for artists. Referrals will be extremely important in the company's marketing strategy. The owners have identified key advertising avenues and tactics to bring in customers and build a reputation for quality.

Murals by Mark & Misty will market the following:

- Custom one-of-a-kind murals

- Night and weekend hours

- No job too small

- You imagine it, we'll create it

Advertising

The business will be showcased in the spring issue of *Art Atlanta* magazine. This should generate some clients rather quickly.

The company will advertise its services by working with:

- Local contractors

- Local interior design companies

- Local baby and kids boutiques

- Local real estate agencies

The company will also advertise using:

- Local newspaper

- Social media

- Internet sites such as Yap.com

The company will also mail flyers to local businesses, including:

- Churches

- Daycare Facilities

- Schools

- Hospitals

- Medical clinics

In addition to conventional advertising, the owners plan to paint murals at a couple of local businesses to showcase their work. Last but not least, they will rely on quality work, great customer service, and fair prices to generate customers through referrals.

FINANCIAL ANALYSIS

Start-up costs

Estimated start-up costs

Supplies/tools	$1,500
Website design	$ 500
Initial advertising	$1,500
Business license	$ 250
Total	**$3,750**

Estimated Monthly Income

Prices for Services

Prices will depend upon mural size, detail, complexity, and scaffolding. Some example prices are listed below.

Service	Price
Baptistery	$1,500–$5,000
Cartoon characters	$200 per character
One wall kids bedroom	$500–$1,500
Small mural (<1 wall)	$500–$800
Princess (2–3 walls)	$3,000–$5,000
Farmyard (1 wall)	$2,000
Superhero (1 wall)	$2,000
Animals (1 wall)	$1,500
Nursery rhymes (1 wall)	$1,500–$3,000

Estimated Monthly Expenses

The salaries paid to the owners will be dependent upon the number of murals painted. The owners will hire art school interns to help as needed but this amount will not be included in the monthly expenses.

Estimated salaries	$6,000
Art supplies	$ 300
Advertising	$ 100
Insurance	$ 100
Total	**$6,500**

Profit/Loss

The owners are strategically starting the business after an article in *Art Atlanta* magazine showcases the duo in its spring edition. They conservatively estimate that they will receive eight jobs from this article during their first month of operation. They anticipate continued momentum from the article for several months and estimate that they will receive eight jobs from this article in the second month and twelve jobs the third month. They expect the number of jobs to remain steady since twelve projects is the maximum amount that they can do without hiring additional full time help. For profit estimation purposes, the jobs will all be in the $1,000 mural category. Each quarter, a bonus will be paid to the full time employees. Each bonus recipient will receive an estimated 10% of the company's available account balance.

After six months, the owners expect to hire an additional artist. The artist's salary will be $3,000 per month plus quarterly bonuses. The addition of a full time artist will allow the company to take on an additional four projects a month. Conservative estimates show sixteen murals painted each month for the remainder of the year. The owners do not expect projects to slow down during the holidays due to businesses or schools wanting work done while closed.

Estimated profits months 1–6

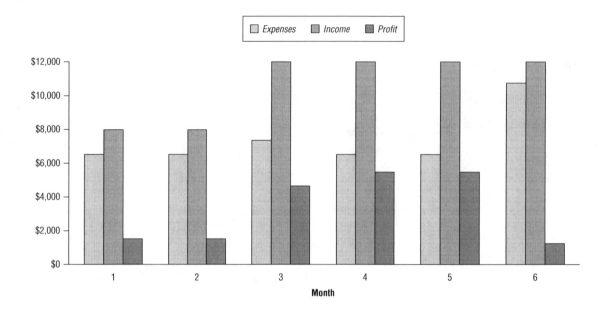

Estimated profits months 7–12

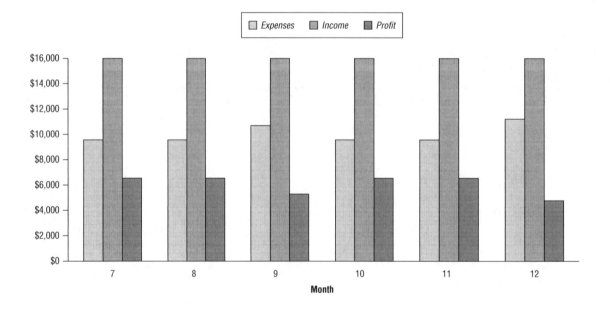

Estimated profits

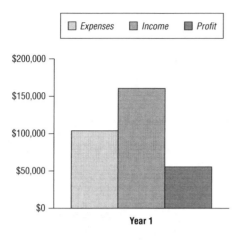

Financing

The owners are personally financing the start-up costs of $3,750. Profit projections indicate that they can easily repay themselves by the end of the first year.

Repayment plan

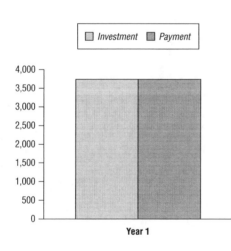

Outdoor Equipment Rental Business

Olson Outdoor LLC

5702 Pine St.
Spencer Cove, MN 76100

Paul Greenland

Olson Outdoor LLC is an outdoor equipment rental business specializing in cross-country skis, snowshoes, kayaks, and mountain bikes.

EXECUTIVE SUMMARY

Olson Outdoor LLC is an outdoor equipment rental business specializing in cross-country skis, snowshoes, kayaks, and mountain bikes. The business is owned and operated by brothers Brian and Mark Olson, who in addition to being business minded are avid outdoor enthusiasts. Located in Spencer Cove, Minnesota, Olson Outdoor begins operations with a three-year contract to provide kayak and cross-country ski rental at Sandy Lake Forest Preserve, which spans 6,000 acres and features a 350-acre lake that is used for swimming, fishing, and boating. Sandy Lake Forest Preserve also offers 80 miles of trails for hiking and cross-country skiing, as well as a 45-mile mountain biking trail system. Olson Outdoor will acquire an existing inventory of equipment from Spencer Cove County Forest Protection District, which no longer has an interest in owning and operating an equipment rental service. In addition to the existing forest preserve equipment inventory, the business will make an investment in new equipment. Olson Outdoor will operate from a leased facility within Sandy Lake Forest Preserve, and will benefit from immediate cash flow from an existing customer base.

INDUSTRY ANALYSIS

According to the Outdoor Industry Association, outdoor recreation is one of the nation's most profitable industry sectors. Personal consumption expenditure data from the Bureau of Economic Analysis reveals that consumer spending on outdoor recreation totaled $646 billion in 2011. This figure was second only to financial services and insurance ($807 billion) and outpatient healthcare ($806 billion), and greater than gasoline and other fuels ($428 billion), motor vehicles and parts ($374 billion), pharmaceuticals ($348 billion), and household utilities ($307 billion). In addition, the outdoor recreation industry employed 6.1 million people that year, ahead of construction (5.5 million), transportation and warehousing (4.3 million), education (3.5 million), information (2.5 million), and oil and gas (2.2 million).

The Outdoor Foundation's 2014 report, *Outdoor Recreation Participation*, reveals that a record 142.6 million Americans engaged in at least one outdoor activity in 2013. This was a notable increase over 2006 levels of 134.4 million. The organization found that stand-up paddling, kayak fishing, and recreational kayaking were among the activities that experienced the strongest participation increases over the previous three years. Participation in these activities increased 24 percent, 20 percent, and 11 percent, respectively.

The Outdoor Foundation's report provides specific details regarding activities that Olson Outdoor will rent equipment for. According to the report, 8.5 million people participated in mountain biking in 2013. Recreational kayaking was enjoyed by 8.7 million people, followed by freestyle skiing (4 million), traditional cross country skiing (3.4 million), snowshoeing (3.0 million), and kayak fishing (1.8 million).

Businesses like Olson Outdoor benefit from several different trade and professional associations, including the Outdoor Industry Association, SnowSports Industries America, and the American Rental Association. These organizations provide members with a wide range of benefits such as education, networking opportunities, industry research, and more.

MARKET ANALYSIS

Olson Outdoor is based in Spencer Cove, Minnesota. According to figures from the Outdoor Industry Association, consumer spending on outdoor recreation activities in Minnesota total almost $12 billion annually. This benefits the state's economy by directly producing 118,000 jobs, $3.4 billion in wages and salaries, and $815 million in state and local tax revenue.

Olson Outdoor begins operations with a three-year contract to provide outdoor equipment rental at Sandy Lake Forest Preserve, which spans 6,000 acres and features a 350-acre lake that is used for swimming, fishing, and boating. Sandy Lake Forest Preserve also offers 80 miles of trails for hiking and cross-country skiing, as well as a 45-mile mountain biking trail system.

The city of Spencer Cove was home to a population of 70,000 people in 2014. The community's average household income was approximately $65,000. After growing nearly 10 percent between 2000 and 2010, Spencer Cove's population is expected to increase nearly 4 percent between 2014 and 2019. In recent years the city has invested more than $100 million in local infrastructure, a significant portion of which has been devoted to attractions and amenities that make Spencer Cove a popular tourist destination and an attractive place to live and work. The city is home to several colleges and universities, and boasts a local population of approximately 35,000 college students. This significant population of active young adults with variable schedules provides Olson Outdoor with a unique customer base compared to other Minnesota communities.

SERVICES

Olson Outdoor will offer the following rental services during its first year of operations:

Snow Sports Equipment Rental (November-March):
Classic Cross-Country Skis (Youth, XS) $25/day

Classic Cross-Country Skis (Adult S, M, L, XL) $30/day

Skate Snow Skis (Adult S, M, L, XL) $35/day

Snowshoes (S, M, L, XL) $20/day

Kayaks (May-October):

Single $10/hour

Double $15/hour

Mountain Bike Rental (April-November):

During Olson Outdoor's second year of operations, mountain bike rental will be introduced. Various adult and youth sizes will be available for rental at the following rates:

Hybrid/Road Bike (Adult, various sizes) $40/day

Mountain Bike (Adult, various sizes) $40/day

Mountain Bike (Youth, various sizes) $30/day

All equipment rentals are subject to:

- $3 discount provided for 24-hour advance online reservations
- All customers must sign a liability waiver
- Credit card deposit required

PERSONNEL

Owners

Olson Outdoor is owned and operated by brothers Brian and Mark Olson, who in addition to being business minded are avid outdoor enthusiasts. Their love for the outdoors began at a young age, when their father introduced them to activities such as hiking, fishing, boating, and cross-country skiing. Both Brian and Mark have competed in the American Birkebeiner, North America's largest cross country ski marathon, and have extensive kayaking experience. However, realizing that running a successful business requires more than passion, the Olson brothers both bring formal education and experience to Olson Outdoor.

After graduating from high school, Brian began working for Northern Road Outfitters, an independently owned sporting-goods store focused on the outdoor adventure and fishing segments. After only three years the owners promoted him to store manager, a position he has held for the past seven years. In that role he has gained valuable customer relations and small business management experience, and has been responsible for managing a staff of 10 employees, as well as purchasing/inventory and sales.

After earning an undergraduate business degree and an MBA from Minnesota Hills University, Mark Olson has spent the last five years working as the North American marketing manager for Akton Scarpeti, an international sporting goods manufacturer. In addition to general corporate marketing experience, Mark also has gained first-hand knowledge of the recreational/outdoor sports market.

Staff

Olson Outdoor will begin operations with one full-time associate and three part-time associates under the day-to-day management of Brian and Mark Olson. During the second year, a manager will be hired to oversee daily operations, allowing the owners to concentrate more on marketing and strategic growth. That year, the business also will add a second full-time associate.

The following table provides details regarding each position and its corresponding salary for the first three years of operations:

Title	2015	2016	2017
Owner	$ 75,000	$100,000	$125,000
Owner	$ 75,000	$100,000	$125,000
Manager	$ 0	$ 40,000	$ 40,800
Associate	$ 20,000	$ 20,400	$ 20,800
Associate	$ 0	$ 20,400	$ 20,800
Associate	$ 10,000	$ 10,200	$ 10,400
Associate	$ 10,000	$ 10,200	$ 10,400
Associate	$ 10,000	$ 10,200	$ 10,400
	$200,000	$311,400	$363,600

Professional and Advisory Support

Brian and Mark Olson will use the local accounting firm, Prairie Tax Services, for assistance with tax preparation and bookkeeping. In addition, they have established a commercial checking account with Central Community Bank, and will utilize a popular mobile point-of-sale service to accept credit card and debit card payments from customers.

GROWTH STRATEGY

The Olson brothers are anticipating strong growth for Olson Outdoor during the business' first three years of operations. The following growth targets have been established:

Year One: Begin operations by providing cross-country ski and kayak rentals to visitors at Sandy Lake. Recoup the owners' initial investment in the business.

Year Two: Expand operations to include mountain bike rentals at Sandy Lake, providing the business with a highly profitable and nearly year-round revenue stream. Increase cross-country skiing and kayak rental revenues by 15 percent through strong marketing initiatives and repeat business incentives from former customers.

Year Three: Purchase bike trailer, as well as additional bike and kayak inventory. Begin offering pre-arranged group bike and kayak rental packages at select locations in a 45-mile radius surrounding Sandy Lake (includes equipment delivery at point of origin and pickup at destination). Increase cross-country skiing and kayak rental revenues by 10 percent and mountain bike rental revenues by 15 percent through strong marketing initiatives and repeat business incentives from former customers. Conduct strategic planning to evaluate the addition of new equipment categories such as canoes, sailboats, fishing gear, and camping equipment and a possible second rental operation at a nearby forest preserve, in years four and five.

OPERATIONS

During its first year, Olson Outdoor will provide outdoor equipment rental services year-round, with the exception of April. The business will rent snow sports equipment from November to March, and kayaks from May through October. Mountain bike rental will be offered from April-November beginning in the second year of operations. Hours will vary depending upon daylight and weather conditions.

Start-up Costs

The owners have agreed to purchase an existing inventory of summer (kayaks, life jackets, and paddles) and winter (ski boots, ski poles, classic and skate-style cross-country skis, and snowshoes) from the county forest preserve at a cost of $24,465. These items are valued as follows:

- Ski Boots (75 pairs): $3,750

- Ski Poles (75 pairs): $2,250

- Snow Shoes (50 pairs): $3,250

- Classic Cross-Country Skis (50 pairs): $4,950

- Cross-Country Skate-Style Skis (25 pairs): $2,475

- Single Kayaks (6): $4,000

- Double Kayaks (six): $3,000

- 84-Inch Kayak Paddles (6): $150

- 89-inch Kayak Paddles (6): $205

- Adult Universal Life Vests (18): $250

- Child Life Vests (18): $185

Both styles of cross-country skis are high-quality, entry-level models that offer excellent performance and stability, as well as high durability for rental operations.

In addition to purchasing the forest preserve's existing inventory, the Olson brothers will purchase some additional equipment to improve availability and replace aging assets.

During the second year of operations, the owners will acquire an inventory of new mountain bikes at a cost of approximately $50,000. These include:

- 15 Hybrid/Road Bikes (Adult, various sizes)

- 30 Mountain Bikes (Adult, various sizes)

- 15 Mountain Bikes (Youth, various sizes)

The owners will provide $50,000 in initial capital from personal savings, and are seeking $150,000 in investment financing in the form of a business loan, which they will repay within the business' first three years.

Location

Located in Spencer Cove, Minnesota, Olson Outdoor will operate from a leased facility at Sandy Lake Forest Preserve, which spans 6,000 acres and features a 350-acre lake that is used for swimming, fishing, and boating. Sandy Lake Forest Preserve also offers 80 miles of trails for hiking and cross-country skiing, as well as a 45-mile mountain biking trail system. Sandy Lake Forest Preserve is managed by the Spencer Cove County Forest Protection District. The business' leased facility includes beachfront access for kayak rentals, a secure fenced area for storing kayaks during off hours, as well as ample indoor storage for summer and winter equipment (e.g., paddles, life jackets, skis, boots, etc.). The facility includes a repair area, a customer service counter, restrooms, a small office with Internet access, overhead door access, and space to accommodate additional/future inventory (e.g., mountain bike rentals). Utilities such as heat, air conditioning, and electricity are included in the annual facility lease cost of $15,000.

MARKETING & SALES

Olson Outdoor has developed a marketing plan that involves the following primary tactics:

1. Printed color fliers promoting the business (distributed at community events and college campuses in Spencer Cove and the surrounding region).

2. Regional print advertising in lifestyle publications and newspapers serving Spencer Cove and the surrounding region.

3. Online "Yellow Page"/directory listings.

4. A Web site with complete details about the business; a listing of rental items, pricing, and terms/conditions; and an advance reservation tool.

5. A social media strategy involving Facebook, Twitter, and Instagram, which will be especially useful in connecting with area college students.

6. A semi-annual (early spring and late fall) direct mail campaign to residents who are (1) self-identified outdoor sports enthusiasts, (2) have household incomes of more than $60,000, and (3) live within a 20-mile radius of Sandy Lake Forest Preserve. The mailer will include details about equipment rentals for the upcoming summer or winter season, coupons, and a special incentive for liking/following the business on social media and opting into Olson Outdoor's e-mail database. A highly targeted list will be purchased from a mailing list broker in Minneapolis for these campaigns.

7. Co-marketing initiatives (TBD) with the Spencer Cove Convention and Visitors Bureau and the Spencer Cove County Forest Protection District.

8. Participation in regional boating, fishing, and outdoor shows.

9. A customer loyalty program that provides a 10 percent discount to those referring a friend or family member to the business.

10. Mobile marketing (displaying the Olson Outdoor name and Web site address on the outside of the owners' vehicles).

11. Constant Contact: Olson Outdoor will utilize this e-mail marketing service to stay in touch with prospects and contacts in the company's database.

FINANCIAL ANALYSIS

On a percentage basis, the Olson brothers anticipate that Olson Outdoor's revenues will break down as follows during the business' first year of operations:

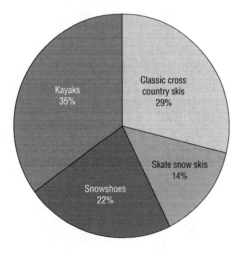

The following table provides a monthly breakdown of Olson Outdoor's projected revenues by category during its first year of operations:

Rental item	Jan.	Feb.	Mar.	Apr.	May	June
Classic cross-country skis (Y)	$ 9,300	$ 7,840	$ 6,200	$0	$ 0	$ 0
Classic cross-country skis (A)	$17,825	$14,700	$11,625	$0	$ 0	$ 0
Skate snow skis	$11,935	$10,780	$ 8,680	$0	$ 0	$ 0
Snowshoes	$23,560	$19,600	$ 3,100	$0	$ 0	$ 0
Kayaks	$ 0	$ 0	$ 0	$0	$14,400	$19,800
	$62,620	**$52,920**	**$29,605**	**$0**	**$14,400**	**$19,800**

Rental item	July	Aug.	Sept.	Oct.	Nov.	Dec.
Classic cross-country skis (Y)	$ 0	$ 0	$ 0	$ 0	$ 4,800	$ 8,060
Classic cross-country skis (A)	$ 0	$ 0	$ 0	$ 0	$ 9,000	$15,500
Skate snow skis	$ 0	$ 0	$ 0	$ 0	$ 6,300	$10,850
Snowshoes	$ 0	$ 0	$ 0	$ 0	$12,000	$20,460
Kayaks	$23,400	$25,200	$23,400	$19,800	$ 0	$ 0
	$23,400	**$25,200**	**$23,400**	**$19,800**	**$32,100**	**$54,870**

A complete set of pro forma financial statements have been prepared and is available upon request. The following table provides a breakdown of Olson Outdoor's projected revenues and expenses during its first three years of operations:

	2015	2016	2017
Sales			
Classic cross country skis	$104,850	$120,578	$132,635
Skate snow skis	$ 48,545	$ 55,827	$ 61,409
Snowshoes	$ 78,720	$ 90,528	$ 99,581
Kayaks	$126,000	$144,900	$159,390
Mountain bike rentals	$ 0	$333,225	$383,209
Group rental packages	$ 0	$ 0	$ 85,000
Total	**$358,115**	**$745,057**	**$921,224**
Expenses			
Advertising & marketing	$ 36,000	$ 75,000	$ 90,000
General/administrative	$ 1,000	$ 1,000	$ 1,000
Legal	$ 1,500	$ 725	$ 725
Accounting	$ 1,500	$ 1,750	$ 2,000
Office supplies	$ 500	$ 600	$ 700
Business insurance	$ 5,310	$ 5,900	$ 6,490
Payroll	$200,000	$311,400	$363,600
Payroll taxes	$ 30,000	$ 46,710	$ 54,540
Facility lease	$ 15,000	$ 15,000	$ 15,000
Postage	$ 225	$ 225	$ 225
New equipment	$ 25,000	$ 65,000	$ 75,000
Replacement equipment	$ 2,500	$ 10,000	$ 10,000
Startup loan	$ 54,756	$ 54,756	$ 54,756
Repairs & maintenance	$ 1,000	$ 1,000	$ 1,000
Total expenses	**$374,291**	**$589,066**	**$675,036**
Net income	**($ 16,176)**	**$155,991**	**$246,188**

ruction Business

utdoor sports education and training services, specializing in cross-
<ing.

EXECUTIVE SU....

Located in Spencer Cove, Minnesota, OutdoorEducators LLC is a provider of outdoor sports and training services, specializing in cross-country skiing, snowboarding, and kayaking. The business is owned by outdoor enthusiasts Jonathan Winters and Steve Johnson. Both Winters and Johnson are members of members the American Canoe Association and the Professional Ski Instructors of America - American Association of Snowboard Instructors. In addition to marketing private and group lessons directly to consumers, the business has been awarded a contract to provide outdoor educational services for the Spencer Cove Park District and will cross-promote services with Olson Outdoor LLC, an equipment rental business located at Sandy Lake Forest Preserve.

INDUSTRY ANALYSIS

According to the Outdoor Industry Association, outdoor recreation is one of the nation's most profitable industry sectors. Personal consumption expenditure data from the Bureau of Economic Analysis reveals that consumer spending on outdoor recreation totaled $646 billion in 2011. This figure was second only to financial services and insurance ($807 billion) and outpatient healthcare ($806 billion), and greater than gasoline and other fuels ($428 billion), motor vehicles and parts ($374 billion), pharmaceuticals ($348 billion), and household utilities ($307 billion). In addition, the outdoor recreation industry employed 6.1 million people that year, ahead of construction (5.5 million), transportation and warehousing (4.3 million), education (3.5 million), information (2.5 million), and oil and gas (2.2 million).

The Outdoor Foundation's 2014 report, *Outdoor Recreation Participation*, reveals that a record 142.6 million Americans engaged in at least one outdoor activity in 2013. This was a notable increase over 2006 levels of 134.4 million. The organization found that stand-up paddling, kayak fishing, and recreational kayaking were among the activities that experienced the strongest participation increases over the previous three years. Participation in these activities increased 24 percent, 20 percent, and 11 percent, respectively.

The Outdoor Foundation's report provides specific details regarding activities that OutdoorEducators will provide training for. According to the report, recreational kayaking was enjoyed by 8.7 million people, followed by freestyle skiing (4.0 million), and traditional cross country skiing (3.4 million).

Businesses like OutdoorEducators benefit from access to several different trade and professional associations, including the American Canoe Association (ACA) and the Professional Ski Instructors of America - American Association of Snowboard Instructors (PSIA-AASI). These organizations provide members with a wide range of benefits such as education, networking opportunities, industry research, and more.

The non-profit PSIA-AASI, which is dedicated to the promotion of skiing and snowboarding through instruction, has approximately 31,500 members. The organization, which has established certification standards for instructors and provides a variety of educational materials, engages in "research and development of instructional programs in alpine skiing, snowboarding, nordic skiing, and adaptive skiing and snowboarding." The ACA, which traces its roots back to 1880, is a non-profit industry organization dedicated to "serving the broader paddling public by providing education related to all aspects of paddling; stewardship support to help protect paddling environments; and sanctioning of programs and events to promote paddlesport competition, exploration and recreation. "

MARKET ANALYSIS

OutdoorEducators is located in Spencer Cove, Minnesota, a community that is home to Sandy Lake Forest Preserve, which spans 6,000 acres and features a 350-acre lake that is used for swimming, fishing, and boating. Sandy Lake Forest Preserve also offers 80 miles of trails for hiking and cross-country skiing, as well as a 45-mile mountain biking trail system. In addition, the community is home to nearly 1,500 acres of parks that are managed by the Spencer Cove Park District.

According to figures from the Outdoor Industry Association, consumer spending on outdoor recreation activities in Minnesota total almost $12 billion annually. This benefits the state's economy by directly producing 118,000 jobs, $3.4 billion in wages and salaries, and $815 million in state and local tax revenue.

The city of Spencer Cove was home to a population of 70,000 people in 2014. The community's average household income was approximately $65,000. After growing nearly 10 percent between 2000 and 2010, Spencer Cove's population is expected to increase nearly 4 percent between 2014 and 2019. In recent years the city has invested more than $100 million in local infrastructure, a significant portion of which has been devoted to attractions and amenities that make Spencer Cove a popular tourist destination and an attractive place to live and work. The city is home to several colleges and universities, and boasts a local population of approximately 35,000 college students. This significant population of active young adults with variable schedules provides OutdoorEducators with a unique customer base compared to other Minnesota communities.

SERVICES

OutdoorEducators provides outdoor sports and training services, specializing in cross-country skiing, snowboarding, and kayaking. The business provides both private and group lessons directly to consumers at different locations throughout Spencer Cove, and also through the Spencer Cove Park District. The following courses have been developed (detailed course descriptions and syllabi available upon request).

Kayaking Courses ($150—3-hour lessons)

I. Paddling Primer (land-based course)—Discusses kayaking equipment, safety, and fundamentals in a classroom environment.

II. Recreation Kayaking Fundamentals—Covers basic recreational paddling skills and safety education in flat-water environments such as reservoirs and inland lakes.

III. Sea Kayaking Fundamentals—Teaches fundamental sea kayaking strokes and safety skills for coastal paddlers. (Offered beginning in year two.)

IV. Intermediate Sea Kayaking—Provides training for near-shore coastal experiences. (Offered beginning in year two.)

V. Advanced Sea Kayaking—Focuses on open-water sea kayaking and advanced coastal techniques. (Offered beginning in year two.)

VI. Great Lakes Kayaking Adventure—Provides experienced sea kayakers with a day trip involving group dynamics in both coastal and open-water environments. (Offered beginning in year three.)

Cross-Country Ski Lessons ($30 group/$60 private—1-hour lessons)

I. Learn to Cross Country Ski (Classic)—Teaches participants fundamental techniques such as rhythm, balance, diagonal stride, weight transfer, snowplow, double poling, and step turns.

II. Intermediate Cross-Country Skiing (Classic)—Builds upon fundamentals from the basic course and teaches participants various double poling techniques and how to ski on different terrains.

III. Learn to Cross Country Ski (Skate)—Teaches participants fundamental techniques such as rhythm, balance, weight transfer, snowplow, V2 alternate open field, V1 uphill, skiing without poles, double poling, and step turns. *Equipment not provided for this class. (Offered beginning in year two.)

IV. Intermediate Cross-Country Skiing (Skate)—Builds upon fundamentals from the basic course and teaches participants various double poling techniques and how to ski on various terrains. *Equipment not provided for this class. (Offered beginning in year two.)

Snowboarding Lessons ($30 group/$60 private—1-hour lessons)

I. Learn to Snowboard—Teaches participants the fundamentals, including equipment orientation, safety, lift use, reading trail maps, balancing, skating, and controlling speed.

II. Intermediate Snowboarding—Covers heel side turns and toe side turns, as well as turn deflections, advanced turning techniques, and instructions for handling difficult terrain.

PERSONNEL

Owners

OutdoorEducators is a partnership owned by outdoor enthusiasts Jonathan Winters and Steve Johnson. Collectively, the owners have more than 25 years of experience in kayaks, including teaching sea kayak and mountaineering courses and guiding trips. In addition, both men are experienced at winter sports, including downhill skiing, snowboarding, and cross-country skiing. Johnson has competed professionally in North America's largest cross-country ski marathon, the American Birkebeiner, four times.

Winters and Johnson have successfully completed Instructor Certification Workshops (ICWs) through the ACA's National Paddlesports Instruction Program. As the ACA explains, its instruction program "has been acknowledged as the 'Gold Standard' of paddlesports education throughout the United States and several foreign countries." Specifically, the owners have completed ICWs in canoeing and kayaking.

The owners also are members of the Professional Ski Instructors of America - American Association of Snowboard Instructors (PSIA-AASI), an organization "committed to providing association members with the most comprehensive, compelling, up-to-date resources for improving the on-snow experience for skiers and snowboarders of every age and ability." PSIA-AASI provides professional certification and certificate programs for instructors in areas such as alpine skiing, Nordic skiing, snowboarding, and adaptive skiing and snowboarding.

A successful investor and independent financial advisor for more than 20 years, Winters brings business experience, as well start-up capital of $50,000, to OutdoorEducators. He will continue to work in the financial services field part-time, while pursuing his passion to work in the outdoor education field. Johnson's career has been spent almost entirely in the field of outdoor education. In addition to working as a staff instructor for several popular resorts, he also has worked as an independent fishing guide in Alaska.

Independent Contractors

OutdoorEducators will develop and maintain a base of independent contractors, allowing the business to scale resources up and down depending on demand, while avoiding the need to hire and manage regular employees.

Professional and Advisory Support

Winters and Johnson will use the local accounting firm, Accurate Accounting, for assistance with tax preparation and bookkeeping. In addition, they have established a commercial checking account with Central Community Bank, and will utilize a popular mobile point-of-sale service to accept credit card and debit card payments from customers. Liability insurance has been obtained from a national provider.

GROWTH STRATEGY

Year One: Begin operations with two full-time instructors (owners) and independent contractor instructors providing courses in paddling and recreational kayaking, as well as classic cross-country skiing and snowboarding. Achieve gross revenues of approximately $1 million and a net profit of $110,147, allowing the owners to recover their initial $50,000 investment (including $30,830 in equipment costs) and provide capital for continued growth and expansion in years two and three.

Year Two: Expand the business to include training in skate-style cross-country skiing, as well as all levels of sea kayaking. Increase gross revenues by at least 15 percent. Begin offering classes through Sam Parkinson Community College's Continuing Education Department.

Year Three: Continue to expand education offerings by introducing kayaking day trips. Increase gross revenues by at least 15 percent.

OPERATIONS

Location

To keep overhead low during OutdoorEducators' formative years, the business initially will operate as a virtual enterprise. Owners Jonathan Winters and Steve Johnson will conduct operations from home offices.

Course Registration

OutdoorEducators' owners will handle customer communications via a dedicated business phone, e-mail, Web site, and social media. Registration for private and group lessons will be managed through a custom designed Web site (registration for courses offered through the Spencer Cove Park District is done directly through the park district).

Start-up Costs

Kayaking Equipment:

- Single Kayaks (12): $8,000

- Double Kayaks (12): $6,000

- 84-Inch Kayak Paddles (12): $300

- 89-inch Kayak Paddles (12): $300

- Adult Universal Life Vests (36): $500

- Kayak Trailer—6 Boat (2): $2,600

Total: $17,700

Winter Sports Equipment

- Ski Boots (50 pairs): $2,500

- Ski Poles (50 pairs): $1,500

- Classic Cross-Country Skis (30 pairs): $2,970

- Snowboards (30): $3,360

- Snowboard Boots (50 pairs): $2,800

Total: $13,130

Legal

Prior to participating in any classes, OutdoorEducators will require all course participants to read and sign a liability release, which has been prepared in partnership with outside legal counsel.

MARKETING & SALES

OutdoorEducators has developed a marketing plan that involves the following primary tactics:

1. Co-promotion with the Spencer Cove Park District (Web site, social media, print and digital catalogs, fliers at park district facilities, etc.).

2. Co-marketing initiatives (TBD) with Olson Outdoor LLC, an equipment rental business located at Sandy Lake Forest Preserve.

3. A media relations strategy in which the owners will pursue guest appearances on the morning and noon shows of major network affiliates to speak about outdoor recreation topics, including tips and primers about skiing, snowboarding, and kayaking. The owners also will do similarly themed radio interviews and write guest columns for regional newspapers and magazines.

4. Printed color fliers promoting the business (distributed at local sporting goods stores, businesses, community events and colleges in and around Spencer Cove).

5. Regional print advertising in lifestyle publications and newspapers serving Spencer Cove and the surrounding region.

6. Gold sponsorship of the Spencer Cove Spiders hockey team, which includes display of the business' name in the local arena and on player uniforms.

7. Online "Yellow Page"/directory listings.

8. A Web site with complete details about the business, including a listing of available courses and corresponding dates and times.

9. A social media strategy involving Facebook, Twitter, and Instagram.

10. Exhibition at regional boating, fishing, and outdoor shows.

11. Mobile marketing (displaying the OutdoorEducators name and Web site address on the outside of the owners' vehicles with removable magnetic signage).

12. E-mail marketing: OutdoorEducators will utilize a popular e-mail marketing service to stay in touch with prospects and customers in the company's database.

FINANCIAL ANALYSIS

Following is a breakdown of projected revenues, by category and month, for OutdoorEducators' first year of operations:

Course	Jan.	Feb.	Mar.	Apr.	May	June
Paddling primer	$ 0	$ 0	$ 0	$22,500	$32,400	$37,800
Recreation kayaking fundamentals	$ 0	$ 0	$ 0	$18,000	$26,100	$33,300
Learn to cross country ski (classic/group)	$ 17,280	$ 15,480	$10,440	$ 0	$ 0	$ 0
Learn to cross country ski (classic/private)	$ 25,920	$ 23,400	$15,480	$ 0	$ 0	$ 0
Intermediate cross-country skiing (classic/group)	$ 12,960	$ 11,700	$ 7,740	$ 0	$ 0	$ 0
Intermediate cross-country skiing (classic/private)	$ 15,840	$ 14,400	$ 9,360	$ 0	$ 0	$ 0
Learn to snowboard (group)	$ 17,280	$ 15,480	$10,440	$ 0	$ 0	$ 0
Learn to snowboard (private)	$ 25,920	$ 23,400	$15,480	$ 0	$ 0	$ 0
Intermediate snowboarding (group)	$ 12,960	$ 11,700	$ 7,740	$ 0	$ 0	$ 0
Intermediate snowboarding (private)	$ 15,840	$ 14,400	$ 9,360	$ 0	$ 0	$ 0
Monthly totals	**$144,000**	**$129,960**	**$86,040**	**$40,500**	**$58,500**	**$71,100**

Course	July	Aug.	Sept.	Oct.	Nov.	Dec.
Paddling primer	$37,800	$37,800	$32,400	$22,500	$ 0	$ 0
Recreation kayaking fundamentals	$33,300	$33,300	$26,100	$18,000	$ 0	$ 0
Learn to cross country ski (classic/group)	$ 0	$ 0	$ 0	$ 0	$10,440	$ 17,280
Learn to cross country ski (classic/private)	$ 0	$ 0	$ 0	$ 0	$15,480	$ 25,920
Intermediate cross-country skiing (classic/group)	$ 0	$ 0	$ 0	$ 0	$ 7,740	$ 12,960
Intermediate cross-country skiing (classic/private)	$ 0	$ 0	$ 0	$ 0	$ 9,360	$ 15,840
Learn to snowboard (group)	$ 0	$ 0	$ 0	$ 0	$10,440	$ 17,280
Learn to snowboard (private)	$ 0	$ 0	$ 0	$ 0	$15,480	$ 25,920
Intermediate snowboarding (group)	$ 0	$ 0	$ 0	$ 0	$ 7,740	$ 12,960
Intermediate snowboarding (private)	$ 0	$ 0	$ 0	$ 0	$ 9,360	$ 15,840
Monthly totals	**$71,100**	**$71,100**	**$58,500**	**$40,500**	**$86,040**	**$144,000**

Financial Highlights

• Gross revenues projected to reach $1,001,340 during OutdoorEducators' first year.

• $590,040 of revenues will be generated by winter sports instruction (59%), and $411,300 from Kayak instruction (41%)

• $110,147 projected net profit will allowing the owners to recover their initial $50,000 investment and provide capital for continued growth and expansion in years two and three.

Expenses

OutdoorEducators' owners anticipate that first-year expenses will be as follows:

• Payroll: $160,000 (16%)

• Independent Contractors: $450,603 (45%)

• Equipment: $30,040 (3%)

- Marketing: $150,201 (15%)

- Operations: $50,000 (5%)

- Administrative: $50,000 (5%)

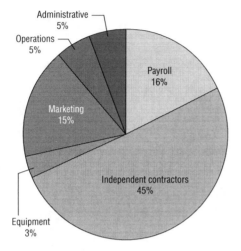

A complete set of pro forma financial statements has been prepared for OutdoorEducators and is available upon request.

SWOT ANALYSIS

Strengths: The owners' extensive capabilities in both summer and winter sports, as well as their certifications and formal experience as educators, provides quality of instruction and a competitive advantage that is difficult to replicate in the local market.

Weaknesses: During its first year of operations, the business will be heavily dependent upon the local park district for the majority of its revenues.

Opportunities: The potential to begin offering courses through the local community college's continuing education department, as well as teambuilding exercises for organizations, provides potentially lucrative opportunities for growth during the business' second and third years of operation.

Threats: Unfavorable and/or unpredictable weather may have an unexpected and negative financial impact on the business.

Pet Daycare and Boarding Services

The Pet Palace, LLC

PO Box 12223
Tucson, AZ 39837

Fran Fletcher

"We treat your pets like royalty."

BUSINESS SUMMARY

The Pet Palace, LLC. is a pet daycare and boarding business in Tucson, Arizona owned and operated by Phoebe Lane. The Pet Palace will be the only business in the area providing both pet daycare services and boarding services. The Pet Palace will provide clients with a caring staff and a safe place to leave their furry family members while at work, on a business trip, weekend getaway or extended vacation.

Previously, Ms. Lane has enjoyed working as a pet groomer and veterinarian assistant. She loves taking care of animals, so starting her own pet daycare and boarding business seemed to be the logical next step.

Pet care is a billion-dollar industry and is expected to increase by 4% each year over the next several years. According to petdemographicsonline.com, the pet population in The Pet Palace's servicing area was 75,000 five years ago, with an estimated 45,000 households owning pets, which will provide a large customer base for the business.

There are three other pet boarding businesses in the area, including two veterinarian offices and a private kennel. Additionally, a few private sitters are available for hire on the website petsit.com. Pet Palace plans to set itself apart by being the only large pet daycare facility in the area and by providing personalized care to precious pets.

The Pet Palace will target individuals who do not like to leave their pets alone and want their pets to be pampered and taken care of while they are away. The Pet Palace's number one goal is to provide its furry clients with individualized services that will meet each customer's needs. This includes older pets that need medication administered or young pets that need extra exercise.

Marketing tactics include offering optional grooming services, transportation to the vet's office, as well as having individual dog runs and a separate area for cats. The Pet Palace will advertise through the local newspaper, radio, social media, and local veterinarian clinics.

Ms. Lane is currently seeking $34,700 in financing to cover start-up costs and any expenses that will be incurred the first month. Conservative projections show a modest profit for the first three months, and then a 10% increase is expected every month thereafter. If profits are made as planned, Ms. Lane will be able to pay off the business loan by the end of the second year.

COMPANY DESCRIPTION

Location

The Pet Palace is located on a small ranch in sunny Tucson, Arizona. The ranch is located approximately 2 miles out of Tucson and is easily accessible from Route 84. The Pet Palace consists of a barn with 12 stalls, a corral, and a fenced in pasture for horses. After construction is complete, The Pet Palace will include a large kennel with 7 individual dog runs, and enough area to board 40 cats and 50 dogs.

Hours of Operation

The Pet Palace is open 24 hours a day/7 days a week.

Personnel

Phoebe Lane (owner)

Ms. Lane loves animals of all kinds. She has five years of experience as a veterinarian assistant and as a pet groomer.

Assistant(s)

One full time and one part time assistant will be hired to assist with daily operations.

Products and Services

Products

- Pet beds

- Pet blankets

- Leashes

- Collars

- Pet shampoo/conditioner

- Brushes/combs

- Hair accessories

- Pet jewelry

- Pet clothes

- Pet bandanas

- Pet toys

Services

The Pet Palace will provide boarding and related services including:

- Medication administration/application

- Meeting special dietary needs

- Exercise/play in private runs

- Hygiene

- Grooming services

- Special care for elderly pets

- Long term boarding

MARKET ANALYSIS

Industry Overview

According to the Bureau of Labor Statistics, pet boarding is categorized under the animal care and service workers field. Jobs in this category are expected to increase by 17% over the next decade. According to the most recent pet survey conducted by the Humane Society, 82.5 million or 68% of American households are pet owners. Pet ownership is expected to increase especially in two-person and retiree households where no kids are present. Boarding combined with pet grooming is a multi-billion dollar industry and projections estimate a 4% increase over the next five years.

According to petdemographicsonline.com, the pet population in The Pet Palace's servicing area was 75,000 five years ago. An estimated 45,000 households in the region have pets, which should supply an ample number of clients.

Target Market

The Pet Palace will target pet owners who travel often for work or pleasure, and want to provide care and companionship while away. This type of pet owner will be willing to pay for the individualized attention that their pet will receive while residing at The Pet Palace.

Competition

There are 3 other boarding businesses in the area, and five individual pet sitters can be found on petsit.com. Two of the boarding businesses are veterinarian offices, and one is a private firm that specializes in boarding horses.

Four Paws Ranch—6077 Prickly Pear Rd., Tucson, AZ

Johnson's Vet Clinic—2224 Lonely Rd, Tucson, AZ

Tucson Vets—7886 N Cactus Blvd., Tucson, AZ

Petsit.com—5 individuals from Tucson are listed on this website at this time; each are limited to 5 pets

GROWTH STRATEGY

The overall growth strategy of The Pet Palace is to become the most popular pet daycare and boarding service in southwest Arizona, with a full kennel every day of the week. The Pet Palace plans to achieve this growth by providing busy customers with a place where they feel that their pets will be given the utmost individualized care.

Another strategy is to build a relationship with each of its furry clients so that the animals will feel comfortable and even enjoy staying at the kennel.

The Pet Palace hopes to achieve financial independence during the first two years of operation. After funding is repaid and the owner has saved additional cash, she will consider expansion.

Sales and Marketing

Referrals are extremely important in any service industry, and pet boarding is no exception. Ms. Lane plans to obtain referrals by going the extra mile to make sure that clients and their owners get the best service possible.

The Pet Palace will host an open house to showcase its facilities to local pet owners. A discount coupon will be given to the first 20 guests, and all guests will receive a refrigerator magnet.

Advertising

In addition to an open house, The Pet Palace will advertise through:

- *The Arizona Shopper*

- Local veterinarian clinics who do not offer boarding services

- Local pet stores, breeders, and shelters

- Company website

- Social media

FINANCIAL ANALYSIS

Start-up Costs

The ranch has an existing barn and corral that will be perfect for horses. The owner will build a kennel that will provide both private and non-private pet quarters. Fencing will be installed to make several dog runs.

Estimated start-up costs

Legal fees	$ 1,000
Kennel construction	$25,000
Business license	$ 250
Website	$ 50
Initial advertising	$ 500
Supplies	$ 2,000
Insurance	$ 500
Total	**$29,300**

Estimated monthly expenses

Electricity	$ 350
Phone/Internet	$ 150
Advertising	$ 50
Loan repayment	$ 488
Insurance	$ 100
Wages owner	$2,000
Wages assistants	$2,000
Inventory	$ 200
Total	**$5,338**

Estimated Monthly Income

The Pet Palace conservatively estimates that it will provide day care for ten dogs a day during the first month of operation while they are trying to become established. Two clients that want to permanently board three horses at The Pet Palace have already contacted the owner. Ms. Lane also estimates that ten pets per week/weekend will be kept over night for two days. All estimated income calculations will use basic services.

Prices for daycare basic services

Pet	Price per day (7 a.m.–6 p.m.)*
Cats	$15
Kittens	$15
Dogs	$15
Puppies	$20
Pot bellied pigs	$15

*Other hours are available for an additional $5 per 30 minutes

If a customer wishes to hold his pet's daycare space, he must pay weekly whether the pet stays or not. The customer will also provide his pet's favorite food, bowl, toy, bed, blanket, etc. or can purchase these items from The Pet Palace.

Additional services will be available to customers for an additional charge. These services are provided to help busy people take care of their pets' basic health needs.

Prices for daycare extra services

Service	Price
Grooming	$40
Vet transport	$20
Bath	$15
Laundry	$10

Prices for basic kennel services

Pet	Per day 24 hrs +
Dog—small	$25
Dog—medium	$25
Dog—large	$25
Puppy	$25
Cat	$15
Kitten	$15
Pot belly pig	$25
Horses	$20
Horses—permanent boarding (owner cares for)	$50 per week
Horses—permanent boarding (pet palace cares for)	$150 per week

Profit/Loss

According to estimated expenses and income data, The Pet Palace will show a small profit the first month, and expects similar profits for the second and third months. Ms. Lane is prepared to personally absorb any profit losses that may occur in the first months of operation by reducing her salary. After the third month, Ms. Lane expects profits to steadily increase by 10% each month as a result of referrals. The estimated profits are shown in the "Annual Profit/Loss" chart.

Monthly profit/loss

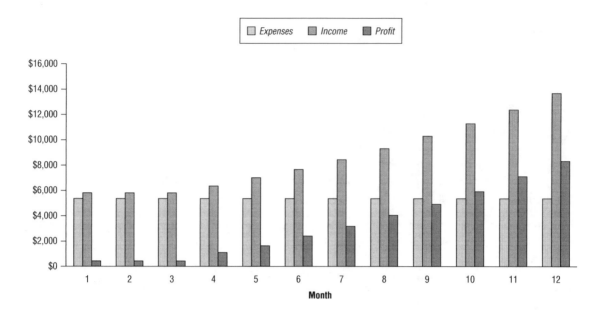

Annual profit/loss

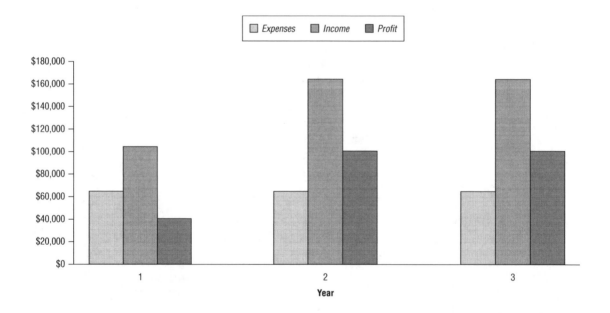

Financing

The Pet Palace is currently seeking financing in the amount of $34,700, which will cover start-up costs and one month's operating expenses. Ms. Lane will seek a business loan from a local bank and will use her property as collateral.

Repayment Plan

Ms. Lane has placed the loan payment in her monthly expenses and is confident that she will be able to repay this loan after three years as illustrated in the "Repayment Plan" chart. At the end of each year, the company will take 20% of its profit and pay a lump sum on the business loan. This will enable repayment of the loan by the end of the second year.

Repayment plan

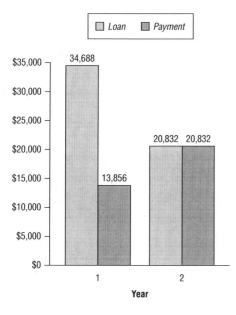

Pipeline Fracture Testing Service

ADSL Pipeline Services Inc.

6712 Hidalgo
Houston, Texas 77056

Gerald Rekve

The sole purpose of this business plan is to raise $4,000,000 of which $2,000,000 has already been secured by client investments with service purchases.

*This plan appeared in a previous volume of **Business Plans Handbook**. It has been updated for this volume.*

EXECUTIVE SUMMARY

ADSL Pipeline Services Inc. is an existing company that was started in 2015 by Ben Francis. The company is a LLC that is held privately by Ben Francis. As part of the growth strategy Mr. Francis is requiring an investment of $6 million dollars to take the company to the next stage. There are no current plans to take the company public. This being said, at some point in the future this will be a possibility and at that time the ownership and investors will make that decision.

At present ADSL Pipeline Services Inc. has clients lined up to buy their products and services. All the patents are held by Ben Francis and are not going to be included in the company's assets. The use of the patent will be leased to ADSL Pipeline Services Inc. for a period of 10 years. Until such point that this changes, Ben Francis will be paid annually for the use of the patent for the VidoMonitor9001.

The sole purpose of this business plan is to raise $6,000,000 of which $3,000,000 has already been secured by client investments with service purchases.

With tensions high in the Middle East, as well as increased security pressure both locally and abroad, we are very confident that our technology is in the right place at the right time.

MISSION STATEMENT

Our mission statement is to provide our clients with state-of-the-art monitoring and tracking equipment that is matched by no other in the market. We will have no significant down times that are a result of any event, whether natural or man-made.

We will provide the best in customer service and provide our clients with fast and up-to-date tracking and monitoring.

We will not let our information get in the hands of any third party that has no right to view our client information.

THE PRODUCTS AND SERVICES

This business plan was written after considerable increase in requests for testing pipelines across North America.

Presently there has been an increase in the number of pipelines that are getting damaged either by natural earth events or vandalism. ADSL Pipeline Services Inc. will send out teams of trained staff to test pipelines, but also install newly engineered monitoring equipment that can not only determine in nano seconds that there has been a breach to the pipeline, but also direct a satellite to actually turn and focus in on the fractured pipeline. This will serve two purposes—first, the engineers can quickly identify the level of damage to the site, and, second, be able to take pictures as well as video of the location within minutes of the fracture happening. This will allow for any vandals to be caught in the act and the police can use this in court to prosecute the vandals.

The VidoMonitor9001 has been produced by a team of engineers at ADSL Pipeline Services Inc. This device has the ability to send signals for up to 3,000 miles using the existing Satellite telephone service and the cellular networks. Working agreements have been reached with all cellular providers in North America. This in itself took considerable amount of work by the customer service staff. The technology used to build the VidoMonitor9001 was considerable. First, the monitor had to have the ability to differentiate between cell calls and Satellite calls by existing clients of the networks. One of the biggest issues with was that fact the crowded cell market left little room for a separate radio signal. The fact that there are still people in North America using the CB Radio technology from the 70's also complicated the matter. There was about $1.8 million dollars invested in the VidoMonitor9001.

The quality of the video and pictures are incredible based on the current technology of digital cameras.

COMPANY START-UP

ADSL Pipeline Services Inc. is already in business and has been operating for the past two years, starting in 2013 by Ben Francis with him investing $2.25 million into the business. Today the company has the products and is in the position to roll out across North America and also in Iraq and other oil producing countries that required this type of monitoring services.

The head office of ADSL Pipeline Services Inc. is located in Houston, Texas with regional monitoring stations setup in Prud Homme, Saskatchewan and Paris, France.

The company is requiring additional investments of $6 million dollars in order to roll out the new service in a timely matter. The entire infrastructure is in place; the money will be used to increase the number of clients, the installation of the monitors, and the monitoring of the systems. Client acquisition is the easy part; with only a limited number of pipeline companies, the customer demand for our products is high.

COMPANY START UP BUDGET

The start up budget for ADSL Pipeline Services Inc. is as follows. While the company already has an existing infrastructure in place, the requirement to increase the volume of monitor installation is at a critical stage. The clients are requesting urgent rollout of the monitors and are willing to pay extra for the installation of them. This being said, we will use the $6 million invested capital to hire both staff and contractors to facilitate the installation of the monitors.

- 4th Quarter of 2015—Spend $1.5 million on production of the monitors.

- 1st quarter 2016—Spend $3 million on subcontractors to start the install.

- The balance of the $6 million will be $1.5 million—this will be used as an operating budget to keep the company liquid while we roll out the installation.

The clients that we have signed contracts with are willing to advance approximately $3 million of payments to us. This will mean our cash flow for the first 6 months of 2016 will be nil. This is where the $1.5 million extra we raise will be used to run the day-to-day operations for 6 months.

Future clients have indicated to us that they are also willing to sign similar agreements, however, we feel this will not be required because of the short timeline we will be bringing in the required revenues to sustain our business.

START-UP BUDGET

Start-up requirements

Start-up expenses

Legal	$ 7,500
Stationery, etc.	$ 1,500
Brochures	$ 4,500
Insurance	$ 1,500
Rent	$ 15,000
Equipment and tools	$ 75,000
Vans (2)	$ 75,000
Total start-up expenses	**$180,000**

Start-up assets

Cash required	$150,000
Start-up inventory	$ 0
Other current assets	$ 0
Long-term assets	$ 75,000
Total assets	**$225,000**
Total requirements	**$405,000**

START-UP FUNDING

Start-up funding

Start-up expenses to fund	$180,000
Start-up assets to fund	$225,000
Total funding required	**$405,000**

Assets

Non-cash assets from start-up	$ 75,000
Cash requirements from start-up	$150,000
Additional cash raised	$ 0
Cash balance on starting date	$225,000

Liabilities and capital

Liabilities

Current borrowing	$ 0
Long-term liabilities	$150,000
Accounts payable (outstanding bills)	$ 0
Other current liabilities (interest-free)	$ 0
Total liabilities	**$150,000**

Capital

Planned investment	$ 0
Owner	$ 90,000
Total planned investment	$ 90,000
Loss at start-up (start-up expenses)	$150,000
Total capital	**$ 90,000**
Total funding	**$750,000**

STAFFING COSTS

Staffing costs

Subcontractors	$3,000,000
Product production	$1,500,000
Staffing existing (1 year)	$3,675,000
Increase in office cost	$ 510,000
Travel	$ 180,000
New staff hire cost	$3,750,000

EQUIPMENT INSTALLATION

ADSL Pipeline Services Inc. was formed by Ben Francis, former CEO of a large gas company based in Texas. Mr. Francis invested $2.25 million of his own money to launch this business. After about two years of R&D, Mr. Francis launched his company in 2015. Right now ADSL Pipeline Services Inc. has about 45 employees. The employees are in all departments from engineering to production and customer service. What is required at the moment is the installation of 1,000 miles of pipe monitors. Each monitor must be installed every 800 feet in areas where there is a straight line or level ground. In areas where there are curves, tree coverage or any obstruction between monitors, the monitor must be installed in eyes sight each other. This task is considerable considering it takes about 40 minutes to install one monitor. Add the drive time and it adds another 15 minutes. So on an average 10 hour work day, a two man crew can install 10 monitors.

Because the set up and installation is considerably more labor intensive, installation staff will be required before we can sign on more clients. This is one of the reasons for this business plan—to attract investors in order to pay our staff or contractors to install the monitors.

THE MONITORING OF THIS NETWORK

Once all the monitors for a client pipeline have been installed, the pipeline will be 100% secure.

The monitoring will be done at our North American geographically-central location. The reason we do it here instead of at our head office in Houston, Texas is simple. We need to make sure the monitoring office is central to all the satellites that fly over North America both day and night. The location chosen is a small town called Prud Homme, Saskatchewan. This location will employ nearly 100 staff, all of which will work shifts around the clock.

Each staff person hired to work in the monitoring station will be required to pass background checks and physiological tests to determine if they have the required strength to work in an environment where the combination of burden and sudden call to attention is required.

On a six-hour shift each one of the staff will monitor anywhere from 500—700 miles of pipeline. When an event happens, that staff member will call it up on the closest satellite to determine what type of event happened, and then start the required process to deal with the event.

STAFFING

The company ADSL Pipeline Services Inc. has approximately 45 staff at the time of this business plan. Here is a breakdown of where the staff is located.

Houston, Texas (Head Office)
- Ben Francis—CEO & Chairmen of the board
- Hadley Brown—CFO
- Betty White—CIO
- Darren Quarters—VP IT
- Mandern Gui—Chief Tech Officer & VP Production
- Harry Brewster—Regional Manager Rollout North America
- Funi Ugiuti—Regional Manager Rollout Middle East
- Franco Dolomote—Regional Manager Rollout UK & Europe & Russia

Prud Homme Monitor Station, Saskatchewan, Canada
- Lily Wasman—Monitor Station Manager
- Gina Grasser—Assistant Station Manager
- Plus 8 monitoring staff
- Will grow to 81 staff when in full operation

UK & Europe—Paris, France Monitor Station
- Manscion Deomo—Monitor Station Manager
- Asitin Grows—Assistant Station Manager
- Plus 4 monitoring staff
- Will grow to 56 staff when in full operation

There is the potential to add new monitoring stations throughout the world. These will be determined on an as-needed basis.

Right now we have 12 crews of 20 contract staff installing the devices where required. Once we get the funding we are requesting, we will see this number grow to about 1,200 installers working from January to July, 2016.

The biggest expense will be the installation of the monitors.

SALES & MARKETING

We will be renting out this monitor service to our clients. The rental fee will be based on a number of factors.

Determinants to Fees

- Number of monitors required

- Location of monitors

- Accessibility of monitors to install crew

The fees for monitoring these devises are as follows.

Installed monitors

- 1—500 = $54 each, monthly

- 501—1000 = $50 each, monthly

- 1001—2000 = $46 each, monthly

- 2001—5000 = $44 each, monthly

- 5000—10,000 = $36 each, monthly

- 10,001 + = $27 each, monthly

Location of monitors

- If location is easy access—meaning less than 1 kilometer from road—no extra fee

- If location is medium hard access—1–3 kilometer from road—one time $9.00 extra fee per monitor

- If terrain is heavy treed/mountain/desert or any other hard access determined by client and us, extra one time fee of $18.00 per monitor

- If in war zone or area staff is at risk of injury, between $68 and $180 per monitor extra one time fee

SALES FORECAST

Our sales forecast for the first year will be in $3 million dollars; year two we will have sales of $5.25 million dollars. Year three we will target to have $6.75 million dollars in sales.

There is some assumptions about our sales—that there is no break down in any of our contracts. This means the contracts not broken by war, weather, earth events, or so on.

MARKETING OF OUR PRODUCTS

Already we have clients signed up for our service; we also have a waiting list of clients who want our service. There is no other competitor out there that offers a direct product to ours. This will change as new companies develop their own technology similar to ours. Right now we have a monopoly for our products and services.

Having said this, we are certain once our clients sign on to our products we will keep them for a long time. In order to insure this as well to make certain that all our clients are happy, we will have on-staff marketing experts who will focus all their energy on winning clients and then retaining them as we move our company forward.

Getting the message out about our products and services will be done as follows.

1. **Trade Show exposure**. We will attend all the trade shows of the products and services for anything to do with oil, gas, etc.

2. **Sales executives**. Our sales executives will target clients across North America and UK, Europe, and the world.

3. **Website and Inter-Network**. The website will be public place where potential clients, media and investors can get information on our company. The Inter-Network will be the place existing clients can get live information on their pipelines; this will also be used to show potential clients how our services work. The Inter-Network will be that of a high security. In fact the security for this network will be similar to that of a bank, because of the potential of the wrong people getting our pipeline information. Only high-level people in the clients' business will be given short-term access to this network and each time a client wants access, one of the senior security staff will actually visit the client site and provide them with short-term access. Short-term means 4 hour limits. Because of the required high security even the senior security staff will have a limit of 2–4 hours per client per visit.

4. **Trade publications advertising**. We will target a variety of trade publications in the oil and gas field and run info-type advertising.

5. **Direct mail**. We will send mailers to potential clients teaching them about our products.

COMPETITION

Investment Capital Required

We are targeting to raise $3 million via investor money and $3 million from prepaid client services. We are very confidant that we will achieve our goals. The $3 million from investors will be paid back over a term of 4 years at 12% interest and monthly installments payments of $15,000 starting month 7 after we have installed all the required monitors for this rollout. The balance of the 12% added to $31,500 per month will start at the end of month 12 after we have installed all the monitors.

The $3 million from clients will be paid back in terms of free service for 6 months. This will mean for 6 months after all monitors are installed, we will be operating with no cash flow other that of new clients who sign up to our service. We know this may be considered risky, however, we know going into month 7 we will have certain cash flow and also we have a $1.5 million dollar reserve in place.

The contractors who have signed on to install the monitors have also put some skin in the game, to use a metaphor. The contractors will be taking 1st stage payment for all work on a monthly basis, based on 70% of contract. Then once the contract is done and all monitors are installed, the contractors will be paid the balance of the 30% in monthly installments over an 8 month period at 3% interest.

We first did not account for this, however the contractors came to us and offered this, knowing that as we roll out more contracts over the years, this will play favor in our books and we will most likely continue to use these contractors in the future–a win-win situation for both us and our contractors.

Our production facilities are already in place and we have subcontracted out certain components of our product, therefore reducing the required investment of capital and equipment as well as staff. We have signed long-term contracts with manufacturers of these extra components.

CLIENTS

Our clients list includes both large and small types of clients.

- Western Pipelines
- Houston Gas Co.
- Wynargard Oil & Gas
- Shell
- Imperial Oil
- Esso
- TransCanada Pipe Lines
- North One Pipe Line
- Kuit Pipe Line Inc.
- Euro Pipes LLC
- UK Petro
- BMO Gas
- AGM Oil Services

STAFF TRAINING & RECRUITMENT

All of our staff will undergo an extensive background check and training prior to gaining employment with our firm. The background check will be done by CSIS in Canada, FBI in USA, and Interpol in UK & Europe. While some think this is over doing it, we maintain that we manage the pipeline infrastructure that could cripple an economy if it is broken down. We have been told by all these agencies that this is a minimum requirement in order for us to operate in this sector. We understand that this is a concern for potential employees; however we know once our staff sees our full services they will understand and adopt the background checks.

The training will be extensive and include software training, security training, and distribution training. On average the training will take place over a period of 8 weeks off site. Each employee is required to achieve a minimum of 75% level of success on any tests conducted during the 8 week training. This will be paid training similar to other oil and gas paid training. If the potential staffer does not achieve the 75%, then they will be retested in the areas they failed. The retesting will be paid by the company. Our goal is that if one of our hiring managers see the potential in you, and they hire you, we will do all we can to make sure you pass the 8 week course. Once employed we will maintain a success follow up every 6 months; this will be to insure our staff is happy and we are happy with their work.

NETWORK MANAGEMENT

Because we are operating a one-of-a-kind network, that not only involves clients, but also involves countries, security agencies, satellite tracking, and so on, we will install a number of failsafe stop gaps to insure our network never goes down. If there is ever a breach in one of our clients lines, we will be there to offer quick as well correct action to correct the event. To track the event, this means we are policing a large and vast global network. We are certain that our follow through services ensure 100% customer satisfaction. The stop gap measures we will implement are not included in this document for security reasons. However we are certain that they will meet all the regularities requirements.

RATIO ANALYSIS

Ratio analysis	Year 1	Year 2	Year 3	Industry profile
Sales growth	10.29%	10.29%	10.20%	4.70%
Percent of total assests				
Accounts receivable	17.96%	17.96%	18.26%	11.20%
Inventory	4.38%	4.38%	4.30%	1.40%
Other current assets	0.00%	0.00%	0.00%	36.30%
Total current assets	73.93%	73.93%	78.43%	48.90%
Long-term assets	26.07%	26.07%	21.57%	51.10%
Total assets	**100.00%**	**100.00%**	**100.00%**	**100.00%**
Current liabilities	9.01%	9.01%	8.87%	26.90%
Long-term liabilities	50.34%	50.34%	40.65%	22.20%
Total liabilities	**59.36%**	**59.36%**	**49.52%**	**49.10%**
Net worth	**40.64%**	**40.64%**	**50.48%**	**50.90%**
Percent of sales				
Sales	100.00%	100.00%	100.00%	100.00%
Gross margin	72.30%	72.30%	73.28%	64.10%
Selling, general & administrative expenses	63.85%	63.85%	67.37%	45.40%
Advertising expenses	4.37%	4.37%	4.76%	0.20%
Profit before interest and taxes	14.55%	14.55%	10.43%	5.20%
Main ratios				
Current	8.2	8.2	8.84	1.79
Quick	7.71	7.71	8.36	1.44
Total debt to total assets	59.36%	59.36%	49.52%	49.10%
Pre-tax return on net worth	64.12%	64.12%	36.71%	4.70%
Pre-tax return on assets	26.06%	26.06%	18.53%	9.30%
Additional ratios				
Net profit margin	8.45%	8.45%	5.91%	n.a.
Return on equity	44.88%	44.88%	25.70%	n.a.
Activity ratios				
Accounts receivable turnover	9.01	9.01	9.01	n.a.
Collection days	39	39	39	n.a.
Inventory turnover	14.24	14.24	14.05	n.a.
Accounts payable turnover	12.17	12.17	12.17	n.a.
Payment days	27	27	29	n.a.
Total asset turnover	2.16	2.16	2.19	n.a.
Debt ratios				
Debt to net worth	1.46	1.46	0.98	n.a.
Current liab. to liab.	0.15	0.15	0.18	n.a.
Liquidity ratios				
Net working capital	$154,750	$154,750	$179,693	n.a.
Interest coverage	5.87	5.87	5.25	n.a.
Additional ratios				
Assets to sales	0.46	0.46	0.46	n.a.
Current debt/total assets	9%	9%	9%	n.a.
Acid test	5.72	5.72	6.3	n.a.
Sales/net worth	5.31	5.31	4.35	n.a.
Dividend payout	0	0	0	n.a.

PROJECTED PROFIT AND LOSS

The following table and chart highlights the projected profit and loss for three years.

Pro forma profit and loss	Year 1	Year 2	Year 3
Sales			
Direct cost of sales	$600,000	$900,000	$1,350,000
Other production expenses	$ 0	$ 0	$0
Total cost of sales	**$600,000**	**$900,000**	**$1,350,000**
Gross margin	$435,000	$510,000	$ 660,000
Gross margin %	72.03%	72.30%	73.28%
Expenses			
Payroll	$180,000	$204,000	$ 249,000
Sales and marketing and other expenses	$ 27,000	$ 34,500	$ 42,000
Utilities	$ 18,000	$ 63,000	$ 93,000
Payroll taxes	$ 27,000	$ 30,600	$ 37,350

PROJECTED CASH FLOW

The following is the projected cash flow for three years.

Pro forma cash flow	Year 1	Year 2	Year 3
Cash from operations			
Cash sales	$116,625	$128,625	$141,750
Cash from receivables	$311,063	$381,882	$420,882
Subtotal cash from operations	**$427,688**	**$510,507**	**$562,632**
Additional cash received			
New investment received	$ 7,500	$ 0	$ 0
Subtotal cash received	**$435,188**	**$510,507**	**$562,632**
Expenditures from operations			
Cash spending	$180,000	$204,000	$249,000
Bill payments	$165,000	$270,000	$285,000

Web Development Business

Lisa Sparks Interactive LLC

29 Lemon Tree Way
Trail View, CO 81000

Paul Greenland

Lisa Sparks Interactive LLC is a full-service Web development agency specializing in mobile interactive projects, especially for the healthcare industry.

EXECUTIVE SUMMARY

Lisa Sparks Interactive LLC is a full-service Web development agency specializing in mobile interactive projects, especially for the healthcare industry. Services include general Web development, Web site design/redesign, mobile application development, database programming, site maintenance, and troubleshooting/debugging. The business is being established by Lisa Sparks, an experienced Web developer who spent the first five years of her career in an agency environment before becoming an in-house developer for Trail View Community Health System.

Lisa Sparks' career experiences have allowed her to gain valuable insight from both the agency and client perspectives. Coupled with an entrepreneurial spirit, strong self-discipline, and a formal two-year Web programming and design degree from Trail View Community College, Sparks is ready to work for herself following 18 months of preparation. She is fortunate to begin operations with two "flagship" clients, for whom she has been freelancing on a part-time basis for 12 months. These include Trail View Aerospace and McMurray Logistics.

INDUSTRY ANALYSIS

According to the U.S. Bureau of Labor Statistics, in 2012 nationwide employment of Web developers totaled 141,400. By 2022 this figure is projected to increase 20 percent (28,500 additional jobs), much faster than the average for all occupations. In mid-2012 Web developers generated a median annual salary of $62,500. At that time, the BLS reported that approximately 25 percent of developers were self-employed.

Some Web developers are represented by the non-profit professional association, WebProfessionals.org (World Organization of Webmasters). According to the organization, which offers education, training, and certification, it is "dedicated to the support of individuals and organizations who create, manage or market web sites."

MARKET ANALYSIS

Primary Market

Because of her extensive experience in the healthcare industry, Lisa Sparks will concentrate marketing efforts for her business on health services providers in her home state of Colorado. According to demographic reports obtained from the Trail View Community Library, there were more than 18,000 such businesses statewide in 2014, including hospitals, family physicians, specialists, optometrists, dentists, orthodontists, and chiropractors. As more consumers rely on mobile technology for all aspects of their lives, healthcare providers are seeking to develop mobile applications with functionality such as appointment requests, appointment reminders, and medical records access.

Hospitals will represent a prime market for Lisa Sparks Interactive. According to the Colorado Hospital Association, there were more than 100 hospitals and health systems throughout the state in 2014. Collectively, these institutions infuse more than $18 billion into the state economy every year, providing care to 9 million outpatients and 555,000 inpatients annually.

Secondary Markets

In addition to healthcare, Lisa Sparks Interactive will concentrate on several other business subcategories within Colorado's services sector, including:

- Business Services (32,507)

- Membership Organizations (11,358)

- Personal Services (10,231)

- Social Services (6,070)

Geography

Lisa Sparks Interactive initially will concentrate on marketing to clients in a 90-mile region around Trail View, making it convenient to meet with customers in person when discussing new projects. A list of prospects, which will be used for direct marketing purposes, has been purchased from Dun & Bradstreet and is available for review upon request.

Competition

There are many independent Web developers operating directly within Lisa Sparks Interactive's geographic market. However, Lisa Sparks has been unable to identify competing developers with her unique blend of healthcare and mobile application development experience. These differentials will help to set her business apart from others in the market.

SERVICES

The majority services provided by Lisa Sparks Interactive will fall into one of the following categories:

1. Back-end Web Development (creating the infrastructure for custom Web sites, based specifically on a client's needs)

2. Mobile Application Development (using the Cocoa application development environment and Objective C to create iOS Apple apps and Java to develop Android apps)

3. Web Design (creating the "look and feel" for both new and existing sites and creating mobile interfaces for traditional sites

4. Compatibility Testing (performing testing to ensure compatibility with various mobile platforms (e.g., Apple, Android, Microsoft, etc.) and PC operating systems

5. Database Programming (PHP and SQL programming)

6. Web Site Maintenance (performing routine/ongoing updates, monitoring site traffic/utilization patterns, search engine optimization, etc.)

7. Troubleshooting/Code Debugging (identifying and correcting site errors, including the identification of security threats)

Process

Lisa Sparks will begin all projects by identifying her client's specific goals and objectives. Although prospective customers typically provide initial details, Sparks will communicate with them to ensure that she has a complete grasp of the project. This typically will involve her providing the client with a list of detailed questions regarding project scope, desired site components and functionality, content/content management system options, hosting arrangements, degree of customization, review/approval processes, and timeframes/deadlines. She may obtain this information via e-mail, telephone, or in-person.

After gathering project-related information, Sparks then will provide the customer with a detailed time and cost estimate. Usually, Sparks will provide clients with a flat project fee, based on her hourly rate of $95. Sparks also will accommodate clients who wish to pay on an hourly basis. This may be advantageous in the case of projects that are ambiguous.

After agreeing upon terms, Lisa Sparks will provide the client with a development agreement. Based on a template obtained from a popular online legal document service, Sparks will customize the agreement based on the specific project/client. Importantly, the agreement will specify payment terms. Sparks typically will require one-third the project fee in advance, another one-third when the project is 50 percent complete, and the final third following successful completion.

PERSONNEL

Lisa Sparks is an experienced Web developer who spent the first five years of her career working for the Boulder, Colorado-based advertising agency, Johnson & Stone, where she worked as an entry-level developer, building a solid base of skills and working on a wide variety of projects. In 2009 she secured a position as an in-house developer for Trail View Community Health System, where she has worked for the past five years.

At Trail View Community Health System, Sparks' responsibilities included:

- Developing custom applications to enhance Web site capabilities
- Developing products that utilize Web services
- Developing reusable/common components
- Maintaining coding standards
- Working with internal customers on application design and development projects
- Researching/learning new/emerging technologies
- Performing debugging, testing, and site modifications
- Collaborating with outside vendors/developers on technology projects

Sparks' career experiences have allowed her to gain valuable insight from both the agency and client perspectives. Her creativity, coupled with an entrepreneurial spirit, strong self-discipline, attention to detail, and a two-year Web programming and design degree from Trail View Community College, has prepared Sparks to work for herself following 18 months of preparation. She has saved six months of salary to provide a financial cushion as her business becomes established.

Lisa Sparks is especially skilled in the area of mobile application development, which will prove to be a strong differential for Lisa Sparks Interactive. While working for Trail View Community Health System, Lisa Sparks benefited from formal training in the development of mobile applications for both the Android and iOS Apple platforms. She put the same knowledge to use on freelance projects, and has developed a niche developing custom mobile apps for her clients.

In addition to her Associates degree, Sparks holds several technology certifications, including:

- Certified Professional Web Designer (CPWDS)

- Certified Professional Web Developer (CPWDV)

- PHP Developer Certificate (W3Schools)

Independent Contractors

When necessary, Lisa Sparks will utilize the assistance of independent programmers and developers. This will give her the ability to "scale up" when projects call for more resources than she can provide independently, without the need to hire additional employees. Sparks already has developed a network of freelancers who are available for project work. In some cases, these independent contractors have skills (for example, ColdFusion knowledge) that she does not possess, allowing her to expand her scope of services.

Professional & Advisory Support

Lisa Sparks utilized a popular online legal document service to establish her limited liability company. Additionally, Lisa Sparks Interactive has established a commercial checking account with Trail View Bank, along with a merchant account for accepting credit card payments. Tax advisory services are provided by Petersfield & Lewis Tax Services.

OPERATIONS

Location

Lisa Sparks initially will operate her business from a home office to keep expenses low. She has designated space within her home to be used exclusively for business purposes, and has subscribed to business class Internet service, allowing her to upload and download large files for clients. Through her cable provider, Sparks has subscribed to an affordable Internet-based telephone service, allowing her to make cost-effective phone calls throughout the United States.

Tools & Equipment

Sparks is fortunate to have many of the tools needed to begin operations. For example, she already has a Macintosh desktop computer, a Mac laptop, and office furniture. Examples of other tools she will use during the day-to-day operation of business include:

- Adobe Creative Suite subscription ($49.99/month)

- Wordpress (free)

- Dropbox for Business: For sharing/accessing files anywhere ($15/month)

- Text Editor (free)

GROWTH STRATEGY

Lisa Sparks is confident that her new business will begin with enough project work to ensure a steady stream of billable hours. Considering this, she has used conservative estimates to establish billable hour targets for the first three years of operations, based on her anticipated average hourly rate of $95 and working 50 weeks per year (allowing two weeks of non-paid time off).

2015: Achieve 1,500 billable hours ($142,500) and net revenue of $10,850. Focus on providing quality development service to flagship clients Trail View Aerospace and McMurray Logistics and building awareness of Lisa Sparks Interactive among healthcare providers in the business' primary market area (especially independent health and dental practices). Gain one new client with ongoing Web development needs.

2016: Achieve 1,750 billable hours ($166,250) and net revenue of $21,330. Continue to focus strongly on maintaining client satisfaction and building awareness in the primary market area. Gain two new clients with ongoing Web development needs.

2017: Achieve 2,000 billable hours ($190,000) and net revenue of $32,269. Begin expanding awareness building activities to the secondary market. Gain three new clients with ongoing Web development needs.

By the third year of operation, Sparks anticipates that she will be at capacity, in terms of being able to provide quality service to her client base. In addition to billing 40 hours of work per week, Sparks acknowledges that additional time will be needed for marketing, as well as administrative tasks such as record keeping and billing. In 2018 (her fourth year of operation), she plans to use the approximately $65,000 in accumulated net revenue to hire a full-time Web developer, but likely will continue operating the agency virtually (e.g., from her home).

MARKETING & SALES

Lisa Sparks Interactive has developed a marketing plan that includes the following primary tactics:

1. A Web site that serves as a prime example of Lisa Sparks' capabilities with both site development and design (including a mobile version). In addition to providing an overview of her capabilities, the site will link to an online portfolio of other sites that Sparks has developed. The site also will prominently feature testimonials from satisfied customers. Sparks also has partnered with a copywriter (an independent contractor with whom she works on projects as needed) to develop five case studies, which demonstrate how he helped clients with different types of projects (e.g., a mobile Web site, custom mobile app, site redesign, custom database project, and new site development).

2. A four-color glossy postcard that can be used for direct mail campaigns and also as a leave-behind following presentations.

3. Presentations. Although some graphic and Web designers have a reputation for being shy, Lisa Sparks enjoys public speaking. For example, in both high school and college she participated in forensics competitions. She will leverage this ability to its fullest, providing her with a competitive differential over other Web designers. Sparks will attempt to give at least one presentation per month to professional and business groups, with a focus on how mobile technologies can take businesses to a new level. This will provide Sparks with an opportunity to showcase her expertise and generate referrals.

4. Direct Mail: A regularly scheduled direct mail campaign targeting prospects in primary and secondary markets specified in the Market Analysis section of this plan (detailed list available upon

request). Trail View Mail Systems, a local mail house, will handle the mailings. Lisa Sparks will follow-up mailings with phone calls in order to maximize the campaign's success.

5. An e-mail marketing campaign targeting members of the Trail View Chamber of Commerce, as well as key prospects (especially healthcare providers) in the primary and secondary market areas. Sparks has obtained e-mail marketing lists from the chamber, as well as a direct marketing broker. She will utilize a popular e-mail marketing service to send messages on behalf of her business. She will then follow-up with e-mails to maximize response rates.

6. A social media strategy involving Twitter, Facebook, and LinkedIn.

7. Membership in the Trail View Chamber of Commerce to gain and maintain visibility among local businesses.

8. Word-of-mouth marketing, whereby Sparks will encourage existing customers to make referrals.

9. Regular bidding activities on freelance marketplaces (e.g., Elance, oDesk, and Guru.com), mainly for short-term projects.

Financial analysis

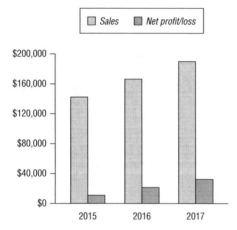

Pro forma profit and loss statement

	2015	2016	2017
Sales	**$142,500**	**$166,250**	**$190,000**
Expenses			
Salary	$ 80,000	$ 90,000	$100,000
Payroll taxes	$ 12,000	$ 13,500	$ 15,000
Accounting & legal	$ 2,500	$ 2,500	$ 2,500
Travel	$ 1,500	$ 2,000	$ 2,500
Marketing	$ 15,000	$ 15,000	$ 15,000
Business insurance	$ 1,500	$ 1,750	$ 2,000
Health insurance	$ 10,200	$ 11,220	$ 11,781
Software/software upgrades	$ 2,500	$ 2,500	$ 2,500
Equipment	$ 5,000	$ 5,000	$ 5,000
Internet/telecommunications	$ 750	$ 750	$ 750
Miscellaneous	$ 700	$ 700	$ 700
Total operating costs	**$131,650**	**$144,920**	**$157,731**
Net profit/loss	**$ 10,850**	**$ 21,330**	**$ 32,269**

BUSINESS PLAN TEMPLATE

USING THIS TEMPLATE

A business plan carefully spells out a company's projected course of action over a period of time, usually the first two to three years after the start-up. In addition, banks, lenders, and other investors examine the information and financial documentation before deciding whether or not to finance a new business venture. Therefore, a business plan is an essential tool in obtaining financing and should describe the business itself in detail as well as all important factors influencing the company, including the market, industry, competition, operations and management policies, problem solving strategies, financial resources and needs, and other vital information. The plan enables the business owner to anticipate costs, plan for difficulties, and take advantage of opportunities, as well as design and implement strategies that keep the company running as smoothly as possible.

This template has been provided as a model to help you construct your own business plan. Please keep in mind that there is no single acceptable format for a business plan, and that this template is in no way comprehensive, but serves as an example.

The business plans provided in this section are fictional and have been used by small business agencies as models for clients to use in compiling their own business plans.

GENERIC BUSINESS PLAN

Main headings included below are topics that should be covered in a comprehensive business plan. They include:

Business Summary

Purpose
Provides a brief overview of your business, succinctly highlighting the main ideas of your plan.

Includes

- Name and Type of Business
- Description of Product/Service
- Business History and Development
- Location
- Market
- Competition
- Management
- Financial Information
- Business Strengths and Weaknesses
- Business Growth

Table of Contents

Purpose
Organized in an Outline Format, the Table of Contents illustrates the selection and arrangement of information contained in your plan.

155

Includes

- Topic Headings and Subheadings
- Page Number References

Business History and Industry Outlook

Purpose

Examines the conception and subsequent development of your business within an industry specific context.

Includes

- Start-up Information
- Owner/Key Personnel Experience
- Location
- Development Problems and Solutions
- Investment/Funding Information
- Future Plans and Goals
- Market Trends and Statistics
- Major Competitors
- Product/Service Advantages
- National, Regional, and Local Economic Impact

Product/Service

Purpose

Introduces, defines, and details the product and/or service that inspired the information of your business.

Includes

- Unique Features
- Niche Served
- Market Comparison
- Stage of Product/Service Development
- Production
- Facilities, Equipment, and Labor
- Financial Requirements
- Product/Service Life Cycle
- Future Growth

Market Examination

Purpose

Assessment of product/service applications in relation to consumer buying cycles.

Includes

- Target Market
- Consumer Buying Habits
- Product/Service Applications
- Consumer Reactions
- Market Factors and Trends
- Penetration of the Market
- Market Share
- Research and Studies
- Cost
- Sales Volume and Goals

Competition

Purpose

Analysis of Competitors in the Marketplace.

Includes

- Competitor Information
- Product/Service Comparison
- Market Niche
- Product/Service Strengths and Weaknesses
- Future Product/Service Development

Marketing

Purpose

Identifies promotion and sales strategies for your product/service.

Includes

- Product/Service Sales Appeal
- Special and Unique Features
- Identification of Customers
- Sales and Marketing Staff
- Sales Cycles

- Type of Advertising/ Promotion
- Pricing
- Competition
- Customer Services

Operations

Purpose

Traces product/service development from production/inception to the market environment.

Includes

- Cost Effective Production Methods
- Facility
- Location

- Equipment
- Labor
- Future Expansion

Administration and Management

Purpose

Offers a statement of your management philosophy with an in-depth focus on processes and procedures.

Includes

- Management Philosophy
- Structure of Organization
- Reporting System
- Methods of Communication
- Employee Skills and Training

- Employee Needs and Compensation
- Work Environment
- Management Policies and Procedures
- Roles and Responsibilities

Key Personnel

Purpose

Describes the unique backgrounds of principle employees involved in business.

Includes

- Owner(s)/Employee Education and Experience
- Positions and Roles

- Benefits and Salary
- Duties and Responsibilities
- Objectives and Goals

Potential Problems and Solutions

Purpose

Discussion of problem solving strategies that change issues into opportunities.

Includes

- Risks
- Litigation
- Future Competition

- Economic Impact
- Problem Solving Skills

Financial Information

Purpose

Secures needed funding and assistance through worksheets and projections detailing financial plans, methods of repayment, and future growth opportunities.

Includes

- Financial Statements
- Bank Loans
- Methods of Repayment
- Tax Returns
- Start-up Costs
- Projected Income (3 years)
- Projected Cash Flow (3 Years)
- Projected Balance Statements (3 years)

Appendices

Purpose

Supporting documents used to enhance your business proposal.

Includes

- Photographs of product, equipment, facilities, etc.
- Copyright/Trademark Documents
- Legal Agreements
- Marketing Materials
- Research and or Studies
- Operation Schedules
- Organizational Charts
- Job Descriptions
- Resumes
- Additional Financial Documentation

Fictional Food Distributor

Commercial Foods, Inc.

3003 Avondale Ave.
Knoxville, TN 37920

This plan demonstrates how a partnership can have a positive impact on a new business. It demonstrates how two individuals can carve a niche in the specialty foods market by offering gourmet foods to upscale restaurants and fine hotels. This plan is fictional and has not been used to gain funding from a bank or other lending institution.

STATEMENT OF PURPOSE

Commercial Foods, Inc. seeks a loan of $75,000 to establish a new business. This sum, together with $5,000 equity investment by the principals, will be used as follows:

- Merchandise inventory $25,000
- Office fixture/equipment $12,000
- Warehouse equipment $14,000
- One delivery truck $10,000
- Working capital $39,000
- Total $100,000

DESCRIPTION OF THE BUSINESS

Commercial Foods, Inc. will be a distributor of specialty food service products to hotels and upscale restaurants in the geographical area of a 50 mile radius of Knoxville. Richard Roberts will direct the sales effort and John Williams will manage the warehouse operation and the office. One delivery truck will be used initially with a second truck added in the third year. We expect to begin operation of the business within 30 days after securing the requested financing.

MANAGEMENT

A. Richard Roberts is a native of Memphis, Tennessee. He is a graduate of Memphis State University with a Bachelor's degree from the School of Business. After graduation, he worked for a major manufacturer of specialty food service products as a detail sales person for five years, and, for the past three years, he has served as a product sales manager for this firm.

B. John Williams is a native of Nashville, Tennessee. He holds a B.S. Degree in Food Technology from the University of Tennessee. His career includes five years as a product development chemist in gourmet food products and five years as operations manager for a food service distributor.

Both men are healthy and energetic. Their backgrounds complement each other, which will ensure the success of Commercial Foods, Inc. They will set policies together and personnel decisions will be made jointly. Initial salaries for the owners will be $1,000 per month for the first few years. The spouses of both principals are successful in the business world and earn enough to support the families.

They have engaged the services of Foster Jones, CPA, and William Hale, Attorney, to assist them in an advisory capacity.

PERSONNEL

The firm will employ one delivery truck driver at a wage of $8.00 per hour. One office worker will be employed at $7.50 per hour. One part-time employee will be used in the office at $5.00 per hour. The driver will load and unload his own trucks. Mr. Williams will assist in the warehouse operation as needed to assist one stock person at $7.00 per hour. An additional delivery truck and driver will be added the third year.

LOCATION

The firm will lease a 20,000 square foot building at 3003 Avondale Ave., in Knoxville, which contains warehouse and office areas equipped with two-door truck docks. The annual rental is $9,000. The building was previously used as a food service warehouse and very little modification to the building will be required.

PRODUCTS AND SERVICES

The firm will offer specialty food service products such as soup bases, dessert mixes, sauce bases, pastry mixes, spices, and flavors, normally used by upscale restaurants and nice hotels. We are going after a niche in the market with high quality gourmet products. There is much less competition in this market than in standard run of the mill food service products. Through their work experiences, the principals have contacts with supply sources and with local chefs.

THE MARKET

We know from our market survey that there are over 200 hotels and upscale restaurants in the area we plan to serve. Customers will be attracted by a direct sales approach. We will offer samples of our products and product application data on use of our products in the finished prepared foods. We will cultivate the chefs in these establishments. The technical background of John Williams will be especially useful here.

COMPETITION

We find that we will be only distributor in the area offering a full line of gourmet food service products. Other foodservice distributors offer only a few such items in conjunction with their standard product line. Our survey shows that many of the chefs are ordering products from Atlanta and Memphis because of a lack of adequate local supply.

SUMMARY

Commercial Foods, Inc. will be established as a foodservice distributor of specialty food in Knoxville. The principals, with excellent experience in the industry, are seeking a $75,000 loan to establish the business. The principals are investing $25,000 as equity capital.

The business will be set up as an S Corporation with each principal owning 50% of the common stock in the corporation.

FICTIONAL HARDWARE STORE

OSHKOSH HARDWARE, INC.

123 Main St.
Oshkosh, WI 54901

The following plan outlines how a small hardware store can survive competition from large discount chains by offering products and providing expert advice in the use of any product it sells. This plan is fictional and has not been used to gain funding from a bank or other lending institution.

EXECUTIVE SUMMARY

Oshkosh Hardware, Inc. is a new corporation that is going to establish a retail hardware store in a strip mall in Oshkosh, Wisconsin. The store will sell hardware of all kinds, quality tools, paint, and housewares. The business will make revenue and a profit by servicing its customers not only with needed hardware but also with expert advice in the use of any product it sells.

Oshkosh Hardware, Inc. will be operated by its sole shareholder, James Smith. The company will have a total of four employees. It will sell its products in the local market. Customers will buy our products because we will provide free advice on the use of all of our products and will also furnish a full refund warranty.

Oshkosh Hardware, Inc. will sell its products in the Oshkosh store staffed by three sales representatives. No additional employees will be needed to achieve its short and long range goals. The primary short range goal is to open the store by October 1, 1994. In order to achieve this goal a lease must be signed by July 1, 1994 and the complete inventory ordered by August 1, 1994.

Mr. James Smith will invest $30,000 in the business. In addition, the company will have to borrow $150,000 during the first year to cover the investment in inventory, accounts receivable, and furniture and equipment. The company will be profitable after six months of operation and should be able to start repayment of the loan in the second year.

THE BUSINESS

The business will sell hardware of all kinds, quality tools, paint, and housewares. We will purchase our products from three large wholesale buying groups.

In general our customers are homeowners who do their own repair and maintenance, hobbyists, and housewives. Our business is unique in that we will have a complete line of all hardware items and will be able to get special orders by overnight delivery. The business makes revenue and profits by servicing our customers not only with needed hardware but also with expert advice in the use of any product we sell. Our major costs for bringing our products to market are cost of merchandise of 36%, salaries of $45,000, and occupancy costs of $60,000.

163

Oshkosh Hardware, Inc.'s retail outlet will be located at 1524 Frontage Road, which is in a newly developed retail center of Oshkosh. Our location helps facilitate accessibility from all parts of town and reduces our delivery costs. The store will occupy 7500 square feet of space. The major equipment involved in our business is counters and shelving, a computer, a paint mixing machine, and a truck.

THE MARKET

Oshkosh Hardware, Inc. will operate in the local market. There are 15,000 potential customers in this market area. We have three competitors who control approximately 98% of the market at present. We feel we can capture 25% of the market within the next four years. Our major reason for believing this is that our staff is technically competent to advise our customers in the correct use of all products we sell.

After a careful market analysis, we have determined that approximately 60% of our customers are men and 40% are women. The percentage of customers that fall into the following age categories are:

Under 16: 0%
17-21: 5%
22-30: 30%
31-40: 30%
41-50: 20%
51-60: 10%
61-70: 5%
Over 70: 0%

The reasons our customers prefer our products is our complete knowledge of their use and our full refund warranty.

We get our information about what products our customers want by talking to existing customers. There seems to be an increasing demand for our product. The demand for our product is increasing in size based on the change in population characteristics.

SALES

At Oshkosh Hardware, Inc. we will employ three sales people and will not need any additional personnel to achieve our sales goals. These salespeople will need several years experience in home repair and power tool usage. We expect to attract 30% of our customers from newspaper ads, 5% of our customers from local directories, 5% of our customers from the yellow pages, 10% of our customers from family and friends, and 50% of our customers from current customers. The most cost effect source will be current customers. In general our industry is growing.

MANAGEMENT

We would evaluate the quality of our management staff as being excellent. Our manager is experienced and very motivated to achieve the various sales and quality assurance objectives we have set. We will use a management information system that produces key inventory, quality assurance, and sales data on a weekly basis. All data is compared to previously established goals for that week, and deviations are the primary focus of the management staff.

GOALS IMPLEMENTATION

The short term goals of our business are:

1. Open the store by October 1, 1994
2. Reach our breakeven point in two months
3. Have sales of $100,000 in the first six months

In order to achieve our first short term goal we must:

1. Sign the lease by July 1, 1994
2. Order a complete inventory by August 1, 1994

In order to achieve our second short term goal we must:

1. Advertise extensively in Sept. and Oct.
2. Keep expenses to a minimum

In order to achieve our third short term goal we must:

1. Promote power tool sales for the Christmas season
2. Keep good customer traffic in Jan. and Feb.

The long term goals for our business are:

1. Obtain sales volume of $600,000 in three years
2. Become the largest hardware dealer in the city
3. Open a second store in Fond du Lac

The most important thing we must do in order to achieve the long term goals for our business is to develop a highly profitable business with excellent cash flow.

FINANCE

Oshkosh Hardware, Inc. Faces some potential threats or risks to our business. They are discount house competition. We believe we can avoid or compensate for this by providing quality products complimented by quality advice on the use of every product we sell. The financial projections we have prepared are located at the end of this document.

JOB DESCRIPTION-GENERAL MANAGER

The General Manager of the business of the corporation will be the president of the corporation. He will be responsible for the complete operation of the retail hardware store which is owned by the corporation. A detailed description of his duties and responsibilities is as follows.

Sales

Train and supervise the three sales people. Develop programs to motivate and compensate these employees. Coordinate advertising and sales promotion effects to achieve sales totals as outlined in budget. Oversee purchasing function and inventory control procedures to insure adequate merchandise at all times at a reasonable cost.

Finance

Prepare monthly and annual budgets. Secure adequate line of credit from local banks. Supervise office personnel to insure timely preparation of records, statements, all government reports, control of receivables and payables, and monthly financial statements.

Administration

Perform duties as required in the areas of personnel, building leasing and maintenance, licenses and permits, and public relations.

Organizations, Agencies, & Consultants

A listing of Associations and Consultants of interest to entrepreneurs, followed by the Small Business Administration Regional Offices, Small Business Development Centers, Service Corps of Retired Executives offices, and Venture Capital and Finance Companies.

Associations

This section contains a listing of associations and other agencies of interest to the small business owner. Entries are listed alphabetically by organization name.

American Business Women's Association
9100 Ward Pkwy.
PO Box 8728
Kansas City, MO 64114-0728
(800)228-0007
E-mail: abwa@abwa.org
Website: http://www.abwa.org
Jeanne Banks, National President

American Franchisee Association
53 W Jackson Blvd., Ste. 1157
Chicago, IL 60604
(312)431-0545
E-mail: info@franchisee.org
Website: http://www.franchisee.org
Susan P. Kezios, President

American Independent Business Alliance
222 S Black Ave.
Bozeman, MT 59715
(406)582-1255
E-mail: info@amiba.net
Website: http://www.amiba.net
Jennifer Rockne, Director

American Small Businesses Association
206 E College St., Ste. 201
Grapevine, TX 76051
800-942-2722
E-mail: info@asbaonline.org
Website: http://www.asbaonline.org/

American Women's Economic Development Corporation
216 East 45th St., 10th Floor
New York, NY 10017
(917)368-6100
Fax: (212)986-7114
E-mail: info@awed.org
Website: http://www.awed.org
Roseanne Antonucci, Exec. Dir.

Association for Enterprise Opportunity
1601 N Kent St., Ste. 1101
Arlington, VA 22209
(703)841-7760
Fax: (703)841-7748
E-mail: aeo@assoceo.org
Website: http://www.microenterprise works.org
Bill Edwards, Exec.Dir.

Association of Small Business Development Centers
c/o Don Wilson
8990 Burke Lake Rd.
Burke, VA 22015
(703)764-9850
Fax: (703)764-1234
E-mail: info@asbdc-us.org
Website: http://www.asbdc-us.org
Don Wilson, Pres./CEO

BEST Employers Association
2505 McCabe Way
Irvine, CA 92614
(949)253-4080
800-433-0088
Fax: (714)553-0883
E-mail: info@bestlife.com
Website: http://www.bestlife.com
Donald R. Lawrenz, CEO

Center for Family Business
PO Box 24219
Cleveland, OH 44124
(440)460-5409
E-mail: grummi@aol.com
Dr. Leon A. Danco, Chm.

Coalition for Government Procurement
1990 M St. NW, Ste. 400
Washington, DC 20036
(202)331-0975
E-mail: info@thecgp.org
Website: http://www.coalgovpro.org
Paul Caggiano, Pres.

Employers of America
PO Box 1874
Mason City, IA 50402-1874
(641)424-3187
800-728-3187
Fax: (641)424-1673
E-mail: employer@employerhelp.org
Website: http://www.employerhelp.org
Jim Collison, Pres.

Family Firm Institute
200 Lincoln St., Ste. 201
Boston, MA 02111
(617)482-3045
Fax: (617)482-3049
E-mail: ffi@ffi.org
Website: http://www.ffi.org
Judy L. Green, Ph.D., Exec.Dir.

Independent Visually Impaired Enterprisers
500 S 3rd St., Apt. H
Burbank, CA 91502
(818)238-9321
E-mail: abazyn@bazyncommunications .com
http://www.acb.org/affiliates
Adris Bazyn, Pres.

International Association for Business Organizations
3 Woodthorn Ct., Ste. 12
Owings Mills, MD 21117
(410)581-1373
E-mail: nahbb@msn.com
Rudolph Lewis, Exec. Officer

International Council for Small Business
The George Washington University School of Business and Public Management
2115 G St. NW, Ste. 403
Washington, DC 20052
(202)994-0704
Fax: (202)994-4930
E-mail: icsb@gwu.edu
Website: http://www.icsb.org
Susan G. Duffy. Admin.

International Small Business Consortium
3309 Windjammer St.
Norman, OK 73072
E-mail: sb@isbc.com
Website: http://www.isbc.com

Kauffman Center for Entrepreneurial Leadership
4801 Rockhill Rd.
Kansas City, MO 64110-2046
(816)932-1000
E-mail: info@kauffman.org
Website: http://www.entreworld.org

National Alliance for Fair Competition
3 Bethesda Metro Center, Ste. 1100
Bethesda, MD 20814
(410)235-7116
Fax: (410)235-7116
E-mail: ampesq@aol.com
Tony Ponticelli, Exec.Dir.

National Association for the Self-Employed
PO Box 612067
DFW Airport
Dallas, TX 75261-2067
(800)232-6273
E-mail: mpetron@nase.org
Website: http://www.nase.org
Robert Hughes, Pres.

National Association of Business Leaders
4132 Shoreline Dr., Ste. J & H
Earth City, MO 63045
Fax: (314)298-9110
E-mail: nabl@nabl.com
Website: http://www.nabl.com/
Gene Blumenthal, Contact

National Association of Private Enterprise
PO Box 15550
Long Beach, CA 90815
888-224-0953
Fax: (714)844-4942

Website: http://www.napeonline.net
Laura Squiers, Exec.Dir.

National Association of Small Business Investment Companies
666 11th St. NW, Ste. 750
Washington, DC 20001
(202)628-5055
Fax: (202)628-5080
E-mail: nasbic@nasbic.org
Website: http://www.nasbic.org
Lee W. Mercer, Pres.

National Business Association
PO Box 700728
5151 Beltline Rd., Ste. 1150
Dallas, TX 75370
(972)458-0900
800-456-0440
Fax: (972)960-9149
E-mail: info@nationalbusiness.org
Website: http://www.nationalbusiness.org
Raj Nisankarao, Pres.

National Business Owners Association
PO Box 111
Stuart, VA 24171
(276)251-7500
(866)251-7505
Fax: (276)251-2217
E-mail: membershipservices@nboa.org
Website: http://www.rvmdb.com.nboa
Paul LaBarr, Pres.

National Center for Fair Competition
PO Box 220
Annandale, VA 22003
(703)280-4622
Fax: (703)280-0942
E-mail: kentonp1@aol.com
Kenton Pattie, Pres.

National Family Business Council
1640 W. Kennedy Rd.
Lake Forest, IL 60045
(847)295-1040
Fax: (847)295-1898
E-mail: lmsnfbc@email.msn.com
Jogn E. Messervey, Pres.

National Federation of Independent Business
53 Century Blvd., Ste. 250
Nashville, TN 37214
(615)872-5800
800-NFIBNOW
Fax: (615)872-5353
Website: http://www.nfib.org
Jack Faris, Pres. and CEO

National Small Business Association
1156 15th St. NW, Ste. 1100
Washington, DC 20005
(202)293-8830
800-345-6728
Fax: (202)872-8543
E-mail: press@nsba.biz
Website: http://www.nsba.biz
Rob Yunich, Dir. of Communications

PUSH Commercial Division
930 E 50th St.
Chicago, IL 60615-2702
(773)373-3366
Fax: (773)373-3571
E-mail: info@rainbowpush.org
Website: http://www.rainbowpush.org
Rev. Willie T. Barrow, Co-Chm.

Research Institute for Small and Emerging Business
722 12th St. NW
Washington, DC 20005
(202)628-8382
Fax: (202)628-8392
E-mail: info@riseb.org
Website: http://www.riseb.org
Allan Neece, Jr., Chm.

Sales Professionals USA
PO Box 149
Arvada, CO 80001
(303)534-4937
888-736-7767
E-mail: salespro@salesprofessionals-usa.com
Website: http://www.salesprofessionals-usa.com
Sharon Herbert, Natl. Pres.

Score Association - Service Corps of Retired Executives
409 3rd St. SW, 6th Fl.
Washington, DC 20024
(202)205-6762
800-634-0245
Fax: (202)205-7636
E-mail: media@score.org
Website: http://www.score.org
W. Kenneth Yancey, Jr., CEO

Small Business and Entrepreneurship Council
1920 L St. NW, Ste. 200
Washington, DC 20036
(202)785-0238
Fax: (202)822-8118
E-mail: membership@sbec.org
Website: http://www.sbecouncil.org
Karen Kerrigan, Pres./CEO

Small Business in Telecommunications
1331 H St. NW, Ste. 500
Washington, DC 20005
(202)347-4511
Fax: (202)347-8607
E-mail: sbt@sbthome.org
Website: http://www.sbthome.org
Lonnie Danchik, Chm.

Small Business Legislative Council
1010 Massachusetts Ave. NW, Ste. 540
Washington, DC 20005
(202)639-8500
Fax: (202)296-5333
E-mail: email@sblc.org
Website: http://www.sblc.org
John Satagaj, Pres.

Small Business Service Bureau
554 Main St.
PO Box 15014
Worcester, MA 01615-0014
(508)756-3513
800-343-0939
Fax: (508)770-0528
E-mail: membership@sbsb.com
Website: http://www.sbsb.com
Francis R. Carroll, Pres.

Small Publishers Association of North America
1618 W Colorado Ave.
Colorado Springs, CO 80904
(719)475-1726
Fax: (719)471-2182
E-mail: span@spannet.org
Website: http://www.spannet.org
Scott Flora, Exec. Dir.

SOHO America
PO Box 941
Hurst, TX 76053-0941
800-495-SOHO
E-mail: soho@1sas.com
Website: http://www.soho.org

Structured Employment Economic Development Corporation
915 Broadway, 17th Fl.
New York, NY 10010
(212)473-0255
Fax: (212)473-0357
E-mail: info@seedco.org
Website: http://www.seedco.org
William Grinker, CEO

Support Services Alliance
107 Prospect St.
Schoharie, NY 12157
800-836-4772
E-mail: info@ssamembers.com

Website: http://www.ssainfo.com
Steve COle, Pres.

United States Association for Small Business and Entrepreneurship
975 University Ave., No. 3260
Madison, WI 53706
(608)262-9982
Fax: (608)263-0818
E-mail: jgillman@wisc.edu
Website: http://www.ususbe.org
Joan Gillman, Exec. Dir.

Consultants

This section contains a listing of consultants specializing in small business development. It is arranged alphabetically by country, then by state or province, then by city, then by firm name.

Canada

Alberta

Tenato
1229A 9th Ave. SE
Calgary, AB, Canada T2G 0S9
(403)242-1127
Fax: (403)261-5693
E-mail: jdrew@tenato.com
Website: http://www.tenato.com

Varsity Consulting Group
School of Business
University of Alberta
Edmonton, AB, Canada T6G 2R6
(780)492-2994
Fax: (780)492-5400

British Columbia

Andrew R. De Boda Consulting
1523 Milford Ave.
Coquitlam, BC, Canada V3J 2V9
(604)936-4527
Fax: (604)936-4527
E-mail: deboda@intergate.bc.ca

Reality Marketing Associates
3049 Sienna Ct.
Coquitlam, BC, Canada V3E 3N7
(604)944-8603
Fax: (604)944-4708
E-mail: info@realityassociates.com
Website: http://www.realityassociates.com

Pinpoint Tactics Business Consulting
5525 West Blvd., Ste. 330
Vancouver, BC, Canada V6M 3W6
(604)263-4698

E-mail: info@pinpointtactics.com
Website: http://www.pinpointtactics.com

Ketch Consulting Inc.
6890 Winnifred Pl.
Victoria, BC, Canada V8M 1N1
(250)661-1208
E-mail: info@ketch.ca
Website: http://www.ketch.ca

Mahigan Consulting Services
334 Skawshen Rd.
West Vancouver, BC, Canada V7P 3T1
(604)210-3833
Fax: (778)285-2736
E-mail: info@mahiganconsulting.com
Website: http://www.mahiganconsulting.com

Nova Scotia

The Marketing Clinic
1384 Bedford Hwy.
Bedford, NS, Canada B4A 1E2
(902)835-4122
Fax: (902)832-9389
E-mail: office@themarketingclinic.ca
Website: http://www.themarketingclinic.ca

Ontario

The Cynton Co.
17 Massey St.
Brampton, ON, Canada L6S 2V6
(905)792-7769
Fax: (905)792-8116
E-mail: cynton@home.com
Website: http://www.cynton.com

CRO Engineering Ltd.
1895 William Hodgins Ln.
Carp, ON, Canada K0A 1L0
(613)839-1108
Fax: (613)839-1406
E-mail: J.Grefford@ieee.ca

Business Plan World
PO Box 1322, Sta. B
Mississauga, ON, Canada L4Y 4B6
(709)643-8544
E-mail: theboss@businessplanworld.com
Website: http://www.businessplanworld.com

JPL Consulting
236 Millard Ave.
Newmarket, ON, Canada L3Y 1Z2
(416)606-9124
E-mail: sales@jplbiz.ca
Website: http://www.jplbiz.ca

Black Eagle Consulting 2000 Inc.
451 Barclay Cres.
Oakville, ON , Canada L6J 6H8
(905)842-3010
Fax: (905)842-9586
E-mail: info@blackeagle.ca
Website: http://www.blackeagle.ca

Care Concepts & Communications
21 Spruce Hill Rd.
Toronto, ON, Canada M4E 3G2
(416)420-8840
E-mail: info@cccbizconsultants.com
Website: http://
www.cccbizconsultants.com

FHG International Inc.
14 Glengrove Ave. W
Toronto, ON, Canada M4R 1N4
(416)402-8000
E-mail: info@fhgi.com
Website: http://www.fhgi.com

Harrison Pricing Strategy Group Inc.
1235 Bay St., Ste. 400
Toronto, ON, Canada M5R 3K4
(416)218-1103
Fax: (416) 827-8595

Ken Wyman & Associates Inc.
64 Lamb Ave.
Toronto, ON, Canada V
(416)362-2926
Fax: (416)362-3039
E-mail: kenwyman@compuserve.com

Quebec

PGP Consulting
17 Linton
Dollard-des-Ormeaux, QC, Canada H9B
1P2
(514)796-7613
Fax: (866)750-0947
E-mail: pierre@pgpconsulting.com
Website: http://www.pgpconsulting.com

Komand Consulting
1250 Rene Levesque Blvd.,W
22nd Fl., Ste. 2200
Montreal, QC, Canada H3B 4W8
(514)934-9281
Fax: (514)934-0770
E-mail: info@komand.ca
Website: http://www.komand.ca

Saskatchewan

Banda Marketing Group
410 - 22nd St. E, Ste. 810
Saskatoon, SK, Canada S7K 5T6
(306) 343-6100

Fax: (306) 652-1340
E-mail: admin@bandagroup.com
Website: http://www.bandagroup.com

Oracle Planning
106 28th St. W
Saskatoon, SK, Canada, S7L 0K2
(306) 717-5001
Fax: (650)618-2742

United states

Alabama

Business Planning Inc.
2090 Columbiana Rd., Ste. 2950
Vestavia Hills, AL 35216
(205)824-8969
Fax: (205)824-8939
E-mail: kmiller@businessplanninginc.
com
Website: http://www.business
planninginc.com

Tradebank of Eastern Alabama
400 S St. E
Talladega, AL 35160
(256)761-9051
Fax: (256)761-9227

Alaska

**Alaska Business Development
Center**
840 K St., Ste. 202
Anchorage, AK 99501
(907)562-0335
Free: 800-478-3474
Fax: (907)562-6988
E-mail: info@abdc.org
Website: http://www.abdc.org

Arizona

Carefree Direct Marketing Corp.
8001 E Serene St.
PO Box 3737
Carefree, AZ 85377-3737
(480)488-4227
Fax: (480)488-2841

Management 2000
39342 S Winding Trl.
Oro Valley, AZ 85737
(520)818-9988
Fax: (520)818-3277
E-mail: m2000@mgmt2000.com
Website: http://www.mgmt2000.com

CMAS
5125 N 16th St.
Phoenix, AZ 85016

(602)395-1001
Fax: (602)604-8180

Moneysoft Inc.
1 E Camelback Rd. #550
Phoenix, AZ 85012
Free: 800-966-7797
E-mail: mbray@moneysoft.com
Website: http://www.moneysoft.com

Harvey C. Skoog
7151 E Addis Ave.
Prescott Valley, AZ 86314
(928)772-1448

The De Angelis Group Inc.
9815 E Bell Rd., Ste. 120
Scottsdale, AZ 85260
(480)609-4868
Fax: (480)452-0401
E-mail: info@thedeangelisgroup.com
Website: http://www.thedeangelisgroup.com

Incendo Marketing L.L.C.
7687 E Thunderhawk Rd., Ste. 100
Scottsdale, AZ 85255
(480)513-4208
Fax: (509)561-9011

Sauerbrun Technology Group Ltd.
7979 E Princess Dr., Ste. 5
Scottsdale, AZ 85255-5878
(602)502-4950
Fax: (602)502-4292
E-mail: info@sauerbrun.com
Website: http://www.sauerbrun.com

Van Cleve Associates
6932 E 2nd St.
Tucson, AZ 85710
(520)296-2587
Fax: (520)296-3358

Variantia
6161 N Canon del Pajaro
Tucson, AZ 85750
(520)577-7680

Louws Management Corp.
PO Box 130
Vail, AZ 85641
(520)664-1881
Fax: (928)222-0086
E-mail: info@louwstraining.com
Website: http://www.louwsmanagement
.com

California

Thomas E. Church & Associates Inc.
PO Box 2439
Aptos, CA 95001
(831) 662-7950

Fax:(831) 684-0173
E-mail: thomase2@trueyellow.net
Website: http://www.thomas_church
.ypgs.net

AB Manley Partners Worldwide L.L.C.
1428 S Marengo Ave.
Alhambra, CA 91803-3096
(626) 457-8841

**Lindquist Consultants-Venture
Planning**
225 Arlington Ave.
Berkeley, CA 94707
(510)524-6685
Fax: (510)527-6604

One Page Business Plan Co.
1798 Fifth St.
Berkeley, CA 94710
(510)705-8400
Fax: (510)705-8403
E-mail: info@onepagebusinessplan.com
Website: http://www.onepagebusiness
plan.com

WordCraft Creative Services
2687 Shasta Rd.
Berkeley, CA 94708
(510) 848-5177
Fax:(510) 868-1006
E-mail: info@wordcraftcreative.com
Website: http://www.wordcraft
creative.com

Growth Partners
1566 La Pradera Dr., Ste. 5
Campbell, CA 95008
(408) 871-7925
Fax: (408) 871-7924
E-mail: mark@growth-partners.com
Website: http://www.growth-partners
.com

The Success Resource
25773 Flanders Pl.
Carmel, CA 93923
(831) 236-0732

W and J PARTNERSHIP
PO Box 2499
18876 Edwin Markham Dr.
Castro Valley, CA 94546
(510)583-7751
Fax: (510)583-7645
E-mail: wamorgan@wjpartnership.com
Website: http://www.wjpartnership.com

JB Associates
21118 Gardena Dr.
Cupertino, CA 95014
(408)257-0214

Fax: (408)257-0216
E-mail: semarang@sirius.com

House Agricultural Consultants
1105 Kennedy Pl., Ste. 1
Davis, CA 95616
(916)753-3361
Fax: (916)753-0464
E-mail: infoag@houseag.com
Website: http://www.houseag.com/

3C Systems Co.
16161 Ventura Blvd., Ste. 815
Encino, CA 91436
(818)907-1302
Fax: (818)907-1357
E-mail: mark@3CSysCo.com
Website: http://www.3CSysCo.com

Technical Management Consultants
3624 Westfall Dr.
Encino, CA 91436-4154
(818)784-0626
Fax: (818)501-5575
E-mail: tmcrs@aol.com

Rainwater-Gish & Associates
317 3rd St., Ste. 3
Eureka, CA 95501
(707)443-0030
Fax: (707)443-5683

MedMarket Diligence L.L.C.
51 Fairfield
Foothill Ranch, CA 92610-1856
(949) 859-3401
Fax: (949) 837-4558
E-mail: info@mediligence.com
Website: http://www.mediligence.com

Global Tradelinks
451 Pebble Beach Pl.
Fullerton, CA 92835
(714)441-2280
Fax: (714)441-2281
E-mail: info@globaltradelinks.com
Website: http://www.globaltradelinks.com

Larson Associates
1440 Harbor Blvd., Ste. 800
Fullerton, CA 92835
(714)529-4121
Fax: (714)572-3606
E-mail: ray@consultlarson.com
Website: http://www.consultlarson.com

Strategic Business Group
800 Cienaga Dr.
Fullerton, CA 92835-1248
(714)449-1040
Fax: (714)525-1631

Burnes Consulting
20537 Wolf Creek Rd.
Grass Valley, CA 95949
(530)346-8188
Free: 800-949-9021
Fax: (530)346-7704
E-mail: kent@burnesconsulting.com
Website: http://www.burnesconsulting
.com

International Health Resources
PO Box 2738
Grass Valley, CA 95945
Website: http://www.futureofhealthcare
.com

Pioneer Business Consultants
9042 Garfield Ave., Ste. 211
Huntington Beach, CA 92646
(714)964-7600

Fluor Daniel Inc.
3353 Michelson Dr.
Irvine, CA 92612-0650
(949)975-2000
Fax: (949)975-5271
E-mail: sales.consulting@fluordaniel.com
Website: http://www.fluor.com

MCS Associates
18881 Von Karman, Ste. 1175
Irvine, CA 92612
(949)263-8700
Fax: (949)263-0770
E-mail: info@mcsassociates.com
Website: http://www.mcsassociates.com

Savvy Communications
9730 Soda Bay Rd., Ste. 5035
Kelseyville, CA 95451-9576
(707) 277-8078
Fax:(707) 277-8079

Sky Blue Consulting Inc.
4165 Executive Dr.
Lafayette, CA 94549
(925) 283-8272

Comprehensive Business Services
3201 Lucas Cir.
Lafayette, CA 94549
(925)283-8272
Fax: (925)283-8272

The Ribble Group
27601 Forbes Rd., Ste. 52
Laguna Niguel, CA 92677
(714)582-1085
Fax: (714)582-6420
E-mail: ribble@deltanet.com

Norris Bernstein, CMC
9309 Marina Pacifica Dr. N
Long Beach, CA 90803

(562)493-5458
Fax: (562)493-5459
E-mail: norris@ctecomputer.com
Website: http://foodconsultants.com/
bernstein/

Horizon Consulting Services
1315 Garthwick Dr.
Los Altos, CA 94024
(415)967-0906
Fax: (650)967-0906

Blue Garnet Associates L.L.C.
8055 W Manchester Ave., Ste. 430
Los Angeles, CA 90293
(310) 439-1930
Fax: (310) 388-1657
E-mail: hello@bluegarnet.net
Website: http://www.bluegarnet.net

CAST Management Consultants Inc.
700 S Flower St., Ste. 1900
Los Angeles, CA 90017
(213) 614-8066
Fax: (213) 614-0760
E-mail: info@castconsultants.com
Website: http://www.castconsultants.com

Rubenstein/Justman Management Consultants
11620 Wilshire Blvd., Ste. 750
Los Angeles, CA 90025
(310)445-5300
Fax: (310)496-1450
E-mail: info@rjmc.net
Website: http://www.rjmc.net

F.J. Schroeder & Associates
1926 Westholme Ave.
Los Angeles, CA 90025
(310)470-2655
Fax: (310)470-6378
E-mail: fjsacons@aol.com
Website: http://www.mcninet.com/
GlobalLook/Fjschroe.html

Western Management Associates
5777 W Century Blvd., Ste. 1220
Los Angeles, CA 90045
(310)645-1091
Free: (888)788-6534
Fax: (310)645-1092
E-mail: gene@cfoforrent.com
Website: http://www.cfoforrent.com

Inspiration Quest Inc.
PO Box 90
Mendocino, CA 95460
(415) 235-6002
E-mail: info@inspirationquest.com
Website: http://www.inspirationquest
.com

Heron Advisory Group
9 Heron Dr.
Mill Valley, CA 94941
(415) 380-8611
Fax: (415) 381-9044
E-mail: janetmca@pacbell.net
Website: http://www.hagroup.biz

Emacula Consulting Group
131 Draeger Dr., Ste. A
Moraga, CA 94556
(925) 388-6083
Fax: (267) 589-3151
E-mail: drochlin@emacula.com
Website: http://www.emacula.com

BizplanSource
1048 Irvine Ave., Ste. 621
Newport Beach, CA 92660
Free: 888-253-0974
Fax: 800-859-8254
E-mail: info@bizplansource.com
Website: http://www.bizplansource.com
Adam Greengrass, President

The Market Connection
20051 SW Birch St., Ste 310
Newport Beach, CA 92660
(949)851-6313
Fax: (949)833-0283

Intelequest Corp.
722 Gailen Ave.
Palo Alto, CA 94303
(415)968-3443
Fax: (415)493-6954
E-mail: frits@iqix.com

Beblie, Brandt & Jacobs Inc.
19 Brista del Lago
Rancho Santa Margarita, CA 92618
(949)589-5120
Fax: (949)203-6225
E-mail: darcy@bbjinc.com

California Business Incubation Network
225 Broadway, Ste. 2250
San Diego, CA 92101
(619)237-0559
Fax: (619)237-0521

The Drake Group
824 Santa Clara Pl.
San Diego, CA 92109-7224
X(858) 488-3911
Fax: (810) 454-4593
E-mail: cdrake@drakegroup.com
Website: http://www.drakegroup.com

G.R. Gordetsky Consultants Inc.
11414 Windy Summit Pl.
San Diego, CA 92127

(858)487-4939
E-mail: gordet@pacbell.net

Noorany Marketing Resources
3830 Valley Centre Dr., Ste. 705
San Diego, CA 92130
(858) 792-9559
Fax: (858) 259-2320
E-mail: heidi@noorany.com
Website: http://www.noorany.com

Freeman, Sullivan & Co.
1101 Montgomery St., 15th Fl.
San Francisco, CA 94104
Website: http://www.fscgroup.com

PKF Consulting Corp.
50 California St., 19th Fl.
San Francisco, CA 94111
(415)788-3102
Fax: (415)433-7844
E-mail: callahan@pkfc.com
Website: http://www.pkfc.com

Welling & Woodard Inc.
1067 Broadway
San Francisco, CA 94133
(415)776-4500
Fax: (415)776-5067

Highland Associates
16174 Highland Dr.
San Jose, CA 95127
(408)272-7008
Fax: (408)272-4040

Leckrone Law Corp.
4010 Moorpark Ave., Ste. 215
San Jose, CA 95117-1843
(408) 243-9898
Fax: (408) 296-6637

ORDIS Inc.
6815 Trinidad Dr.
San Jose, CA 95120-2056
(408)268-3321
Free: 800-446-7347
Fax: (408)268-3582
E-mail: ordis@ordis.com
Website: http://www.ordis.com

Bay Area Tax Consultants and Bayhill Financial Consultants
1840 Gateway Dr.
San Mateo, CA 94404
(650)378-1373
Fax: (650)585-5444
E-mail: admin@baytax.com
Website: http://www.baytax.com/

Helfert Associates
111 St. Matthews, Ste. 307
San Mateo, CA 94401

(650)377-0540
Fax: (650)377-0472

Mykytyn Consulting Group Inc.
185 N Redwood Dr., Ste. 200
San Rafael, CA 94903
(415)491-1770
Fax: (415)491-1251
E-mail: info@mcgi.com

Omega Management Systems Inc.
3 Mount Darwin Ct.
San Rafael, CA 94903-1109
(415)499-1300
Fax: (415)492-9490
E-mail: information@omegamgt.com

Manex Consulting
2010 Crow Canyon Pl., Ste. 320
San Ramon, CA 94583
(925) 807-5100
Website: http://www.manexconsulting
.com

Brincko Associates Inc.
530 Wilshire Blvd., Ste. 201
Santa Monica, CA 90401
(310)553-4523
Fax: (310)553-6782

hE Myth
131B Stony Cir., Ste. 2000
Santa Rosa, CA 95401
(541)552-4600
Free: 800-300-3531
E-mail: info@emyth.com
Website: http://www.emyth.com

Figueroa Farms L.L.C.
PO Box 206
Santa Ynez, CA 93460
(805) 686-4890
Fax: (805) 686-2887
E-mail: info@figueroafarms.com
Website: http://www.FigueroaFarms.com

Reilly, Connors & Ray
1743 Canyon Rd.
Spring Valley, CA 91977
(619)698-4808
Fax: (619)460-3892
E-mail: davidray@adnc.com

RJR Associates
1639 Lewiston Dr.
Sunnyvale, CA 94087
(408)737-7720
E-mail: bobroy@rjrassoc.com
Website: http://www.rjrassoc.com

Schwafel Associates
333 Cobalt Way, Ste. 107
Sunnyvale, CA 94085

(408)720-0649
Fax: (408)720-1796
E-mail: schwafel@ricochet.net
Website: http://www.patca.org

The International Coverting Institute
5200 Badger Rd
Terrebonne, CA 97760
(503) 548-1447
Fax: (503) 548-1618

GlobalReady
1521 Kirk Ave.
Thousand Oaks, CA 91360
(805) 427-4131
E-mail: info@globalready.com
Website: http://www.globalready.com

Staubs Business Services
23320 S Vermont Ave.
Torrance, CA 90502-2940
(310)830-9128
Fax: (310)830-9128
E-mail: Harry_L_Staubs@Lamg.com

Enterprise Management Corp.
17461 Irvine Blvd., Ste. M
Tustin, CA 92780
(714) 505-1925
Fax: (714) 505-9691
E-mail: cfotogo@companycfo.com
Website: http://www.companycfo.com

Out of Your Mind . . . and Into the Marketplace
13381 White Sands Dr.
Tustin, CA 92780-4565
(714)544-0248
Free: 800-419-1513
Fax: (714)730-1414
Website: http://www.business-plan.com

Ingman Company Inc.
7949 Woodley Ave., Ste. 120
Van Nuys, CA 91406-1232
(805)650-9353
Fax: (805)984-2979

Innovative Technology Associates
3639 E Harbor Blvd., Ste. 203E
Ventura, CA 93001
(805)650-9353

Grid Technology Associates
20404 Tufts Cir.
Walnut, CA 91789
(909)444-0922
Fax: (909)444-0922

Bell Springs Publishing
PO Box 1240
Willits, CA 95490
(707)459-6372

E-mail: bellsprings@sabernet
Website: http://www.bellsprings.com

Hutchinson Consulting and Appraisal
23245 Sylvan St., Ste. 103
Woodland Hills, CA 91367
(818)888-8175
Free: 800-977-7548
Fax: (818)888-8220
E-mail: r.f.hutchinson-cpa@worldnet
.att.net

Colorado

Sam Boyer & Associates
4255 S Buckley Rd., No. 136
Aurora, CO 80013
(303)766-1557
Free: 800-785-0485
Fax: (303)766-8740
E-mail: samboyer@samboyer.com
Website: http://www.samboyer.com/

Associated Enterprises Ltd.
183 Pauls Ln.
Bailey, CO 80421

Comer & Associates LLC
5255 Holmes Pl.
Boulder, CO 80303
(303) 786-7986
Fax: (303)895-2347
E-mail: jerry@comerassociates.com
Website: http://www.comerassociates
.com

Ameriwest Business Consultants Inc.
3725 E. Wade Ln.
Colorado Springs, CO 80917
(719)380-7096
Fax: (719)380-7096
E-mail: email@abchelp.com
Website: http://www.abchelp.com

GVNW Consulting Inc.
2270 La Montana Way
Colorado Springs, CO 80936
(719)594-5800
Fax: (719)594-5803
Website: http://www.gvnw.com

M-Squared Inc.
755 San Gabriel Pl.
Colorado Springs, CO 80906
(719)576-2554
Fax: (719)576-2554

Foxhall Consulting Services
2532 Dahlia St.
Denver, CO 80207
(303)355-7995
Fax: (303)377-0716

E-mail: michael@foxhallconsulting.com
Website: http://www.foxhallconsulting
.com

KLA Associates
2352 Humboldt St.
Denver, CO 80205-5332
(303)830-8042

Wilson Hughes Consulting LLC
2100 Humboldt St., Ste. 302
Denver, CO 80205
Website: http://www.wilsonhughes
consultingllc.com

Co-Active Communications Corp.
400 Inverness Pkwy., Ste. 200
Englewood, CO 80112-6415
(303)771-6181
Fax: (303)771-0080

Thornton Financial FNIC
1024 Centre Ave., Bldg. E
Fort Collins, CO 80526-1849
(970)221-2089
Fax: (970)484-5206

Extelligent Inc.
8400 E Crescent Pky., Ste. 600
Greenwood Village, CO 80111
(720)201-5672
E-mail: info@extelligent.com
Website: http://www.extelligent.com

**Western Capital Holdings Inc.10050 E
Applwood Dr.**
Parker, CO 80138
(303)841-1022
Fax: (303)770-1945

Connecticut

Christiansen Consulting
56 Scarborough St.
Hartford, CT 06105
(860)586-8265
Fax: (860)233-3420
Website: http://www.Christiansen
Consulting.com

Follow-up News
185 Pine St., Ste. 818
Manchester, CT 06040
(860)647-7542
Free: 800-708-0696
Fax: (860)646-6544
E-mail: Followupnews@aol.com

Musevue360
555 Millbrook Rd.
Middletown, CT 06457
(860)463-7722
Fax: (860)346-3013

E-mail: jennifer.eifrig@musevue360.com
Website: http://www.musevue360.com

Alltis Corp.
747 Farmington Ave., Ste. 6
New Britain, CT 06053
(860)224-1300
Fax: (860)224-1700
E-mail: info@alltis.com
Website: http://www.alltis.com

Kalba International Inc.
116 McKinley Ave.
New Haven, CT 06515
(203)397-2199
Fax: (781)240-2657
E-mail: kalba@comcast.net
Website: http://www.kalbainternational
.com

Lovins & Associates Consulting
357 Whitney Ave.
New Haven, CT 06511
(203)787-3367
Fax: (203)624-7599
E-mail: Alovinsphd@aol.com
Website: http://www.lovinsgroup.com

JC Ventures Inc.
4 Arnold St.
Old Greenwich, CT 06870-1203
(203)698-1990
Free: 800-698-1997
Fax: (203)698-2638

**Charles L. Hornung
Associates**
52 Ned's Mountain Rd.
Ridgefield, CT 06877
(203)431-0297

Greenwich Associates
6 High Ridge Park
Stamford, CT 06905
(203)629-1200
Fax: (203)629-1229
E-mail: lisa@greenwich.com
Website: http://www.greenwich.com

Management Practice Inc.
216 W Hill Rd.
Stamford, CT 06902
(203)973-0535
Fax: (203)978-9034
E-mail: mpayne@mpiweb.com
Website: http://www.mpiweb.com

RealBusinessPlans.com
156 Westport Rd.
Wilton, CT 06897
(914)837-2886

E-mail: ct@realbusinessplans.com
Website: http://www.RealBusinessPlans
.com

Wellspring Consulting LLC
198 Amity Rd., 2nd Fl.
Woodbridge, CT 06525
(203)387-7192
Fax: (203)387-1345
E-mail: info@wellspringconsulting.net
Website: http://www.wellspring
consulting.net

Delaware

Focus Marketing
61-7 Habor Dr.
Claymont, DE 19703
(302)793-3064

Daedalus Ventures Ltd.
PO Box 1474
Hockessin, DE 19707
(302)239-6758
Fax: (302)239-9991
E-mail: daedalus@mail.del.net

The Formula Group
PO Box 866
Hockessin, DE 19707
(302)456-0952
Fax: (302)456-1354
E-mail: formula@netaxs.com

Selden Enterprises Inc.
2502 Silverside Rd., Ste. 1
Wilmington, DE 19810-3740
(302)529-7113
Fax: (302)529-7442
E-mail: selden2@bellatlantic.net
Website: http://www.seldenenterprises
.com

District of Columbia

The Breen Consulting Group LLC
1101 Pennsylvania Ave, NW, 7th Fl.
Washington, DC 20004
(877)881-4688
E-mail: sales@joebreen.com
Website: http://www.joebreen.com

Catalysr IpF
1514Upshur St. NW
Washington, DC 20011
(202)230-2662
E-mail: contact@catalystipf.com
Website: http://www.catalystipf.com

Smith, Dawson & Andrews Inc.
1150 Connecticut Ave., Ste. 1025
Washington, DC 20036
(202)835-0740

Fax: (202)775-8526
E-mail: webmaster@sda-inc.com
Website: http://www.sda-inc.com

1000 Cranes LLC
1425 K St. NW, Ste. 350
Washington, DC 20005
(202)587-2737
E-mail: info@1000cranes.com
Website: http://www.1000cranes.com

Florida

BackBone, Inc.
20404 Hacienda Court
Boca Raton, FL 33498
(561)470-0965
Fax: 516-908-4038
E-mail: BPlans@backboneinc.com
Website: http://www.backboneinc.com

Dr. Eric H Shaw and Associates
500 South Ocean Blvd., Ste. 2105
Boca Raton, FL 33432
(561)338-5151
E-mail: ericshaw@bellsouth.net
Website: http://www.ericshaw.com

E.N. Rysso & Associates
180 Bermuda Petrel Ct.
Daytona Beach, FL 32119
(386)760-3028
E-mail: erysso@aol.com

Eric Sands Consulting Services
6750 N. Andrews Ave., Ste. 200
Fort Lauderdale, FL 33309
(954)721-4767
Fax: (954)720-2815
E-mail: easands@aol.com
Website: http://www.ericsandsconsultig
.com

F.A. McGee Inc.
800 Claughton Island Dr., Ste. 401
Miami, FL 33131
(305)377-9123

Strategic Business Planning Co.
12000 Biscayne Blvd., Ste. 203
Miami, FL 33181
(954)704-9100
E-mail: info@bizplan.com
Website: http://www.bizplan.com

Professional Planning Associates, Inc.
1440 NE 35th St.
Oakland Park, FL 33334
(954)829-2523
Fax:(954)537-7945
E-mail: Mgoldstein@proplana.com
Website: http://proplana.com
Michael Goldstein, President

Hunter G. Jackson Jr.
3409 Canoga Dr.
Orlando, FL 32861-8272
(407)245-7682
E-mail: hunterjackson@juno.com

F. Newton Parks
210 El Brillo Way
Palm Beach, FL 33480
(561)833-1727
Fax: (561)833-4541

Hughes Consulting Services LLC
522 Alternate 19
Palm Harbor, FL 34683
(727)631-2536
Fax: (727)474-9818
Website: http://consultinghughes.com

Avery Business Development Services
2506 St. Michel Ct.
Ponte Vedra Beach, FL 32082
(904)280-8840
Fax: (904)285-6033

Dufresne Consulting Group Inc.
10014 N Dale Mabry, Ste. 101
Tampa, FL 33618-4426
(813)264-4775
Fax: (813)264-9300
Website: http://www.dcgconsult.com

Tunstall Consulting LLC
13153 N. Dale Mabry Hwy., Ste. 200
Tampa, FL 33618
(813)968-4461
Fax: (813)961-2315
Website: http://www.tunstallconsulting
.com

The Business Planning Institute, LLC.
580 Village Blvd., Ste. 150
West Palm Beach, FL 33409
(561)236-5533
Fax: (561)689-5546
Website: http://www.bpiplans.com

Georgia

Fountainhead Consulting Group, Inc.
3970 Old Milton Pkwy, Ste. 210
Atlanta, GA 30005
(770)642-4220
Website: http://www.fountainhead
consultinggroup.com/

CHScottEnterprises
227 Sandy Springs P., NE, Ste. 720702
Atlanta, GA 30358
(770)356-4808
E-mail: info@chscottenterprises.com
Website: http://www.chscottenter
prises.com

US Business Plan Inc.
1200 Barrett Pky., Ste. 4-400
Kennesaw, GA 30144
(770)794-8000
Website: http://www.usbusinessplan.com

Business Ventures Corp.
1650 Oakbrook Dr., Ste. 405
Norcross, GA 30093
(770)729-8000
Fax: (770)729-8028

Tom C. Davis CPA LLC
1808-A Plum St.
Valdosta, GA 31601
(229)247-9801
Fax:(229) 244-7704
E-mail: mail@tcdcpa.com
Website: http://www.tcdcpa.com/

Illinois

TWD and Associates
431 S Patton
Arlington Heights, IL 60005
(847)398-6410
Fax: (847)255-5095
E-mail: tdoo@aol.com

Management Planning Associates Inc.
2275 Half Day Rd., Ste. 350
Bannockburn, IL 60015-1277
(847)945-2421
Fax: (847)945-2425

Phil Faris Associates
86 Old Mill Ct.
Barrington, IL 60010
(847)382-4888
Fax: (847)382-4890
E-mail: pfaris@meginsnet.net

Seven Continents Technology
787 Stonebridge
Buffalo Grove, IL 60089
(708)577-9653
Fax: (708)870-1220

Grubb & Blue Inc.
2404 Windsor Pl.
Champaign, IL 61820
(217)366-0052
Fax: (217)356-0117

ACE Accounting Service Inc.
3128 N Bernard St.
Chicago, IL 60618
(773)463-7854
Fax: (773)463-7854

AON Consulting Worldwide
200 E Randolph St., 10th Fl.
Chicago, IL 60601

(312)381-4800
Free: 800-438-6487
Fax: (312)381-0240
Website: http://www.aon.com

FMS Consultants
5801 N Sheridan Rd., Ste. 3D
Chicago, IL 60660
(773)561-7362
Fax: (773)561-6274

Grant Thornton
800 1 Prudential Plz.
130 E Randolph St.
Chicago, IL 60601
(312)856-0001
Fax: (312)861-1340
E-mail: gtinfo@gt.com
Website: http://www.grantthornton.com

Kingsbury International Ltd.
5341 N Glenwood Ave.
Chicago, IL 60640
(773)271-3030
Fax: (773)728-7080
E-mail: jetlag@mcs.com
Website: http://www.kingbiz.com

MacDougall & Blake Inc.
1414 N Wells St., Ste. 311
Chicago, IL 60610-1306
(312)587-3330
Fax: (312)587-3699
E-mail: jblake@compuserve.com

James C. Osburn Ltd.
6445 N. Western Ave., Ste. 304
Chicago, IL 60645
(773)262-4428
Fax: (773)262-6755
E-mail: osburnltd@aol.com

Tarifero & Tazewell Inc.
211 S Clark
Chicago, IL 60690
(312)665-9714
Fax: (312)665-9716

Human Energy Design Systems
620 Roosevelt Dr.
Edwardsville, IL 62025
(618)692-0258
Fax: (618)692-0819

China Business Consultants Group
931 Dakota Cir.
Naperville, IL 60563
(630)778-7992
Fax: (630)778-7915
E-mail: cbcq@aol.com

Center for Workforce Effectiveness
500 Skokie Blvd., Ste. 222
Northbrook, IL 60062
(847)559-8777

Fax: (847)559-8778
E-mail: office@cwelink.com
Website: http://www.cwelink.com

Smith Associates
1320 White Mountain Dr.
Northbrook, IL 60062
(847)480-7200
Fax: (847)480-9828

Francorp Inc.
20200 Governors Dr.
Olympia Fields, IL 60461
(708)481-2900
Free: 800-372-6244
Fax: (708)481-5885
E-mail: francorp@aol.com
Website: http://www.francorpinc.com

Camber Business Strategy Consultants
1010 S Plum Tree Ct
Palatine, IL 60078-0986
(847)202-0101
Fax: (847)705-7510
E-mail: camber@ameritech.net

Partec Enterprise Group
5202 Keith Dr.
Richton Park, IL 60471
(708)503-4047
Fax: (708)503-9468

Rockford Consulting Group Ltd.
Century Plz., Ste. 206
7210 E State St.
Rockford, IL 61108
(815)229-2900
Free: 800-667-7495
Fax: (815)229-2612
E-mail: rligus@RockfordConsulting.com
Website: http://www.Rockford
Consulting.com

RSM McGladrey Inc.
1699 E Woodfield Rd., Ste. 300
Schaumburg, IL 60173-4969
(847)413-6900
Fax: (847)517-7067
Website: http://www.rsmmcgladrey.com

A.D. Star Consulting
320 Euclid
Winnetka, IL 60093
(847)446-7827
Fax: (847)446-7827
E-mail: startwo@worldnet.att.net

Indiana

Bingham Economic Development Advisors
8900 Keystone Xing
Indianapolis, IN 46240
(317)968-5576

Ketchum Consulting Group
7575 Copperfield Way
Indianapolis, IN 46256
(317)845-5411
Fax: (317)842-9941

Cox and Company
3930 Mezzanine Dr. Ste A
Lafayette, IN, 47905
(765)449-4495
Fax: (765)449-1218
E-mail: stan@coxpa.com

Iowa

McCord Consulting Group Inc.
3425 Sycamore Ct. NE
Cedar Rapids, IA 52402
(319)378-0077
Fax: (319)378-1577
E-mail: sam@mccordgroup.com

Management Solutions L.L.C.
3815 Lincoln Pl. Dr.
Des Moines, IA 50312
(515)277-6408
Fax: (515)277-3506

Kansas

Aspire Business Development
10955 Lowell Ave., Ste. 400
Overland Park, KS 66210
(913)660-9400
Free: (888)548-1504
Website: http://www.aspirekc.com

Maine

Pan Atlantic SMS Group Inc.
6 City Ctr., Ste. 200
Portland, ME 04101
(207)871-8622
Fax: (207)772-4842
E-mail: pmurphy@panatlanticsmsgroup.
com
Website: http://www.panatlanticsms
group.com

Maryland

Clemons & Associates Inc.
5024-R Campbell Blvd.
Baltimore, MD 21236
(410)931-8100
Fax: (410)931-8111
E-mail: info@clemonsmgmt.com
Website: http://www.clemonsmgmt.com

Employee Benefits Group Inc.
4405 E West Hwy., Ste. 202
Bethesda, MD 20814
(301) 718-4637

Fax: (301) 907-0176
E-mail: info@ebg.com
Website: http://www.ebg.com

Burdeshaw Associates Ltd.
4701 Sangamore Rd.
Bethesda, MD 20816-2508
(301)229-5800
Fax: (301)229-5045
E-mail: jstacy@burdeshaw.com
Website: http://www.burdeshaw.com

Michael E. Cohen
5225 Pooks Hill Rd., Ste. 1119 S
Bethesda, MD 20814
(301)530-5738
Fax: (301)530-2988
E-mail: mecohen@crosslink.net

World Development Group Inc.
5800 Madaket Rd., Ste. 100
Bethesda, MD 20816
(301) 320-0971
Fax: (301) 320-0978
E-mail: wdg@worlddg.com
Website: http://www.worlddg.com

Creative Edge Consulting
6047 Wild Ginger Ct.
Columbia, MD 21044
(443) 545-5863
Website: http://www.creativeedge
consulting.org

Paul Yelder Consulting
9581 Standon Pl.
Columbia, MD 21045
(410) 740-8417
E-mail: consulting@yelder.com
Website: http://www.yelder.com

Hammer Marketing Resources
19118 Silver Maple Ct.
Hagerstown, MD 21742
(301) 733-8891
Fax: (305) 675-3277

Strategies
8 Park Center Ct., Ste. 200
Owings Mills, MD 21117
(410)363-6669
Fax: (410)363-1231
E-mail: info@strategiescorp.net
Website: http://www.strategiescorp.net

Managance Consulting and Coaching
1708 Chester Mill Rd.
Silver Spring, MD 20906
(301) 260-9503
E-mail: info@managance.com
Website: http://www.managance.com

Andrew Sussman & Associates
13731 Kretsinger
Smithsburg, MD 21783
(301)824-2943
Fax: (301)824-2943

Massachusetts

Geibel Marketing and Public Relations
PO Box 611
Belmont, MA 02478-0005
(617)484-8285
Fax: (617)489-3567
E-mail: jgeibel@geibelpr.com
Website: http://www.geibelpr.com

Bain & Co.
131 Dartmouth St.
Boston, MA 02116
(617)572-2000
Fax: (617)572-2427
E-mail: corporate.inquiries@bain.com
Website: http://www.bain.com

Fairmont Consulting Group
470 Atlantic Ave., 4th Fl.
Boston, MA 02210
(617)217-2401
Fax: (617)939-0262
E-mail: info@fairmontcg.com
Website: http://www.fairmontcg.com

Information & Research Associates
PO Box 3121
Framingham, MA 01701
(508)788-0784

Walden Consultants Ltd.
252 Pond St.
Hopkinton, MA 01748
(508)435-4882
Fax: (508)435-3971
Website: http://www.waldenconsultants
.com

Consulting Resources Corp.
6 Northbrook Park
Lexington, MA 02420
(781)863-1222
Fax: (781)863-1441
E-mail: res@consultingresources.net
Website: http://www.consultingre
sources.net

Mehr & Co.
31 Woodcliffe Rd.
Lexington, MA 02421
(781)372-1055

Real Resources
27 Indian Hill Rd.
Medfield, MA 02052
(508)359-6780

VMB Associates Inc.
115 Ashland St.
Melrose, MA 02176
(781)665-0623
Fax: (425)732-7142
E-mail: vmbinc@aol.com

The Company Doctor
14 Pudding Stone Ln.
Mendon, MA 01756
(508)478-1747
Fax: (508)478-0520

Data and Strategies Group Inc.
190 N Main St.
Natick, MA 01760
(508)653-9990
Fax: (508)653-7799
E-mail: dsginc@dsggroup.com
Website: http://www.dsggroup.com

The Enterprise Group
73 Parker Rd.
Needham, MA 02494
(617)444-6631
Fax: (617)433-9991
E-mail: lsacco@world.std.com
Website: http://www.enterprise-group
.com

PSMJ Resources Inc.
10 Midland Ave.
Newton, MA 02458
(617)965-0055
Free: 800-537-7765
Fax: (617)965-5152
E-mail: psmj@tiac.net
Website: http://www.psmj.com

Non Profit Capital Management
41 Main St.
Sterling, MA 01564
(781)933-6726
Fax: (781)933-6734

Michigan

BBC Entrepreneurial Training & Consulting LLC
803 N Main St.
Ann Arbor, MI 48104
(734)930-9741
Fax: (734)930-6629
E-mail: info@bioconsultants.com
Website: http://www.bioconsultants.com

Center for Simplified Strategic Planning Inc.
2219 Packard Rd., Ste. 13
Ann Arbor, MI 48104
(734)995-3465
E-mail: tidd@cssp.com
Website: http://www.cssp.com

Walter Frederick Consulting
1719 South Blvd.
Ann Arbor, MI 48104
(313)662-4336
Fax: (313)769-7505

Aimattech Consulting LLC
568 Woodway Ct., Ste. 1
Bloomfield Hills, MI 48302
(248) 540-3758
Fax: (248) 540-3011
E-mail: dpwconsult@aol.com
Website: http://www.aimattech.com

QualSAT International Inc.
30777 NW Highway., Ste. 101
Farmington Hills, MI 48334
866-899-0020
Fax: (248)932-3801
E-mail: info@qualsat.com
Website: http://www.qualsat.com

Fox Enterprises
6220 W Freeland Rd.
Freeland, MI 48623
(989)695-9170
Fax: (989)695-9174

T. L. Cramer Associates LLC
1788 Broadstone Rd.
Grosse Pointe Woods, MI 48236
(313)332-0182
E-mail: info@tlcramerassociates.com
Website: http://www.tlcramerassociates
.com

G.G.W. and Associates
1213 Hampton
Jackson, MI 49203
(517)782-2255
Fax: (517)782-2255

BHM Associates Inc.
2817 Canterbury Dr.
Midland, MI 48642
(989) 631-7109
E-mail: smiller@bhmassociates.net
Website: http://www.bhmassociates.net

MarketingHelp Inc.
6647 Riverwoods Ct. NE
Rockford, MI 49341
(616) 866-1198
Website: http://www.mktghelp.com

Rehmann, Robson PC
5800 Gratiot
Saginaw, MI 48605
(989)799-9580
Fax: (989)799-0227
E-mail: info@rehmann.com
Website: http://www.rehmann.com

Private Ventures Inc.
16000 W 9 Mile Rd., Ste. 504
Southfield, MI 48075
(248)569-1977
Free: 800-448-7614
Fax: (248)569-1838
E-mail: pventuresi@aol.com

JGK Associates
14464 Kerner Dr.
Sterling Heights, MI 48313
(810)247-9055
Fax: (248)822-4977
E-mail: kozlowski@home.com

Cool & Associates Inc.
921 Village Green Ln., Ste. 1068
Waterford, MI 48328
(248)683-1130
E-mail: jcool@cool-associates.com
Website: http://www.cool-associates.com

Griffioen Consulting Group Inc.
6689 Orchard Lake Rd., Ste. 295
West Bloomfield, MI 48322
(888)262-5850
Fax: (248)855-4084
Website: http://www.griffioenconsulting
.com

Minnesota

Health Fitness Corp.
31700 W 82nd St., Ste. 200
Minneapolis, MN 55431
(952)831-6830
E-mail: info@hfit.com
Website: http://www.hfit.com

Consatech Inc.
PO Box 1047
Burnsville, MN 55337
(612)953-1088
Fax: (612)435-2966

Kaes Analytics Inc.
14960 Ironwood Ct.
Eden Prairie, MN 55346
(952)942-2912

DRI Consulting
2 Otter Ln.
Saint Paul, MN 55127
(651)415-1400
Fax: (651)415-9968
E-mail: dric@dric.com
Website: http://www.dric.com

Markin Consulting
12072 87th Pl. N
Maple Grove, MN 55369
(763)493-3568
Fax: (763)322-5013

E-mail: markin@markinconsulting.com
Website: http://www.markinconsulting
.com

**Minnesota Cooperation Office for
Small Business & Job Creation Inc.**
5001 W 80th St., Ste. 825
Minneapolis, MN 55437
(612)830-1230
Fax: (612)830-1232
E-mail: mncoop@msn.com
Website: http://www.mnco.org

Power Systems Research
1365 Corporate Center Curve, 2nd Fl.
St. Paul, MN 55121
(612)905-8400
Free: (888)625-8612
Fax: (612)454-0760
E-mail: Barb@Powersys.com
Website: http://www.powersys.com

Missouri

**Business Planning and Development
Corp.**
4030 Charlotte St.
Kansas City, MO 64110
(816)753-0495
E-mail: humph@bpdev.demon.co.uk
Website: http://www.bpdev.demon.co.uk

CFO Service
10336 Donoho
St. Louis, MO 63131
(314)750-2940
E-mail: jskae@cfoservice.com
Website: http://www.cfoservice.com

Nebraska

**International Management Consulting
Group Inc.**
1309 Harlan Dr., Ste. 205
Bellevue, NE 68005
(402)291-4545
Free: 800-665-IMCG
Fax: (402)291-4343
E-mail: imcg@neonramp.com
Website: http://www.mgtconsulting.com

**Heartland Management Consulting
Group**
1904 Barrington Pky.
Papillion, NE 68046
(402)952-5339
Fax: (402)339-1319

Nevada

The DuBois Group
865 Tahoe Blvd., Ste. 108
Incline Village, NV 89451

(775)832-0550
Free: 800-375-2935
Fax: (775)832-0556
E-mail: DuBoisGrp@aol.com

New Hampshire

Wolff Consultants
10 Buck Rd.
Hanover, NH 03755
(603)643-6015

BPT Consulting Associates Ltd.
12 Parmenter Rd., Ste. B-6
Londonderry, NH 03053
(603)437-8484
Free: (888)278-0030
Fax: (603)434-5388
E-mail: bptcons@tiac.net
Website: http://www.bptconsulting.com

New Jersey

Delta Planning Inc.
138 Hillcrest Dr.
Denville, NJ 07834
(913)625-1742
Free: 800-672-0762
Fax: (973)625-3531
E-mail: DeltaP@worldnet.att.net
Website: http://deltaplanning.com

Kumar Associates Inc.
1004 Cumbermeade Rd.
Fort Lee, NJ 07024
(201)224-9480
Fax: (201)585-2343
E-mail: mail@kumarassociates.com
Website: http://kumarassociates.com

John Hall & Company Inc.
14 Houston Rd.
Little Falls, NJ 07424
(973)680-4449
Fax: (973)680-4581
E-mail: jhcompany@aol.com

Market Focus
12 Maryland Rd.
Maplewood, NJ 07040
(973)378-2470
Fax: (973)378-2470
E-mail: mcss66@marketfocus.com

Distinctive Marketing Inc.
516 Bloomfield Ave., Ste. 7
Montclair, NJ 07042
(973)746-9114
Fax: (973)783-5555
Website: http://www.distinctive
mktg.com

Vanguard Communications Corp.
45 S Park Pl., Ste. 210
Morristown, NJ 07960
(973)605-8000
Fax: (973)605-8329
Website: http://www.vanguard.net/

Bedminster Group Inc.
16 Arrowhead Dr.
Neshanic Station, NJ 08853
(908)347-0006
Fax: (908)369-4767
E-mail: info@bedminstergroup.com
Website: http://www.bedminstergroup
.com

ConMar International Ltd.
1405 Rte. 18, Ste. 200
Old Bridge, NJ 08857
(732)607-6415
Fax: (732)607-6480
Website: http://www.conmar-intl.com

PA Consulting Group
600 Alexander Pk., Ste. 209A
Princeton, NJ 08540
(609)806-0800
Fax: (609)936-8811
E-mail: info@paconsulting.com
Website: http://www.pa-consulting.com

Aurora Marketing Management Inc.
66 Witherspoon St., Ste. 600
Princeton, NJ 08542
(908)904-1125
Fax: (908)359-1108
E-mail: aurora2@voicenet.com
Website: http://www.auroramarketing
.net

Schkeeper Inc.
130-6 Bodman Pl.
Red Bank, NJ 07701
(732)219-1965
Fax: (732)530-3703
Website: http://www.schkeeper.com

Henry Branch Associates
2502 Harmon Cove Twr.
Secaucus, NJ 07094
(201)866-2008
Fax: (201)601-0101
E-mail: hbranch161@home.com

Robert Gibbons & Company Inc.
46 Knoll Rd.
Tenafly, NJ 07670-1050
(201)871-3933
Fax: (201)871-2173

PMC Management Consultants Inc.
6 Thistle Ln.
Three Bridges, NJ 08887-0332

(908)788-1014
Free: 800-PMC-0250
Fax: (908)806-7287
E-mail: inguiry@pmc-management.com
Website: http://www.pmc-management
.com

R.W. Bankart & Associates
20 Valley Ave., Ste. D-2
Westwood, NJ 07675-3607
(201)664-7672

New Mexico

Vondle & Associates Inc.
4926 Calle de Tierra, NE
Albuquerque, NM 87111
(505)292-8961
Fax: (505)296-2790
E-mail: vondle@aol.com

InfoNewMexico
2207 Black Hills Rd., NE
Rio Rancho, NM 87124
(505)891-2462
Fax: (505)896-8971

New York

Powers Research and Training Institute
PO Box 78
Bayville, NY 11709
(516)628-2250
Fax: (516)628-2252
E-mail: powercocch@compuserve.com
Website: http://www.nancypowers.com

Consortium House
296 Wittenberg Rd.
Bearsville, NY 12409
(845)679-8867
Fax: (845)679-9248
E-mail: eugenegs@aol.com
Website: http://www.chpub.com

Progressive Finance Corp.
3549 Tiemann Ave.
Bronx, NY 10469
(718)405-9029
Free: 800-225-8381
Fax: (718)405-1170

Wave Hill Associates Inc.
2621 Palisade Ave., Ste. 15-C
Bronx, NY 10463
(718)549-7368
Fax: (718)601-9670
E-mail: pepper@compuserve.com

Management Insight
96 Arlington Rd.
Buffalo, NY 14221
(716)631-3319

Fax: (716)631-0203
E-mail: michalski@foodservice
insight.com
Website: http://www.foodserviceinsight
.com

Samani International Enterprises,
Marions Panyaught Consultancy
2028 Parsons
Flushing, NY 11357-3436
(917)287-8087
Fax: 800-873-8939
E-mail: vjp2@biostrategist.com
Website: http://www.biostrategist.com

Marketing Resources Group
71-58 Austin St.
Forest Hills, NY 11375
(718)261-8882

Mangabay Business Plans &
Development

Subsidiary of Innis Asset Allocation
125-10 Queens Blvd., Ste. 2202
Kew Gardens, NY 11415
(905)527-1947
Fax: 509-472-1935
E-mail: mangabay@mangabay.com
Website: http://www.mangabay.com
Lee Toh, Managing Partner

ComputerEase Co.
1301 Monmouth Ave.
Lakewood, NY 08701
(212)406-9464
Fax: (914)277-5317
E-mail: crawfordc@juno.com

Boice Dunham Group
30 W 13th St.
New York, NY 10011
(212)924-2200
Fax: (212)924-1108

Elizabeth Capen
27 E 95th St.
New York, NY 10128
(212)427-7654
Fax: (212)876-3190

Haver Analytics
60 E 42nd St., Ste. 2424
New York, NY 10017
(212)986-9300
Fax: (212)986-5857
E-mail: data@haver.com
Website: http://www.haver.com

The Jordan, Edmiston Group Inc.
150 E 52nd Ave., 18th Fl.
New York, NY 10022
(212)754-0710
Fax: (212)754-0337

KPMG International
345 Park Ave.
New York, NY 10154-0102
(212)758-9700
Fax: (212)758-9819
Website: http://www.kpmg.com

Mahoney Cohen Consulting Corp.
111 W 40th St., 12th Fl.
New York, NY 10018
(212)490-8000
Fax: (212)790-5913

Management Practice Inc.
342 Madison Ave.
New York, NY 10173-1230
(212)867-7948
Fax: (212)972-5188
Website: http://www.mpiweb.com

Moseley Associates Inc.
342 Madison Ave., Ste. 1414
New York, NY 10016
(212)213-6673
Fax: (212)687-1520

Practice Development Counsel
60 Sutton Pl. S
New York, NY 10022
(212)593-1549
Fax: (212)980-7940
E-mail: pwhaserot@pdcounsel.com
Website: http://www.pdcounsel.com

Unique Value International Inc.
575 Madison Ave., 10th Fl.
New York, NY 10022-1304
(212)605-0590
Fax: (212)605-0589

The Van Tulleken Co.
126 E 56th St.
New York, NY 10022
(212)355-1390
Fax: (212)755-3061
E-mail: newyork@vantulleken.com

Vencon Management Inc.
301 W 53rd St.
New York, NY 10019
(212)581-8787
Fax: (212)397-4126
Website: http://www.venconinc.com

Werner International Inc.
55 E 52nd, 29th Fl.
New York, NY 10055
(212)909-1260
Fax: (212)909-1273
E-mail: richard.downing@rgh.com
Website: http://www.wernertex.com

Zimmerman Business Consulting Inc.
44 E 92nd St., Ste. 5-B
New York, NY 10128
(212)860-3107
Fax: (212)860-7730
E-mail: ljzzbci@aol.com
Website: http://www.zbcinc.com

Overton Financial
7 Allen Rd.
Peekskill, NY 10566
(914)737-4649
Fax: (914)737-4696

Stromberg Consulting
2500 Westchester Ave.
Purchase, NY 10577
(914)251-1515
Fax: (914)251-1562
E-mail: strategy@stromberg_
consulting.com
Website: http://www.stromberg_
consulting.com

Innovation Management
Consulting Inc.
209 Dewitt Rd.
Syracuse, NY 13214-2006
(315)425-5144
Fax: (315)445-8989
E-mail: missonneb@axess.net

M. Clifford Agress
891 Fulton St.
Valley Stream, NY 11580
(516)825-8955
Fax: (516)825-8955

Destiny Kinal Marketing Consultancy
105 Chemung St.
Waverly, NY 14892
(607)565-8317
Fax: (607)565-4083

Valutis Consulting Inc.
5350 Main St., Ste. 7
Williamsville, NY 14221-5338
(716)634-2553
Fax: (716)634-2554
E-mail: valutis@localnet.com
Website: http://www.valutisconsulting
.com

North Carolina

Best Practices L.L.C.
6320 Quadrangle Dr., Ste. 200
Chapel Hill, NC 27514
(919)403-0251
Fax: (919)403-0144
E-mail: best@best:in/class
Website: http://www.best-in-class.com

Norelli & Co.
1340 Harding Pl.
Charlotte, NC 28204
(704)376-5484
Fax: (704)376-5485
E-mail: consult@norelli.com
Website: http://www.norelli.com

North Dakota

Center for Innovation
Ina Mae Rude Entrepreneur Ctr.
4200 James Ray Dr.
Grand Forks, ND 58203
(701)777-3132
Fax: (701)777-2339
E-mail: info@innovators.net
Website: http://www.innovators.net

Ohio

Transportation Technology Services
208 Harmon Rd.
Aurora, OH 44202
(330)562-3596

Empro Systems Inc.
4777 Red Bank Expy., Ste. 1
Cincinnati, OH 45227-1542
(513)271-2042
Fax: (513)271-2042

Alliance Management International Ltd.
1440 Windrow Ln.
Cleveland, OH 44147-3200
(440)838-1922
Fax: (440)838-0979
E-mail: bgruss@amiltd.com
Website: http://www.amiltd.com

Bozell Kamstra Public Relations
1301 E 9th St., Ste. 3400
Cleveland, OH 44114
(216)623-1511
Fax: (216)623-1501
E-mail: jfeniger@cleveland.bozell
kamstra.com
Website: http://www.bozellkamstra.com

Cory Dillon Associates
111 Schreyer Pl. E
Columbus, OH 43214
(614)262-8211
Fax: (614)262-3806

Holcomb Gallagher Adams
300 Marconi, Ste. 303
Columbus, OH 43215
(614)221-3343
Fax: (614)221-3367
E-mail: riadams@acme.freenet.oh.us

Young & Associates
PO Box 711
Kent, OH 44240
(330)678-0524
Free: 800-525-9775
Fax: (330)678-6219
E-mail: online@younginc.com
Website: http://www.younginc.com

Robert A. Westman & Associates
8981 Inversary Dr. SE
Warren, OH 44484-2551
(330)856-4149
Fax: (330)856-2564

Oklahoma

Innovative Partners L.L.C.
4900 Richmond Sq., Ste. 100
Oklahoma City, OK 73118
(405)840-0033
Fax: (405)843-8359
E-mail: ipartners@juno.com

Oregon

INTERCON - The International Converting Institute
5200 Badger Rd.
Crooked River Ranch, OR 97760
(541)548-1447
Fax: (541)548-1618
E-mail: johnbowler@crookedriverranch
.com

Talbott ARM
HC 60, Box 5620
Lakeview, OR 97630
(541)635-8587
Fax: (503)947-3482

Management Technology Associates Ltd.
2768 SW Sherwood Dr, Ste. 105
Portland, OR 97201-2251
(503)224-5220
Fax: (503)224-5334
E-mail: lcuster@mta-ltd.com
Website: http://www.mgmt-tech.com

Pennsylvania

Healthscope Inc.
400 Lancaster Ave.
Devon, PA 19333
(610)687-6199
Fax: (610)687-6376
E-mail: health@voicenet.com
Website: http://www.healthscope.net/

Elayne Howard & Associates Inc.
3501 Masons Mill Rd., Ste. 501
Huntingdon Valley, PA 19006-3509
(215)657-9550

GRA Inc.
115 West Ave., Ste. 201
Jenkintown, PA 19046
(215)884-7500
Fax: (215)884-1385
E-mail: gramail@gra-inc.com
Website: http://www.gra-inc.com

Mifflin County Industrial Development Corp.
Mifflin County Industrial Plz.
6395 SR 103 N
Bldg. 50
Lewistown, PA 17044
(717)242-0393
Fax: (717)242-1842
E-mail: mcide@acsworld.net

Autech Products
1289 Revere Rd.
Morrisville, PA 19067
(215)493-3759
Fax: (215)493-9791
E-mail: autech4@yahoo.com

Advantage Associates
434 Avon Dr.
Pittsburgh, PA 15228
(412)343-1558
Fax: (412)362-1684
E-mail: ecocba1@aol.com

Regis J. Sheehan & Associates
Pittsburgh, PA 15220
(412)279-1207

James W. Davidson Company Inc.
23 Forest View Rd.
Wallingford, PA 19086
(610)566-1462

Puerto Rico

Diego Chevere & Co.
Metro Parque 7, Ste. 204
Metro Office
Caparra Heights, PR 00920
(787)774-9595
Fax: (787)774-9566
E-mail: dcco@coqui.net

Manuel L. Porrata and Associates
898 Munoz Rivera Ave., Ste. 201
San Juan, PR 00927
(787)765-2140
Fax: (787)754-3285
E-mail: m_porrata@manuelporrata.com
Website: http://manualporrata.com

South Carolina

Aquafood Business Associates
PO Box 13267
Charleston, SC 29422

(843)795-9506
Fax: (843)795-9477
E-mail: rraba@aol.com

Profit Associates Inc.
PO Box 38026
Charleston, SC 29414
(803)763-5718
Fax: (803)763-5719
E-mail: bobrog@awod.com
Website: http://www.awod.com/gallery/
business/proasc

Strategic Innovations International
12 Executive Ct.
Lake Wylie, SC 29710
(803)831-1225
Fax: (803)831-1177
E-mail: stratinnov@aol.com
Website: http://www.strategic
innovations.com

Minus Stage
Box 4436
Rock Hill, SC 29731
(803)328-0705
Fax: (803)329-9948

Tennessee

Daniel Petchers & Associates
8820 Fernwood CV
Germantown, TN 38138
(901)755-9896

Business Choices
1114 Forest Harbor, Ste. 300
Hendersonville, TN 37075-9646
(615)822-8692
Free: 800-737-8382
Fax: (615)822-8692
E-mail: bz-ch@juno.com

RCFA Healthcare Management Services L.L.C.
9648 Kingston Pke., Ste. 8
Knoxville, TN 37922
(865)531-0176
Free: 800-635-4040
Fax: (865)531-0722
E-mail: info@rcfa.com
Website: http://www.rcfa.com

Growth Consultants of America
3917 Trimble Rd.
Nashville, TN 37215
(615)383-0550
Fax: (615)269-8940
E-mail: 70244.451@compuserve.com

Texas

Integrated Cost Management Systems Inc.
6001 W I-20, Ste. 209
Arlington, TX 76094-0206
(817)475-2945
E-mail: abm@icms.net
Website: http://www.icms.net

Business Resource Software Inc.
1779 Wells Branch Pky.
Austin, TX 78728
Free: 800-423-1228
Fax: (512)251-4401
E-mail: info@brs-inc.com
Website: http://www.brs-inc.com

Erisa Adminstrative Services Inc.
12325 Hymeadow Dr., Bldg. 4
Austin, TX 78750-1847
(512)250-9020
Fax: (512)250-9487
Website: http://www.cserisa.com

R. Miller Hicks & Co.
1011 W 11th St.
Austin, TX 78703
(512)477-7000
Fax: (512)477-9697
E-mail: millerhicks@rmhicks.com
Website: http://www.rmhicks.com

Pragmatic Tactics Inc.
3303 Westchester Ave.
College Station, TX 77845
(409)696-5294
Free: 800-570-5294
Fax: (409)696-4994
E-mail: ptactics@aol.com
Website: http://www.ptatics.com

Zaetric Business Solutions LLC
27350 Blueberry Hill, Ste. 14
Conroe, TX 77385
(713)621-4885
Fax: (713)824-1654
E-mail: inquiries@zaetric.com
Website: http://www.zaetric.com

Perot Systems
12404 Park Central Dr.
Dallas, TX 75251
(972)340-5000
Free: 800-688-4333
Fax: (972)455-4100
E-mail: corp.comm@ps.net
Website: http://www.perotsystems.com

ReGENERATION Partners
3811 Turtle Creek Blvd., Ste. 300
Dallas, TX 75219

(214)559-3999
Free: 800-406-1112
E-mail: info@regeneration-partner.com
Website: http://www.regeneration-
partners.com

High Technology Associates
5739 Longmont Ln.
Houston, TX 77057
(713)963-9300
Fax: (713)963-8341
E-mail: baker@hta-usa.com
Website: http://www.high-technology-
associates.com

SynerImages LLC
1 Riverway, Ste. 1700
Houston, TX 77056
(713)840-6442
Fax: (713)963-8341
Website: http://www.synerimages.com

PROTEC
4607 Linden Pl.
Pearland, TX 77584
(281)997-9872
Fax: (281)997-9895
E-mail: p.oman@ix.netcom.com

Bastian Public Relations
614 San Dizier
San Antonio, TX 78232
(210)404-1839
E-mail: lisa@bastianpr.com
Website: http://www.bastianpr.com
Lisa Bastian CBC

Business Strategy Development Consultants
PO Box 690365
San Antonio, TX 78269
(210)696-8000
Free: 800-927-BSDC
Fax: (210)696-8000

Utah

Vector Resources
7651 S Main St., Ste. 106
Midvale, UT 84047-7158
(801) 352-8500
Fax: (801) 352-8506
E-mail: info@vectorresources.com
Website: http://www.vectorresources
.com

StreetMaker Inc.
524 West 440 South
Orem, UT 84058-6115
(801)607-2246
Fax: (800)561-4928
E-mail: contact@streetmaker.com
Website: http://www.streetmaker.com

Biomedical Management Resources
PO Box 521125
Salt Lake City, UT 84152-1125
(801)272-4668
Fax: (801)277-3290
E-mail: SeniorManagement@Biomedical
Management.com
Website: http://www.biomedical
management.com

Marriott Consulting Inc.
6945 S Knudsen Ridge Cir.
Salt Lake City, UT 84121
(801)944-5000
Fax: (801)947-9022
E-mail: info@marriottconsulting.com
Website: http://www.marriott
consulting.com

Virginia

Crown Consulting Inc.
1400 Key Blvd., Ste. 1100
Arlington, VA 22209
(703)650-0663
Fax: (703)243-1280
E-mail: info@crownci.com
Website: http://www.crownci.com

Dare Mighty Things
901 N Glebe Rd., Ste. 1005
Arlington, VA 22203
(703)752-4331
Fax: (703)752-4332
E-mail: info@daremightythings.com
Website: http://www.daremightythings
.com

Elliott B. Jaffa
2530-B S Walter Reed Dr.
Arlington, VA 22206
(703)931-0040

Koach Enterprises - USA
5529 N 18th St.
Arlington, VA 22205
(703)241-8361
Fax: (703)241-8623

AMX International Inc.
9016 Triple Ridge Rd.
Fairfax Station, VA 22039-3003
(703)864-7046
Fax: (703)690-9994
E-mail: info@amxi.com
Website: http://www.amxi.com

Joel Greenstein & Associates
6212 Nethercombe Ct.
McLean, VA 22101
(703) 893-1888

John C. Randall and Associates Inc.
10197 Georgetown Rd.
Mechanicsville, VA 23116
(804)746-4450

Charles Scott Pugh (Investor)
4101 Pittaway Dr.
Richmond, VA 23235-1022
(804)560-0979
Fax: (804)560-4670

Robert Martens & Co.
2226 Floyd Ave.
Richmond, VA 23220
(804) 342-8850
Fax: (804)342-8860
E-mail: rm@robertmartens.com
Website: http://www.robertmartens.com

William W. Garry Inc.
PO Box 61662
Virginia Beach, VA 23466
(757) 467-7874
E-mail: drbillgarry@freeyellow.com

Regis J. Sheehan & Associates
500 Belmont Bay Dr.
Woodbridge, VA 22191-5445
(703)491-7377

Washington

Burlington Consultants
10900 NE 8th St., Ste. 900
Bellevue, WA 98004
(425)688-3060
Fax: (425)454-4383
E-mail: partners@burlington
consultants.com
Website: http://www.burlington
consultants.com

Perry L. Smith Consulting
800 Bellevue Way NE, Ste. 400
Bellevue, WA 98004-4208
(425)462-2072
Fax: (425)462-5638

St. Charles Consulting Group
1420 NW Gilman Blvd.
Issaquah, WA 98027
(425)557-8708
Fax: (425)557-8731
E-mail: info@stcharlesconsulting.com
Website: http://www.stcharlesconsulting
.com

**Independent Automotive Training
Services**
PO Box 334
Kirkland, WA 98083
(425)822-5715
E-mail: ltunney@autosvccon.com
Website: http://www.autosvccon.com

Kahle Associate Inc.
6203 204th Dr. NE
Redmond, WA 98053
(425)836-8763
Fax: (425)868-3770
E-mail: randykahle@kahleassociates.com
Website: http://www.kahleassociates.com

Dan Collin
3419 Wallingord Ave N, No. 2
Seattle, WA 98103
(206)634-9469
E-mail: dc@dancollin.com
Website: http://members.home.net/
dcollin/

ECG Management Consultants Inc.
1111 3rd Ave., Ste. 2700
Seattle, WA 98101-3201
(206)689-2200
Fax: (206)689-2209
E-mail: ecg@ecgmc.com
Website: http://www.ecgmc.com

**Northwest Trade Adjustment
Assistance Center**
900 4th Ave., Ste. 2430
Seattle, WA 98164-1001
(206)622-2730
Free: 800-667-8087
Fax: (206)622-1105
E-mail: matchingfunds@nwtaac.org
Website: http://www.taacenters.org

Business Planning Consultants
S 3510 Ridgeview Dr.
Spokane, WA 99206
(509)928-0332
Fax: (509)921-0842
E-mail: bpci@nextdim.com

West Virginia

**Stanley & Associates Inc./
BusinessandMarketingPlans.com**
1687 Robert C. Byrd Dr.
Beckley, WV 25801
(304)252-0324
Free: 888-752-6720
Fax: (304)252-0470
E-mail: cclay@charterinternet.com
Website: http://www.Businessand
MarketingPlans.com
Christopher Clay

Wisconsin

White & Associates Inc.
5349 Somerset Ln. S
Greenfield, WI 53221
(414)281-7373
Fax: (414)281-7006
E-mail: wnaconsult@aol.com

Small business administration regional offices

This section contains a listing of Small Business Administration offices arranged numerically by region. Service areas are provided. Contact the appropriate office for a referral to the nearest field office, or visit the Small Business Administration online at www.sba.gov.

Region 1

U.S. Small Business Administration
Region I Office
10 Causeway St., Ste. 812
Boston, MA 02222-1093
Phone: (617)565-8415
Fax: (617)565-8420
Serves Connecticut, Maine, Massachusetts, New Hampshire, Rhode Island, and Vermont.

Region 2

U.S. Small Business Administration
Region II Office
26 Federal Plaza, Ste. 3108
New York, NY 10278
Phone: (212)264-1450
Fax: (212)264-0038
Serves New Jersey, New York, Puerto Rico, and the Virgin Islands.

Region 3

U.S. Small Business Administration
Region III Office
1150 First Avenue Suite 1001
King of Prussia, PA 19406
(610)382-3092
Serves Delaware, the District of Columbia, Maryland, Pennsylvania, Virginia, and West Virginia.

Region 4

U.S. Small Business Administration
Region IV Office
233 Peachtree St. NE
Harris Tower 1800
Atlanta, GA 30303
Phone: (404)331-4999
Fax: (404)331-2354
Serves Alabama, Florida, Georgia, Kentucky, Mississippi, North Carolina, South Carolina, and Tennessee.

Region 5

U.S. Small Business Administration
Region V Office
500 W. Madison St.
Citicorp Center, Ste. 1150
Chicago, IL 60661
Phone: (312)353-0357
Fax: (312)353-3426
Serves Illinois, Indiana, Michigan, Minnesota, Ohio, and Wisconsin.

Region 6

U.S. Small Business Administration
Region VI Office
4300 Amon Carter Blvd., Ste. 108
Fort Worth, TX 76155
Phone: (817)684-5581
Fax: (817)684-5588
Serves Arkansas, Louisiana, New Mexico, Oklahoma, and Texas.

Region 7

U.S. Small Business Administration
Region VII Office
1000 Walnut Suite 530
Kansas City, MO 64106
Phone: (816)426-4840
Fax: (816)426-4848
Serves Iowa, Kansas, Missouri, and Nebraska.

Region 8

U.S. Small Business Administration
Region VIII Office
721 19th St., Ste. 400
Denver, CO 80202
Phone: (303)844-0500
Fax: (303)844-0506
Serves Colorado, Montana, North Dakota, South Dakota, Utah, and Wyoming.

Region 9

U.S. Small Business Administration
Region IX Office
330 N Brand Blvd., Ste. 1200
Glendale, CA 91203
Phone: (818)552-3437
Fax: (818)552-0344
Serves American Samoa, Arizona, California, Guam, Hawaii, Nevada, and the Trust Territory of the Pacific Islands.

Region 10

U.S. Small Business Administration
Region X Office
2401 Fourth Ave., Ste. 400
Seattle, WA 98121
Phone: (206)553-5676
Fax: (206)553-4155
Serves Alaska, Idaho, Oregon, and Washington.

Small business development centers

This section contains a listing of all Small Business Development Centers, organized alphabetically by state/U.S. territory, then by city, then by agency name.

Alabama

Alabama SBDC

UNIVERSITY OF ALABAMA
2800 Milan Court Suite 124
Birmingham, AL 35211-6908
Phone: 205-943-6750
Fax: 205-943-6752
E-Mail: wcampbell@provost.uab.edu
Website: http://www.asbdc.org
Mr. William Campbell Jr, State Director

Alaska

Alaska SBDC

UNIVERSITY OF ALASKA - ANCHORAGE
430 West Seventh Avenue, Suite 110
Anchorage, AK 99501
Phone: 907-274 -7232
Fax: 907-272-0565
E-Mail: Isaac.Vanderburg@aksbdc.org
Website: http://www.aksbdc.org
Isaac Vanderburg, State Director

American Samoa

American Samoa SBDC

AMERICAN SAMOA COMMUNITY COLLEGE
P.O. Box 2609
Pago Pago, American Samoa 96799
Phone: 011-684-699-4830
Fax: 011-684-699-6132
E-Mail: hthweatt.sbdc@hotmail.com
Website: www.as-sbdc.org
Mr. Herbert Thweatt, Director

Arizona

Arizona SBDC

MARICOPA COUNTY COMMUNITY COLLEGE
2411 West 14th Street, Suite 114
Tempe, AZ 85281
Phone: 480-731-8720
Fax: 480-731-8729

E-Mail: janice.washington@domail
.maricopa.edu
Website: http://www.azsbdc.net
Janice Washington, State Director

Arkansas

Arkansas SBDC

UNIVERSITY OF ARKANSAS

2801 South University Avenue
Little Rock, AR 72204
Phone: 501-683-7700
Fax: 501-683-7720
E-Mail: jmroderick@ualr.edu
Website: http://asbtdc.org
Ms. Janet M. Roderick, State Director

California

**California - Northern California
Regional SBDC**

Northern California SBDC

HUMBOLDT STATE UNIVERSITY

1 Harpst Street 2006A, 209 Siemens Hall
Arcata, CA, 95521
Phone: 707-826-3920
Fax: 707-826-3912
E-Mail: Kristin.Johnson@humboldt.edu
Website: https://www.norcalsbdc.org
Kristin Johnson, Regional Director

California - Northern California SBDC

**CALIFORNIA STATE UNIVERSITY -
CHICO**

35 Main St., Rm 203rr
Chico, CA 95929-0765
Phone: 530-898-5443
Fax: 530-898-4734
E-Mail: dripke@csuchico.edu
Website: https://www.necsbdc.org
Mr. Dan Ripke, Interim Regional
Director

**California - San Diego and
Imperial SBDC**

**SOUTHWESTERN COMMUNITY
COLLEGE**

880 National City Boulevard, Suite 103
National City, CA 91950
Phone: 619-216-6721
Fax: 619-216-6692
E-Mail: awilson@swccd.edu
Website: http://www.SBDCRegional
Network.org
Aleta Wilson, Regional Director

California - UC Merced SBDC

UC Merced Lead Center

**UNIVERSITY OF CALIFORNIA -
MERCED**

550 East Shaw, Suite 105A
Fresno, CA 93710
Phone: 559-241-6590
Fax: 559-241-7422
E-Mail: dhowerton@ucmerced.edu
Website: http://sbdc.ucmerced.edu
Diane Howerton, State Director

**California - Orange County/Inland
Empire SBDC**

Tri-County Lead SBDC

**CALIFORNIA STATE UNIVERSITY -
FULLERTON**

800 North State College Boulevard,
SGMH 5313
Fullerton, CA 92834
Phone: 714-278-5168
Fax: 714-278-7101
E-Mail: kmpayne@fullerton.edu
Website: http://www.leadsbdc.org
Katrina Payne Smith, Lead Center
Director

California - Los Angeles Region SBDC

LONG BEACH CITY COLLEGE

4900 E. Conant Street, Building 2
Long Beach, CA 90808
Phone: 562-938-5006
Fax: 562-938-5030
E-Mail: jtorres@lbcc.edu
Website: http://www.smallbizla.org
Jesse Torres, Lead Center Director

Colorado

Colorado SBDC

COLORADO SBDC

1625 Broadway, Suite 2700
Denver, CO 80202
Phone: 303-892-3864
Fax: 303-892-3848
E-Mail: Kelly.Manning@state.co.us
Website: http://www.www.coloradosbdc
.org
Ms. Kelly Manning, State Director

Connecticut

Connecticut SBDC

UNIVERSITY OF CONNECTICUT
2100 Hillside Road, Unit 1044
Storrs, CT 06269
Phone: 855-428-7232

E-Mail: ecarter@uconn.edu
Website: www.ctsbdc.com
Emily Carter, State Director

Delaware

Delaware SBDC

DELAWARE TECHNOLOGY PARK

1 Innovation Way, Suite 301
Newark, DE 19711
Phone: 302-831-4283
Fax: 302-831-1423
E-Mail: jmbowman@udel.edu
Website: http://www.delawaresbdc.org
Mike Bowman, State Director

District of Columbia

District of Columbia SBDC

HOWARD UNIVERSITY

2600 6th Street, NW Room 128
Washington, DC 20059
Phone: 202-806-1550
Fax: 202-806-1777
E-Mail: darrell.brown@howard.edu
Website: http://www.dcsbdc.com/
Darrell Brown, Executive Director

Florida

Florida SBDC

UNIVERSITY OF WEST FLORIDA

11000 University Parkway, Building 38
Pensacola, FL 32514
Phone: 850-473-7800
Fax: 850-473-7813
E-Mail: mmyhre@uwf.edu
Website: http://www.floridasbdc.com
Michael Myhre, State Director

Georgia

Georgia SBDC

UNIVERSITY OF GEORGIA

1180 East Broad Street
Athens, GA 30602
Phone: 706-542-6762
Fax: 706-542-7935
E-mail: aadams@georgiasbdc.org
Website: http://www.georgiasbdc.org
Mr. Allan Adams, State Director

Guam

**Guam Small Business Development
Center**

UNIVERSITY OF GUAM
Pacific Islands SBDC
P.O. Box 5014 - U.O.G. Station

Mangilao, GU 96923
Phone: 671-735-2590
Fax: 671-734-2002
E-mail: casey@pacificsbdc.com
Website: http://www.uog.edu/sbdc
Mr. Casey Jeszenka, Director

Hawaii

Hawaii SBDC

UNIVERSITY OF HAWAII - HILO

200 W. Kawili Street, Suite 107
Hilo, HI 96720
Phone: 808-974-7515
Fax: 808-974-7683
E-Mail: cathy.wiltse@hisbdc.org
Website: http://www.hisbdc.org
Cathy Wiltse, State Director

Idaho

Idaho SBDC

BOISE STATE UNIVERSITY

1910 University Drive
Boise, ID 83725
Phone: 208-426-3838
Fax: 208-426-3877
E-mail: ksewell@boisestate.edu
Website: http://www.idahosbdc.org
Katie Sewell, State Director

Illinois

Illinois SBDC

DEPARTMENT OF COMMERCE AND ECONOMIC OPPORTUNITY

500 E. Monroe
Springfield, IL 62701
Phone: 217-524-5700
Fax: 217-524-0171
E-mail: mark.petrilli@illinois.gov
Website: http://www.ilsbdc.biz
Mr. Mark Petrilli, State Director

Indiana

Indiana SBDC

INDIANA ECONOMIC DEVELOPMENT CORPORATION

One North Capitol, Suite 700
Indianapolis, IN 46204
Phone: 317-232-8805
Fax: 317-232-8872
E-mail: JSchpok@iedc.in.gov
Website: http://www.isbdc.org
Jacob Schpok, State Director

Iowa

Iowa SBDC

IOWA STATE UNIVERSITY

2321 North Loop Drive, Suite 202
Ames, IA 50010
Phone: 515-294-2030
Fax: 515-294-6522
E-mail: lshimkat@iastate.edu
Website: http://www.iowasbdc.org
Lisa Shimkat, State Director

Kansas

Kansas SBDC

FORT HAYS STATE UNIVERSITY

214 SW Sixth Street, Suite 301
Topeka, KS 66603
Phone: 785-296-6514
Fax: 785-291-3261
E-mail: panichello@ksbdc.net
Website: http://www.fhsu.edu/ksbdc
Greg Panichello, State Director

Kentucky

Kentucky SBDC

UNIVERSITY OF KENTUCKY

One Quality Street
Lexington, KY 40507
Phone: 859-257-7668
Fax: 859-323-1907
E-mail: lrnaug0@uky.edu
Website: http://www.ksbdc.org
Becky Naugle, State Director

Louisiana

Louisiana SBDC

UNIVERSITY OF LOUISIANA - MONROE

College of Business Administration
700 University Avenue
Monroe, LA 71209
Phone: 318-342-5507
Fax: 318-342-5510
E-mail: rkessler@lsbdc.org
Website: http://www.lsbdc.org
Rande Kessler, State Director

Maine

Maine SBDC

UNIVERSITY OF SOUTHERN MAINE

96 Falmouth Street P.O. Box 9300
Portland, ME 04104
Phone: 207-780-4420
Fax: 207-780-4810

E-mail: mark.delisle@maine.edu
Website: http://www.mainesbdc.org
Mark Delisle, State Director

Maryland

Maryland SBDC

UNIVERSITY OF MARYLAND

7100 Baltimore Avenue, Suite 401
College Park, MD 20742
Phone: 301-403-8300
Fax: 301-403-8303
E-mail: rsprow@mdsbdc.umd.edu
Website: http://www.mdsbdc.umd.edu
Renee Sprow, State Director

Massachusetts

Massachusetts SBDC

UNIVERSITY OF MASSACHUSETTS

23 Tillson Farm Road
Amherst, MA 01003
Phone: 413-545-6301
Fax: 413-545-1273
E-mail: gparkin@msbdc.umass.edu
Website: http://www.www.msbdc.org
Georgianna Parkin, State Director

Michigan

Michigan SBTDC

GRAND VALLEY STATE UNIVERSITY

510 West Fulton Avenue
Grand Rapids, MI 49504
Phone: 616-331-7480
Fax: 616-331-7485
E-mail: boesen@gvsu.edu
Website: http://www.misbtdc.org
Nancy Boese, State Director

Minnesota

Minnesota SBDC

MINNESOTA SMALL BUSINESS DEVELOPMENT CENTER

1st National Bank Building
332 Minnesota Street, Suite E200
St. Paul, MN 55101-1349
Phone: 651-259-7420
Fax: 651-296-5287
E-mail: Bruce.Strong@state.mn.us
Website: http://www.mnsbdc.com
Bruce H. Strong, State Director

Mississippi

Mississippi SBDC

UNIVERSITY OF MISSISSIPPI

122 Jeanette Phillips Drive
P.O. Box 1848

University, MS 38677
Phone: 662-915-5001
Fax: 662-915-5650
E-mail: wgurley@olemiss.edu
Website: http://www.mssbdc.org
Doug Gurley, Jr., State Director

Missouri

Missouri SBDC

UNIVERSITY OF MISSOURI

410 South 6th Street, ?200
Engineering North
Columbia, MO 65211
Phone: 573-882-9206
Fax: 573-884-4297
E-mail: bouchardc@missouri.edu
Website: http://www.missouribusiness.net
Chris Bouchard, State Director

Montana

Montana SBDC

DEPARTMENT OF COMMERCE

301 S. Park Avenue, Room 114
Helena, MT 59601
Phone: 406-841-2746
Fax: 406-841-2728
E-mail: adesch@mt.gov
Website: http://www.sbdc.mt.gov
Ms. Ann Desch, State Director

Nebraska

Nebraska SBDC

UNIVERSITY OF NEBRASKA - OMAHA

200 Mammel Hall, 67th & Pine Streets
Omaha, NE 68182
Phone: 402-554-2521
Fax: 402-554-3473
E-mail: rbernier@unomaha.edu
Website: http://nbdc.unomaha.edu
Robert Bernier, State Director

Nevada

Nevada SBDC

UNIVERSITY OF NEVADA - RENO

Reno College of Business, Room 411
Reno, NV 89557-0100
Phone: 775-784-1717
Fax: 775-784-4337
E-mail: males@unr.edu
Website: http://www.nsbdc.org
Sam Males, State Director

New Hampshire

New Hampshire SBDC

UNIVERSITY OF NEW HAMPSHIRE

10 Garrison Avenue
Durham, NH 03824-3593
Phone: 603-862-2200
Fax: 603-862-4876
E-mail: Mary.Collins@unh.edu
Website: http://www.nhsbdc.org
Mary Collins, State Director

New Jersey

New Jersey SBDC

RUTGERS UNIVERSITY

1 Washington Park, 3rd Floor
Newark, NJ 07102
Phone: 973-353-1927
Fax: 973-353-1110
E-mail: bhopper@njsbdc.com
Website: http://www.njsbdc.com
Brenda Hopper, State Director

New Mexico

New Mexico SBDC

SANTA FE COMMUNITY COLLEGE

6401 Richards Avenue
Santa Fe, NM 87508
Phone: 505-428-1362
Fax: 505-428-1469
E-mail: russell.wyrick@sfcc.edu
Website: http://www.nmsbdc.org
Russell Wyrick, State Director

New York

New York SBDC

STATE UNIVERSITY OF NEW YORK

22 Corporate Woods, 3rd Floor
Albany, NY 12246
Phone: 518-443-5398
Fax: 518-443-5275
E-mail: j.king@nyssbdc.org
Website: http://www.nyssbdc.org
Jim King, State Director

North Carolina

North Carolina SBDTC

UNIVERSITY OF NORTH CAROLINA

5 West Hargett Street, Suite 600
Raleigh, NC 27601
Phone: 919-715-7272
Fax: 919-715-7777
E-mail: sdaugherty@sbtdc.org
Website: http://www.sbtdc.org
Scott Daugherty, State Director

North Dakota

North Dakota SBDC

UNIVERSITY OF NORTH DAKOTA

1200 Memorial Highway, PO Box 5509
Bismarck, ND 58506
Phone: 701-328-5375
Fax: 701-250-4304
E-mail: dkmartin@ndsbdc.org
Website: http://www.ndsbdc.org
David Martin, State Director

Ohio

Ohio SBDC

OHIO DEPARTMENT OF DEVELOPMENT

77 South High Street, 28th Floor
Columbus, OH 43216
Phone: 614-466-2711
Fax: 614-466-1789
E-mail: ezra.escudero@development.ohio.gov
Website: http://www.ohiosbdc.org
Ezra Escudero, State Director

Oklahoma

Oklahoma SBDC

SOUTHEAST OKLAHOMA STATE UNIVERSITY

1405 N. 4th Avenue, PMB 2584
Durant, OK 74701
Phone: 580-745-2955
Fax: 580-745-7471
E-mail: wcarter@se.edu
Website: http://www.osbdc.org
Grady Pennington, State Director

Oregon

Oregon SBDC

LANE COMMUNITY COLLEGE

1445 Willamette Street, Suite 5
Eugene, OR 97401
Phone: 541-463-5250
Fax: 541-345-6006
E-mail: gregorym@lanecc.edu
Website: http://www.bizcenter.org
Mark Gregory, State Director

Pennsylvania

Pennsylvania SBDC

UNIVERSITY OF PENNSYLVANIA

The Wharton School
3819-33 Chestnut Street, Suite 325
Philadelphia, PA 19104

Phone: 215-898-1219
Fax: 215-573-2135
E-mail: cconroy@wharton.upenn.edu
Website: http://pasbdc.org
Christian Conroy, State Director

Puerto Rico

Puerto Rico SBDC

INTER-AMERICAN UNIVERSITY OF PUERTO RICO

416 Ponce de Leon Avenue, Union Plaza, Tenth Floor
Hato Rey, PR 00918
Phone: 787-763-6811
Fax: 787-763-6875
E-mail: cmarti@prsbdc.org
Website: http://www.prsbdc.org
Carmen Marti, Executive Director

Rhode Island

Rhode Island SBDC

UNIVERSITY OF RHODE ISLAND

75 Lower College Road, 2nd Floor
Kingston, RI 02881
Phone: 401-874-4576
E-mail: gsonnenfeld@uri.edu
Website: http://www.risbdc.org
Gerald Sonnenfeld, State Director

South Carolina

South Carolina SBDC

UNIVERSITY OF SOUTH CAROLINA

Moore School of Business

1014 Greene Street
Columbia, SC 29208
Phone: 803-777-0749
Fax: 803-777-6876
E-mail: michele.abraham@moore.sc.edu
Website: http://www.scsbdc.com
Michele Abraham, State Director

South Dakota

South Dakota SBDC

UNIVERSITY OF SOUTH DAKOTA

414 East Clark Street, Patterson Hall
Vermillion, SD 57069
Phone: 605-677-5103
Fax: 605-677-5427
E-mail: jeff.eckhoff@usd.edu
Website: http://www.usd.edu/sbdc
Jeff Eckhoff, State Director

Tennessee

Tennessee SBDC

MIDDLE TENNESSEE STATE UNIVERSITY

3050 Medical Center Parkway, Ste. 200
Nashville, TN 37129
Phone: 615-849-9999
Fax: 615-893-7089
E-mail: pgeho@tsbdc.org
Website: http://www.tsbdc.org
Patrick Geho, State Director

Texas

Texas-North SBDC

DALLAS COUNTY COMMUNITY COLLEGE

1402 Corinth Street
Dallas, TX 75215
Phone: 214-860-5832
Fax: 214-860-5813
E-mail: m.langford@dcccd.edu
Website: http://www.ntsbdc.org
Mark Langford, Region Director

Texas Gulf Coast SBDC

UNIVERSITY OF HOUSTON

2302 Fannin, Suite 200
Houston, TX 77002
Phone: 713-752-8444
Fax: 713-756-1500
E-mail: fyoung@uh.edu
Website: http://sbdcnetwork.uh.edu
Mike Young, Executive Director

Texas-NW SBDC

TEXAS TECH UNIVERSITY

2579 South Loop 289, Suite 114
Lubbock, TX 79423
Phone: 806-745-3973
Fax: 806-745-6207
E-mail: c.bean@nwtsbdc.org
Website: http://www.nwtsbdc.org
Craig Bean, Executive Director

Texas-South-West Texas Border Region SBDC

UNIVERSITY OF TEXAS - SAN ANTONIO

501 West Durango Boulevard
San Antonio, TX 78207-4415
Phone: 210-458-2480
Fax: 210-458-2425
E-mail: albert.salgado@utsa.edu
Website: https://www.txsbdc.org
Alberto Salgado, Region Director

Utah

Utah SBDC

SALT LAKE COMMUNITY COLLEGE

9750 South 300 West
Salt Lake City, UT 84070
Phone: 801-957-5384
Fax: 801-985-5300
E-mail: Sherm.Wilkinson@slcc.edu
Website: http://www.utahsbdc.org
Sherm Wilkinson, State Director

Vermont

Vermont SBDC

VERMONT TECHNICAL COLLEGE

PO Box 188, 1 Main Street
Randolph Center, VT 05061-0188
Phone: 802-728-9101
Fax: 802-728-3026
E-mail: lrossi@vtsbdc.org
Website: http://www.vtsbdc.org
Linda Rossi, State Director

Virgin Islands

Virgin Islands SBDC

UNIVERSITY OF THE VIRGIN ISLANDS

8000 Nisky Center, Suite 720
St. Thomas, VI 00802
Phone: 340-776-3206
Fax: 340-775-3756
E-mail: ldottin@uvi.edu
Website: http://www.sbdcvi.org
Leonor Dottin, State Director

Virginia

Virginia SBDC

GEORGE MASON UNIVERSITY

4031 University Drive, Suite100
Fairfax, VA 22030
Phone: 703-277-7727
Fax: 703-352-8518
E-mail: jkeenan@gmu.edu
Website: http://www.virginiasbdc.org
Jody Keenan, Director

Washington

Washington SBDC

WASHINGTON STATE UNIVERSITY

1235 N. Post Street, Suite 201
Spokane, WA 99201
Phone: 509-358-7765
Fax: 509-358-7764
E-mail: duane.fladland@wsbdc.org
Website: http://www.wsbdc.org
Duane Fladland, State Director

West Virginia

West Virginia SBDC

WEST VIRGINIA DEVELOPMENT OFFICE
Capital Complex, Building 6, Room 652
1900 Kanawha Boulevard
Charleston, WV 25305
Phone: 304-957-2087
Fax: 304-558-0127
E-mail: Kristina.J.Oliver@wv.gov
Website: http://www.wvsbdc.org
Mr. Conley Salyor, State Director

Wisconsin

Wisconsin SBDC

UNIVERSITY OF WISCONSIN
432 North Lake Street, Room 423
Madison, WI 53706
Phone: 608-263-7794
Fax: 608-263-7830
E-mail: bon.wikenheiser@uwex.edu
Website: http://www.uwex.edu/sbdc
Bon Wikenheiser, State Director

Wyoming

Wyoming SBDC

UNIVERSITY OF WYOMING
1000 E. University Ave., Dept. 3922
Laramie, WY 82071-3922
Phone: 307-766-3405
Fax: 307-766-3406
E-mail: jkline@uwyo.edu
Website: http://www.wyomingentre
preneur.biz
Jill Kline, Acting State Director

Service corps of retired executives (score) offices

This section contains a listing of all SCORE offices organized alphabetically by state/U.S. territory, then by city, then by agency name.

Alabama

SCORE Office (Northeast Alabama)
1400 Commerce Blvd., Northeast
Anniston, AL 36207
(256)241-6111

SCORE Office (North Alabama)
1731 1st Ave. North, Ste. 200
Birmingham, AL 35203
(205)264-8425
Fax: (205)934-0538

SCORE Office (Baldwin County)
327 Fairhope Avenue
Fairhope, AL 36532
(251)928-6387

SCORE Office (Mobile)
451 Government Street
Mobile, AL 36652
(251)431-8614
Fax: (251)431-8646

SCORE Office (Alabama Capitol City)
600 S. Court St.
Montgomery, AL 36104
(334)240-6868
Fax: (334)240-6869

SCORE Office (Tuscaloosa)
2200 University Blvd.
Tuscaloosa, AL 35402
(205)758-7588

Alaska

SCORE Office (Anchorage)
420 L St., Ste. 300
Anchorage, AK 99501
(907)271-4022
Fax: (907)271-4545

Arizona

SCORE Office (Greater Phoenix)
2828 N. Central Ave., Ste. 800
Phoenix, AZ 85004
(602)745-7250
Fax: (602)745-7210
E-mail: e-mail@SCORE-phoenix.org
Website: http://www.greaterphoenix
.score.org/

SCORE Office (Northern Arizona)
1228 Willow Creek Rd., Ste. 2
Prescott, AZ 86301
(928)778-7438
Fax: (928)778-0812
Website: http://www.northernarizona
.score.org/

SCORE Office (Southern Arizona)
1400 W Speedway Blvd.
Tucson, AZ 85745
(520)505-3636
Fax: (520)670-5011
Website: http://www.southernarizona
.score.org/

Arkansas

SCORE Office (South Central)
201 N. Jackson Ave.
El Dorado, AR 71730-5803
(870)863-6113
Fax: (870)863-6115

SCORE Office (Northwest Arkansas)
614 E. Emma St., Room M412
Springdale, AR 72764
(479)725-1809
Website: http://www.northwestarkansas
.score.org

SCORE Office (Little Rock)
2120 Riverfront Dr., Ste. 250
Little Rock, AR 72202-1747
(501)324-7379
Fax: (501)324-5199
Website: http://www.littlerock.score.org

SCORE Office (Southeast Arkansas)
P.O. Box 5069
Pine Bluff, AR 71611-5069
(870)535-0110
Fax: (870)535-1643

California

SCORE Office (Bakersfield)
P.O. Box 2426
Bakersfield, CA 93303
(661)861-9249
Fax: (661)395-4134
Website: http://www.bakersfield.score.org

SCORE Office (Santa Cruz County)
716 G Capitola Ave.
Capitola, CA 95010
(831)621-3735
Fax: (831)475-6530
Website: http://santacruzcounty.score.org

SCORE Office (Greater Chico Area)
1324 Mangrove St., Ste. 114
Chico, CA 95926
(530)342-8932
Fax: (530)342-8932
Website: http://www.greaterchicoarea
.score.org

SCORE Office (El Centro)
1850 W. Main St, Ste. C
El Centro, CA 92243
(760)337-2692
Website: http://www.sandiego.score.org/

SCORE Office (Central Valley)
801 R St., Ste. 201
Fresno, CA 93721
(559)487-5605
Fax: (559)487-5636
Website: http://www.centralvalley.score
.org

SCORE Office (Los Angeles)
330 N. Brand Blvd., Ste. 190
Glendale, CA 91203-2304
(818)552-3206

Fax: (818)552-3323
Website: http://www.greaterlosangeles.
score.org

SCORE Office (Modesto Merced)
1880 W. Wardrobe Ave.
Merced, CA 95340
(209)725-2033
Fax: (209)577-2673
Website: http://www.modestomerced.
score.org

SCORE Office (Monterey Bay)
Monterey Chamber of Commerce
30 Ragsdale Dr.
Monterey, CA 93940
(831)648-5360
Website: http://www.montereybay.score
.org

SCORE Office (East Bay)
492 9th St., Ste. 350
Oakland, CA 94607
(510)273-6611
Fax: (510)273-6015
E-mail: webmaster@eastbayscore.org
Website: http://www.eastbay.score.org/

SCORE Office (Ventura County)
400 E. Esplanade Dr., Ste. 301
Oxnard, CA 93036
(805)204-6022
Fax: (805)650-1414
Website: http://www.ventura.score.org

SCORE Office (Coachella)
43100 Cook St., Ste. 104
Palm Desert, CA 92211
(760)773-6507
Fax: (760)773-6514
Website: http://www.coachellavalley
.score.org

SCORE Office (Antelope Valley)
1212 E. Avenue, S Ste. A3
Palmdale, CA 93550
(661)947-7679
Website: http://www.antelopevalley
.score.org/

SCORE Office (Inland Empire)
11801 Pierce St., 2nd Fl.
Riverside, CA 92505
(951)-652-4390
Fax: (951)929-8543
Website: http://www.inlandempire
.score.org/

SCORE Office (Sacramento)
4990 Stockton Blvd.
Sacramento, CA 95820
(916)635-9085

Fax: (916)635-9089
Website: http://www.sacramento
.score.org

SCORE Office (San Diego)
550 West C. St., Ste. 550
San Diego, CA 92101-3540
(619)557-7272
Website: http://www.sandiego.score.org/

SCORE Office (San Francisco)
455 Market St., 6th Fl.
San Francisco, CA 94105
(415)744-6827
Fax: (415)744-6750
E-mail: sfscore@sfscore.
Website: http://www.sanfrancisco
.score.org/

SCORE Office (Silicon Valley)
234 E. Gish Rd., Ste. 100
San Jose, CA 95112
(408)453-6237
Fax: (408)494-0214
E-mail: info@svscore.org
Website: http://www.siliconvalley
.score.org/

SCORE Office (San Luis Obispo)
711 Tank Farm Rd., Ste. 210
San Luis Obispo, CA 93401
(805)547-0779
Website: http://www.sanluisobispo
.score.org

SCORE Office (Orange County)
200 W. Santa Anna Blvd., Ste. 700
Santa Ana, CA 92701
(714)550-7369
Fax: (714)550-0191
Website: http://www.orangecounty.
score.org

SCORE Office (Santa Barbara)
924 Anacapa St.
Santa Barbara, CA 93101
(805)563-0084
Website: http://www.santabarbara
.score.org/

SCORE Office (North Coast)
777 Sonoma Ave., Rm. 115E
Santa Rosa, CA 95404
(707)571-8342
Fax: (707)541-0331
Website: http://www.northcoast.score
.org

SCORE Office (Tuolumne County)
222 S. Shepherd St.
Sonora, CA 95370
(209)532-4316

Fax: (209)588-0673
Website: http://www.tuolumnecounty
.score.org/

Colorado

SCORE Office (Colorado Springs)
3595 E. Fountain Blvd., Ste. E-1
Colorado Springs, CO 80910
(719)636-3074
Fax: (719)635-1571
Website: http://www.coloradosprings
.score.org/

SCORE Office (Denver)
US Custom's House, 4th Fl.
721 19th St.
Denver, CO 80202
(303)844-3985
Fax: (303)844-6490
Website: http://www.denver.score.org/

SCORE Office (Tri-River)
1102 Grand Ave.
Glenwood Springs, CO 81601
(970)945-6589

SCORE Office (Grand Junction)
2591 B & 3/4 Rd.
Grand Junction, CO 81503
(970)243-5242

SCORE Office (Gunnison)
608 N. 11th
Gunnison, CO 81230
(303)641-4422

SCORE Office (Montrose)
1214 Peppertree Dr.
Montrose, CO 81401
(970)249-6080

SCORE Office (Pagosa Springs)
PO Box 4381
Pagosa Springs, CO 81157
(970)731-4890

SCORE Office (Rifle)
0854 W. Battlement Pky., Apt. C106
Parachute, CO 81635
(970)285-9390

SCORE Office (Pueblo)
302 N. Santa Fe
Pueblo, CO 81003
(719)542-1704
Fax: (719)542-1624
Website: http://www.pueblo.score.org

SCORE Office (Ridgway)
143 Poplar Pl.
Ridgway, CO 81432

SCORE Office (Silverton)
PO Box 480
Silverton, CO 81433
(303)387-5430

SCORE Office (Minturn)
PO Box 2066
Vail, CO 81658
(970)476-1224

Connecticut

SCORE Office (Greater Bridgeport)
230 Park Ave.
Bridgeport, CT 06604
(203)450-9484
Fax: (203)576-4388

SCORE Office (Western Connecticut)
155 Deer Hill Ave.
Danbury, CT 06010
(203)794-1404
Website: http://www.westernconnecticut
.score.org

SCORE Office (Greater Hartford County)
330 Main St., 2nd Fl.
Hartford, CT 06106
(860)240-4700
Fax: (860)240-4659
Website: http://www.greaterhartford
.score.org

SCORE Office (Manchester)
20 Hartford Rd.
Manchester, CT 06040
(203)646-2223
Fax: (203)646-5871

SCORE Office (New Britain)
185 Main St., Ste. 431
New Britain, CT 06051
(203)827-4492
Fax: (203)827-4480

SCORE Office (New Haven)
60 Sargent Dr.
New Haven, CT 06511
(203)865-7645
Website: http://www.newhaven.score.org

SCORE Office (Fairfield County)
111 East Ave.
Norwalk, CT 06851
(203)847-7348
Fax: (203)849-9308
Website: http://www.fairfieldcounty
.score.org

SCORE Office (Southeastern Connecticut)
665 Boston Post Rd.
Old Saybrook, CT 06475

(860)388-9508
Website: http://www.southeastern
connecticut.score.org

SCORE Office (Northwest Connecticut)
 333 Kennedy Dr.
Torrington, CT 06790
(560)482-6586
Website: http://www.northwest
connecticut.score.org

Delaware

SCORE Office (Dover)
Treadway Towers
PO Box 576
Dover, DE 19903
(302)678-0892
Fax: (302)678-0189

SCORE Office (Lewes)
PO Box 1
Lewes, DE 19958
(302)645-8073
Fax: (302)645-8412

SCORE Office (Milford)
204 NE Front St.
Milford, DE 19963
(302)422-3301

SCORE Office (Wilmington)
824 Market St., Ste. 610
Wilmington, DE 19801
(302)573-6652
Fax: (302)573-6092
Website: http://www.scoredelaware.com

District of Columbia

SCORE Office (George Mason University)
409 3rd St. SW, 4th Fl.
Washington, DC 20024
800-634-0245

SCORE Office (Washington DC)
1110 Vermont Ave. NW, 9th Fl.
Washington, DC 20043
(202)606-4000
Fax: (202)606-4225
E-mail: dcscore@hotmail.com
Website: http://www.scoredc.org/

Florida

SCORE Office (Desota County Chamber of Commerce)
16 South Velucia Ave.
Arcadia, FL 34266
(941)494-4033

SCORE Office (Suncoast/Pinellas)
Airport Business Ctr.
4707 - 140th Ave. N, No. 311
Clearwater, FL 33755
(813)532-6800
Fax: (813)532-6800

SCORE Office (DeLand)
336 N. Woodland Blvd.
DeLand, FL 32720
(904)734-4331
Fax: (904)734-4333

SCORE Office (South Palm Beach)
1050 S. Federal Hwy., Ste. 132
Delray Beach, FL 33483
(561)278-7752
Fax: (561)278-0288

SCORE Office (Ft. Lauderdale)
Federal Bldg., Ste. 123
299 E. Broward Blvd.
Ft. Lauderdale, FL 33301
(954)356-7263
Fax: (954)356-7145

SCORE Office (Southwest Florida)
The Renaissance
8695 College Pky., Ste. 345 & 346
Ft. Myers, FL 33919
(941)489-2935
Fax: (941)489-1170

SCORE Office (Treasure Coast)
Professional Center, Ste. 2
3220 S. US, No. 1
Ft. Pierce, FL 34982
(561)489-0548

SCORE Office (Gainesville)
101 SE 2nd Pl., Ste. 104
Gainesville, FL 32601
(904)375-8278

SCORE Office (Hialeah Dade Chamber)
59 W. 5th St.
Hialeah, FL 33010
(305)887-1515
Fax: (305)887-2453

SCORE Office (Daytona Beach)
921 Nova Rd., Ste. A
Holly Hills, FL 32117
(904)255-6889
Fax: (904)255-0229
E-mail: score87@dbeach.com

SCORE Office (South Broward)
3475 Sheridian St., Ste. 203
Hollywood, FL 33021
(305)966-8415

SCORE Office (Citrus County)
5 Poplar Ct.
Homosassa, FL 34446
(352)382-1037

SCORE Office (Jacksonville)
7825 Baymeadows Way, Ste. 100-B
Jacksonville, FL 32256
(904)443-1911
Fax: (904)443-1980
E-mail: scorejax@juno.com
Website: http://www.scorejax.org/

SCORE Office (Jacksonville Satellite)
3 Independent Dr.
Jacksonville, FL 32256
(904)366-6600
Fax: (904)632-0617

SCORE Office (Central Florida)
5410 S. Florida Ave., No. 3
Lakeland, FL 33801
(941)687-5783
Fax: (941)687-6225

SCORE Office (Lakeland)
100 Lake Morton Dr.
Lakeland, FL 33801
(941)686-2168

SCORE Office (St. Petersburg)
800 W. Bay Dr., Ste. 505
Largo, FL 33712
(813)585-4571

SCORE Office (Leesburg)
9501 US Hwy. 441
Leesburg, FL 34788-8751
(352)365-3556
Fax: (352)365-3501

SCORE Office (Cocoa)
1600 Farno Rd., Unit 205
Melbourne, FL 32935
(407)254-2288

SCORE Office (Melbourne)
Melbourne Professional Complex
1600 Sarno, Ste. 205
Melbourne, FL 32935
(407)254-2288
Fax: (407)245-2288

SCORE Office (Merritt Island)
1600 Sarno Rd., Ste. 205
Melbourne, FL 32935
(407)254-2288
Fax: (407)254-2288

SCORE Office (Space Coast)
Melbourn Professional Complex
1600 Sarno, Ste. 205
Melbourne, FL 32935
(407)254-2288
Fax: (407)254-2288

SCORE Office (Dade)
49 NW 5th St.
Miami, FL 33128
(305)371-6889
Fax: (305)374-1882
E-mail: score@netrox.net
Website: http://www.netrox.net/~score/

SCORE Office (Naples of Collier)
International College
2654 Tamiami Trl. E
Naples, FL 34112
(941)417-1280
Fax: (941)417-1281
E-mail: score@naples.net
Website: http://www.naples.net/clubs/
score/index.htm

SCORE Office (Pasco County)
6014 US Hwy. 19, Ste. 302
New Port Richey, FL 34652
(813)842-4638

SCORE Office (Southeast Volusia)
115 Canal St.
New Smyrna Beach, FL 32168
(904)428-2449
Fax: (904)423-3512

SCORE Office (Ocala)
110 E. Silver Springs Blvd.
Ocala, FL 34470
(352)629-5959

Clay County SCORE Office
Clay County Chamber of Commerce
1734 Kingsdey Ave.
PO Box 1441
Orange Park, FL 32073
(904)264-2651
Fax: (904)269-0363

SCORE Office (Orlando)
80 N. Hughey Ave.
Rm. 445 Federal Bldg.
Orlando, FL 32801
(407)648-6476
Fax: (407)648-6425

SCORE Office (Emerald Coast)
19 W. Garden St., No. 325
Pensacola, FL 32501
(904)444-2060
Fax: (904)444-2070

SCORE Office (Charlotte County)
201 W. Marion Ave., Ste. 211
Punta Gorda, FL 33950
(941)575-1818
E-mail: score@gls3c.com
Website: http://www.charlotte-florida
.com/business/scorepg01.htm

SCORE Office (St. Augustine)
1 Riberia St.
St. Augustine, FL 32084
(904)829-5681
Fax: (904)829-6477

SCORE Office (Bradenton)
2801 Fruitville, Ste. 280
Sarasota, FL 34237
(813)955-1029

SCORE Office (Manasota)
2801 Fruitville Rd., Ste. 280
Sarasota, FL 34237
(941)955-1029
Fax: (941)955-5581
E-mail: score116@gte.net
Website: http://www.score-suncoast.org/

SCORE Office (Tallahassee)
200 W. Park Ave.
Tallahassee, FL 32302
(850)487-2665

SCORE Office (Hillsborough)
4732 Dale Mabry Hwy. N, Ste. 400
Tampa, FL 33614-6509
(813)870-0125

SCORE Office (Lake Sumter)
122 E. Main St.
Tavares, FL 32778-3810
(352)365-3556

SCORE Office (Titusville)
2000 S. Washington Ave.
Titusville, FL 32780
(407)267-3036
Fax: (407)264-0127

SCORE Office (Venice)
257 N. Tamiami Trl.
Venice, FL 34285
(941)488-2236
Fax: (941)484-5903

SCORE Office (Palm Beach)
500 Australian Ave. S, Ste. 100
West Palm Beach, FL 33401
(561)833-1672
Fax: (561)833-1712

SCORE Office (Wildwood)
103 N. Webster St.
Wildwood, FL 34785

Georgia

SCORE Office (Atlanta)
Harris Tower, Suite 1900
233 Peachtree Rd., NE
Atlanta, GA 30309
(404)347-2442
Fax: (404)347-1227

SCORE Office (Augusta)
3126 Oxford Rd.
Augusta, GA 30909
(706)869-9100

SCORE Office (Columbus)
School Bldg.
PO Box 40
Columbus, GA 31901
(706)327-3654

SCORE Office (Dalton-Whitfield)
305 S. Thorton Ave.
Dalton, GA 30720
(706)279-3383

SCORE Office (Gainesville)
PO Box 374
Gainesville, GA 30503
(770)532-6206
Fax: (770)535-8419

SCORE Office (Macon)
711 Grand Bldg.
Macon, GA 31201
(912)751-6160

SCORE Office (Brunswick)
4 Glen Ave.
St. Simons Island, GA 31520
(912)265-0620
Fax: (912)265-0629

SCORE Office (Savannah)
111 E. Liberty St., Ste. 103
Savannah, GA 31401
(912)652-4335
Fax: (912)652-4184
E-mail: info@scoresav.org
Website: http://www.coastalempire.com/
score/index.htm

Guam

SCORE Office (Guam)
Pacific News Bldg., Rm. 103
238 Archbishop Flores St.
Agana, GU 96910-5100
(671)472-7308

Hawaii

SCORE Office (Hawaii, Inc.)
1111 Bishop St., Ste. 204
PO Box 50207
Honolulu, HI 96813
(808)522-8132
Fax: (808)522-8135
E-mail: hnlscore@juno.com

SCORE Office (Kahului)
250 Alamaha, Unit N16A
Kahului, HI 96732
(808)871-7711

SCORE Office (Maui, Inc.)
590 E. Lipoa Pkwy., Ste. 227
Kihei, HI 96753
(808)875-2380

Idaho

SCORE Office (Treasure Valley)
1020 Main St., No. 290
Boise, ID 83702
(208)334-1696
Fax: (208)334-9353

SCORE Office (Eastern Idaho)
2300 N. Yellowstone, Ste. 119
Idaho Falls, ID 83401
(208)523-1022
Fax: (208)528-7127

Illinois

SCORE Office (Fox Valley)
40 W. Downer Pl.
PO Box 277
Aurora, IL 60506
(630)897-9214
Fax: (630)897-7002

SCORE Office (Greater Belvidere)
419 S. State St.
Belvidere, IL 61008
(815)544-4357
Fax: (815)547-7654

SCORE Office (Bensenville)
1050 Busse Hwy. Suite 100
Bensenville, IL 60106
(708)350-2944
Fax: (708)350-2979

SCORE Office (Central Illinois)
402 N. Hershey Rd.
Bloomington, IL 61704
(309)644-0549
Fax: (309)663-8270
E-mail: webmaster@central-illinois-score
.org
Website: http://www.central-illinois-score
.org/

SCORE Office (Southern Illinois)
150 E. Pleasant Hill Rd.
Box 1
Carbondale, IL 62901
(618)453-6654
Fax: (618)453-5040

SCORE Office (Chicago)
Northwest Atrium Ctr.
500 W. Madison St., No. 1250
Chicago, IL 60661
(312)353-7724
Fax: (312)886-5688
Website: http://www.mcs.net/~bic/

SCORE Office (Chicago–Oliver Harvey College)
Pullman Bldg.
1000 E. 11th St., 7th Fl.
Chicago, IL 60628
Fax: (312)468-8086

SCORE Office (Danville)
28 W. N. Street
Danville, IL 61832
(217)442-7232
Fax: (217)442-6228

SCORE Office (Decatur)
Milliken University
1184 W. Main St.
Decatur, IL 62522
(217)424-6297
Fax: (217)424-3993
E-mail: charding@mail.millikin.edu
Website: http://www.millikin.edu/
academics/Tabor/score.html

SCORE Office (Downers Grove)
925 Curtis
Downers Grove, IL 60515
(708)968-4050
Fax: (708)968-8368

SCORE Office (Elgin)
24 E. Chicago, 3rd Fl.
PO Box 648
Elgin, IL 60120
(847)741-5660
Fax: (847)741-5677

SCORE Office (Freeport Area)
26 S. Galena Ave.
Freeport, IL 61032
(815)233-1350
Fax: (815)235-4038

SCORE Office (Galesburg)
292 E. Simmons St.
PO Box 749
Galesburg, IL 61401
(309)343-1194
Fax: (309)343-1195

SCORE Office (Glen Ellyn)
500 Pennsylvania
Glen Ellyn, IL 60137
(708)469-0907
Fax: (708)469-0426

SCORE Office (Greater Alton)
Alden Hall
5800 Godfrey Rd.
Godfrey, IL 62035-2466
(618)467-2280

Fax: (618)466-8289
Website: http://www.altonweb.com/score/

SCORE Office (Grayslake)
19351 W. Washington St.
Grayslake, IL 60030
(708)223-3633
Fax: (708)223-9371

SCORE Office (Harrisburg)
303 S. Commercial
Harrisburg, IL 62946-1528
(618)252-8528
Fax: (618)252-0210

SCORE Office (Joliet)
100 N. Chicago
Joliet, IL 60432
(815)727-5371
Fax: (815)727-5374

SCORE Office (Kankakee)
101 S. Schuyler Ave.
Kankakee, IL 60901
(815)933-0376
Fax: (815)933-0380

SCORE Office (Macomb)
216 Seal Hall, Rm. 214
Macomb, IL 61455
(309)298-1128
Fax: (309)298-2520

SCORE Office (Matteson)
210 Lincoln Mall
Matteson, IL 60443
(708)709-3750
Fax: (708)503-9322

SCORE Office (Mattoon)
1701 Wabash Ave.
Mattoon, IL 61938
(217)235-5661
Fax: (217)234-6544

SCORE Office (Quad Cities)
622 19th St.
Moline, IL 61265
(309)797-0082
Fax: (309)757-5435
E-mail: score@qconline.com
Website: http://www.qconline.com/
business/score/

SCORE Office (Naperville)
131 W. Jefferson Ave.
Naperville, IL 60540
(708)355-4141
Fax: (708)355-8355

SCORE Office (Northbrook)
2002 Walters Ave.
Northbrook, IL 60062

(847)498-5555
Fax: (847)498-5510

SCORE Office (Palos Hills)
10900 S. 88th Ave.
Palos Hills, IL 60465
(847)974-5468
Fax: (847)974-0078

SCORE Office (Peoria)
124 SW Adams, Ste. 300
Peoria, IL 61602
(309)676-0755
Fax: (309)676-7534

SCORE Office (Prospect Heights)
1375 Wolf Rd.
Prospect Heights, IL 60070
(847)537-8660
Fax: (847)537-7138

SCORE Office (Quincy Tri-State)
300 Civic Center Plz., Ste. 245
Quincy, IL 62301
(217)222-8093
Fax: (217)222-3033

SCORE Office (River Grove)
2000 5th Ave.
River Grove, IL 60171
(708)456-0300
Fax: (708)583-3121

SCORE Office (Northern Illinois)
515 N. Court St.
Rockford, IL 61103
(815)962-0122
Fax: (815)962-0122

SCORE Office (St. Charles)
103 N. 1st Ave.
St. Charles, IL 60174-1982
(847)584-8384
Fax: (847)584-6065

SCORE Office (Springfield)
511 W. Capitol Ave., Ste. 302
Springfield, IL 62704
(217)492-4416
Fax: (217)492-4867

SCORE Office (Sycamore)
112 Somunak St.
Sycamore, IL 60178
(815)895-3456
Fax: (815)895-0125

SCORE Office (University)
Hwy. 50 & Stuenkel Rd. Ste. C3305
University Park, IL 60466
(708)534-5000
Fax: (708)534-8457

Indiana

SCORE Office (Anderson)
205 W. 11th St.
Anderson, IN 46015
(317)642-0264

SCORE Office (Bloomington)
Star Center
216 W. Allen
Bloomington, IN 47403
(812)335-7334
E-mail: wtfische@indiana.edu
Website: http://www.brainfreezemedia
.com/score527/

SCORE Office (South East Indiana)
500 Franklin St.
Box 29
Columbus, IN 47201
(812)379-4457

SCORE Office (Corydon)
310 N. Elm St.
Corydon, IN 47112
(812)738-2137
Fax: (812)738-6438

SCORE Office (Crown Point)
Old Courthouse Sq. Ste. 206
PO Box 43
Crown Point, IN 46307
(219)663-1800

SCORE Office (Elkhart)
418 S. Main St.
Elkhart, IN 46515
(219)293-1531
Fax: (219)294-1859

SCORE Office (Evansville)
1100 W. Lloyd Expy., Ste. 105
Evansville, IN 47708
(812)426-6144

SCORE Office (Fort Wayne)
1300 S. Harrison St.
Ft. Wayne, IN 46802
(219)422-2601
Fax: (219)422-2601

SCORE Office (Gary)
973 W. 6th Ave., Rm. 326
Gary, IN 46402
(219)882-3918

SCORE Office (Hammond)
7034 Indianapolis Blvd.
Hammond, IN 46324
(219)931-1000
Fax: (219)845-9548

SCORE Office (Indianapolis)
429 N. Pennsylvania St., Ste. 100
Indianapolis, IN 46204-1873

(317)226-7264
Fax: (317)226-7259
E-mail: inscore@indy.net
Website: http://www.score-indianapolis
.org/

SCORE Office (Jasper)
PO Box 307
Jasper, IN 47547-0307
(812)482-6866

SCORE Office (Kokomo/Howard Counties)
106 N. Washington St.
Kokomo, IN 46901
(765)457-5301
Fax: (765)452-4564

SCORE Office (Logansport)
300 E. Broadway, Ste. 103
Logansport, IN 46947
(219)753-6388

SCORE Office (Madison)
301 E. Main St.
Madison, IN 47250
(812)265-3135
Fax: (812)265-2923

SCORE Office (Marengo)
Rt. 1 Box 224D
Marengo, IN 47140
Fax: (812)365-2793

SCORE Office (Marion/Grant Counties)
215 S. Adams
Marion, IN 46952
(765)664-5107

SCORE Office (Merrillville)
255 W. 80th Pl.
Merrillville, IN 46410
(219)769-8180
Fax: (219)736-6223

SCORE Office (Michigan City)
200 E. Michigan Blvd.
Michigan City, IN 46360
(219)874-6221
Fax: (219)873-1204

SCORE Office (South Central Indiana)
4100 Charleston Rd.
New Albany, IN 47150-9538
(812)945-0066

SCORE Office (Rensselaer)
104 W. Washington
Rensselaer, IN 47978

SCORE Office (Salem)
210 N. Main St.
Salem, IN 47167

(812)883-4303
Fax: (812)883-1467

SCORE Office (South Bend)
300 N. Michigan St.
South Bend, IN 46601
(219)282-4350
E-mail: chair@southbend-score.org
Website: http://www.southbend-score.org/

SCORE Office (Valparaiso)
150 Lincolnway
Valparaiso, IN 46383
(219)462-1105
Fax: (219)469-5710

SCORE Office (Vincennes)
27 N. 3rd
PO Box 553
Vincennes, IN 47591
(812)882-6440
Fax: (812)882-6441

SCORE Office (Wabash)
PO Box 371
Wabash, IN 46992
(219)563-1168
Fax: (219)563-6920

Iowa

SCORE Office (Burlington)
Federal Bldg.
300 N. Main St.
Burlington, IA 52601
(319)752-2967

SCORE Office (Cedar Rapids)
2750 1st Ave. NE, Ste 350
Cedar Rapids, IA 52401-1806
(319)362-6405
Fax: (319)362-7861
E:mail: score@scorecr.org
Website: http://www.scorecr.org

SCORE Office (Illowa)
333 4th Ave. S
Clinton, IA 52732
(319)242-5702

SCORE Office (Council Bluffs)
7 N. 6th St.
Council Bluffs, IA 51502
(712)325-1000

SCORE Office (Northeast Iowa)
3404 285th St.
Cresco, IA 52136
(319)547-3377

SCORE Office (Des Moines)
Federal Bldg., Rm. 749
210 Walnut St.

Des Moines, IA 50309-2186
(515)284-4760

SCORE Office (Ft. Dodge)
Federal Bldg., Rm. 436
205 S. 8th St.
Ft. Dodge, IA 50501
(515)955-2622

SCORE Office (Independence)
110 1st. St. east
Independence, IA 50644
(319)334-7178
Fax: (319)334-7179

SCORE Office (Iowa City)
210 Federal Bldg.
PO Box 1853
Iowa City, IA 52240-1853
(319)338-1662

SCORE Office (Keokuk)
401 Main St.
Pierce Bldg., No. 1
Keokuk, IA 52632
(319)524-5055

SCORE Office (Central Iowa)
Fisher Community College
709 S. Center
Marshalltown, IA 50158
(515)753-6645

SCORE Office (River City)
15 West State St.
Mason City, IA 50401
(515)423-5724

SCORE Office (South Central)
SBDC, Indian Hills Community College
525 Grandview Ave.
Ottumwa, IA 52501
(515)683-5127
Fax: (515)683-5263

SCORE Office (Dubuque)
10250 Sundown Rd.
Peosta, IA 52068
(319)556-5110

SCORE Office (Southwest Iowa)
614 W. Sheridan
Shenandoah, IA 51601
(712)246-3260

SCORE Office (Sioux City)
Federal Bldg.
320 6th St.
Sioux City, IA 51101
(712)277-2324
Fax: (712)277-2325

SCORE Office (Iowa Lakes)
122 W. 5th St.
Spencer, IA 51301
(712)262-3059

SCORE Office (Vista)
119 W. 6th St.
Storm Lake, IA 50588
(712)732-3780

SCORE Office (Waterloo)
215 E. 4th
Waterloo, IA 50703
(319)233-8431

Kansas

SCORE Office (Southwest Kansas)
501 W. Spruce
Dodge City, KS 67801
(316)227-3119

SCORE Office (Emporia)
811 Homewood
Emporia, KS 66801
(316)342-1600

SCORE Office (Golden Belt)
1307 Williams
Great Bend, KS 67530
(316)792-2401

SCORE Office (Hays)
PO Box 400
Hays, KS 67601
(913)625-6595

SCORE Office (Hutchinson)
1 E. 9th St.
Hutchinson, KS 67501
(316)665-8468
Fax: (316)665-7619

SCORE Office (Southeast Kansas)
404 Westminster Pl.
PO Box 886
Independence, KS 67301
(316)331-4741

SCORE Office (McPherson)
306 N. Main
PO Box 616
McPherson, KS 67460
(316)241-3303

SCORE Office (Salina)
120 Ash St.
Salina, KS 67401
(785)243-4290
Fax: (785)243-1833

SCORE Office (Topeka)
1700 College
Topeka, KS 66621
(785)231-1010

SCORE Office (Wichita)
100 E. English, Ste. 510
Wichita, KS 67202

(316)269-6273
Fax: (316)269-6499

SCORE Office (Ark Valley)
205 E. 9th St.
Winfield, KS 67156
(316)221-1617

Kentucky

SCORE Office (Ashland)
PO Box 830
Ashland, KY 41105
(606)329-8011
Fax: (606)325-4607

SCORE Office (Bowling Green)
812 State St.
PO Box 51
Bowling Green, KY 42101
(502)781-3200
Fax: (502)843-0458

SCORE Office (Tri-Lakes)
508 Barbee Way
Danville, KY 40422-1548
(606)231-9902

SCORE Office (Glasgow)
301 W. Main St.
Glasgow, KY 42141
(502)651-3161
Fax: (502)651-3122

SCORE Office (Hazard)
B & I Technical Center
100 Airport Gardens Rd.
Hazard, KY 41701
(606)439-5856
Fax: (606)439-1808

SCORE Office (Lexington)
410 W. Vine St., Ste. 290, Civic C
Lexington, KY 40507
(606)231-9902
Fax: (606)253-3190
E-mail: scorelex@uky.campus.mci.net

SCORE Office (Louisville)
188 Federal Office Bldg.
600 Dr. Martin L. King Jr. Pl.
Louisville, KY 40202
(502)582-5976

SCORE Office (Madisonville)
257 N. Main
Madisonville, KY 42431
(502)825-1399
Fax: (502)825-1396

SCORE Office (Paducah)
Federal Office Bldg.
501 Broadway, Rm. B-36

Paducah, KY 42001
(502)442-5685

Louisiana

SCORE Office (Central Louisiana)
802 3rd St.
Alexandria, LA 71309
(318)442-6671

SCORE Office (Baton Rouge)
564 Laurel St.
PO Box 3217
Baton Rouge, LA 70801
(504)381-7130
Fax: (504)336-4306

SCORE Office (North Shore)
2 W. Thomas
Hammond, LA 70401
(504)345-4457
Fax: (504)345-4749

SCORE Office (Lafayette)
804 St. Mary Blvd.
Lafayette, LA 70505-1307
(318)233-2705
Fax: (318)234-8671
E-mail: score302@aol.com

SCORE Office (Lake Charles)
120 W. Pujo St.
Lake Charles, LA 70601
(318)433-3632

SCORE Office (New Orleans)
365 Canal St., Ste. 3100
New Orleans, LA 70130
(504)589-2356
Fax: (504)589-2339

SCORE Office (Shreveport)
400 Edwards St.
Shreveport, LA 71101
(318)677-2536
Fax: (318)677-2541

Maine

SCORE Office (Augusta)
40 Western Ave.
Augusta, ME 04330
(207)622-8509

SCORE Office (Bangor)
Peabody Hall, Rm. 229
One College Cir.
Bangor, ME 04401
(207)941-9707

SCORE Office (Central & Northern Arroostock)
111 High St.
Caribou, ME 04736

(207)492-8010
Fax: (207)492-8010

SCORE Office (Penquis)
South St.
Dover Foxcroft, ME 04426
(207)564-7021

SCORE Office (Maine Coastal)
Mill Mall
Box 1105
Ellsworth, ME 04605-1105
(207)667-5800
E-mail: score@arcadia.net

SCORE Office (Lewiston-Auburn)
BIC of Maine-Bates Mill Complex
35 Canal St.
Lewiston, ME 04240-7764
(207)782-3708
Fax: (207)783-7745

SCORE Office (Portland)
66 Pearl St., Rm. 210
Portland, ME 04101
(207)772-1147
Fax: (207)772-5581
E-mail: Score53@score.maine.org
Website: http://www.score.maine.org/
chapter53/

SCORE Office (Western Mountains)
255 River St.
PO Box 252
Rumford, ME 04257-0252
(207)369-9976

SCORE Office (Oxford Hills)
166 Main St.
South Paris, ME 04281
(207)743-0499

Maryland

SCORE Office (Southern Maryland)
2525 Riva Rd., Ste. 110
Annapolis, MD 21401
(410)266-9553
Fax: (410)573-0981
E-mail: score390@aol.com
Website: http://members.aol.com/
score390/index.htm

SCORE Office (Baltimore)
The City Crescent Bldg., 6th Fl.
10 S. Howard St.
Baltimore, MD 21201
(410)962-2233
Fax: (410)962-1805

SCORE Office (Bel Air)
108 S. Bond St.
Bel Air, MD 21014

(410)838-2020
Fax: (410)893-4715

SCORE Office (Bethesda)
7910 Woodmont Ave., Ste. 1204
Bethesda, MD 20814
(301)652-4900
Fax: (301)657-1973

SCORE Office (Bowie)
6670 Race Track Rd.
Bowie, MD 20715
(301)262-0920
Fax: (301)262-0921

SCORE Office (Dorchester County)
203 Sunburst Hwy.
Cambridge, MD 21613
(410)228-3575

SCORE Office (Upper Shore)
210 Marlboro Ave.
Easton, MD 21601
(410)822-4606
Fax: (410)822-7922

SCORE Office (Frederick County)
43A S. Market St.
Frederick, MD 21701
(301)662-8723
Fax: (301)846-4427

SCORE Office (Gaithersburg)
9 Park Ave.
Gaithersburg, MD 20877
(301)840-1400
Fax: (301)963-3918

SCORE Office (Glen Burnie)
103 Crain Hwy. SE
Glen Burnie, MD 21061
(410)766-8282
Fax: (410)766-9722

SCORE Office (Hagerstown)
111 W. Washington St.
Hagerstown, MD 21740
(301)739-2015
Fax: (301)739-1278

SCORE Office (Laurel)
7901 Sandy Spring Rd. Ste. 501
Laurel, MD 20707
(301)725-4000
Fax: (301)725-0776

SCORE Office (Salisbury)
300 E. Main St.
Salisbury, MD 21801
(410)749-0185
Fax: (410)860-9925

Massachusetts

SCORE Office (NE Massachusetts)
100 Cummings Ctr., Ste. 101 K
Beverly, MA 01923
(978)922-9441
Website: http://www1.shore.net/~score/

SCORE Office (Boston)
10 Causeway St., Rm. 265
Boston, MA 02222-1093
(617)565-5591
Fax: (617)565-5598
E-mail: boston-score-20@worldnet
.att.net
Website: http://www.scoreboston.org/

SCORE office (Bristol/Plymouth County)
53 N. 6th St., Federal Bldg.
Bristol, MA 02740
(508)994-5093

SCORE Office (SE Massachusetts)
60 School St.
Brockton, MA 02401
(508)587-2673
Fax: (508)587-1340
Website: http://www.metrosouth
chamber.com/score.html

SCORE Office (North Adams)
820 N. State Rd.
Cheshire, MA 01225
(413)743-5100

SCORE Office (Clinton Satellite)
1 Green St.
Clinton, MA 01510
Fax: (508)368-7689

SCORE Office (Greenfield)
PO Box 898
Greenfield, MA 01302
(413)773-5463
Fax: (413)773-7008

SCORE Office (Haverhill)
87 Winter St.
Haverhill, MA 01830
(508)373-5663
Fax: (508)373-8060

SCORE Office (Hudson Satellite)
PO Box 578
Hudson, MA 01749
(508)568-0360
Fax: (508)568-0360

SCORE Office (Cape Cod)
Independence Pk., Ste. 5B
270 Communications Way
Hyannis, MA 02601

(508)775-4884
Fax: (508)790-2540

SCORE Office (Lawrence)
264 Essex St.
Lawrence, MA 01840
(508)686-0900
Fax: (508)794-9953

SCORE Office (Leominster Satellite)
110 Erdman Way
Leominster, MA 01453
(508)840-4300
Fax: (508)840-4896

SCORE Office (Bristol/Plymouth Counties)
53 N. 6th St., Federal Bldg.
New Bedford, MA 02740
(508)994-5093

SCORE Office (Newburyport)
29 State St.
Newburyport, MA 01950
(617)462-6680

SCORE Office (Pittsfield)
66 West St.
Pittsfield, MA 01201
(413)499-2485

SCORE Office (Haverhill-Salem)
32 Derby Sq.
Salem, MA 01970
(508)745-0330
Fax: (508)745-3855

SCORE Office (Springfield)
1350 Main St.
Federal Bldg.
Springfield, MA 01103
(413)785-0314

SCORE Office (Carver)
12 Taunton Green, Ste. 201
Taunton, MA 02780
(508)824-4068
Fax: (508)824-4069

SCORE Office (Worcester)
33 Waldo St.
Worcester, MA 01608
(508)753-2929
Fax: (508)754-8560

Michigan

SCORE Office (Allegan)
PO Box 338
Allegan, MI 49010
(616)673-2479

SCORE Office (Ann Arbor)
425 S. Main St., Ste. 103
Ann Arbor, MI 48104
(313)665-4433

SCORE Office (Battle Creek)
34 W. Jackson Ste. 4A
Battle Creek, MI 49017-3505
(616)962-4076
Fax: (616)962-6309

SCORE Office (Cadillac)
222 Lake St.
Cadillac, MI 49601
(616)775-9776
Fax: (616)768-4255

SCORE Office (Detroit)
477 Michigan Ave., Rm. 515
Detroit, MI 48226
(313)226-7947
Fax: (313)226-3448

SCORE Office (Flint)
708 Root Rd., Rm. 308
Flint, MI 48503
(810)233-6846

SCORE Office (Grand Rapids)
111 Pearl St. NW
Grand Rapids, MI 49503-2831
(616)771-0305
Fax: (616)771-0328
E-mail: scoreone@iserv.net
Website: http://www.iserv.net/
~scoreone/

SCORE Office (Holland)
480 State St.
Holland, MI 49423
(616)396-9472

SCORE Office (Jackson)
209 East Washington
PO Box 80
Jackson, MI 49204
(517)782-8221
Fax: (517)782-0061

SCORE Office (Kalamazoo)
345 W. Michigan Ave.
Kalamazoo, MI 49007
(616)381-5382
Fax: (616)384-0096
E-mail: score@nucleus.net

SCORE Office (Lansing)
117 E. Allegan
PO Box 14030
Lansing, MI 48901
(517)487-6340
Fax: (517)484-6910

SCORE Office (Livonia)
15401 Farmington Rd.
Livonia, MI 48154
(313)427-2122
Fax: (313)427-6055

SCORE Office (Madison Heights)
26345 John R
Madison Heights, MI 48071
(810)542-5010
Fax: (810)542-6821

SCORE Office (Monroe)
111 E. 1st
Monroe, MI 48161
(313)242-3366
Fax: (313)242-7253

SCORE Office (Mt. Clemens)
58 S/B Gratiot
Mt. Clemens, MI 48043
(810)463-1528
Fax: (810)463-6541

SCORE Office (Muskegon)
PO Box 1087
230 Terrace Plz.
Muskegon, MI 49443
(616)722-3751
Fax: (616)728-7251

SCORE Office (Petoskey)
401 E. Mitchell St.
Petoskey, MI 49770
(616)347-4150

SCORE Office (Pontiac)
Executive Office Bldg.
1200 N. Telegraph Rd.
Pontiac, MI 48341
(810)975-9555

SCORE Office (Pontiac)
PO Box 430025
Pontiac, MI 48343
(810)335-9600

SCORE Office (Port Huron)
920 Pinegrove Ave.
Port Huron, MI 48060
(810)985-7101

SCORE Office (Rochester)
71 Walnut Ste. 110
Rochester, MI 48307
(810)651-6700
Fax: (810)651-5270

SCORE Office (Saginaw)
901 S. Washington Ave.
Saginaw, MI 48601
(517)752-7161
Fax: (517)752-9055

SCORE Office (Upper Peninsula)
2581 I-75 Business Spur
Sault Ste. Marie, MI 49783
(906)632-3301

SCORE Office (Southfield)
21000 W. 10 Mile Rd.
Southfield, MI 48075
(810)204-3050
Fax: (810)204-3099

SCORE Office (Traverse City)
202 E. Grandview Pkwy.
PO Box 387
Traverse City, MI 49685
(616)947-5075
Fax: (616)946-2565

SCORE Office (Warren)
30500 Van Dyke, Ste. 118
Warren, MI 48093
(810)751-3939

Minnesota

SCORE Office (Aitkin)
Aitkin, MN 56431
(218)741-3906

SCORE Office (Albert Lea)
202 N. Broadway Ave.
Albert Lea, MN 56007
(507)373-7487

SCORE Office (Austin)
PO Box 864
Austin, MN 55912
(507)437-4561
Fax: (507)437-4869

SCORE Office (South Metro)
Ames Business Ctr.
2500 W. County Rd., No. 42
Burnsville, MN 55337
(612)898-5645
Fax: (612)435-6972
E-mail: southmetro@scoreminn.org
Website: http://www.scoreminn.org/
southmetro/

SCORE Office (Duluth)
1717 Minnesota Ave.
Duluth, MN 55802
(218)727-8286
Fax: (218)727-3113
E-mail: duluth@scoreminn.org
Website: http://www.scoreminn.org

SCORE Office (Fairmont)
PO Box 826
Fairmont, MN 56031
(507)235-5547
Fax: (507)235-8411

SCORE Office (Southwest Minnesota)
112 Riverfront St.
Box 999
Mankato, MN 56001

(507)345-4519
Fax: (507)345-4451
Website: http://www.scoreminn.org/

SCORE Office (Minneapolis)
North Plaza Bldg., Ste. 51
5217 Wayzata Blvd.
Minneapolis, MN 55416
(612)591-0539
Fax: (612)544-0436
Website: http://www.scoreminn.org/

SCORE Office (Owatonna)
PO Box 331
Owatonna, MN 55060
(507)451-7970
Fax: (507)451-7972

SCORE Office (Red Wing)
2000 W. Main St., Ste. 324
Red Wing, MN 55066
(612)388-4079

SCORE Office (Southeastern Minnesota)
220 S. Broadway, Ste. 100
Rochester, MN 55901
(507)288-1122
Fax: (507)282-8960
Website: http://www.scoreminn.org/

SCORE Office (Brainerd)
St. Cloud, MN 56301

SCORE Office (Central Area)
1527 Northway Dr.
St. Cloud, MN 56301
(320)240-1332
Fax: (320)255-9050
Website: http://www.scoreminn.org/

SCORE Office (St. Paul)
350 St. Peter St., No. 295
Lowry Professional Bldg.
St. Paul, MN 55102
(651)223-5010
Fax: (651)223-5048
Website: http://www.scoreminn.org/

SCORE Office (Winona)
Box 870
Winona, MN 55987
(507)452-2272
Fax: (507)454-8814

SCORE Office (Worthington)
1121 3rd Ave.
Worthington, MN 56187
(507)372-2919
Fax: (507)372-2827

Mississippi

SCORE Office (Delta)
915 Washington Ave.
PO Box 933
Greenville, MS 38701
(601)378-3141

SCORE Office (Gulfcoast)
1 Government Plaza
2909 13th St., Ste. 203
Gulfport, MS 39501
(228)863-0054

SCORE Office (Jackson)
1st Jackson Center, Ste. 400
101 W. Capitol St.
Jackson, MS 39201
(601)965-5533

SCORE Office (Meridian)
5220 16th Ave.
Meridian, MS 39305
(601)482-4412

Missouri

SCORE Office (Lake of the Ozark)
University Extension
113 Kansas St.
PO Box 1405
Camdenton, MO 65020
(573)346-2644
Fax: (573)346-2694
E-mail: score@cdoc.net
Website: http://sites.cdoc.net/score/

Chamber of Commerce (Cape Girardeau)
PO Box 98
Cape Girardeau, MO 63702-0098
(314)335-3312

SCORE Office (Mid-Missouri)
1705 Halstead Ct.
Columbia, MO 65203
(573)874-1132

SCORE Office (Ozark-Gateway)
1486 Glassy Rd.
Cuba, MO 65453-1640
(573)885-4954

SCORE Office (Kansas City)
323 W. 8th St., Ste. 104
Kansas City, MO 64105
(816)374-6675
Fax: (816)374-6692
E-mail: SCOREBIC@AOL.COM
Website: http://www.crn.org/score/

SCORE Office (Sedalia)
Lucas Place
323 W. 8th St., Ste.104

Kansas City, MO 64105
(816)374-6675

SCORE office (Tri-Lakes)
PO Box 1148
Kimberling, MO 65686
(417)739-3041

SCORE Office (Tri-Lakes)
HCRI Box 85
Lampe, MO 65681
(417)858-6798

SCORE Office (Mexico)
111 N. Washington St.
Mexico, MO 65265
(314)581-2765

SCORE Office (Southeast Missouri)
Rte. 1, Box 280
Neelyville, MO 63954
(573)989-3577

SCORE office (Poplar Bluff Area)
806 Emma St.
Poplar Bluff, MO 63901
(573)686-8892

SCORE Office (St. Joseph)
3003 Frederick Ave.
St. Joseph, MO 64506
(816)232-4461

SCORE Office (St. Louis)
815 Olive St., Rm. 242
St. Louis, MO 63101-1569
(314)539-6970
Fax: (314)539-3785
E-mail: info@stlscore.org
Website: http://www.stlscore.org/

SCORE Office (Lewis & Clark)
425 Spencer Rd.
St. Peters, MO 63376
(314)928-2900
Fax: (314)928-2900
E-mail: score01@mail.win.org

SCORE Office (Springfield)
620 S. Glenstone, Ste. 110
Springfield, MO 65802-3200
(417)864-7670
Fax: (417)864-4108

SCORE office (Southeast Kansas)
1206 W. First St.
Webb City, MO 64870
(417)673-3984

Montana

SCORE Office (Billings)
815 S. 27th St.
Billings, MT 59101
(406)245-4111

SCORE Office (Bozeman)
1205 E. Main St.
Bozeman, MT 59715
(406)586-5421

SCORE Office (Butte)
1000 George St.
Butte, MT 59701
(406)723-3177

SCORE Office (Great Falls)
710 First Ave. N
Great Falls, MT 59401
(406)761-4434
E-mail: scoregtf@in.tch.com

SCORE Office (Havre, Montana)
518 First St.
Havre, MT 59501
(406)265-4383

SCORE Office (Helena)
Federal Bldg.
301 S. Park
Helena, MT 59626-0054
(406)441-1081

SCORE Office (Kalispell)
2 Main St.
Kalispell, MT 59901
(406)756-5271
Fax: (406)752-6665

SCORE Office (Missoula)
723 Ronan
Missoula, MT 59806
(406)327-8806
E-mail: score@safeshop.com
Website: http://missoula.bigsky.net/
score/

Nebraska

SCORE Office (Columbus)
Columbus, NE 68601
(402)564-2769

SCORE Office (Fremont)
92 W. 5th St.
Fremont, NE 68025
(402)721-2641

SCORE Office (Hastings)
Hastings, NE 68901
(402)463-3447

SCORE Office (Lincoln)
8800 O St.
Lincoln, NE 68520
(402)437-2409

SCORE Office (Panhandle)
150549 CR 30
Minatare, NE 69356

(308)632-2133
Website: http://www.tandt.com/SCORE

SCORE Office (Norfolk)
3209 S. 48th Ave.
Norfolk, NE 68106
(402)564-2769

SCORE Office (North Platte)
3301 W. 2nd St.
North Platte, NE 69101
(308)532-4466

SCORE Office (Omaha)
11145 Mill Valley Rd.
Omaha, NE 68154
(402)221-3606
Fax: (402)221-3680
E-mail: infoctr@ne.uswest.net
Website: http://www.tandt.com/score/

Nevada

SCORE Office (Incline Village)
969 Tahoe Blvd.
Incline Village, NV 89451
(702)831-7327
Fax: (702)832-1605

SCORE Office (Carson City)
301 E. Stewart
PO Box 7527
Las Vegas, NV 89125
(702)388-6104

SCORE Office (Las Vegas)
300 Las Vegas Blvd. S, Ste. 1100
Las Vegas, NV 89101
(702)388-6104

SCORE Office (Northern Nevada)
SBDC, College of Business
Administration
Univ. of Nevada
Reno, NV 89557-0100
(702)784-4436
Fax: (702)784-4337

New Hampshire

SCORE Office (North Country)
PO Box 34
Berlin, NH 03570
(603)752-1090

SCORE Office (Concord)
143 N. Main St., Rm. 202A
PO Box 1258
Concord, NH 03301
(603)225-1400
Fax: (603)225-1409

SCORE Office (Dover)
299 Central Ave.
Dover, NH 03820

(603)742-2218
Fax: (603)749-6317

SCORE Office (Monadnock)
34 Mechanic St.
Keene, NH 03431-3421
(603)352-0320

SCORE Office (Lakes Region)
67 Water St., Ste. 105
Laconia, NH 03246
(603)524-9168

SCORE Office (Upper Valley)
Citizens Bank Bldg., Rm. 310
20 W. Park St.
Lebanon, NH 03766
(603)448-3491
Fax: (603)448-1908
E-mail: billt@valley.net
Website: http://www.valley.net/~score/

SCORE Office (Merrimack Valley)
275 Chestnut St., Rm. 618
Manchester, NH 03103
(603)666-7561
Fax: (603)666-7925

SCORE Office (Mt. Washington Valley)
PO Box 1066
North Conway, NH 03818
(603)383-0800

SCORE Office (Seacoast)
195 Commerce Way, Unit-A
Portsmouth, NH 03801-3251
(603)433-0575

New Jersey

SCORE Office (Somerset)
Paritan Valley Community College,
Rte. 28
Branchburg, NJ 08807
(908)218-8874
E-mail: nj-score@grizbiz.com.
Website: http://www.nj-score.org/

SCORE Office (Chester)
5 Old Mill Rd.
Chester, NJ 07930
(908)879-7080

SCORE Office (Greater Princeton)
4 A George Washington Dr.
Cranbury, NJ 08512
(609)520-1776

SCORE Office (Freehold)
36 W. Main St.
Freehold, NJ 07728
(908)462-3030
Fax: (908)462-2123

SCORE Office (North West)
Picantinny Innovation Ctr.
3159 Schrader Rd.
Hamburg, NJ 07419
(973)209-8525
Fax: (973)209-7252
E-mail: nj-score@grizbiz.com
Website: http://www.nj-score.org/

SCORE Office (Monmouth)
765 Newman Springs Rd.
Lincroft, NJ 07738
(908)224-2573
E-mail: nj-score@grizbiz.com
Website: http://www.nj-score.org/

SCORE Office (Manalapan)
125 Symmes Dr.
Manalapan, NJ 07726
(908)431-7220

SCORE Office (Jersey City)
2 Gateway Ctr., 4th Fl.
Newark, NJ 07102
(973)645-3982
Fax: (973)645-2375

SCORE Office (Newark)
2 Gateway Center, 15th Fl.
Newark, NJ 07102-5553
(973)645-3982
Fax: (973)645-2375
E-mail: nj-score@grizbiz.com
Website: http://www.nj-score.org

SCORE Office (Bergen County)
327 E. Ridgewood Ave.
Paramus, NJ 07652
(201)599-6090
E-mail: nj-score@grizbiz.com
Website: http://www.nj-score.org/

SCORE Office (Pennsauken)
4900 Rte. 70
Pennsauken, NJ 08109
(609)486-3421

SCORE Office (Southern New Jersey)
4900 Rte. 70
Pennsauken, NJ 08109
(609)486-3421
E-mail: nj-score@grizbiz.com
Website: http://www.nj-score.org/

SCORE Office (Greater Princeton)
216 Rockingham Row
Princeton Forrestal Village
Princeton, NJ 08540
(609)520-1776
Fax: (609)520-9107
E-mail: nj-score@grizbiz.com
Website: http://www.nj-score.org/

SCORE Office (Shrewsbury)
Hwy. 35
Shrewsbury, NJ 07702
(908)842-5995
Fax: (908)219-6140

SCORE Office (Ocean County)
33 Washington St.
Toms River, NJ 08754
(732)505-6033
E-mail: nj-score@grizbiz.com
Website: http://www.nj-score.org/

SCORE Office (Wall)
2700 Allaire Rd.
Wall, NJ 07719
(908)449-8877

SCORE Office (Wayne)
2055 Hamburg Tpke.
Wayne, NJ 07470
(201)831-7788
Fax: (201)831-9112

New Mexico

SCORE Office (Albuquerque)
525 Buena Vista, SE
Albuquerque, NM 87106
(505)272-7999
Fax: (505)272-7963

SCORE Office (Las Cruces)
Loretto Towne Center
505 S. Main St., Ste. 125
Las Cruces, NM 88001
(505)523-5627
Fax: (505)524-2101
E-mail: score.397@zianet.com

SCORE Office (Roswell)
Federal Bldg., Rm. 237
Roswell, NM 88201
(505)625-2112
Fax: (505)623-2545

SCORE Office (Santa Fe)
Montoya Federal Bldg.
120 Federal Place, Rm. 307
Santa Fe, NM 87501
(505)988-6302
Fax: (505)988-6300

New York

SCORE Office (Northeast)
1 Computer Dr. S
Albany, NY 12205
(518)446-1118
Fax: (518)446-1228

SCORE Office (Auburn)
30 South St.
PO Box 675

Auburn, NY 13021
(315)252-7291

SCORE Office (South Tier Binghamton)
Metro Center, 2nd Fl.
49 Court St.
PO Box 995
Binghamton, NY 13902
(607)772-8860

SCORE Office (Queens County City)
12055 Queens Blvd., Rm. 333
Borough Hall, NY 11424
(718)263-8961

SCORE Office (Buffalo)
Federal Bldg., Rm. 1311
111 W. Huron St.
Buffalo, NY 14202
(716)551-4301
Website: http://www2.pcom.net/score/
buf45.html

SCORE Office (Canandaigua)
Chamber of Commerce Bldg.
113 S. Main St.
Canandaigua, NY 14424
(716)394-4400
Fax: (716)394-4546

SCORE Office (Chemung)
333 E. Water St., 4th Fl.
Elmira, NY 14901
(607)734-3358

SCORE Office (Geneva)
Chamber of Commerce Bldg.
PO Box 587
Geneva, NY 14456
(315)789-1776
Fax: (315)789-3993

SCORE Office (Glens Falls)
84 Broad St.
Glens Falls, NY 12801
(518)798-8463
Fax: (518)745-1433

SCORE Office (Orange County)
40 Matthews St.
Goshen, NY 10924
(914)294-8080
Fax: (914)294-6121

SCORE Office (Huntington Area)
151 W. Carver St.
Huntington, NY 11743
(516)423-6100

SCORE Office (Tompkins County)
904 E. Shore Dr.
Ithaca, NY 14850
(607)273-7080

SCORE Office (Long Island City)
120-55 Queens Blvd.
Jamaica, NY 11424
(718)263-8961
Fax: (718)263-9032

SCORE Office (Chatauqua)
101 W. 5th St.
Jamestown, NY 14701
(716)484-1103

SCORE Office (Westchester)
2 Caradon Ln.
Katonah, NY 10536
(914)948-3907
Fax: (914)948-4645
E-mail: score@w-w-w.com
Website: http://w-w-w.com/score/

SCORE Office (Queens County)
Queens Borough Hall
120-55 Queens Blvd. Rm. 333
Kew Gardens, NY 11424
(718)263-8961
Fax: (718)263-9032

SCORE Office (Brookhaven)
3233 Rte. 112
Medford, NY 11763
(516)451-6563
Fax: (516)451-6925

SCORE Office (Melville)
35 Pinelawn Rd., Rm. 207-W
Melville, NY 11747
(516)454-0771

SCORE Office (Nassau County)
400 County Seat Dr., No. 140
Mineola, NY 11501
(516)571-3303
E-mail: Counse1998@aol.com
Website: http://members.aol.com/
Counse1998/Default.htm

SCORE Office (Mt. Vernon)
4 N. 7th Ave.
Mt. Vernon, NY 10550
(914)667-7500

SCORE Office (New York)
26 Federal Plz., Rm. 3100
New York, NY 10278
(212)264-4507
Fax: (212)264-4963
E-mail: score1000@erols.com
Website: http://users.erols.com/
score-nyc/

SCORE Office (Newburgh)
47 Grand St.
Newburgh, NY 12550
(914)562-5100

SCORE Office (Owego)
188 Front St.
Owego, NY 13827
(607)687-2020

SCORE Office (Peekskill)
1 S. Division St.
Peekskill, NY 10566
(914)737-3600
Fax: (914)737-0541

SCORE Office (Penn Yan)
2375 Rte. 14A
Penn Yan, NY 14527
(315)536-3111

SCORE Office (Dutchess)
110 Main St.
Poughkeepsie, NY 12601
(914)454-1700

SCORE Office (Rochester)
601 Keating Federal Bldg., Rm. 410
100 State St.
Rochester, NY 14614
(716)263-6473
Fax: (716)263-3146
Website: http://www.ggw.org/score/

SCORE Office (Saranac Lake)
30 Main St.
Saranac Lake, NY 12983
(315)448-0415

SCORE Office (Suffolk)
286 Main St.
Setauket, NY 11733
(516)751-3886

SCORE Office (Staten Island)
130 Bay St.
Staten Island, NY 10301
(718)727-1221

SCORE Office (Ulster)
Clinton Bldg., Rm. 107
Stone Ridge, NY 12484
(914)687-5035
Fax: (914)687-5015
Website: http://www.scoreulster.org/

SCORE Office (Syracuse)
401 S. Salina, 5th Fl.
Syracuse, NY 13202
(315)471-9393

SCORE Office (Utica)
SUNY Institute of Technology, Route 12
Utica, NY 13504-3050
(315)792-7553

SCORE Office (Watertown)
518 Davidson St.
Watertown, NY 13601

(315)788-1200
Fax: (315)788-8251

North Carolina

SCORE office (Asheboro)
317 E. Dixie Dr.
Asheboro, NC 27203
(336)626-2626
Fax: (336)626-7077

SCORE Office (Asheville)
Federal Bldg., Rm. 259
151 Patton
Asheville, NC 28801-5770
(828)271-4786
Fax: (828)271-4009

SCORE Office (Chapel Hill)
104 S. Estes Dr.
PO Box 2897
Chapel Hill, NC 27514
(919)967-7075

SCORE Office (Coastal Plains)
PO Box 2897
Chapel Hill, NC 27515
(919)967-7075
Fax: (919)968-6874

SCORE Office (Charlotte)
200 N. College St., Ste. A-2015
Charlotte, NC 28202
(704)344-6576
Fax: (704)344-6769
E-mail: CharlotteSCORE47@AOL.com
Website: http://www.charweb.org/
business/score/

SCORE Office (Durham)
411 W. Chapel Hill St.
Durham, NC 27707
(919)541-2171

SCORE Office (Gastonia)
PO Box 2168
Gastonia, NC 28053
(704)864-2621
Fax: (704)854-8723

SCORE Office (Greensboro)
400 W. Market St., Ste. 103
Greensboro, NC 27401-2241
(910)333-5399

SCORE Office (Henderson)
PO Box 917
Henderson, NC 27536
(919)492-2061
Fax: (919)430-0460

SCORE Office (Hendersonville)
Federal Bldg., Rm. 108
W. 4th Ave. & Church St.

Hendersonville, NC 28792
(828)693-8702
E-mail: score@circle.net
Website: http://www.wncguide.com/
score/Welcome.html

SCORE Office (Unifour)
PO Box 1828
Hickory, NC 28603
(704)328-6111

SCORE Office (High Point)
1101 N. Main St.
High Point, NC 27262
(336)882-8625
Fax: (336)889-9499

SCORE Office (Outer Banks)
Collington Rd. and Mustain
Kill Devil Hills, NC 27948
(252)441-8144

SCORE Office (Down East)
312 S. Front St., Ste. 6
New Bern, NC 28560
(252)633-6688
Fax: (252)633-9608

SCORE Office (Kinston)
PO Box 95
New Bern, NC 28561
(919)633-6688

SCORE Office (Raleigh)
Century Post Office Bldg., Ste. 306
300 Federal St. Mall
Raleigh, NC 27601
(919)856-4739
E-mail: jendres@ibm.net
Website: http://www.intrex.net/score96/
score96.htm

SCORE Office (Sanford)
1801 Nash St.
Sanford, NC 27330
(919)774-6442
Fax: (919)776-8739

SCORE Office (Sandhills Area)
1480 Hwy. 15-501
PO Box 458
Southern Pines, NC 28387
(910)692-3926

SCORE Office (Wilmington)
Corps of Engineers Bldg.
96 Darlington Ave., Ste. 207
Wilmington, NC 28403
(910)815-4576
Fax: (910)815-4658

North Dakota

SCORE Office (Bismarck-Mandan)
700 E. Main Ave., 2nd Fl.
PO Box 5509
Bismarck, ND 58506-5509
(701)250-4303

SCORE Office (Fargo)
657 2nd Ave., Rm. 225
Fargo, ND 58108-3083
(701)239-5677

SCORE Office (Upper Red River)
4275 Technology Dr., Rm. 156
Grand Forks, ND 58202-8372
(701)777-3051

SCORE Office (Minot)
100 1st St. SW
Minot, ND 58701-3846
(701)852-6883
Fax: (701)852-6905

Ohio

SCORE Office (Akron)
1 Cascade Plz., 7th Fl.
Akron, OH 44308
(330)379-3163
Fax: (330)379-3164

SCORE Office (Ashland)
Gill Center
47 W. Main St.
Ashland, OH 44805
(419)281-4584

SCORE Office (Canton)
116 Cleveland Ave. NW, Ste. 601
Canton, OH 44702-1720
(330)453-6047

SCORE Office (Chillicothe)
165 S. Paint St.
Chillicothe, OH 45601
(614)772-4530

SCORE Office (Cincinnati)
Ameritrust Bldg., Rm. 850
525 Vine St.
Cincinnati, OH 45202
(513)684-2812
Fax: (513)684-3251
Website: http://
www.score.chapter34.org/

SCORE Office (Cleveland)
Eaton Center, Ste. 620
1100 Superior Ave.
Cleveland, OH 44114-2507
(216)522-4194
Fax: (216)522-4844

SCORE Office (Columbus)
2 Nationwide Plz., Ste. 1400
Columbus, OH 43215-2542
(614)469-2357
Fax: (614)469-2391
E-mail: info@scorecolumbus.org
Website: http://www.scorecolumbus.org/

SCORE Office (Dayton)
Dayton Federal Bldg., Rm. 505
200 W. Second St.
Dayton, OH 45402-1430
(513)225-2887
Fax: (513)225-7667

SCORE Office (Defiance)
615 W. 3rd St.
PO Box 130
Defiance, OH 43512
(419)782-7946

SCORE Office (Findlay)
123 E. Main Cross St.
PO Box 923
Findlay, OH 45840
(419)422-3314

SCORE Office (Lima)
147 N. Main St.
Lima, OH 45801
(419)222-6045
Fax: (419)229-0266

SCORE Office (Mansfield)
55 N. Mulberry St.
Mansfield, OH 44902
(419)522-3211

SCORE Office (Marietta)
Thomas Hall
Marietta, OH 45750
(614)373-0268

SCORE Office (Medina)
County Administrative Bldg.
144 N. Broadway
Medina, OH 44256
(216)764-8650

SCORE Office (Licking County)
50 W. Locust St.
Newark, OH 43055
(614)345-7458

SCORE Office (Salem)
2491 State Rte. 45 S
Salem, OH 44460
(216)332-0361

SCORE Office (Tiffin)
62 S. Washington St.
Tiffin, OH 44883
(419)447-4141
Fax: (419)447-5141

SCORE Office (Toledo)
608 Madison Ave, Ste. 910
Toledo, OH 43624
(419)259-7598
Fax: (419)259-6460

SCORE Office (Heart of Ohio)
377 W. Liberty St.
Wooster, OH 44691
(330)262-5735
Fax: (330)262-5745

SCORE Office (Youngstown)
306 Williamson Hall
Youngstown, OH 44555
(330)746-2687

Oklahoma

SCORE Office (Anadarko)
PO Box 366
Anadarko, OK 73005
(405)247-6651

SCORE Office (Ardmore)
410 W. Main
Ardmore, OK 73401
(580)226-2620

SCORE Office (Northeast Oklahoma)
210 S. Main
Grove, OK 74344
(918)787-2796
Fax: (918)787-2796
E-mail: Score595@greencis.net

SCORE Office (Lawton)
4500 W. Lee Blvd., Bldg. 100, Ste. 107
Lawton, OK 73505
(580)353-8727
Fax: (580)250-5677

SCORE Office (Oklahoma City)
210 Park Ave., No. 1300
Oklahoma City, OK 73102
(405)231-5163
Fax: (405)231-4876
E-mail: score212@usa.net

SCORE Office (Stillwater)
439 S. Main
Stillwater, OK 74074
(405)372-5573
Fax: (405)372-4316

SCORE Office (Tulsa)
616 S. Boston, Ste. 406
Tulsa, OK 74119
(918)581-7462
Fax: (918)581-6908
Website: http://www.ionet.net/~tulscore/

Oregon

SCORE Office (Bend)
63085 N. Hwy. 97
Bend, OR 97701
(541)923-2849
Fax: (541)330-6900

SCORE Office (Willamette)
1401 Willamette St.
PO Box 1107
Eugene, OR 97401-4003
(541)465-6600
Fax: (541)484-4942

SCORE Office (Florence)
3149 Oak St.
Florence, OR 97439
(503)997-8444
Fax: (503)997-8448

SCORE Office (Southern Oregon)
33 N. Central Ave., Ste. 216
Medford, OR 97501
(541)776-4220
E-mail: pgr134f@prodigy.com

SCORE Office (Portland)
1515 SW 5th Ave., Ste. 1050
Portland, OR 97201
(503)326-3441
Fax: (503)326-2808
E-mail: gr134@prodigy.com

SCORE Office (Salem)
416 State St. (corner of Liberty)
Salem, OR 97301
(503)370-2896

Pennsylvania

SCORE Office (Altoona-Blair)
1212 12th Ave.
Altoona, PA 16601-3493
(814)943-8151

SCORE Office (Lehigh Valley)
Rauch Bldg. 37
Lehigh University
621 Taylor St.
Bethlehem, PA 18015
(610)758-4496
Fax: (610)758-5205

SCORE Office (Butler County)
100 N. Main St.
PO Box 1082
Butler, PA 16003
(412)283-2222
Fax: (412)283-0224

SCORE Office (Harrisburg)
4211 Trindle Rd.
Camp Hill, PA 17011

(717)761-4304
Fax: (717)761-4315

SCORE Office (Cumberland Valley)
75 S. 2nd St.
Chambersburg, PA 17201
(717)264-2935

SCORE Office (Monroe County-Stroudsburg)
556 Main St.
East Stroudsburg, PA 18301
(717)421-4433

SCORE Office (Erie)
120 W. 9th St.
Erie, PA 16501
(814)871-5650
Fax: (814)871-7530

SCORE Office (Bucks County)
409 Hood Blvd.
Fairless Hills, PA 19030
(215)943-8850
Fax: (215)943-7404

SCORE Office (Hanover)
146 Broadway
Hanover, PA 17331
(717)637-6130
Fax: (717)637-9127

SCORE Office (Harrisburg)
100 Chestnut, Ste. 309
Harrisburg, PA 17101
(717)782-3874

SCORE Office (East Montgomery County)
Baederwood Shopping Center
1653 The Fairways, Ste. 204
Jenkintown, PA 19046
(215)885-3027

SCORE Office (Kittanning)
2 Butler Rd.
Kittanning, PA 16201
(412)543-1305
Fax: (412)543-6206

SCORE Office (Lancaster)
118 W. Chestnut St.
Lancaster, PA 17603
(717)397-3092

SCORE Office (Westmoreland County)
300 Fraser Purchase Rd.
Latrobe, PA 15650-2690
(412)539-7505
Fax: (412)539-1850

SCORE Office (Lebanon)
252 N. 8th St.
PO Box 899

Lebanon, PA 17042-0899
(717)273-3727
Fax: (717)273-7940

SCORE Office (Lewistown)
3 W. Monument Sq., Ste. 204
Lewistown, PA 17044
(717)248-6713
Fax: (717)248-6714

SCORE Office (Delaware County)
602 E. Baltimore Pike
Media, PA 19063
(610)565-3677
Fax: (610)565-1606

SCORE Office (Milton Area)
112 S. Front St.
Milton, PA 17847
(717)742-7341
Fax: (717)792-2008

SCORE Office (Mon-Valley)
435 Donner Ave.
Monessen, PA 15062
(412)684-4277
Fax: (412)684-7688

SCORE Office (Monroeville)
William Penn Plaza
2790 Mosside Blvd., Ste. 295
Monroeville, PA 15146
(412)856-0622
Fax: (412)856-1030

SCORE Office (Airport Area)
986 Brodhead Rd.
Moon Township, PA 15108-2398
(412)264-6270
Fax: (412)264-1575

SCORE Office (Northeast)
8601 E. Roosevelt Blvd.
Philadelphia, PA 19152
(215)332-3400
Fax: (215)332-6050

SCORE Office (Philadelphia)
1315 Walnut St., Ste. 500
Philadelphia, PA 19107
(215)790-5050
Fax: (215)790-5057
E-mail: score46@bellatlantic.net
Website: http://www.pgweb.net/score46/

SCORE Office (Pittsburgh)
1000 Liberty Ave., Rm. 1122
Pittsburgh, PA 15222
(412)395-6560
Fax: (412)395-6562

SCORE Office (Tri-County)
801 N. Charlotte St.
Pottstown, PA 19464
(610)327-2673

SCORE Office (Reading)
601 Penn St.
Reading, PA 19601
(610)376-3497

SCORE Office (Scranton)
Oppenheim Bldg.
116 N. Washington Ave., Ste. 650
Scranton, PA 18503
(717)347-4611
Fax: (717)347-4611

SCORE Office (Central Pennsylvania)
200 Innovation Blvd., Ste. 242-B
State College, PA 16803
(814)234-9415
Fax: (814)238-9686
Website: http://countrystore.org/
business/score.htm

SCORE Office (Monroe-Stroudsburg)
556 Main St.
Stroudsburg, PA 18360
(717)421-4433

SCORE Office (Uniontown)
Federal Bldg.
Pittsburg St.
PO Box 2065 DTS
Uniontown, PA 15401
(412)437-4222
E-mail: uniontownscore@lcsys.net

SCORE Office (Warren County)
315 2nd Ave.
Warren, PA 16365
(814)723-9017

SCORE Office (Waynesboro)
323 E. Main St.
Waynesboro, PA 17268
(717)762-7123
Fax: (717)962-7124

SCORE Office (Chester County)
Government Service Center, Ste. 281
601 Westtown Rd.
West Chester, PA 19382-4538
(610)344-6910
Fax: (610)344-6919
E-mail: score@locke.ccil.org

SCORE Office (Wilkes-Barre)
7 N. Wilkes-Barre Blvd.
Wilkes Barre, PA 18702-5241
(717)826-6502
Fax: (717)826-6287

SCORE Office (North Central Pennsylvania)
240 W. 3rd St., Rm. 227
PO Box 725
Williamsport, PA 17703

(717)322-3720
Fax: (717)322-1607
E-mail: score234@mail.csrlink.net
Website: http://www.lycoming.org/score/

SCORE Office (York)
Cyber Center
2101 Pennsylvania Ave.
York, PA 17404
(717)845-8830
Fax: (717)854-9333

Puerto Rico

SCORE Office (Puerto Rico & Virgin Islands)
PO Box 12383-96
San Juan, PR 00914-0383
(787)726-8040
Fax: (787)726-8135

Rhode Island

SCORE Office (Barrington)
281 County Rd.
Barrington, RI 02806
(401)247-1920
Fax: (401)247-3763

SCORE Office (Woonsocket)
640 Washington Hwy.
Lincoln, RI 02865
(401)334-1000
Fax: (401)334-1009

SCORE Office (Wickford)
8045 Post Rd.
North Kingstown, RI 02852
(401)295-5566
Fax: (401)295-8987

SCORE Office (J.G.E. Knight)
380 Westminster St.
Providence, RI 02903
(401)528-4571
Fax: (401)528-4539
Website: http://www.riscore.org

SCORE Office (Warwick)
3288 Post Rd.
Warwick, RI 02886
(401)732-1100
Fax: (401)732-1101

SCORE Office (Westerly)
74 Post Rd.
Westerly, RI 02891
(401)596-7761
800-732-7636
Fax: (401)596-2190

South Carolina

SCORE Office (Aiken)
PO Box 892
Aiken, SC 29802
(803)641-1111
800-542-4536
Fax: (803)641-4174

SCORE Office (Anderson)
Anderson Mall
3130 N. Main St.
Anderson, SC 29621
(864)224-0453

SCORE Office (Coastal)
284 King St.
Charleston, SC 29401
(803)727-4778
Fax: (803)853-2529

SCORE Office (Midlands)
Strom Thurmond Bldg., Rm. 358
1835 Assembly St., Rm 358
Columbia, SC 29201
(803)765-5131
Fax: (803)765-5962
Website: http://www.scoremidlands.org/

SCORE Office (Piedmont)
Federal Bldg., Rm. B-02
300 E. Washington St.
Greenville, SC 29601
(864)271-3638

SCORE Office (Greenwood)
PO Drawer 1467
Greenwood, SC 29648
(864)223-8357

SCORE Office (Hilton Head Island)
52 Savannah Trail
Hilton Head, SC 29926
(803)785-7107
Fax: (803)785-7110

SCORE Office (Grand Strand)
937 Broadway
Myrtle Beach, SC 29577
(803)918-1079
Fax: (803)918-1083
E-mail: score381@aol.com

SCORE Office (Spartanburg)
PO Box 1636
Spartanburg, SC 29304
(864)594-5000
Fax: (864)594-5055

South Dakota

SCORE Office (West River)
Rushmore Plz. Civic Ctr.
444 Mount Rushmore Rd., No. 209

Rapid City, SD 57701
(605)394-5311
E-mail: score@gwtc.net

SCORE Office (Sioux Falls)
First Financial Center
110 S. Phillips Ave., Ste. 200
Sioux Falls, SD 57104-6727
(605)330-4231
Fax: (605)330-4231

Tennessee

SCORE Office (Chattanooga)
Federal Bldg., Rm. 26
900 Georgia Ave.
Chattanooga, TN 37402
(423)752-5190
Fax: (423)752-5335

SCORE Office (Cleveland)
PO Box 2275
Cleveland, TN 37320
(423)472-6587
Fax: (423)472-2019

SCORE Office (Upper Cumberland Center)
1225 S. Willow Ave.
Cookeville, TN 38501
(615)432-4111
Fax: (615)432-6010

SCORE Office (Unicoi County)
PO Box 713
Erwin, TN 37650
(423)743-3000
Fax: (423)743-0942

SCORE Office (Greeneville)
115 Academy St.
Greeneville, TN 37743
(423)638-4111
Fax: (423)638-5345

SCORE Office (Jackson)
194 Auditorium St.
Jackson, TN 38301
(901)423-2200

SCORE Office (Northeast Tennessee)
1st Tennessee Bank Bldg.
2710 S. Roan St., Ste. 584
Johnson City, TN 37601
(423)929-7686
Fax: (423)461-8052

SCORE Office (Kingsport)
151 E. Main St.
Kingsport, TN 37662
(423)392-8805

SCORE Office (Greater Knoxville)
Farragot Bldg., Ste. 224
530 S. Gay St.
Knoxville, TN 37902
(423)545-4203
E-mail: scoreknox@ntown.com
Website: http://www.scoreknox.org/

SCORE Office (Maryville)
201 S. Washington St.
Maryville, TN 37804-5728
(423)983-2241
800-525-6834
Fax: (423)984-1386

SCORE Office (Memphis)
Federal Bldg., Ste. 390
167 N. Main St.
Memphis, TN 38103
(901)544-3588

SCORE Office (Nashville)
50 Vantage Way, Ste. 201
Nashville, TN 37228-1500
(615)736-7621

Texas

SCORE Office (Abilene)
2106 Federal Post Office and Court Bldg.
Abilene, TX 79601
(915)677-1857

SCORE Office (Austin)
2501 S. Congress
Austin, TX 78701
(512)442-7235
Fax: (512)442-7528

SCORE Office (Golden Triangle)
450 Boyd St.
Beaumont, TX 77704
(409)838-6581
Fax: (409)833-6718

SCORE Office (Brownsville)
3505 Boca Chica Blvd., Ste. 305
Brownsville, TX 78521
(210)541-4508

SCORE Office (Brazos Valley)
3000 Briarcrest, Ste. 302
Bryan, TX 77802
(409)776-8876
E-mail: 102633.2612@compuserve.com

SCORE Office (Cleburne)
Watergarden Pl., 9th Fl., Ste. 400
Cleburne, TX 76031
(817)871-6002

SCORE Office (Corpus Christi)
651 Upper North Broadway, Ste. 654
Corpus Christi, TX 78477

(512)888-4322
Fax: (512)888-3418

SCORE Office (Dallas)
6260 E. Mockingbird
Dallas, TX 75214-2619
(214)828-2471
Fax: (214)821-8033

SCORE Office (El Paso)
10 Civic Center Plaza
El Paso, TX 79901
(915)534-0541
Fax: (915)534-0513

SCORE Office (Bedford)
100 E. 15th St., Ste. 400
Ft. Worth, TX 76102
(817)871-6002

SCORE Office (Ft. Worth)
100 E. 15th St., No. 24
Ft. Worth, TX 76102
(817)871-6002
Fax: (817)871-6031
E-mail: fwbac@onramp.net

SCORE Office (Garland)
2734 W. Kingsley Rd.
Garland, TX 75041
(214)271-9224

SCORE Office (Granbury Chamber of Commerce)
416 S. Morgan
Granbury, TX 76048
(817)573-1622
Fax: (817)573-0805

SCORE Office (Lower Rio Grande Valley)
222 E. Van Buren, Ste. 500
Harlingen, TX 78550
(956)427-8533
Fax: (956)427-8537

SCORE Office (Houston)
9301 Southwest Fwy., Ste. 550
Houston, TX 77074
(713)773-6565
Fax: (713)773-6550

SCORE Office (Irving)
3333 N. MacArthur Blvd., Ste. 100
Irving, TX 75062
(214)252-8484
Fax: (214)252-6710

SCORE Office (Lubbock)
1205 Texas Ave., Rm. 411D
Lubbock, TX 79401
(806)472-7462
Fax: (806)472-7487

SCORE Office (Midland)
Post Office Annex
200 E. Wall St., Rm. P121
Midland, TX 79701
(915)687-2649

SCORE Office (Orange)
1012 Green Ave.
Orange, TX 77630-5620
(409)883-3536
800-528-4906
Fax: (409)886-3247

SCORE Office (Plano)
1200 E. 15th St.
PO Drawer 940287
Plano, TX 75094-0287
(214)424-7547
Fax: (214)422-5182

SCORE Office (Port Arthur)
4749 Twin City Hwy., Ste. 300
Port Arthur, TX 77642
(409)963-1107
Fax: (409)963-3322

SCORE Office (Richardson)
411 Belle Grove
Richardson, TX 75080
(214)234-4141
800-777-8001
Fax: (214)680-9103

SCORE Office (San Antonio)
Federal Bldg., Rm. A527
727 E. Durango
San Antonio, TX 78206
(210)472-5931
Fax: (210)472-5935

SCORE Office (Texarkana State College)
819 State Line Ave.
Texarkana, TX 75501
(903)792-7191
Fax: (903)793-4304

SCORE Office (East Texas)
RTDC
1530 SSW Loop 323, Ste. 100
Tyler, TX 75701
(903)510-2975
Fax: (903)510-2978

SCORE Office (Waco)
401 Franklin Ave.
Waco, TX 76701
(817)754-8898
Fax: (817)756-0776
Website: http://www.brc-waco.com/

SCORE Office (Wichita Falls)
Hamilton Bldg.
900 8th St.

Wichita Falls, TX 76307
(940)723-2741
Fax: (940)723-8773

Utah

SCORE Office (Northern Utah)
160 N. Main
Logan, UT 84321
(435)746-2269

SCORE Office (Ogden)
1701 E. Windsor Dr.
Ogden, UT 84604
(801)629-8613
E-mail: score158@netscape.net

SCORE Office (Central Utah)
1071 E. Windsor Dr.
Provo, UT 84604
(801)373-8660

SCORE Office (Southern Utah)
225 South 700 East
St. George, UT 84770
(435)652-7751

SCORE Office (Salt Lake)
310 S Main St.
Salt Lake City, UT 84101
(801)746-2269
Fax: (801)746-2273

Vermont

SCORE Office (Champlain Valley)
Winston Prouty Federal Bldg.
11 Lincoln St., Rm. 106
Essex Junction, VT 05452
(802)951-6762

SCORE Office (Montpelier)
87 State St., Rm. 205
PO Box 605
Montpelier, VT 05601
(802)828-4422
Fax: (802)828-4485

SCORE Office (Marble Valley)
256 N. Main St.
Rutland, VT 05701-2413
(802)773-9147

SCORE Office (Northeast Kingdom)
20 Main St.
PO Box 904
St. Johnsbury, VT 05819
(802)748-5101

Virgin Islands

SCORE Office (St. Croix)
United Plaza Shopping Center
PO Box 4010, Christiansted

St. Croix, VI 00822
(809)778-5380

SCORE Office (St. Thomas-St. John)
Federal Bldg., Rm. 21
Veterans Dr.
St. Thomas, VI 00801
(809)774-8530

Virginia

SCORE Office (Arlington)
2009 N. 14th St., Ste. 111
Arlington, VA 22201
(703)525-2400

SCORE Office (Blacksburg)
141 Jackson St.
Blacksburg, VA 24060
(540)552-4061

SCORE Office (Bristol)
20 Volunteer Pkwy.
Bristol, VA 24203
(540)989-4850

SCORE Office (Central Virginia)
1001 E. Market St., Ste. 101
Charlottesville, VA 22902
(804)295-6712
Fax: (804)295-7066

SCORE Office (Alleghany Satellite)
241 W. Main St.
Covington, VA 24426
(540)962-2178
Fax: (540)962-2179

SCORE Office (Central Fairfax)
3975 University Dr., Ste. 350
Fairfax, VA 22030
(703)591-2450

SCORE Office (Falls Church)
PO Box 491
Falls Church, VA 22040
(703)532-1050
Fax: (703)237-7904

SCORE Office (Glenns)
Glenns Campus
Box 287
Glenns, VA 23149
(804)693-9650

SCORE Office (Peninsula)
6 Manhattan Sq.
PO Box 7269
Hampton, VA 23666
(757)766-2000
Fax: (757)865-0339
E-mail: score100@seva.net

SCORE Office (Tri-Cities)
108 N. Main St.
Hopewell, VA 23860
(804)458-5536

SCORE Office (Lynchburg)
Federal Bldg.
1100 Main St.
Lynchburg, VA 24504-1714
(804)846-3235

SCORE Office (Greater Prince William)
8963 Center St
Manassas, VA 20110
(703)368-4813
Fax: (703)368-4733

SCORE Office (Martinsvile)
115 Broad St.
Martinsville, VA 24112-0709
(540)632-6401
Fax: (540)632-5059

SCORE Office (Hampton Roads)
Federal Bldg., Rm. 737
200 Grandby St.
Norfolk, VA 23510
(757)441-3733
Fax: (757)441-3733
E-mail: scorehr60@juno.com

SCORE Office (Norfolk)
Federal Bldg., Rm. 737
200 Granby St.
Norfolk, VA 23510
(757)441-3733
Fax: (757)441-3733

SCORE Office (Virginia Beach)
Chamber of Commerce
200 Grandby St., Rm 737
Norfolk, VA 23510
(804)441-3733

SCORE Office (Radford)
1126 Norwood St.
Radford, VA 24141
(540)639-2202

SCORE Office (Richmond)
Federal Bldg.
400 N. 8th St., Ste. 1150
PO Box 10126
Richmond, VA 23240-0126
(804)771-2400
Fax: (804)771-8018
E-mail: scorechapter12@yahoo.com
Website: http://www.cvco.org/score/

SCORE Office (Roanoke)
Federal Bldg., Rm. 716
250 Franklin Rd.
Roanoke, VA 24011

(540)857-2834
Fax: (540)857-2043
E-mail: scorerva@juno.com
Website: http://hometown.aol.com/
scorerv/Index.html

SCORE Office (Fairfax)
8391 Old Courthouse Rd., Ste. 300
Vienna, VA 22182
(703)749-0400

SCORE Office (Greater Vienna)
513 Maple Ave. West
Vienna, VA 22180
(703)281-1333
Fax: (703)242-1482

SCORE Office (Shenandoah Valley)
301 W. Main St.
Waynesboro, VA 22980
(540)949-8203
Fax: (540)949-7740
E-mail: score427@intelos.net

SCORE Office (Williamsburg)
201 Penniman Rd.
Williamsburg, VA 23185
(757)229-6511
E-mail: wacc@williamsburgcc.com

SCORE Office (Northern Virginia)
1360 S. Pleasant Valley Rd.
Winchester, VA 22601
(540)662-4118

Washington

SCORE Office (Gray's Harbor)
506 Duffy St.
Aberdeen, WA 98520
(360)532-1924
Fax: (360)533-7945

SCORE Office (Bellingham)
101 E. Holly St.
Bellingham, WA 98225
(360)676-3307

SCORE Office (Everett)
2702 Hoyt Ave.
Everett, WA 98201-3556
(206)259-8000

SCORE Office (Gig Harbor)
3125 Judson St.
Gig Harbor, WA 98335
(206)851-6865

SCORE Office (Kennewick)
PO Box 6986
Kennewick, WA 99336
(509)736-0510

SCORE Office (Puyallup)
322 2nd St. SW
PO Box 1298
Puyallup, WA 98371
(206)845-6755
Fax: (206)848-6164

SCORE Office (Seattle)
1200 6th Ave., Ste. 1700
Seattle, WA 98101
(206)553-7320
Fax: (206)553-7044
E-mail: score55@aol.com
Website: http://www.scn.org/civic/
score-online/index55.html

SCORE Office (Spokane)
801 W. Riverside Ave., No. 240
Spokane, WA 99201
(509)353-2820
Fax: (509)353-2600
E-mail: score@dmi.net
Website: http://www.dmi.net/score/

SCORE Office (Clover Park)
PO Box 1933
Tacoma, WA 98401-1933
(206)627-2175

SCORE Office (Tacoma)
1101 Pacific Ave.
Tacoma, WA 98402
(253)274-1288
Fax: (253)274-1289

SCORE Office (Fort Vancouver)
1701 Broadway, S-1
Vancouver, WA 98663
(360)699-1079

SCORE Office (Walla Walla)
500 Tausick Way
Walla Walla, WA 99362
(509)527-4681

SCORE Office (Mid-Columbia)
1113 S. 14th Ave.
Yakima, WA 98907
(509)574-4944
Fax: (509)574-2943
Website: http://www.ellensburg.com/
~score/

West Virginia

SCORE Office (Charleston)
1116 Smith St.
Charleston, WV 25301
(304)347-5463
E-mail: score256@juno.com

SCORE Office (Virginia Street)
1116 Smith St., Ste. 302
Charleston, WV 25301
(304)347-5463

SCORE Office (Marion County)
PO Box 208
Fairmont, WV 26555-0208
(304)363-0486

SCORE Office (Upper Monongahela Valley)
1000 Technology Dr., Ste. 1111
Fairmont, WV 26555
(304)363-0486
E-mail: score537@hotmail.com

SCORE Office (Huntington)
1101 6th Ave., Ste. 220
Huntington, WV 25701-2309
(304)523-4092

SCORE Office (Wheeling)
1310 Market St.
Wheeling, WV 26003
(304)233-2575
Fax: (304)233-1320

Wisconsin

SCORE Office (Fox Cities)
227 S. Walnut St.
Appleton, WI 54913
(920)734-7101
Fax: (920)734-7161

SCORE Office (Beloit)
136 W. Grand Ave., Ste. 100
PO Box 717
Beloit, WI 53511
(608)365-8835
Fax: (608)365-9170

SCORE Office (Eau Claire)
Federal Bldg., Rm. B11
510 S. Barstow St.
Eau Claire, WI 54701
(715)834-1573
E-mail: score@ecol.net
Website: http://www.ecol.net/~score/

SCORE Office (Fond du Lac)
207 N. Main St.
Fond du Lac, WI 54935
(414)921-9500
Fax: (414)921-9559

SCORE Office (Green Bay)
835 Potts Ave.
Green Bay, WI 54304
(414)496-8930
Fax: (414)496-6009

SCORE Office (Janesville)
20 S. Main St., Ste. 11
PO Box 8008
Janesville, WI 53547
(608)757-3160
Fax: (608)757-3170

SCORE Office (La Crosse)
712 Main St.
La Crosse, WI 54602-0219
(608)784-4880

SCORE Office (Madison)
505 S. Rosa Rd.
Madison, WI 53719
(608)441-2820

SCORE Office (Manitowoc)
1515 Memorial Dr.
PO Box 903
Manitowoc, WI 54221-0903
(414)684-5575
Fax: (414)684-1915

**SCORE Office
(Milwaukee)**
310 W. Wisconsin Ave., Ste. 425
Milwaukee, WI 53203
(414)297-3942
Fax: (414)297-1377

**SCORE Office
(Central Wisconsin)**
1224 Lindbergh Ave.
Stevens Point, WI 54481
(715)344-7729

SCORE Office (Superior)
Superior Business Center Inc.
1423 N. 8th St.
Superior, WI 54880
(715)394-7388
Fax: (715)393-7414

SCORE Office (Waukesha)
223 Wisconsin Ave.
Waukesha, WI 53186-4926
(414)542-4249

SCORE Office (Wausau)
300 3rd St., Ste. 200
Wausau, WI 54402-6190
(715)845-6231

**SCORE Office
(Wisconsin Rapids)**
2240 Kingston Rd.
Wisconsin Rapids, WI 54494
(715)423-1830

Wyoming

SCORE Office (Casper)
Federal Bldg., No. 2215
100 East B St.
Casper, WY 82602
(307)261-6529
Fax: (307)261-6530

Venture capital & financing companies

This section contains a listing of financing and loan companies in the United States and Canada. These listing are arranged alphabetically by country, then by state or province, then by city, then by organization name.

Canada

Alberta

Launchworks Inc.
1902J 11th St., S.E.
Calgary, AB, Canada T2G 3G2
(403)269-1119
Fax: (403)269-1141
Website: http://www.launchworks.com

Native Venture Capital Company, Inc.
21 Artist View Point, Box 7
Site 25, RR 12
Calgary, AB, Canada T3E 6W3
(903)208-5380

Miralta Capital Inc.
4445 Calgary Trail South
888 Terrace Plaza Alberta
Edmonton, AB, Canada T6H 5R7
(780)438-3535
Fax: (780)438-3129

Vencap Equities Alberta Ltd.
10180-101st St., Ste. 1980
Edmonton, AB, Canada T5J 3S4
(403)420-1171
Fax: (403)429-2541

British Columbia

Discovery Capital
5th Fl., 1199 West Hastings
Vancouver, BC, Canada V6E 3T5
(604)683-3000
Fax: (604)662-3457
E-mail: info@discoverycapital.com
Website: http://www.discoverycapital.com

Greenstone Venture Partners
1177 West Hastings St.
Ste. 400
Vancouver, BC, Canada V6E 2K3
(604)717-1977
Fax: (604)717-1976
Website: http://www.greenstonevc.com

Growthworks Capital
2600-1055 West Georgia St.
Box 11170 Royal Centre

Vancouver, BC, Canada V6E 3R5
(604)895-7259
Fax: (604)669-7605
Website: http://www.wofund.com

MDS Discovery Venture Management, Inc.
555 W. Eighth Ave., Ste. 305
Vancouver, BC, Canada V5Z 1C6
(604)872-8464
Fax: (604)872-2977
E-mail: info@mds-ventures.com

Ventures West Management Inc.
1285 W. Pender St., Ste. 280
Vancouver, BC, Canada V6E 4B1
(604)688-9495
Fax: (604)687-2145
Website: http://www.ventureswest.com

Nova Scotia

ACF Equity Atlantic Inc.
Purdy's Wharf Tower II
Ste. 2106
Halifax, NS, Canada B3J 3R7
(902)421-1965
Fax: (902)421-1808

Montgomerie, Huck & Co.
146 Bluenose Dr.
PO Box 538
Lunenburg, NS, Canada B0J 2C0
(902)634-7125
Fax: (902)634-7130

Ontario

IPS Industrial Promotion Services Ltd.
60 Columbia Way, Ste. 720
Markham, ON, Canada L3R 0C9
(905)475-9400
Fax: (905)475-5003

Betwin Investments Inc.
Box 23110
Sault Ste. Marie, ON, Canada P6A 6W6
(705)253-0744
Fax: (705)253-0744

Bailey & Company, Inc.
594 Spadina Ave.
Toronto, ON, Canada M5S 2H4
(416)921-6930
Fax: (416)925-4670

BCE Capital
200 Bay St.
South Tower, Ste. 3120
Toronto, ON, Canada M5J 2J2
(416)815-0078
Fax: (416)941-1073
Website: http://www.bcecapital.com

Castlehill Ventures

55 University Ave., Ste. 500
Toronto, ON, Canada M5J 2H7
(416)862-8574
Fax: (416)862-8875

CCFL Mezzanine Partners of Canada

70 University Ave.
Ste. 1450
Toronto, ON, Canada M5J 2M4
(416)977-1450
Fax: (416)977-6764
E-mail: info@ccfl.com
Website: http://www.ccfl.com

Celtic House International

100 Simcoe St., Ste. 100
Toronto, ON, Canada M5H 3G2
(416)542-2436
Fax: (416)542-2435
Website: http://www.celtic-house.com

Clairvest Group Inc.

22 St. Clair Ave. East
Ste. 1700
Toronto, ON, Canada M4T 2S3
(416)925-9270
Fax: (416)925-5753

Crosbie & Co., Inc.

One First Canadian Place
9th Fl.
PO Box 116
Toronto, ON, Canada M5X 1A4
(416)362-7726
Fax: (416)362-3447
E-mail: info@crosbieco.com
Website: http://www.crosbieco.com

Drug Royalty Corp.

Eight King St. East
Ste. 202
Toronto, ON, Canada M5C 1B5
(416)863-1865
Fax: (416)863-5161

Grieve, Horner, Brown & Asculai

8 King St. E, Ste. 1704
Toronto, ON, Canada M5C 1B5
(416)362-7668
Fax: (416)362-7660

Jefferson Partners

77 King St. West
Ste. 4010
PO Box 136
Toronto, ON, Canada M5K 1H1
(416)367-1533
Fax: (416)367-5827
Website: http://www.jefferson.com

J.L. Albright Venture Partners

Canada Trust Tower, 161 Bay St.
Ste. 4440
PO Box 215
Toronto, ON, Canada M5J 2S1
(416)367-2440
Fax: (416)367-4604
Website: http://www.jlaventures.com

McLean Watson Capital Inc.

One First Canadian Place
Ste. 1410
PO Box 129
Toronto, ON, Canada M5X 1A4
(416)363-2000
Fax: (416)363-2010
Website: http://www.mcleanwatson.com

Middlefield Capital Fund

One First Canadian Place
85th Fl.
PO Box 192
Toronto, ON, Canada M5X 1A6
(416)362-0714
Fax: (416)362-7925
Website: http://www.middlefield.com

Mosaic Venture Partners

24 Duncan St.
Ste. 300
Toronto, ON, Canada M5V 3M6
(416)597-8889
Fax: (416)597-2345

Onex Corp.

161 Bay St.
PO Box 700
Toronto, ON, Canada M5J 2S1
(416)362-7711
Fax: (416)362-5765

Penfund Partners Inc.

145 King St. West
Ste. 1920
Toronto, ON, Canada M5H 1J8
(416)865-0300
Fax: (416)364-6912
Website: http://www.penfund.com

Primaxis Technology Ventures Inc.

1 Richmond St. West, 8th Fl.
Toronto, ON, Canada M5H 3W4
(416)313-5210
Fax: (416)313-5218
Website: http://www.primaxis.com

Priveq Capital Funds

240 Duncan Mill Rd., Ste. 602
Toronto, ON, Canada M3B 3P1
(416)447-3330
Fax: (416)447-3331
E-mail: priveq@sympatico.ca

Roynat Ventures

40 King St. West, 26th Fl.
Toronto, ON, Canada M5H 1H1
(416)933-2667
Fax: (416)933-2783
Website: http://www.roynatcapital.com

Tera Capital Corp.

366 Adelaide St. East, Ste. 337
Toronto, ON, Canada M5A 3X9
(416)368-1024
Fax: (416)368-1427

Working Ventures Canadian Fund Inc.

250 Bloor St. East, Ste. 1600
Toronto, ON, Canada M4W 1E6
(416)934-7718
Fax: (416)929-0901
Website: http://www.workingventures.ca

Quebec

Altamira Capital Corp.

202 University
Niveau de Maisoneuve, Bur. 201
Montreal, QC, Canada H3A 2A5
(514)499-1656
Fax: (514)499-9570

Federal Business Development Bank

Venture Capital Division
Five Place Ville Marie, Ste. 600
Montreal, QC, Canada H3B 5E7
(514)283-1896
Fax: (514)283-5455

Hydro-Quebec Capitech Inc.

75 Boul, Rene Levesque Quest
Montreal, QC, Canada H2Z 1A4
(514)289-4783
Fax: (514)289-5420
Website: http://www.hqcapitech.com

Investissement Desjardins

2 complexe Desjardins
C.P. 760
Montreal, QC, Canada H5B 1B8
(514)281-7131
Fax: (514)281-7808
Website: http://www.desjardins.com/id

Marleau Lemire Inc.

One Place Ville-Marie, Ste. 3601
Montreal, QC, Canada H3B 3P2
(514)877-3800
Fax: (514)875-6415

Speirs Consultants Inc.

365 Stanstead
Montreal, QC, Canada H3R 1X5
(514)342-3858
Fax: (514)342-1977

Tecnocap Inc.
4028 Marlowe
Montreal, QC, Canada H4A 3M2
(514)483-6009
Fax: (514)483-6045
Website: http://www.technocap.com

Telsoft Ventures
1000, Rue de la Gauchetiere
Quest, 25eme Etage
Montreal, QC, Canada H3B 4W5
(514)397-8450
Fax: (514)397-8451

Saskatchewan

Saskatchewan Government Growth Fund
1801 Hamilton St., Ste. 1210
Canada Trust Tower
Regina, SK, Canada S4P 4B4
(306)787-2994
Fax: (306)787-2086

United states

Alabama

FHL Capital Corp.
600 20th Street North
Suite 350
Birmingham, AL 35203
(205)328-3098
Fax: (205)323-0001

Harbert Management Corp.
One Riverchase Pkwy. South
Birmingham, AL 35244
(205)987-5500
Fax: (205)987-5707
Website: http://www.harbert.net

Jefferson Capital Fund
PO Box 13129
Birmingham, AL 35213
(205)324-7709

Private Capital Corp.
100 Brookwood Pl., 4th Fl.
Birmingham, AL 35209
(205)879-2722
Fax: (205)879-5121

21st Century Health Ventures
One Health South Pkwy.
Birmingham, AL 35243
(256)268-6250
Fax: (256)970-8928

FJC Growth Capital Corp.
200 W. Side Sq., Ste. 340
Huntsville, AL 35801
(256)922-2918
Fax: (256)922-2909

Hickory Venture Capital Corp.
301 Washington St. NW
Suite 301
Huntsville, AL 35801
(256)539-1931
Fax: (256)539-5130
E-mail: hvcc@hvcc.com
Website: http://www.hvcc.com

Southeastern Technology Fund
7910 South Memorial Pkwy., Ste. F
Huntsville, AL 35802
(256)883-8711
Fax: (256)883-8558

Cordova Ventures
4121 Carmichael Rd., Ste. 301
Montgomery, AL 36106
(334)271-6011
Fax: (334)260-0120
Website: http://www.cordovaventures
.com

**Small Business Clinic of Alabama/AG
Bartholomew & Associates**
PO Box 231074
Montgomery, AL 36123-1074
(334)284-3640

Arizona

Miller Capital Corp.
4909 E. McDowell Rd.
Phoenix, AZ 85008
(602)225-0504
Fax: (602)225-9024
Website: http://www.themillergroup.com

The Columbine Venture Funds
9449 North 90th St., Ste. 200
Scottsdale, AZ 85258
(602)661-9222
Fax: (602)661-6262

Koch Ventures
17767 N. Perimeter Dr., Ste. 101
Scottsdale, AZ 85255
(480)419-3600
Fax: (480)419-3606
Website: http://www.kochventures.com

McKee & Co.
7702 E. Doubletree Ranch Rd.
Suite 230
Scottsdale, AZ 85258
(480)368-0333
Fax: (480)607-7446

Merita Capital Ltd.
7350 E. Stetson Dr., Ste. 108-A
Scottsdale, AZ 85251
(480)947-8700
Fax: (480)947-8766

**Valley Ventures / Arizona Growth
Partners L.P.**
6720 N. Scottsdale Rd., Ste. 208
Scottsdale, AZ 85253
(480)661-6600
Fax: (480)661-6262

Estreetcapital.com
660 South Mill Ave., Ste. 315
Tempe, AZ 85281
(480)968-8400
Fax: (480)968-8480
Website: http://www.estreetcapital.com

Coronado Venture Fund
PO Box 65420
Tucson, AZ 85728-5420
(520)577-3764
Fax: (520)299-8491

Arkansas

Arkansas Capital Corp.
225 South Pulaski St.
Little Rock, AR 72201
(501)374-9247
Fax: (501)374-9425
Website: http://www.arcapital.com

California

Sundance Venture Partners, L.P.
100 Clocktower Place, Ste. 130
Carmel, CA 93923
(831)625-6500
Fax: (831)625-6590

Westar Capital (Costa Mesa)
949 South Coast Dr., Ste. 650
Costa Mesa, CA 92626
(714)481-5160
Fax: (714)481-5166
E-mail: mailbox@westarcapital.com
Website: http://www.westarcapital.com

Alpine Technology Ventures
20300 Stevens Creek Boulevard, Ste. 495
Cupertino, CA 95014
(408)725-1810
Fax: (408)725-1207
Website: http://www.alpineventures.com

Bay Partners
10600 N. De Anza Blvd.
Cupertino, CA 95014-2031
(408)725-2444
Fax: (408)446-4502
Website: http://www.baypartners.com

Novus Ventures
20111 Stevens Creek Blvd., Ste. 130
Cupertino, CA 95014
(408)252-3900

Fax: (408)252-1713
Website: http://www.novusventures.com

Triune Capital
19925 Stevens Creek Blvd., Ste. 200
Cupertino, CA 95014
(310)284-6800
Fax: (310)284-3290

Acorn Ventures
268 Bush St., Ste. 2829
Daly City, CA 94014
(650)994-7801
Fax: (650)994-3305
Website: http://www.acornventures.com

Digital Media Campus
2221 Park Place
El Segundo, CA 90245
(310)426-8000
Fax: (310)426-8010
E-mail: info@thecampus.com
Website: http://
www.digitalmediacampus.com

BankAmerica Ventures / BA Venture Partners
950 Tower Ln., Ste. 700
Foster City, CA 94404
(650)378-6000
Fax: (650)378-6040
Website: http://www.baventurepartners
.com

Starting Point Partners
666 Portofino Lane
Foster City, CA 94404
(650)722-1035
Website: http://
www.startingpointpartners.com

Opportunity Capital Partners
2201 Walnut Ave., Ste. 210
Fremont, CA 94538
(510)795-7000
Fax: (510)494-5439
Website: http://www.ocpcapital.com

Imperial Ventures Inc.
9920 S. La Cienega Boulevar, 14th Fl.
Inglewood, CA 90301
(310)417-5409
Fax: (310)338-6115

Ventana Global (Irvine)
18881 Von Karman Ave., Ste. 1150
Irvine, CA 92612
(949)476-2204
Fax: (949)752-0223
Website: http://www.ventanaglobal.com

Integrated Consortium Inc.
50 Ridgecrest Rd.
Kentfield, CA 94904

(415)925-0386
Fax: (415)461-2726

Enterprise Partners
979 Ivanhoe Ave., Ste. 550
La Jolla, CA 92037
(858)454-8833
Fax: (858)454-2489
Website: http://www.epvc.com

Domain Associates
28202 Cabot Rd., Ste. 200
Laguna Niguel, CA 92677
(949)347-2446
Fax: (949)347-9720
Website: http://www.domainvc.com

Cascade Communications Ventures
60 E. Sir Francis Drake Blvd., Ste. 300
Larkspur, CA 94939
(415)925-6500
Fax: (415)925-6501

Allegis Capital
One First St., Ste. Two
Los Altos, CA 94022
(650)917-5900
Fax: (650)917-5901
Website: http://www.allegiscapital.com

Aspen Ventures
1000 Fremont Ave., Ste. 200
Los Altos, CA 94024
(650)917-5670
Fax: (650)917-5677
Website: http://www.aspenventures.com

AVI Capital L.P.
1 First St., Ste. 2
Los Altos, CA 94022
(650)949-9862
Fax: (650)949-8510
Website: http://www.avicapital.com

Bastion Capital Corp.
1999 Avenue of the Stars, Ste. 2960
Los Angeles, CA 90067
(310)788-5700
Fax: (310)277-7582
E-mail: ga@bastioncapital.com
Website: http://www.bastioncapital.com

Davis Group
PO Box 69953
Los Angeles, CA 90069-0953
(310)659-6327
Fax: (310)659-6337

Developers Equity Corp.
1880 Century Park East, Ste. 211
Los Angeles, CA 90067
(213)277-0300

Far East Capital Corp.
350 S. Grand Ave., Ste. 4100
Los Angeles, CA 90071
(213)687-1361
Fax: (213)617-7939
E-mail: free@fareastnationalbank.com

Kline Hawkes & Co.
11726 San Vicente Blvd., Ste. 300
Los Angeles, CA 90049
(310)442-4700
Fax: (310)442-4707
Website: http://www.klinehawkes.com

Lawrence Financial Group
701 Teakwood
PO Box 491773
Los Angeles, CA 90049
(310)471-4060
Fax: (310)472-3155

Riordan Lewis & Haden
300 S. Grand Ave., 29th Fl.
Los Angeles, CA 90071
(213)229-8500
Fax: (213)229-8597

Union Venture Corp.
445 S. Figueroa St., 9th Fl.
Los Angeles, CA 90071
(213)236-4092
Fax: (213)236-6329

Wedbush Capital Partners
1000 Wilshire Blvd.
Los Angeles, CA 90017
(213)688-4545
Fax: (213)688-6642
Website: http://www.wedbush.com

Advent International Corp.
2180 Sand Hill Rd., Ste. 420
Menlo Park, CA 94025
(650)233-7500
Fax: (650)233-7515
Website: http://www.adventinternational
.com

Altos Ventures
2882 Sand Hill Rd., Ste. 100
Menlo Park, CA 94025
(650)234-9771
Fax: (650)233-9821
Website: http://www.altosvc.com

Applied Technology
1010 El Camino Real, Ste. 300
Menlo Park, CA 94025
(415)326-8622
Fax: (415)326-8163

APV Technology Partners
535 Middlefield, Ste. 150
Menlo Park, CA 94025

(650)327-7871
Fax: (650)327-7631
Website: http://www.apvtp.com

August Capital Management
2480 Sand Hill Rd., Ste. 101
Menlo Park, CA 94025
(650)234-9900
Fax: (650)234-9910
Website: http://www.augustcap.com

Baccharis Capital Inc.
2420 Sand Hill Rd., Ste. 100
Menlo Park, CA 94025
(650)324-6844
Fax: (650)854-3025

Benchmark Capital
2480 Sand Hill Rd., Ste. 200
Menlo Park, CA 94025
(650)854-8180
Fax: (650)854-8183
E-mail: info@benchmark.com
Website: http://www.benchmark.com

Bessemer Venture Partners (Menlo Park)
535 Middlefield Rd., Ste. 245
Menlo Park, CA 94025
(650)853-7000
Fax: (650)853-7001
Website: http://www.bvp.com

The Cambria Group
1600 El Camino Real Rd., Ste. 155
Menlo Park, CA 94025
(650)329-8600
Fax: (650)329-8601
Website: http://www.cambriagroup.com

Canaan Partners
2884 Sand Hill Rd., Ste. 115
Menlo Park, CA 94025
(650)854-8092
Fax: (650)854-8127
Website: http://www.canaan.com

Capstone Ventures
3000 Sand Hill Rd., Bldg. One, Ste. 290
Menlo Park, CA 94025
(650)854-2523
Fax: (650)854-9010
Website: http://www.capstonevc.com

Comdisco Venture Group (Silicon Valley)
3000 Sand Hill Rd., Bldg. 1, Ste. 155
Menlo Park, CA 94025
(650)854-9484
Fax: (650)854-4026

Commtech International
535 Middlefield Rd., Ste. 200
Menlo Park, CA 94025

(650)328-0190
Fax: (650)328-6442

Compass Technology Partners
1550 El Camino Real, Ste. 275
Menlo Park, CA 94025-4111
(650)322-7595
Fax: (650)322-0588
Website: http://www.compasstech
partners.com

Convergence Partners
3000 Sand Hill Rd., Ste. 235
Menlo Park, CA 94025
(650)854-3010
Fax: (650)854-3015
Website: http://www.convergence
partners.com

The Dakota Group
PO Box 1025
Menlo Park, CA 94025
(650)853-0600
Fax: (650)851-4899
E-mail: info@dakota.com

Delphi Ventures
3000 Sand Hill Rd.
Bldg. One, Ste. 135
Menlo Park, CA 94025
(650)854-9650
Fax: (650)854-2961
Website: http://www.delphiventures.com

El Dorado Ventures
2884 Sand Hill Rd., Ste. 121
Menlo Park, CA 94025
(650)854-1200
Fax: (650)854-1202
Website: http://www.eldorado
ventures.com

Glynn Ventures
3000 Sand Hill Rd., Bldg. 4, Ste. 235
Menlo Park, CA 94025
(650)854-2215

Indosuez Ventures
2180 Sand Hill Rd., Ste. 450
Menlo Park, CA 94025
(650)854-0587
Fax: (650)323-5561
Website: http://www.indosuezventures
.com

Institutional Venture Partners
3000 Sand Hill Rd., Bldg. 2, Ste. 290
Menlo Park, CA 94025
(650)854-0132
Fax: (650)854-5762
Website: http://www.ivp.com

Interwest Partners (Menlo Park)
3000 Sand Hill Rd., Bldg. 3, Ste. 255
Menlo Park, CA 94025-7112
(650)854-8585
Fax: (650)854-4706
Website: http://www.interwest.com

Kleiner Perkins Caufield & Byers (Menlo Park)
2750 Sand Hill Rd.
Menlo Park, CA 94025
(650)233-2750
Fax: (650)233-0300
Website: http://www.kpcb.com

Magic Venture Capital LLC
1010 El Camino Real, Ste. 300
Menlo Park, CA 94025
(650)325-4149

Matrix Partners
2500 Sand Hill Rd., Ste. 113
Menlo Park, CA 94025
(650)854-3131
Fax: (650)854-3296
Website: http://www.matrixpartners.com

Mayfield Fund
2800 Sand Hill Rd.
Menlo Park, CA 94025
(650)854-5560
Fax: (650)854-5712
Website: http://www.mayfield.com

McCown De Leeuw and Co. (Menlo Park)
3000 Sand Hill Rd., Bldg. 3, Ste. 290
Menlo Park, CA 94025-7111
(650)854-6000
Fax: (650)854-0853
Website: http://www.mdcpartners.com

Menlo Ventures
3000 Sand Hill Rd., Bldg. 4, Ste. 100
Menlo Park, CA 94025
(650)854-8540
Fax: (650)854-7059
Website: http://www.menloventures.com

Merrill Pickard Anderson & Eyre
2480 Sand Hill Rd., Ste. 200
Menlo Park, CA 94025
(650)854-8600
Fax: (650)854-0345

New Enterprise Associates (Menlo Park)
2490 Sand Hill Rd.
Menlo Park, CA 94025
(650)854-9499
Fax: (650)854-9397
Website: http://www.nea.com

Onset Ventures
2400 Sand Hill Rd., Ste. 150
Menlo Park, CA 94025
(650)529-0700
Fax: (650)529-0777
Website: http://www.onset.com

Paragon Venture Partners
3000 Sand Hill Rd., Bldg. 1, Ste. 275
Menlo Park, CA 94025
(650)854-8000
Fax: (650)854-7260

**Pathfinder Venture Capital Funds
(Menlo Park)**
3000 Sand Hill Rd., Bldg. 3, Ste. 255
Menlo Park, CA 94025
(650)854-0650
Fax: (650)854-4706

Rocket Ventures
3000 Sandhill Rd., Bldg. 1, Ste. 170
Menlo Park, CA 94025
(650)561-9100
Fax: (650)561-9183
Website: http://www.rocketventures.com

Sequoia Capital
3000 Sand Hill Rd., Bldg. 4, Ste. 280
Menlo Park, CA 94025
(650)854-3927
Fax: (650)854-2977
E-mail: sequoia@sequioacap.com
Website: http://www.sequoiacap.com

Sierra Ventures
3000 Sand Hill Rd., Bldg. 4, Ste. 210
Menlo Park, CA 94025
(650)854-1000
Fax: (650)854-5593
Website: http://www.sierraventures.com

Sigma Partners
2884 Sand Hill Rd., Ste. 121
Menlo Park, CA 94025-7022
(650)853-1700
Fax: (650)853-1717
E-mail: info@sigmapartners.com
Website: http://www.sigmapartners.com

Sprout Group (Menlo Park)
3000 Sand Hill Rd.
Bldg. 3, Ste. 170
Menlo Park, CA 94025
(650)234-2700
Fax: (650)234-2779
Website: http://www.sproutgroup.com

TA Associates (Menlo Park)
70 Willow Rd., Ste. 100
Menlo Park, CA 94025
(650)328-1210

Fax: (650)326-4933
Website: http://www.ta.com

Thompson Clive & Partners Ltd.
3000 Sand Hill Rd., Bldg. 1, Ste. 185
Menlo Park, CA 94025-7102
(650)854-0314
Fax: (650)854-0670
E-mail: mail@tcvc.com
Website: http://www.tcvc.com

Trinity Ventures Ltd.
3000 Sand Hill Rd., Bldg. 1, Ste. 240
Menlo Park, CA 94025
(650)854-9500
Fax: (650)854-9501
Website: http://www.trinityventures.com

U.S. Venture Partners
2180 Sand Hill Rd., Ste. 300
Menlo Park, CA 94025
(650)854-9080
Fax: (650)854-3018
Website: http://www.usvp.com

USVP-Schlein Marketing Fund
2180 Sand Hill Rd., Ste. 300
Menlo Park, CA 94025
(415)854-9080
Fax: (415)854-3018
Website: http://www.usvp.com

Venrock Associates
2494 Sand Hill Rd., Ste. 200
Menlo Park, CA 94025
(650)561-9580
Fax: (650)561-9180
Website: http://www.venrock.com

Brad Peery Capital Inc.
145 Chapel Pkwy.
Mill Valley, CA 94941
(415)389-0625
Fax: (415)389-1336

Dot Edu Ventures
650 Castro St., Ste. 270
Mountain View, CA 94041
(650)575-5638
Fax: (650)325-5247
Website: http://www.doteduventures
.com

Forrest, Binkley & Brown
840 Newport Ctr. Dr., Ste. 480
Newport Beach, CA 92660
(949)729-3222
Fax: (949)729-3226
Website: http://www.fbbvc.com

Marwit Capital LLC
180 Newport Center Dr., Ste. 200
Newport Beach, CA 92660
(949)640-6234

Fax: (949)720-8077
Website: http://www.marwit.com

**Kaiser Permanente / National Venture
Development**
1800 Harrison St., 22nd Fl.
Oakland, CA 94612
(510)267-4010
Fax: (510)267-4036
Website: http://www.kpventures.com

Nu Capital Access Group, Ltd.
7677 Oakport St., Ste. 105
Oakland, CA 94621
(510)635-7345
Fax: (510)635-7068

Inman and Bowman
4 Orinda Way, Bldg. D, Ste. 150
Orinda, CA 94563
(510)253-1611
Fax: (510)253-9037

Accel Partners (San Francisco)
428 University Ave.
Palo Alto, CA 94301
(650)614-4800
Fax: (650)614-4880
Website: http://www.accel.com

Advanced Technology Ventures
485 Ramona St., Ste. 200
Palo Alto, CA 94301
(650)321-8601
Fax: (650)321-0934
Website: http://www.atvcapital.com

Anila Fund
400 Channing Ave.
Palo Alto, CA 94301
(650)833-5790
Fax: (650)833-0590
Website: http://www.anila.com

**Asset Management Company
Venture Capital**
2275 E. Bayshore, Ste. 150
Palo Alto, CA 94303
(650)494-7400
Fax: (650)856-1826
E-mail: postmaster@assetman.com
Website: http://www.assetman.com

**BancBoston Capital / BancBoston
Ventures**
435 Tasso St., Ste. 250
Palo Alto, CA 94305
(650)470-4100
Fax: (650)853-1425
Website: http://www.bancbostoncapital
.com

Charter Ventures
525 University Ave., Ste. 1400
Palo Alto, CA 94301
(650)325-6953
Fax: (650)325-4762
Website: http://www.charterventures
.com

Communications Ventures
505 Hamilton Avenue, Ste. 305
Palo Alto, CA 94301
(650)325-9600
Fax: (650)325-9608
Website: http://www.comven.com

HMS Group
2468 Embarcadero Way
Palo Alto, CA 94303-3313
(650)856-9862
Fax: (650)856-9864

Jafco America Ventures, Inc.
505 Hamilton Ste. 310
Palto Alto, CA 94301
(650)463-8800
Fax: (650)463-8801
Website: http://www.jafco.com

New Vista Capital
540 Cowper St., Ste. 200
Palo Alto, CA 94301
(650)329-9333
Fax: (650)328-9434
E-mail: fgreene@nvcap.com
Website: http://www.nvcap.com

Norwest Equity Partners (Palo Alto)
245 Lytton Ave., Ste. 250
Palo Alto, CA 94301-1426
(650)321-8000
Fax: (650)321-8010
Website: http://www.norwestvp.com

Oak Investment Partners
525 University Ave., Ste. 1300
Palo Alto, CA 94301
(650)614-3700
Fax: (650)328-6345
Website: http://www.oakinv.com

Patricof & Co. Ventures, Inc. (Palo Alto)
2100 Geng Rd., Ste. 150
Palo Alto, CA 94303
(650)494-9944
Fax: (650)494-6751
Website: http://www.patricof.com

RWI Group
835 Page Mill Rd.
Palo Alto, CA 94304
(650)251-1800

Fax: (650)213-8660
Website: http://www.rwigroup.com

Summit Partners (Palo Alto)
499 Hamilton Ave., Ste. 200
Palo Alto, CA 94301
(650)321-1166
Fax: (650)321-1188
Website: http://www.summitpartners
.com

Sutter Hill Ventures
755 Page Mill Rd., Ste. A-200
Palo Alto, CA 94304
(650)493-5600
Fax: (650)858-1854
E-mail: shv@shv.com

Vanguard Venture Partners
525 University Ave., Ste. 600
Palo Alto, CA 94301
(650)321-2900
Fax: (650)321-2902
Website: http://www.vanguardventures
.com

Venture Growth Associates
2479 East Bayshore St., Ste. 710
Palo Alto, CA 94303
(650)855-9100
Fax: (650)855-9104

Worldview Technology Partners
435 Tasso St., Ste. 120
Palo Alto, CA 94301
(650)322-3800
Fax: (650)322-3880
Website: http://www.worldview.com

Draper, Fisher, Jurvetson / Draper Associates
400 Seaport Ct., Ste.250
Redwood City, CA 94063
(415)599-9000
Fax: (415)599-9726
Website: http://www.dfj.com

Gabriel Venture Partners
350 Marine Pkwy., Ste. 200
Redwood Shores, CA 94065
(650)551-5000
Fax: (650)551-5001
Website: http://www.gabrielvp.com

Hallador Venture Partners, L.L.C.
740 University Ave., Ste. 110
Sacramento, CA 95825-6710
(916)920-0191
Fax: (916)920-5188
E-mail: chris@hallador.com

Emerald Venture Group
12396 World Trade Dr., Ste. 116
San Diego, CA 92128

(858)451-1001
Fax: (858)451-1003
Website: http://www.emeraldventure
.com

Forward Ventures
9255 Towne Centre Dr.
San Diego, CA 92121
(858)677-6077
Fax: (858)452-8799
E-mail: info@forwardventure.com
Website: http://www.forwardventure
.com

Idanta Partners Ltd.
4660 La Jolla Village Dr., Ste. 850
San Diego, CA 92122
(619)452-9690
Fax: (619)452-2013
Website: http://www.idanta.com

Kingsbury Associates
3655 Nobel Dr., Ste. 490
San Diego, CA 92122
(858)677-0600
Fax: (858)677-0800

Kyocera International Inc.
Corporate Development
8611 Balboa Ave.
San Diego, CA 92123
(858)576-2600
Fax: (858)492-1456

Sorrento Associates, Inc.
4370 LaJolla Village Dr., Ste. 1040
San Diego, CA 92122
(619)452-3100
Fax: (619)452-7607
Website: http://www.sorrentoventures
.com

Western States Investment Group
9191 Towne Ctr. Dr., Ste. 310
San Diego, CA 92122
(619)678-0800
Fax: (619)678-0900

Aberdare Ventures
One Embarcadero Center, Ste. 4000
San Francisco, CA 94111
(415)392-7442
Fax: (415)392-4264
Website: http://www.aberdare.com

Acacia Venture Partners
101 California St., Ste. 3160
San Francisco, CA 94111
(415)433-4200
Fax: (415)433-4250
Website: http://www.acaciavp.com

Access Venture Partners
319 Laidley St.
San Francisco, CA 94131
(415)586-0132
Fax: (415)392-6310
Website: http://www.accessventure
partners.com

Alta Partners
One Embarcadero Center, Ste. 4050
San Francisco, CA 94111
(415)362-4022
Fax: (415)362-6178
E-mail: alta@altapartners.com
Website: http://www.altapartners.com

Bangert Dawes Reade Davis & Thom
220 Montgomery St., Ste. 424
San Francisco, CA 94104
(415)954-9900
Fax: (415)954-9901
E-mail: bdrdt@pacbell.net

Berkeley International Capital Corp.
650 California St., Ste. 2800
San Francisco, CA 94108-2609
(415)249-0450
Fax: (415)392-3929
Website: http://www.berkeleyvc.com

Blueprint Ventures LLC
456 Montgomery St., 22nd Fl.
San Francisco, CA 94104
(415)901-4000
Fax: (415)901-4035
Website: http://www.blueprint
ventures.com

Blumberg Capital Ventures
580 Howard St., Ste. 401
San Francisco, CA 94105
(415)905-5007
Fax: (415)357-5027
Website: http://www.blumberg-
capital.com

Burr, Egan, Deleage, and Co. (San Francisco)
1 Embarcadero Center, Ste. 4050
San Francisco, CA 94111
(415)362-4022
Fax: (415)362-6178

Burrill & Company
120 Montgomery St., Ste. 1370
San Francisco, CA 94104
(415)743-3160
Fax: (415)743-3161
Website: http://www.burrillandco.com

CMEA Ventures
235 Montgomery St., Ste. 920
San Francisco, CA 94401

(415)352-1520
Fax: (415)352-1524
Website: http://www.cmeaventures.com

Crocker Capital
1 Post St., Ste. 2500
San Francisco, CA 94101
(415)956-5250
Fax: (415)959-5710

Dominion Ventures, Inc.
44 Montgomery St., Ste. 4200
San Francisco, CA 94104
(415)362-4890
Fax: (415)394-9245

Dorset Capital
Pier 1
Bay 2
San Francisco, CA 94111
(415)398-7101
Fax: (415)398-7141
Website: http://www.dorsetcapital.com

Gatx Capital
Four Embarcadero Center, Ste. 2200
San Francisco, CA 94904
(415)955-3200
Fax: (415)955-3449

IMinds
135 Main St., Ste. 1350
San Francisco, CA 94105
(415)547-0000
Fax: (415)227-0300
Website: http://www.iminds.com

LF International Inc.
360 Post St., Ste. 705
San Francisco, CA 94108
(415)399-0110
Fax: (415)399-9222
Website: http://www.lfvc.com

Newbury Ventures
535 Pacific Ave., 2nd Fl.
San Francisco, CA 94133
(415)296-7408
Fax: (415)296-7416
Website: http://www.newburyven.com

Quest Ventures (San Francisco)
333 Bush St., Ste. 1750
San Francisco, CA 94104
(415)782-1414
Fax: (415)782-1415

Robertson-Stephens Co.
555 California St., Ste. 2600
San Francisco, CA 94104
(415)781-9700

Fax: (415)781-2556
Website: http://www.omegaadventures
.com

Rosewood Capital, L.P.
One Maritime Plaza, Ste. 1330
San Francisco, CA 94111-3503
(415)362-5526
Fax: (415)362-1192
Website: http://www.rosewoodvc.com

Ticonderoga Capital Inc.
555 California St., No. 4950
San Francisco, CA 94104
(415)296-7900
Fax: (415)296-8956

21st Century Internet Venture Partners
Two South Park
2nd Floor
San Francisco, CA 94107
(415)512-1221
Fax: (415)512-2650
Website: http://www.21vc.com

VK Ventures
600 California St., Ste.1700
San Francisco, CA 94111
(415)391-5600
Fax: (415)397-2744

Walden Group of Venture Capital Funds
750 Battery St., Seventh Floor
San Francisco, CA 94111
(415)391-7225
Fax: (415)391-7262

Acer Technology Ventures
2641 Orchard Pkwy.
San Jose, CA 95134
(408)433-4945
Fax: (408)433-5230

Authosis
226 Airport Pkwy., Ste. 405
San Jose, CA 95110
(650)814-3603
Website: http://www.authosis.com

Western Technology Investment
2010 N. First St., Ste. 310
San Jose, CA 95131
(408)436-8577
Fax: (408)436-8625
E-mail: mktg@westerntech.com

Drysdale Enterprises
177 Bovet Rd., Ste. 600
San Mateo, CA 94402
(650)341-6336
Fax: (650)341-1329
E-mail: drysdale@aol.com

Greylock
2929 Campus Dr., Ste. 400
San Mateo, CA 94401
(650)493-5525
Fax: (650)493-5575
Website: http://www.greylock.com

Technology Funding
2000 Alameda de las Pulgas, Ste. 250
San Mateo, CA 94403
(415)345-2200
Fax: (415)345-1797

2M Invest Inc.
1875 S. Grant St.
Suite 750
San Mateo, CA 94402
(650)655-3765
Fax: (650)372-9107
E-mail: 2minfo@2minvest.com
Website: http://www.2minvest.com

Phoenix Growth Capital Corp.
2401 Kerner Blvd.
San Rafael, CA 94901
(415)485-4569
Fax: (415)485-4663

NextGen Partners LLC
1705 East Valley Rd.
Santa Barbara, CA 93108
(805)969-8540
Fax: (805)969-8542
Website: http://www.nextgenpartners.com

Denali Venture Capital
1925 Woodland Ave.
Santa Clara, CA 95050
(408)690-4838
Fax: (408)247-6979
E-mail: wael@denaliventurecapital.com
Website: http://www.denaliventurecapital.com

Dotcom Ventures LP
3945 Freedom Circle, Ste. 740
Santa Clara, CA 95045
(408)919-9855
Fax: (408)919-9857
Website: http://www.dotcomventuresatl.com

Silicon Valley Bank
3003 Tasman
Santa Clara, CA 95054
(408)654-7400
Fax: (408)727-8728

Al Shugart International
920 41st Ave.
Santa Cruz, CA 95062

(831)479-7852
Fax: (831)479-7852
Website: http://www.alshugart.com

Leonard Mautner Associates
1434 Sixth St.
Santa Monica, CA 90401
(213)393-9788
Fax: (310)459-9918

Palomar Ventures
100 Wilshire Blvd., Ste. 450
Santa Monica, CA 90401
(310)260-6050
Fax: (310)656-4150
Website: http://www.palomarventures.com

Medicus Venture Partners
12930 Saratoga Ave., Ste. D8
Saratoga, CA 95070
(408)447-8600
Fax: (408)447-8599
Website: http://www.medicusvc.com

Redleaf Venture Management
14395 Saratoga Ave., Ste. 130
Saratoga, CA 95070
(408)868-0800
Fax: (408)868-0810
E-mail: nancy@redleaf.com
Website: http://www.redleaf.com

Artemis Ventures
207 Second St., Ste. E
3rd Fl.
Sausalito, CA 94965
(415)289-2500
Fax: (415)289-1789
Website: http://www.artemisventures.com

Deucalion Venture Partners
19501 Brooklime
Sonoma, CA 95476
(707)938-4974
Fax: (707)938-8921

Windward Ventures
PO Box 7688
Thousand Oaks, CA 91359-7688
(805)497-3332
Fax: (805)497-9331

National Investment Management, Inc.
2601 Airport Dr., Ste.210
Torrance, CA 90505
(310)784-7600
Fax: (310)784-7605

Southern California Ventures
406 Amapola Ave. Ste. 125
Torrance, CA 90501

(310)787-4381
Fax: (310)787-4382

Sandton Financial Group
21550 Oxnard St., Ste. 300
Woodland Hills, CA 91367
(818)702-9283

Woodside Fund
850 Woodside Dr.
Woodside, CA 94062
(650)368-5545
Fax: (650)368-2416
Website: http://www.woodsidefund.com

Colorado

Colorado Venture Management
Ste. 300
Boulder, CO 80301
(303)440-4055
Fax: (303)440-4636

Dean & Associates
4362 Apple Way
Boulder, CO 80301
Fax: (303)473-9900

Roser Ventures LLC
1105 Spruce St.
Boulder, CO 80302
(303)443-6436
Fax: (303)443-1885
Website: http://www.roserventures.com

Sequel Venture Partners
4430 Arapahoe Ave., Ste. 220
Boulder, CO 80303
(303)546-0400
Fax: (303)546-9728
E-mail: tom@sequelvc.com
Website: http://www.sequelvc.com

New Venture Resources
445C E. Cheyenne Mtn. Blvd.
Colorado Springs, CO 80906-4570
(719)598-9272
Fax: (719)598-9272

The Centennial Funds
1428 15th St.
Denver, CO 80202-1318
(303)405-7500
Fax: (303)405-7575
Website: http://www.centennial.com

Rocky Mountain Capital Partners
1125 17th St., Ste. 2260
Denver, CO 80202
(303)291-5200
Fax: (303)291-5327

Sandlot Capital LLC
600 South Cherry St., Ste. 525
Denver, CO 80246
(303)893-3400
Fax: (303)893-3403
Website: http://www.sandlotcapital.com

Wolf Ventures
50 South Steele St., Ste. 777
Denver, CO 80209
(303)321-4800
Fax: (303)321-4848
E-mail: businessplan@wolfventures.com
Website: http://www.wolfventures.com

The Columbine Venture Funds
5460 S. Quebec St., Ste. 270
Englewood, CO 80111
(303)694-3222
Fax: (303)694-9007

Investment Securities of Colorado, Inc.
4605 Denice Dr.
Englewood, CO 80111
(303)796-9192

Kinship Partners
6300 S. Syracuse Way, Ste. 484
Englewood, CO 80111
(303)694-0268
Fax: (303)694-1707
E-mail: block@vailsys.com

Boranco Management, L.L.C.
1528 Hillside Dr.
Fort Collins, CO 80524-1969
(970)221-2297
Fax: (970)221-4787

Aweida Ventures
890 West Cherry St., Ste. 220
Louisville, CO 80027
(303)664-9520
Fax: (303)664-9530
Website: http://www.aweida.com

Access Venture Partners
8787 Turnpike Dr., Ste. 260
Westminster, CO 80030
(303)426-8899
Fax: (303)426-8828

Connecticut

Medmax Ventures, LP
1 Northwestern Dr., Ste. 203
Bloomfield, CT 06002
(860)286-2960
Fax: (860)286-9960

James B. Kobak & Co.
Four Mansfield Place
Darien, CT 06820

(203)656-3471
Fax: (203)655-2905

Orien Ventures
1 Post Rd.
Fairfield, CT 06430
(203)259-9933
Fax: (203)259-5288

ABP Acquisition Corporation
115 Maple Ave.
Greenwich, CT 06830
(203)625-8287
Fax: (203)447-6187

Catterton Partners
9 Greenwich Office Park
Greenwich, CT 06830
(203)629-4901
Fax: (203)629-4903
Website: http://www.cpequity.com

Consumer Venture Partners
3 Pickwick Plz.
Greenwich, CT 06830
(203)629-8800
Fax: (203)629-2019

Insurance Venture Partners
31 Brookside Dr., Ste. 211
Greenwich, CT 06830
(203)861-0030
Fax: (203)861-2745

The NTC Group
Three Pickwick Plaza
Ste. 200
Greenwich, CT 06830
(203)862-2800
Fax: (203)622-6538

Regulus International Capital Co., Inc.
140 Greenwich Ave.
Greenwich, CT 06830
(203)625-9700
Fax: (203)625-9706

Axiom Venture Partners
City Place II
185 Asylum St., 17th Fl.
Hartford, CT 06103
(860)548-7799
Fax: (860)548-7797
Website: http://www.axiomventures.com

Conning Capital Partners
City Place II
185 Asylum St.
Hartford, CT 06103-4105
(860)520-1289
Fax: (860)520-1299
E-mail: pe@conning.com
Website: http://www.conning.com

First New England Capital L.P.
100 Pearl St.
Hartford, CT 06103
(860)293-3333
Fax: (860)293-3338
E-mail: info@firstnewenglandcapital.com
Website: http://www.firstnewengland
capital.com

Northeast Ventures
One State St., Ste. 1720
Hartford, CT 06103
(860)547-1414
Fax: (860)246-8755

Windward Holdings
38 Sylvan Rd.
Madison, CT 06443
(203)245-6870
Fax: (203)245-6865

Advanced Materials Partners, Inc.
45 Pine St.
PO Box 1022
New Canaan, CT 06840
(203)966-6415
Fax: (203)966-8448
E-mail: wkb@amplink.com

RFE Investment Partners
36 Grove St.
New Canaan, CT 06840
(203)966-2800
Fax: (203)966-3109
Website: http://www.rfeip.com

Connecticut Innovations, Inc.
999 West St.
Rocky Hill, CT 06067
(860)563-5851
Fax: (860)563-4877
E-mail: pamela.hartley@ctinnovations. com
Website: http://www.ctinnovations.com

Canaan Partners
105 Rowayton Ave.
Rowayton, CT 06853
(203)855-0400
Fax: (203)854-9117
Website: http://www.canaan.com

Landmark Partners, Inc.
10 Mill Pond Ln.
Simsbury, CT 06070
(860)651-9760
Fax: (860)651-8890
Website: http://www.landmarkpartners. com

Sweeney & Company
PO Box 567
Southport, CT 06490
(203)255-0220
Fax: (203)255-0220
E-mail: sweeney@connix.com

Baxter Associates, Inc.
PO Box 1333
Stamford, CT 06904
(203)323-3143
Fax: (203)348-0622

Beacon Partners Inc.
6 Landmark Sq., 4th Fl.
Stamford, CT 06901-2792
(203)359-5776
Fax: (203)359-5876

Collinson, Howe, and Lennox, LLC
1055 Washington Blvd., 5th Fl.
Stamford, CT 06901
(203)324-7700
Fax: (203)324-3636
E-mail: info@chlmedical.com
Website: http://www.chlmedical.com

Prime Capital Management Co.
550 West Ave.
Stamford, CT 06902
(203)964-0642
Fax: (203)964-0862

Saugatuck Capital Co.
1 Canterbury Green
Stamford, CT 06901
(203)348-6669
Fax: (203)324-6995
Website: http://www.saugatuckcapital
.com

Soundview Financial Group Inc.
22 Gatehouse Rd.
Stamford, CT 06902
(203)462-7200
Fax: (203)462-7350
Website: http://www.sndv.com

TSG Ventures, L.L.C.
177 Broad St., 12th Fl.
Stamford, CT 06901
(203)406-1500
Fax: (203)406-1590

Whitney & Company
177 Broad St.
Stamford, CT 06901
(203)973-1400
Fax: (203)973-1422
Website: http://www.jhwhitney.com

**Cullinane & Donnelly Venture
Partners L.P.**
970 Farmington Ave.
West Hartford, CT 06107
(860)521-7811

**The Crestview Investment and
Financial Group**
431 Post Rd. E, Ste. 1
Westport, CT 06880-4403

(203)222-0333
Fax: (203)222-0000

**Marketcorp Venture Associates,
L.P. (MCV)**
274 Riverside Ave.
Westport, CT 06880
(203)222-3030
Fax: (203)222-3033

Oak Investment Partners (Westport)
1 Gorham Island
Westport, CT 06880
(203)226-8346
Fax: (203)227-0372
Website: http://www.oakinv.com

Oxford Bioscience Partners
315 Post Rd. W
Westport, CT 06880-5200
(203)341-3300
Fax: (203)341-3309
Website: http://www.oxbio.com

Prince Ventures (Westport)
25 Ford Rd.
Westport, CT 06880
(203)227-8332
Fax: (203)226-5302

LTI Venture Leasing Corp.
221 Danbury Rd.
Wilton, CT 06897
(203)563-1100
Fax: (203)563-1111
Website: http://www.ltileasing.com

Delaware

Blue Rock Capital
5803 Kennett Pike, Ste. A
Wilmington, DE 19807
(302)426-0981
Fax: (302)426-0982
Website: http://www.bluerockcapital
.com

District of Columbia

Allied Capital Corp.
1919 Pennsylvania Ave. NW
Washington, DC 20006-3434
(202)331-2444
Fax: (202)659-2053
Website: http://www.alliedcapital.com

Atlantic Coastal Ventures, L.P.
3101 South St. NW
Washington, DC 20007
(202)293-1166
Fax: (202)293-1181
Website: http://www.atlanticcv.com

Columbia Capital Group, Inc.
1660 L St. NW, Ste. 308
Washington, DC 20036
(202)775-8815
Fax: (202)223-0544

Core Capital Partners
901 15th St., NW
9th Fl.
Washington, DC 20005
(202)589-0090
Fax: (202)589-0091
Website: http://www.core-capital.com

Next Point Partners
701 Pennsylvania Ave. NW, Ste. 900
Washington, DC 20004
(202)661-8703
Fax: (202)434-7400
E-mail: mf@nextpoint.vc
Website: http://www.nextpointvc.com

**Telecommunications
Development Fund**
2020 K. St. NW
Ste. 375
Washington, DC 20006
(202)293-8840
Fax: (202)293-8850
Website: http://www.tdfund.com

Wachtel & Co., Inc.
1101 4th St. NW
Washington, DC 20005-5680
(202)898-1144

Winslow Partners LLC
1300 Connecticut Ave. NW
Washington, DC 20036-1703
(202)530-5000
Fax: (202)530-5010
E-mail: winslow@winslowpartners.com

Women's Growth Capital Fund
1054 31st St., NW
Ste. 110
Washington, DC 20007
(202)342-1431
Fax: (202)341-1203
Website: http://www.wgcf.com

Florida

Sigma Capital Corp.
22668 Caravelle Circle
Boca Raton, FL 33433
(561)368-9783

**North American Business
Development Co., L.L.C.**
111 East Las Olas Blvd.
Ft. Lauderdale, FL 33301
(305)463-0681

Fax: (305)527-0904
Website: http://www.northamerican
fund.com

Chartwell Capital Management Co. Inc.
1 Independent Dr., Ste. 3120
Jacksonville, FL 32202
(904)355-3519
Fax: (904)353-5833
E-mail: info@chartwellcap.com

CEO Advisors
1061 Maitland Center Commons
Ste. 209
Maitland, FL 32751
(407)660-9327
Fax: (407)660-2109

Henry & Co.
8201 Peters Rd., Ste. 1000
Plantation, FL 33324
(954)797-7400

Avery Business Development Services
2506 St. Michel Ct.
Ponte Vedra, FL 32082
(904)285-6033

New South Ventures
5053 Ocean Blvd.
Sarasota, FL 34242
(941)358-6000
Fax: (941)358-6078
Website: http://www.newsouth
ventures.com

Venture Capital Management Corp.
PO Box 2626
Satellite Beach, FL 32937
(407)777-1969

Florida Capital Venture Ltd.
325 Florida Bank Plaza
100 W. Kennedy Blvd.
Tampa, FL 33602
(813)229-2294
Fax: (813)229-2028

Quantum Capital Partners
339 South Plant Ave.
Tampa, FL 33606
(813)250-1999
Fax: (813)250-1998
Website: http://www.quantumcapital
partners.com

South Atlantic Venture Fund
614 W. Bay St.
Tampa, FL 33606-2704
(813)253-2500
Fax: (813)253-2360
E-mail: venture@southatlantic.com
Website: http://www.southatlantic.com

LM Capital Corp.
120 S. Olive, Ste. 400
West Palm Beach, FL 33401
(561)833-9700
Fax: (561)655-6587
Website: http://www.lmcapital
securities.com

Georgia

Venture First Associates
4811 Thornwood Dr.
Acworth, GA 30102
(770)928-3733
Fax: (770)928-6455

Alliance Technology Ventures
8995 Westside Pkwy., Ste. 200
Alpharetta, GA 30004
(678)336-2000
Fax: (678)336-2001
E-mail: info@atv.com
Website: http://www.atv.com

Cordova Ventures
2500 North Winds Pkwy., Ste. 475
Alpharetta, GA 30004
(678)942-0300
Fax: (678)942-0301
Website: http://www.cordovaventures
.com

Advanced Technology Development Fund
1000 Abernathy, Ste. 1420
Atlanta, GA 30328-5614
(404)668-2333
Fax: (404)668-2333

CGW Southeast Partners
12 Piedmont Center, Ste. 210
Atlanta, GA 30305
(404)816-3255
Fax: (404)816-3258
Website: http://www.cgwlp.com

Cyberstarts
1900 Emery St., NW
3rd Fl.
Atlanta, GA 30318
(404)267-5000
Fax: (404)267-5200
Website: http://www.cyberstarts.com

EGL Holdings, Inc.
10 Piedmont Center, Ste. 412
Atlanta, GA 30305
(404)949-8300
Fax: (404)949-8311

Equity South
1790 The Lenox Bldg.
3399 Peachtree Rd. NE

Atlanta, GA 30326
(404)237-6222
Fax: (404)261-1578

Five Paces
3400 Peachtree Rd., Ste. 200
Atlanta, GA 30326
(404)439-8300
Fax: (404)439-8301
Website: http://www.fivepaces.com

Frontline Capital, Inc.
3475 Lenox Rd., Ste. 400
Atlanta, GA 30326
(404)240-7280
Fax: (404)240-7281

Fuqua Ventures LLC
1201 W. Peachtree St. NW, Ste. 5000
Atlanta, GA 30309
(404)815-4500
Fax: (404)815-4528
Website: http://www.fuquaventures.com

Noro-Moseley Partners
4200 Northside Pkwy., Bldg. 9
Atlanta, GA 30327
(404)233-1966
Fax: (404)239-9280
Website: http://www.noro-moseley.com

Renaissance Capital Corp.
34 Peachtree St. NW, Ste. 2230
Atlanta, GA 30303
(404)658-9061
Fax: (404)658-9064

River Capital, Inc.
Two Midtown Plaza
1360 Peachtree St. NE, Ste. 1430
Atlanta, GA 30309
(404)873-2166
Fax: (404)873-2158

State Street Bank & Trust Co.
3414 Peachtree Rd. NE, Ste. 1010
Atlanta, GA 30326
(404)364-9500
Fax: (404)261-4469

UPS Strategic Enterprise Fund
55 Glenlake Pkwy. NE
Atlanta, GA 30328
(404)828-8814
Fax: (404)828-8088
E-mail: jcacyce@ups.com
Website: http://www.ups.com/sef/
sef_home

Wachovia
191 Peachtree St. NE, 26th Fl.
Atlanta, GA 30303
(404)332-1000

Fax: (404)332-1392
Website: http://www.wachovia.com/wca

Brainworks Ventures
4243 Dunwoody Club Dr.
Chamblee, GA 30341
(770)239-7447

First Growth Capital Inc.
Best Western Plaza, Ste. 105
PO Box 815
Forsyth, GA 31029
(912)781-7131

Financial Capital Resources, Inc.
21 Eastbrook Bend, Ste. 116
Peachtree City, GA 30269
(404)487-6650

Hawaii

HMS Hawaii Management Partners
Davies Pacific Center
841 Bishop St., Ste. 860
Honolulu, HI 96813
(808)545-3755
Fax: (808)531-2611

Idaho

Sun Valley Ventures
160 Second St.
Ketchum, ID 83340
(208)726-5005
Fax: (208)726-5094

Illinois

Open Prairie Ventures
115 N. Neil St., Ste. 209
Champaign, IL 61820
(217)351-7000
Fax: (217)351-7051
E-mail: inquire@openprairie.com
Website: http://www.openprairie.com

ABN AMRO Private Equity
208 S. La Salle St., 10th Fl.
Chicago, IL 60604
(312)855-7079
Fax: (312)553-6648
Website: http://www.abnequity.com

Alpha Capital Partners, Ltd.
122 S. Michigan Ave., Ste. 1700
Chicago, IL 60603
(312)322-9800
Fax: (312)322-9808
E-mail: acp@alphacapital.com

Ameritech Development Corp.
30 S. Wacker Dr., 37th Fl.
Chicago, IL 60606

(312)750-5083
Fax: (312)609-0244

Apex Investment Partners
225 W. Washington, Ste. 1450
Chicago, IL 60606
(312)857-2800
Fax: (312)857-1800
E-mail: apex@apexvc.com
Website: http://www.apexvc.com

Arch Venture Partners
8725 W. Higgins Rd., Ste. 290
Chicago, IL 60631
(773)380-6600
Fax: (773)380-6606
Website: http://www.archventure.com

The Bank Funds
208 South LaSalle St., Ste. 1680
Chicago, IL 60604
(312)855-6020
Fax: (312)855-8910

Batterson Venture Partners
303 W. Madison St., Ste. 1110
Chicago, IL 60606-3309
(312)269-0300
Fax: (312)269-0021
Website: http://www.battersonvp.com

William Blair Capital Partners, L.L.C.
222 W. Adams St., Ste. 1300
Chicago, IL 60606
(312)364-8250
Fax: (312)236-1042
E-mail: privateequity@wmblair.com
Website: http://www.wmblair.com

Bluestar Ventures
208 South LaSalle St., Ste. 1020
Chicago, IL 60604
(312)384-5000
Fax: (312)384-5005
Website: http://www.bluestarventures
.com

The Capital Strategy Management Co.
233 S. Wacker Dr.
Box 06334
Chicago, IL 60606
(312)444-1170

DN Partners
77 West Wacker Dr., Ste. 4550
Chicago, IL 60601
(312)332-7960
Fax: (312)332-7979

Dresner Capital Inc.
29 South LaSalle St., Ste. 310
Chicago, IL 60603
(312)726-3600
Fax: (312)726-7448

Eblast Ventures LLC
11 South LaSalle St., 5th Fl.
Chicago, IL 60603
(312)372-2600
Fax: (312)372-5621
Website: http://www.eblastventures.com

Essex Woodlands Health Ventures, L.P.
190 S. LaSalle St., Ste. 2800
Chicago, IL 60603
(312)444-6040
Fax: (312)444-6034
Website: http://www.essexwood
lands.com

First Analysis Venture Capital
233 S. Wacker Dr., Ste. 9500
Chicago, IL 60606
(312)258-1400
Fax: (312)258-0334
Website: http://www.firstanalysis.com

Frontenac Co.
135 S. LaSalle St., Ste.3800
Chicago, IL 60603
(312)368-0044
Fax: (312)368-9520
Website: http://www.frontenac.com

GTCR Golder Rauner, LLC
6100 Sears Tower
Chicago, IL 60606
(312)382-2200
Fax: (312)382-2201
Website: http://www.gtcr.com

High Street Capital LLC
311 South Wacker Dr., Ste. 4550
Chicago, IL 60606
(312)697-4990
Fax: (312)697-4994
Website: http://www.highstr.com

IEG Venture Management, Inc.
70 West Madison
Chicago, IL 60602
(312)644-0890
Fax: (312)454-0369
Website: http://www.iegventure.com

JK&B Capital
180 North Stetson, Ste. 4500
Chicago, IL 60601
(312)946-1200
Fax: (312)946-1103
E-mail: gspencer@jkbcapital.com
Website: http://www.jkbcapital.com

Kettle Partners L.P.
350 W. Hubbard, Ste. 350
Chicago, IL 60610
(312)329-9300

Fax: (312)527-4519

Website: http://www.kettlevc.com

Lake Shore Capital Partners
20 N. Wacker Dr., Ste. 2807
Chicago, IL 60606
(312)803-3536
Fax: (312)803-3534

LaSalle Capital Group Inc.
70 W. Madison St., Ste. 5710
Chicago, IL 60602
(312)236-7041
Fax: (312)236-0720

Linc Capital, Inc.
303 E. Wacker Pkwy., Ste. 1000
Chicago, IL 60601
(312)946-2670
Fax: (312)938-4290
E-mail: bdemars@linccap.com

Madison Dearborn Partners, Inc.
3 First National Plz., Ste. 3800
Chicago, IL 60602
(312)895-1000
Fax: (312)895-1001
E-mail: invest@mdcp.com
Website: http://www.mdcp.com

Mesirow Private Equity Investments Inc.
350 N. Clark St.
Chicago, IL 60610
(312)595-6950
Fax: (312)595-6211
Website: http://www.meisrow
financial.com

Mosaix Ventures LLC
1822 North Mohawk
Chicago, IL 60614
(312)274-0988
Fax: (312)274-0989
Website: http://www.mosaixventures.
com

Nesbitt Burns
111 West Monroe St.
Chicago, IL 60603
(312)416-3855
Fax: (312)765-8000
Website: http://www.harrisbank.com

Polestar Capital, Inc.
180 N. Michigan Ave., Ste. 1905
Chicago, IL 60601
(312)984-9090
Fax: (312)984-9877
E-mail: wl@polestarvc.com
Website: http://www.polestarvc.com

Prince Ventures (Chicago)
10 S. Wacker Dr., Ste. 2575
Chicago, IL 60606-7407
(312)454-1408
Fax: (312)454-9125

Prism Capital
444 N. Michigan Ave.
Chicago, IL 60611
(312)464-7900
Fax: (312)464-7915
Website: http://www.prismfund.com

Third Coast Capital
900 N. Franklin St., Ste. 700
Chicago, IL 60610
(312)337-3303
Fax: (312)337-2567
E-mail: manic@earthlink.com
Website: http://www.thirdcoast
capital.com

Thoma Cressey Equity Partners
4460 Sears Tower, 92nd Fl.
233 S. Wacker Dr.
Chicago, IL 60606
(312)777-4444
Fax: (312)777-4445
Website: http://www.thomacressey.com

Tribune Ventures
435 N. Michigan Ave., Ste. 600
Chicago, IL 60611
(312)527-8797
Fax: (312)222-5993
Website: http://www.tribune
ventures.com

Wind Point Partners (Chicago)
676 N. Michigan Ave., Ste. 330
Chicago, IL 60611
(312)649-4000
Website: http://www.wppartners.com

Marquette Venture Partners
520 Lake Cook Rd., Ste. 450
Deerfield, IL 60015
(847)940-1700
Fax: (847)940-1724
Website: http://
www.marquetteventures.com

Duchossois Investments Limited, LLC
845 Larch Ave.
Elmhurst, IL 60126
(630)530-6105
Fax: (630)993-8644
Website: http://www.duchtec.com

Evanston Business Investment Corp.
1840 Oak Ave.
Evanston, IL 60201

(847)866-1840
Fax: (847)866-1808
E-mail: t-parkinson@nwu.com
Website: http://www.ebic.com

Inroads Capital Partners L.P.
1603 Orrington Ave., Ste. 2050
Evanston, IL 60201-3841
(847)864-2000
Fax: (847)864-9692

The Cerulean Fund/WGC Enterprises
1701 E. Lake Ave., Ste. 170
Glenview, IL 60025
(847)657-8002
Fax: (847)657-8168

Ventana Financial Resources, Inc.
249 Market Sq.
Lake Forest, IL 60045
(847)234-3434

Beecken, Petty & Co.
901 Warrenville Rd., Ste. 205
Lisle, IL 60532
(630)435-0300
Fax: (630)435-0370
E-mail: hep@bpcompany.com
Website: http://www.bpcompany.com

Allstate Private Equity
3075 Sanders Rd., Ste. G5D
Northbrook, IL 60062-7127
(847)402-8247
Fax: (847)402-0880

KB Partners
1101 Skokie Blvd., Ste. 260
Northbrook, IL 60062-2856
(847)714-0444
Fax: (847)714-0445
E-mail: keith@kbpartners.com
Website: http://www.kbpartners.com

Transcap Associates Inc.
900 Skokie Blvd., Ste. 210
Northbrook, IL 60062
(847)753-9600
Fax: (847)753-9090

Graystone Venture Partners, L.L.C. / Portage Venture Partners
One Northfield Plaza, Ste. 530
Northfield, IL 60093
(847)446-9460
Fax: (847)446-9470
Website: http://www.portage
ventures.com

Motorola Inc.
1303 E. Algonquin Rd.
Schaumburg, IL 60196-1065
(847)576-4929

Fax: (847)538-2250
Website: http://www.mot.com/mne

Indiana

Irwin Ventures LLC
500 Washington St.
Columbus, IN 47202
(812)373-1434
Fax: (812)376-1709
Website: http://www.irwinventures.com

Cambridge Venture Partners
4181 East 96th St., Ste. 200
Indianapolis, IN 46240
(317)814-6192
Fax: (317)944-9815

CID Equity Partners
One American Square, Ste. 2850
Box 82074
Indianapolis, IN 46282
(317)269-2350
Fax: (317)269-2355
Website: http://www.cidequity.com

Gazelle Techventures
6325 Digital Way, Ste. 460
Indianapolis, IN 46278
(317)275-6800
Fax: (317)275-1101
Website: http://www.gazellevc.com

Monument Advisors Inc.
Bank One Center/Circle
111 Monument Circle, Ste. 600
Indianapolis, IN 46204-5172
(317)656-5065
Fax: (317)656-5060
Website: http://www.monumentadv.com

MWV Capital Partners
201 N. Illinois St., Ste. 300
Indianapolis, IN 46204
(317)237-2323
Fax: (317)237-2325
Website: http://www.mwvcapital.com

First Source Capital Corp.
100 North Michigan St.
PO Box 1602
South Bend, IN 46601
(219)235-2180
Fax: (219)235-2227

Iowa

Allsop Venture Partners
118 Third Ave. SE, Ste. 837
Cedar Rapids, IA 52401
(319)368-6675
Fax: (319)363-9515

InvestAmerica Investment Advisors, Inc.
101 2nd St. SE, Ste. 800
Cedar Rapids, IA 52401
(319)363-8249
Fax: (319)363-9683

Pappajohn Capital Resources
2116 Financial Center
Des Moines, IA 50309
(515)244-5746
Fax: (515)244-2346
Website: http://www.pappajohn.com

Berthel Fisher & Company Planning Inc.
701 Tama St.
PO Box 609
Marion, IA 52302
(319)497-5700
Fax: (319)497-4244

Kansas

Enterprise Merchant Bank
7400 West 110th St., Ste. 560
Overland Park, KS 66210
(913)327-8500
Fax: (913)327-8505

Kansas Venture Capital, Inc. (Overland Park)
6700 Antioch Plz., Ste. 460
Overland Park, KS 66204
(913)262-7117
Fax: (913)262-3509
E-mail: jdalton@kvci.com

Child Health Investment Corp.
6803 W. 64th St., Ste. 208
Shawnee Mission, KS 66202
(913)262-1436
Fax: (913)262-1575
Website: http://www.chca.com

Kansas Technology Enterprise Corp.
214 SW 6th, 1st Fl.
Topeka, KS 66603-3719
(785)296-5272
Fax: (785)296-1160
E-mail: ktec@ktec.com
Website: http://www.ktec.com

Kentucky

Kentucky Highlands Investment Corp.
362 Old Whitley Rd.
London, KY 40741
(606)864-5175
Fax: (606)864-5194
Website: http://www.khic.org

Chrysalis Ventures, L.L.C.
1850 National City Tower
Louisville, KY 40202
(502)583-7644
Fax: (502)583-7648
E-mail: bobsany@chrysalisventures.com
Website: http://www.chrysalisventures.com

Humana Venture Capital
500 West Main St.
Louisville, KY 40202
(502)580-3922
Fax: (502)580-2051
E-mail: gemont@humana.com
George Emont, Director

Summit Capital Group, Inc.
6510 Glenridge Park Pl., Ste. 8
Louisville, KY 40222
(502)332-2700

Louisiana

Bank One Equity Investors, Inc.
451 Florida St.
Baton Rouge, LA 70801
(504)332-4421
Fax: (504)332-7377

Advantage Capital Partners
LLE Tower
909 Poydras St., Ste. 2230
New Orleans, LA 70112
(504)522-4850
Fax: (504)522-4950
Website: http://www.advantagecap.com

Maine

CEI Ventures / Coastal Ventures LP
2 Portland Fish Pier, Ste. 201
Portland, ME 04101
(207)772-5356
Fax: (207)772-5503
Website: http://www.ceiventures.com

Commwealth Bioventures, Inc.
4 Milk St.
Portland, ME 04101
(207)780-0904
Fax: (207)780-0913

Maryland

Annapolis Ventures LLC
151 West St., Ste. 302
Annapolis, MD 21401
(443)482-9555
Fax: (443)482-9565
Website: http://www.annapolisventures.com

Delmag Ventures
220 Wardour Dr.
Annapolis, MD 21401
(410)267-8196
Fax: (410)267-8017
Website: http://www.delmagventures
.com

Abell Venture Fund
111 S. Calvert St., Ste. 2300
Baltimore, MD 21202
(410)547-1300
Fax: (410)539-6579
Website: http://www.abell.org

ABS Ventures (Baltimore)
1 South St., Ste. 2150
Baltimore, MD 21202
(410)895-3895
Fax: (410)895-3899
Website: http://www.absventures.com

Anthem Capital, L.P.
16 S. Calvert St., Ste. 800
Baltimore, MD 21202-1305
(410)625-1510
Fax: (410)625-1735
Website: http://www.anthemcapital.com

Catalyst Ventures
1119 St. Paul St.
Baltimore, MD 21202
(410)244-0123
Fax: (410)752-7721

Maryland Venture Capital Trust
217 E. Redwood St., Ste. 2200
Baltimore, MD 21202
(410)767-6361
Fax: (410)333-6931

New Enterprise Associates (Baltimore)
1119 St. Paul St.
Baltimore, MD 21202
(410)244-0115
Fax: (410)752-7721
Website: http://www.nea.com

T. Rowe Price Threshold Partnerships
100 E. Pratt St., 8th Fl.
Baltimore, MD 21202
(410)345-2000
Fax: (410)345-2800

Spring Capital Partners
16 W. Madison St.
Baltimore, MD 21201
(410)685-8000
Fax: (410)727-1436
E-mail: mailbox@springcap.com

Arete Corporation
3 Bethesda Metro Ctr., Ste. 770
Bethesda, MD 20814

(301)657-6268
Fax: (301)657-6254
Website: http://www.arete-microgen.com

Embryon Capital
7903 Sleaford Place
Bethesda, MD 20814
(301)656-6837
Fax: (301)656-8056

Potomac Ventures
7920 Norfolk Ave., Ste. 1100
Bethesda, MD 20814
(301)215-9240
Website: http://
www.potomacventures.com

Toucan Capital Corp.
3 Bethesda Metro Center, Ste. 700
Bethesda, MD 20814
(301)961-1970
Fax: (301)961-1969
Website: http://www.toucancapital.com

Kinetic Ventures LLC
2 Wisconsin Cir., Ste. 620
Chevy Chase, MD 20815
(301)652-8066
Fax: (301)652-8310
Website: http://
www.kineticventures.com

Boulder Ventures Ltd.
4750 Owings Mills Blvd.
Owings Mills, MD 21117
(410)998-3114
Fax: (410)356-5492
Website: http://
www.boulderventures.com

Grotech Capital Group
9690 Deereco Rd., Ste. 800
Timonium, MD 21093
(410)560-2000
Fax: (410)560-1910
Website: http://www.grotech.com

Massachusetts

Adams, Harkness & Hill, Inc.
60 State St.
Boston, MA 02109
(617)371-3900

Advent International
75 State St., 29th Fl.
Boston, MA 02109
(617)951-9400
Fax: (617)951-0566
Website: http://www.adventinernational
.com

American Research and Development
30 Federal St.
Boston, MA 02110-2508
(617)423-7500
Fax: (617)423-9655

Ascent Venture Partners
255 State St., 5th Fl.
Boston, MA 02109
(617)270-9400
Fax: (617)270-9401
E-mail: info@ascentvp.com
Website: http://www.ascentvp.com

Atlas Venture
222 Berkeley St.
Boston, MA 02116
(617)488-2200
Fax: (617)859-9292
Website: http://www.atlasventure.com

Axxon Capital
28 State St., 37th Fl.
Boston, MA 02109
(617)722-0980
Fax: (617)557-6014
Website: http://www.axxoncapital.com

BancBoston Capital/BancBoston Ventures
175 Federal St., 10th Fl.
Boston, MA 02110
(617)434-2509
Fax: (617)434-6175
Website: http://www.bancbostoncapital.
com

Boston Capital Ventures
Old City Hall
45 School St.
Boston, MA 02108
(617)227-6550
Fax: (617)227-3847
E-mail: info@bcv.com
Website: http://www.bcv.com

Boston Financial & Equity Corp.
20 Overland St.
PO Box 15071
Boston, MA 02215
(617)267-2900
Fax: (617)437-7601
E-mail: debbie@bfec.com

Boston Millennia Partners
30 Rowes Wharf
Boston, MA 02110
(617)428-5150
Fax: (617)428-5160
Website: http://www.millenniapartners
.com

Bristol Investment Trust
842A Beacon St.
Boston, MA 02215-3199
(617)566-5212
Fax: (617)267-0932

Brook Venture Management LLC
50 Federal St., 5th Fl.
Boston, MA 02110
(617)451-8989
Fax: (617)451-2369
Website: http://www.brookventure.com

Burr, Egan, Deleage, and Co. (Boston)
200 Clarendon St., Ste. 3800
Boston, MA 02116
(617)262-7770
Fax: (617)262-9779

Cambridge/Samsung Partners
One Exeter Plaza
Ninth Fl.
Boston, MA 02116
(617)262-4440
Fax: (617)262-5562

Chestnut Street Partners, Inc.
75 State St., Ste. 2500
Boston, MA 02109
(617)345-7220
Fax: (617)345-7201
E-mail: chestnut@chestnutp.com

Claflin Capital Management, Inc.
10 Liberty Sq., Ste. 300
Boston, MA 02109
(617)426-6505
Fax: (617)482-0016
Website: http://www.claflincapital.com

Copley Venture Partners
99 Summer St., Ste. 1720
Boston, MA 02110
(617)737-1253
Fax: (617)439-0699

Corning Capital / Corning Technology Ventures
121 High Street, Ste. 400
Boston, MA 02110
(617)338-2656
Fax: (617)261-3864
Website: http://www.corningventures
.com

Downer & Co.
211 Congress St.
Boston, MA 02110
(617)482-6200
Fax: (617)482-6201
E-mail: cdowner@downer.com
Website: http://www.downer.com

Fidelity Ventures
82 Devonshire St.
Boston, MA 02109
(617)563-6370
Fax: (617)476-9023
Website: http://www.fidelityventures.com

Greylock Management Corp. (Boston)
1 Federal St.
Boston, MA 02110-2065
(617)423-5525
Fax: (617)482-0059

Gryphon Ventures
222 Berkeley St., Ste.1600
Boston, MA 02116
(617)267-9191
Fax: (617)267-4293
E-mail: all@gryphoninc.com

Halpern, Denny & Co.
500 Boylston St.
Boston, MA 02116
(617)536-6602
Fax: (617)536-8535

Harbourvest Partners, LLC
1 Financial Center, 44th Fl.
Boston, MA 02111
(617)348-3707
Fax: (617)350-0305
Website: http://www.hvpllc.com

Highland Capital Partners
2 International Pl.
Boston, MA 02110
(617)981-1500
Fax: (617)531-1550
E-mail: info@hcp.com
Website: http://www.hcp.com

Lee Munder Venture Partners
John Hancock Tower T-53
200 Clarendon St.
Boston, MA 02103
(617)380-5600
Fax: (617)380-5601
Website: http://www.leemunder.com

M/C Venture Partners
75 State St., Ste. 2500
Boston, MA 02109
(617)345-7200
Fax: (617)345-7201
Website: http://www.mcventurepartners
.com

Massachusetts Capital Resources Co.
420 Boylston St.
Boston, MA 02116
(617)536-3900
Fax: (617)536-7930

Massachusetts Technology Development Corp. (MTDC)
148 State St.
Boston, MA 02109
(617)723-4920
Fax: (617)723-5983
E-mail: jhodgman@mtdc.com
Website: http://www.mtdc.com

New England Partners
One Boston Place, Ste. 2100
Boston, MA 02108
(617)624-8400
Fax: (617)624-8999
Website: http://www.nepartners.com

North Hill Ventures
Ten Post Office Square
11th Fl.
Boston, MA 02109
(617)788-2112
Fax: (617)788-2152
Website: http://www.northhillventures
.com

OneLiberty Ventures
150 Cambridge Park Dr.
Boston, MA 02140
(617)492-7280
Fax: (617)492-7290
Website: http://www.oneliberty.com

Schroder Ventures
Life Sciences
60 State St., Ste. 3650
Boston, MA 02109
(617)367-8100
Fax: (617)367-1590
Website: http://www.shroderventures.com

Shawmut Capital Partners
75 Federal St., 18th Fl.
Boston, MA 02110
(617)368-4900
Fax: (617)368-4910
Website: http://www.shawmutcapital.com

Solstice Capital LLC
15 Broad St., 3rd Fl.
Boston, MA 02109
(617)523-7733
Fax: (617)523-5827
E-mail: solticecapital@solcap.com

Spectrum Equity Investors
One International Pl., 29th Fl.
Boston, MA 02110
(617)464-4600
Fax: (617)464-4601
Website: http://www.spectrumequity.com

Spray Venture Partners
One Walnut St.
Boston, MA 02108
(617)305-4140
Fax: (617)305-4144
Website: http://www.sprayventure.com

The Still River Fund
100 Federal St., 29th Fl.
Boston, MA 02110
(617)348-2327
Fax: (617)348-2371
Website: http://www.stillriverfund.com

Summit Partners
600 Atlantic Ave., Ste. 2800
Boston, MA 02210-2227
(617)824-1000
Fax: (617)824-1159
Website: http://www.summitpartners.com

TA Associates, Inc. (Boston)
High Street Tower
125 High St., Ste. 2500
Boston, MA 02110
(617)574-6700
Fax: (617)574-6728
Website: http://www.ta.com

TVM Techno Venture Management
101 Arch St., Ste. 1950
Boston, MA 02110
(617)345-9320
Fax: (617)345-9377
E-mail: info@tvmvc.com
Website: http://www.tvmvc.com

UNC Ventures
64 Burough St.
Boston, MA 02130-4017
(617)482-7070
Fax: (617)522-2176

**Venture Investment Management
Company (VIMAC)**
177 Milk St.
Boston, MA 02190-3410
(617)292-3300
Fax: (617)292-7979
E-mail: bzeisig@vimac.com
Website: http://www.vimac.com

MDT Advisers, Inc.
125 Cambridge Park Dr.
Cambridge, MA 02140-2314
(617)234-2200
Fax: (617)234-2210
Website: http://www.mdtai.com

TTC Ventures
One Main St., 6th Fl.
Cambridge, MA 02142

(617)528-3137
Fax: (617)577-1715
E-mail: info@ttcventures.com

Zero Stage Capital Co. Inc.
101 Main St., 17th Fl.
Cambridge, MA 02142
(617)876-5355
Fax: (617)876-1248
Website: http://www.zerostage.com

Atlantic Capital
164 Cushing Hwy.
Cohasset, MA 02025
(617)383-9449
Fax: (617)383-6040
E-mail: info@atlanticcap.com
Website: http://www.atlanticcap.com

Seacoast Capital Partners
55 Ferncroft Rd.
Danvers, MA 01923
(978)750-1300
Fax: (978)750-1301
E-mail: gdeli@seacoastcapital.com
Website: http://www.seacoastcapital.com

Sage Management Group
44 South Street
PO Box 2026
East Dennis, MA 02641
(508)385-7172
Fax: (508)385-7272
E-mail: sagemgt@capecod.net

Applied Technology
1 Cranberry Hill
Lexington, MA 02421-7397
(617)862-8622
Fax: (617)862-8367

Royalty Capital Management
5 Downing Rd.
Lexington, MA 02421-6918
(781)861-8490

Argo Global Capital
210 Broadway, Ste. 101
Lynnfield, MA 01940
(781)592-5250
Fax: (781)592-5230
Website: http://www.gsmcapital.com

Industry Ventures
6 Bayne Lane
Newburyport, MA 01950
(978)499-7606
Fax: (978)499-0686
Website: http://www.industryventures
.com

Softbank Capital Partners
10 Langley Rd., Ste. 202
Newton Center, MA 02459

(617)928-9300
Fax: (617)928-9305
E-mail: clax@bvc.com

**Advanced Technology Ventures
(Boston)**
281 Winter St., Ste. 350
Waltham, MA 02451
(781)290-0707
Fax: (781)684-0045
E-mail: info@atvcapital.com
Website: http://www.atvcapital.com

Castile Ventures
890 Winter St., Ste. 140
Waltham, MA 02451
(781)890-0060
Fax: (781)890-0065
Website: http://www.castileventures.com

Charles River Ventures
1000 Winter St., Ste. 3300
Waltham, MA 02451
(781)487-7060
Fax: (781)487-7065
Website: http://www.crv.com

Comdisco Venture Group (Waltham)
Totton Pond Office Center
400-1 Totten Pond Rd.
Waltham, MA 02451
(617)672-0250
Fax: (617)398-8099

Marconi Ventures
890 Winter St., Ste. 310
Waltham, MA 02451
(781)839-7177
Fax: (781)522-7477
Website: http://www.marconi.com

Matrix Partners
Bay Colony Corporate Center
1000 Winter St., Ste.4500
Waltham, MA 02451
(781)890-2244
Fax: (781)890-2288
Website: http://www.matrixpartners.com

North Bridge Venture Partners
950 Winter St. Ste. 4600
Waltham, MA 02451
(781)290-0004
Fax: (781)290-0999
E-mail: eta@nbvp.com

Polaris Venture Partners
Bay Colony Corporate Ctr.
1000 Winter St., Ste. 3500
Waltham, MA 02451
(781)290-0770
Fax: (781)290-0880

Organizations, Agencies, & Consultants

E-mail: partners@polarisventures.com
Website: http://www.polarisventures
.com

Seaflower Ventures
Bay Colony Corporate Ctr.
1000 Winter St. Ste. 1000
Waltham, MA 02451
(781)466-9552
Fax: (781)466-9553
E-mail: moot@seaflower.com
Website: http://www.seaflower.com

Ampersand Ventures
55 William St., Ste. 240
Wellesley, MA 02481
(617)239-0700
Fax: (617)239-0824
E-mail: info@ampersandventures.com
Website: http://www.ampersandventures
.com

Battery Ventures (Boston)
20 William St., Ste. 200
Wellesley, MA 02481
(781)577-1000
Fax: (781)577-1001
Website: http://www.battery.com

Commonwealth Capital Ventures, L.P.
20 William St., Ste.225
Wellesley, MA 02481
(781)237-7373
Fax: (781)235-8627
Website: http://www.ccvlp.com

Fowler, Anthony & Company
20 Walnut St.
Wellesley, MA 02481
(781)237-4201
Fax: (781)237-7718

Gemini Investors
20 William St.
Wellesley, MA 02481
(781)237-7001
Fax: (781)237-7233

Grove Street Advisors Inc.
20 William St., Ste. 230
Wellesley, MA 02481
(781)263-6100
Fax: (781)263-6101
Website: http://www.grovestreetadvisors
.com

Mees Pierson Investeringsmaat B.V.
20 William St., Ste. 210
Wellesley, MA 02482
(781)239-7600
Fax: (781)239-0377

Norwest Equity Partners
40 William St., Ste. 305
Wellesley, MA 02481-3902
(781)237-5870
Fax: (781)237-6270
Website: http://www.norwestvp.com

**Bessemer Venture Partners
(Wellesley Hills)**
83 Walnut St.
Wellesley Hills, MA 02481
(781)237-6050
Fax: (781)235-7576
E-mail: travis@bvpny.com
Website: http://www.bvp.com

Venture Capital Fund of New England
20 Walnut St., Ste. 120
Wellesley Hills, MA 02481-2175
(781)239-8262
Fax: (781)239-8263

Prism Venture Partners
100 Lowder Brook Dr., Ste. 2500
Westwood, MA 02090
(781)302-4000
Fax: (781)302-4040
E-mail: dwbaum@prismventure.com

Palmer Partners LP
200 Unicorn Park Dr.
Woburn, MA 01801
(781)933-5445
Fax: (781)933-0698

Michigan

Arbor Partners, L.L.C.
130 South First St.
Ann Arbor, MI 48104
(734)668-9000
Fax: (734)669-4195
Website: http://www.arborpartners.com

EDF Ventures
425 N. Main St.
Ann Arbor, MI 48104
(734)663-3213
Fax: (734)663-7358
E-mail: edf@edfvc.com
Website: http://www.edfvc.com

White Pines Management, L.L.C.
2401 Plymouth Rd., Ste. B
Ann Arbor, MI 48105
(734)747-9401
Fax: (734)747-9704
E-mail: ibund@whitepines.com
Website: http://www.whitepines.com

Wellmax, Inc.
3541 Bendway Blvd., Ste. 100
Bloomfield Hills, MI 48301

(248)646-3554
Fax: (248)646-6220

Venture Funding, Ltd.
Fisher Bldg.
3011 West Grand Blvd., Ste. 321
Detroit, MI 48202
(313)871-3606
Fax: (313)873-4935

**Investcare Partners L.P. / GMA
Capital LLC**
32330 W. Twelve Mile Rd.
Farmington Hills, MI 48334
(248)489-9000
Fax: (248)489-8819
E-mail: gma@gmacapital.com
Website: http://www.gmacapital.com

Liberty Bidco Investment Corp.
30833 Northwestern Highway, Ste. 211
Farmington Hills, MI 48334
(248)626-6070
Fax: (248)626-6072

Seaflower Ventures
5170 Nicholson Rd.
PO Box 474
Fowlerville, MI 48836
(517)223-3335
Fax: (517)223-3337
E-mail: gibbons@seaflower.com
Website: http://www.seaflower.com

Ralph Wilson Equity Fund LLC
15400 E. Jefferson Ave.
Gross Pointe Park, MI 48230
(313)821-9122
Fax: (313)821-9101
Website: http://www.RalphWilsonEquity
Fund.com
J. Skip Simms, President

Minnesota

Development Corp. of Austin
1900 Eighth Ave., NW
Austin, MN 55912
(507)433-0346
Fax: (507)433-0361
E-mail: dca@smig.net
Website: http://www.spamtownusa.com

Northeast Ventures Corp.
802 Alworth Bldg.
Duluth, MN 55802
(218)722-9915
Fax: (218)722-9871

Medical Innovation Partners, Inc.
6450 City West Pkwy.
Eden Prairie, MN 55344-3245
(612)828-9616
Fax: (612)828-9596

St. Paul Venture Capital, Inc.
10400 Vicking Dr., Ste. 550
Eden Prairie, MN 55344
(612)995-7474
Fax: (612)995-7475
Website: http://www.stpaulvc.com

Cherry Tree Investments, Inc.
7601 France Ave. S, Ste. 150
Edina, MN 55435
(612)893-9012
Fax: (612)893-9036
Website: http://www.cherrytree.com

Shared Ventures, Inc.
6550 York Ave. S
Edina, MN 55435
(612)925-3411

Sherpa Partners LLC
5050 Lincoln Dr., Ste. 490
Edina, MN 55436
(952)942-1070
Fax: (952)942-1071
Website: http://www.sherpapartners.com

Affinity Capital Management
901 Marquette Ave., Ste. 1810
Minneapolis, MN 55402
(612)252-9900
Fax: (612)252-9911
Website: http://www.affinitycapital.com

Artesian Capital
1700 Foshay Tower
821 Marquette Ave.
Minneapolis, MN 55402
(612)334-5600
Fax: (612)334-5601
E-mail: artesian@artesian.com

Coral Ventures
60 S. 6th St., Ste. 3510
Minneapolis, MN 55402
(612)335-8666
Fax: (612)335-8668
Website: http://www.coralventures.com

Crescendo Venture Management, L.L.C.
800 LaSalle Ave., Ste. 2250
Minneapolis, MN 55402
(612)607-2800
Fax: (612)607-2801
Website: http://www.crescendoventures
.com

Gideon Hixon Venture
1900 Foshay Tower
821 Marquette Ave.
Minneapolis, MN 55402
(612)904-2314
Fax: (612)204-0913

Norwest Equity Partners
3600 IDS Center
80 S. 8th St.
Minneapolis, MN 55402
(612)215-1600
Fax: (612)215-1601
Website: http://www.norwestvp.com

Oak Investment Partners (Minneapolis)
4550 Norwest Center
90 S. 7th St.
Minneapolis, MN 55402
(612)339-9322
Fax: (612)337-8017
Website: http://www.oakinv.com

Pathfinder Venture Capital Funds (Minneapolis)
7300 Metro Blvd., Ste. 585
Minneapolis, MN 55439
(612)835-1121
Fax: (612)835-8389
E-mail: jahrens620@aol.com

U.S. Bancorp Piper Jaffray Ventures, Inc.
800 Nicollet Mall, Ste. 800
Minneapolis, MN 55402
(612)303-5686
Fax: (612)303-1350
Website: http://www.paperjaffrey
ventures.com

The Food Fund, Ltd. Partnership
5720 Smatana Dr., Ste. 300
Minnetonka, MN 55343
(612)939-3950
Fax: (612)939-8106

Mayo Medical Ventures
200 First St. SW
Rochester, MN 55905
(507)266-4586
Fax: (507)284-5410
Website: http://www.mayo.edu

Missouri

Bankers Capital Corp.
3100 Gillham Rd.
Kansas City, MO 64109
(816)531-1600
Fax: (816)531-1334

Capital for Business, Inc. (Kansas City)
1000 Walnut St., 18th Fl.
Kansas City, MO 64106
(816)234-2357
Fax: (816)234-2952
Website: http://www.capitalforbusiness
.com

De Vries & Co. Inc.
800 West 47th St.
Kansas City, MO 64112
(816)756-0055
Fax: (816)756-0061

InvestAmerica Venture Group Inc. (Kansas City)
Commerce Tower
911 Main St., Ste. 2424
Kansas City, MO 64105
(816)842-0114
Fax: (816)471-7339

Kansas City Equity Partners
233 W. 47th St.
Kansas City, MO 64112
(816)960-1771
Fax: (816)960-1777
Website: http://www.kcep.com

Bome Investors, Inc.
8000 Maryland Ave., Ste. 1190
St. Louis, MO 63105
(314)721-5707
Fax: (314)721-5135
Website: http://www.gatewayventures.com

Capital for Business, Inc. (St. Louis)
11 S. Meramac St., Ste. 1430
St. Louis, MO 63105
(314)746-7427
Fax: (314)746-8739
Website: http://www.capitalforbusiness
.com

Crown Capital Corp.
540 Maryville Centre Dr., Ste. 120
Saint Louis, MO 63141
(314)576-1201
Fax: (314)576-1525
Website: http://www.crown- cap.com

Gateway Associates L.P.
8000 Maryland Ave., Ste. 1190
St. Louis, MO 63105
(314)721-5707
Fax: (314)721-5135

Harbison Corp.
8112 Maryland Ave., Ste. 250
Saint Louis, MO 63105
(314)727-8200
Fax: (314)727-0249

Nebraska

Heartland Capital Fund, Ltd.
PO Box 642117
Omaha, NE 68154
(402)778-5124
Fax: (402)445-2370
Website: http://www.heartlandcapital
fund.com

Odin Capital Group
1625 Farnam St., Ste. 700
Omaha, NE 68102
(402)346-6200
Fax: (402)342-9311
Website: http://www.odincapital.com

Nevada

Edge Capital Investment Co. LLC
1350 E. Flamingo Rd., Ste. 3000
Las Vegas, NV 89119
(702)438-3343
E-mail: info@edgecapital.net
Website: http://www.edgecapital.net

The Benefit Capital Companies Inc.
PO Box 542
Logandale, NV 89021
(702)398-3222
Fax: (702)398-3700

Millennium Three Venture Group LLC
6880 South McCarran Blvd., Ste. A-11
Reno, NV 89509
(775)954-2020
Fax: (775)954-2023
Website: http://www.m3vg.com

New Jersey

Alan I. Goldman & Associates
497 Ridgewood Ave.
Glen Ridge, NJ 07028
(973)857-5680
Fax: (973)509-8856

CS Capital Partners LLC
328 Second St., Ste. 200
Lakewood, NJ 08701
(732)901-1111
Fax: (212)202-5071
Website: http://www.cs-capital.com

Edison Venture Fund
1009 Lenox Dr., Ste. 4
Lawrenceville, NJ 08648
(609)896-1900
Fax: (609)896-0066
E-mail: info@edisonventure.com
Website: http://www.edisonventure.com

Tappan Zee Capital Corp. (New Jersey)
201 Lower Notch Rd.
PO Box 416
Little Falls, NJ 07424
(973)256-8280
Fax: (973)256-2841

The CIT Group/Venture Capital, Inc.
650 CIT Dr.
Livingston, NJ 07039
(973)740-5429

Fax: (973)740-5555
Website: http://www.cit.com

Capital Express, L.L.C.
1100 Valleybrook Ave.
Lyndhurst, NJ 07071
(201)438-8228
Fax: (201)438-5131
E-mail: niles@capitalexpress.com
Website: http://www.capitalexpress.com

Westford Technology Ventures, L.P.
17 Academy St.
Newark, NJ 07102
(973)624-2131
Fax: (973)624-2008

Accel Partners
1 Palmer Sq.
Princeton, NJ 08542
(609)683-4500
Fax: (609)683-4880
Website: http://www.accel.com

Cardinal Partners
221 Nassau St.
Princeton, NJ 08542
(609)924-6452
Fax: (609)683-0174
Website: http://www.cardinalhealth
partners.com

Domain Associates L.L.C.
One Palmer Sq., Ste. 515
Princeton, NJ 08542
(609)683-5656
Fax: (609)683-9789
Website: http://www.domainvc.com

Johnston Associates, Inc.
181 Cherry Valley Rd.
Princeton, NJ 08540
(609)924-3131
Fax: (609)683-7524
E-mail: jaincorp@aol.com

Kemper Ventures
Princeton Forrestal Village
155 Village Blvd.
Princeton, NJ 08540
(609)936-3035
Fax: (609)936-3051

Penny Lane Parnters
One Palmer Sq., Ste. 309
Princeton, NJ 08542
(609)497-4646
Fax: (609)497-0611

Early Stage Enterprises L.P.
995 Route 518
Skillman, NJ 08558
(609)921-8896

Fax: (609)921-8703
Website: http://www.esevc.com

MBW Management Inc.
1 Springfield Ave.
Summit, NJ 07901
(908)273-4060
Fax: (908)273-4430

BCI Advisors, Inc.
Glenpointe Center W.
Teaneck, NJ 07666
(201)836-3900
Fax: (201)836-6368
E-mail: info@bciadvisors.com
Website: http://www.bci partners.com

Demuth, Folger & Wetherill / DFW Capital Partners
Glenpointe Center E., 5th Fl.
300 Frank W. Burr Blvd.
Teaneck, NJ 07666
(201)836-2233
Fax: (201)836-5666
Website: http://www.dfwcapital.com

First Princeton Capital Corp.
189 Berdan Ave., No. 131
Wayne, NJ 07470-3233
(973)278-3233
Fax: (973)278-4290
Website: http://www.lytellcatt.net

Edelson Technology Partners
300 Tice Blvd.
Woodcliff Lake, NJ 07675
(201)930-9898
Fax: (201)930-8899
Website: http://www.edelsontech.com

New Mexico

Bruce F. Glaspell & Associates
10400 Academy Rd. NE, Ste. 313
Albuquerque, NM 87111
(505)292-4505
Fax: (505)292-4258

High Desert Ventures, Inc.
6101 Imparata St. NE, Ste. 1721
Albuquerque, NM 87111
(505)797-3330
Fax: (505)338-5147

New Business Capital Fund, Ltd.
5805 Torreon NE
Albuquerque, NM 87109
(505)822-8445

SBC Ventures
10400 Academy Rd. NE, Ste. 313
Albuquerque, NM 87111

(505)292-4505
Fax: (505)292-4528

Technology Ventures Corp.
1155 University Blvd. SE
Albuquerque, NM 87106
(505)246-2882
Fax: (505)246-2891

New York

**Small Business Technology
Investment Fund**
99 Washington Ave., Ste. 1731
Albany, NY 12210
(518)473-9741
Fax: (518)473-6876

Rand Capital Corp.
2200 Rand Bldg.
Buffalo, NY 14203
(716)853-0802
Fax: (716)854-8480
Website: http://www.randcapital.com

Seed Capital Partners
620 Main St.
Buffalo, NY 14202
(716)845-7520
Fax: (716)845-7539
Website: http://www.seedcp.com

Coleman Venture Group
5909 Northern Blvd.
PO Box 224
East Norwich, NY 11732
(516)626-3642
Fax: (516)626-9722

Vega Capital Corp.
45 Knollwood Rd.
Elmsford, NY 10523
(914)345-9500
Fax: (914)345-9505

Herbert Young Securities, Inc.
98 Cuttermill Rd.
Great Neck, NY 11021
(516)487-8300
Fax: (516)487-8319

**Sterling/Carl Marks Capital,
Inc.**
175 Great Neck Rd., Ste. 408
Great Neck, NY 11021
(516)482-7374
Fax: (516)487-0781
E-mail: stercrlmar@aol.com
Website: http://www.serlingcarlmarks
.com

Impex Venture Management Co.
PO Box 1570
Green Island, NY 12183
(518)271-8008
Fax: (518)271-9101

Corporate Venture Partners L.P.
200 Sunset Park
Ithaca, NY 14850
(607)257-6323
Fax: (607)257-6128

Arthur P. Gould & Co.
One Wilshire Dr.
Lake Success, NY 11020
(516)773-3000
Fax: (516)773-3289

Dauphin Capital Partners
108 Forest Ave.
Locust Valley, NY 11560
(516)759-3339
Fax: (516)759-3322
Website: http://www.dauphincapital.com

550 Digital Media Ventures
555 Madison Ave., 10th Fl.
New York, NY 10022
Website: http://www.550dmv.com

Aberlyn Capital Management Co., Inc.
500 Fifth Ave.
New York, NY 10110
(212)391-7750
Fax: (212)391-7762

Adler & Company
342 Madison Ave., Ste. 807
New York, NY 10173
(212)599-2535
Fax: (212)599-2526

Alimansky Capital Group, Inc.
605 Madison Ave., Ste. 300
New York, NY 10022-1901
(212)832-7300
Fax: (212)832-7338

Allegra Partners
515 Madison Ave., 29th Fl.
New York, NY 10022
(212)826-9080
Fax: (212)759-2561

The Argentum Group
The Chyrsler Bldg.
405 Lexington Ave.
New York, NY 10174
(212)949-6262
Fax: (212)949-8294
Website: http://www.argentumgroup.com

Axavision Inc.
14 Wall St., 26th Fl.
New York, NY 10005
(212)619-4000
Fax: (212)619-7202

Bedford Capital Corp.
18 East 48th St., Ste. 1800
New York, NY 10017
(212)688-5700
Fax: (212)754-4699
E-mail: info@bedfordnyc.com
Website: http://www.bedfordnyc.com

Bloom & Co.
950 Third Ave.
New York, NY 10022
(212)838-1858
Fax: (212)838-1843

Bristol Capital Management
300 Park Ave., 17th Fl.
New York, NY 10022
(212)572-6306
Fax: (212)705-4292

**Citicorp Venture Capital Ltd.
(New York City)**
399 Park Ave., 14th Fl.
Zone 4
New York, NY 10043
(212)559-1127
Fax: (212)888-2940

CM Equity Partners
135 E. 57th St.
New York, NY 10022
(212)909-8428
Fax: (212)980-2630

Cohen & Co., L.L.C.
800 Third Ave.
New York, NY 10022
(212)317-2250
Fax: (212)317-2255
E-mail: nlcohen@aol.com

Cornerstone Equity Investors, L.L.C.
717 5th Ave., Ste. 1100
New York, NY 10022
(212)753-0901
Fax: (212)826-6798
Website: http://www.cornerstone-equity
.com

CW Group, Inc.
1041 3rd Ave., 2nd fl.
New York, NY 10021
(212)308-5266
Fax: (212)644-0354
Website: http://www.cwventures.com

DH Blair Investment Banking Corp.
44 Wall St., 2nd Fl.
New York, NY 10005
(212)495-5000
Fax: (212)269-1438

Dresdner Kleinwort Capital
75 Wall St.
New York, NY 10005
(212)429-3131
Fax: (212)429-3139
Website: http://www.dresdnerkb.com

East River Ventures, L.P.
645 Madison Ave., 22nd Fl.
New York, NY 10022
(212)644-2322
Fax: (212)644-5498

Easton Hunt Capital Partners
641 Lexington Ave., 21st Fl.
New York, NY 10017
(212)702-0950
Fax: (212)702-0952
Website: http://www.eastoncapital.com

Elk Associates Funding Corp.
747 3rd Ave., Ste. 4C
New York, NY 10017
(212)355-2449
Fax: (212)759-3338

EOS Partners, L.P.
320 Park Ave., 22nd Fl.
New York, NY 10022
(212)832-5800
Fax: (212)832-5815
E-mail: mfirst@eospartners.com
Website: http://www.eospartners.com

Euclid Partners
45 Rockefeller Plaza, Ste. 3240
New York, NY 10111
(212)218-6880
Fax: (212)218-6877
E-mail: graham@euclidpartners.com
Website: http://www.euclidpartners.com

Evergreen Capital Partners, Inc.
150 East 58th St.
New York, NY 10155
(212)813-0758
Fax: (212)813-0754

Exeter Capital L.P.
10 E. 53rd St.
New York, NY 10022
(212)872-1172
Fax: (212)872-1198
E-mail: exeter@usa.net

Financial Technology Research Corp.
518 Broadway
Penthouse

New York, NY 10012
(212)625-9100
Fax: (212)431-0300
E-mail: fintek@financier.com

4C Ventures
237 Park Ave., Ste. 801
New York, NY 10017
(212)692-3680
Fax: (212)692-3685
Website: http://www.4cventures.com

Fusient Ventures
99 Park Ave., 20th Fl.
New York, NY 10016
(212)972-8999
Fax: (212)972-9876
E-mail: info@fusient.com
Website: http://www.fusient.com

Generation Capital Partners
551 Fifth Ave., Ste. 3100
New York, NY 10176
(212)450-8507
Fax: (212)450-8550
Website: http://www.genpartners.com

Golub Associates, Inc.
555 Madison Ave.
New York, NY 10022
(212)750-6060
Fax: (212)750-5505

Hambro America Biosciences Inc.
650 Madison Ave., 21st Floor
New York, NY 10022
(212)223-7400
Fax: (212)223-0305

Hanover Capital Corp.
505 Park Ave., 15th Fl.
New York, NY 10022
(212)755-1222
Fax: (212)935-1787

Harvest Partners, Inc.
280 Park Ave, 33rd Fl.
New York, NY 10017
(212)559-6300
Fax: (212)812-0100
Website: http://www.harvpart.com

Holding Capital Group, Inc.
10 E. 53rd St., 30th Fl.
New York, NY 10022
(212)486-6670
Fax: (212)486-0843

Hudson Venture Partners
660 Madison Ave., 14th Fl.
New York, NY 10021-8405
(212)644-9797
Fax: (212)644-7430
Website: http://www.hudsonptr.com

IBJS Capital Corp.
1 State St., 9th Fl.
New York, NY 10004
(212)858-2018
Fax: (212)858-2768

InterEquity Capital Partners, L.P.
220 5th Ave.
New York, NY 10001
(212)779-2022
Fax: (212)779-2103
Website: http://www.interequity-capital
.com

The Jordan Edmiston Group Inc.
150 East 52nd St., 18th Fl.
New York, NY 10022
(212)754-0710
Fax: (212)754-0337

Josephberg, Grosz and Co., Inc.
633 3rd Ave., 13th Fl.
New York, NY 10017
(212)974-9926
Fax: (212)397-5832

J.P. Morgan Capital Corp.
60 Wall St.
New York, NY 10260-0060
(212)648-9000
Fax: (212)648-5002
Website: http://www.jpmorgan.com

The Lambda Funds
380 Lexington Ave., 54th Fl.
New York, NY 10168
(212)682-3454
Fax: (212)682-9231

Lepercq Capital Management Inc.
1675 Broadway
New York, NY 10019
(212)698-0795
Fax: (212)262-0155

Loeb Partners Corp.
61 Broadway, Ste. 2400
New York, NY 10006
(212)483-7000
Fax: (212)574-2001

Madison Investment Partners
660 Madison Ave.
New York, NY 10021
(212)223-2600
Fax: (212)223-8208

MC Capital Inc.
520 Madison Ave., 16th Fl.
New York, NY 10022
(212)644-0841
Fax: (212)644-2926

McCown, De Leeuw and Co.
(New York)
65 E. 55th St., 36th Fl.
New York, NY 10022
(212)355-5500
Fax: (212)355-6283
Website: http://www.mdcpartners.com

Morgan Stanley Venture Partners
1221 Avenue of the Americas, 33rd Fl.
New York, NY 10020
(212)762-7900
Fax: (212)762-8424
E-mail: msventures@ms.com
Website: http://www.msvp.com

Nazem and Co.
645 Madison Ave., 12th Fl.
New York, NY 10022
(212)371-7900
Fax: (212)371-2150

Needham Capital Management, L.L.C.
445 Park Ave.
New York, NY 10022
(212)371-8300
Fax: (212)705-0299
Website: http://www.needhamco.com

Norwood Venture Corp.
1430 Broadway, Ste. 1607
New York, NY 10018
(212)869-5075
Fax: (212)869-5331
E-mail: nvc@mail.idt.net
Website: http://www.norven.com

Noveltek Venture Corp.
521 Fifth Ave., Ste. 1700
New York, NY 10175
(212)286-1963

Paribas Principal, Inc.
787 7th Ave.
New York, NY 10019
(212)841-2005
Fax: (212)841-3558

Patricof & Co. Ventures, Inc.
(New York)
445 Park Ave.
New York, NY 10022
(212)753-6300
Fax: (212)319-6155
Website: http://www.patricof.com

The Platinum Group, Inc.
350 Fifth Ave, Ste. 7113
New York, NY 10118
(212)736-4300
Fax: (212)736-6086
Website: http://www.platinumgroup.com

Pomona Capital
780 Third Ave., 28th Fl.
New York, NY 10017
(212)593-3639
Fax: (212)593-3987
Website: http://www.pomonacapital.com

Prospect Street Ventures
10 East 40th St., 44th Fl.
New York, NY 10016
(212)448-0702
Fax: (212)448-9652
E-mail: wkohler@prospectstreet.com
Website: http://www.prospectstreet.com

Regent Capital Management
505 Park Ave., Ste. 1700
New York, NY 10022
(212)735-9900
Fax: (212)735-9908

Rothschild Ventures, Inc.
1251 Avenue of the Americas, 51st Fl.
New York, NY 10020
(212)403-3500
Fax: (212)403-3652
Website: http://www.nmrothschild.com

Sandler Capital Management
767 Fifth Ave., 45th Fl.
New York, NY 10153
(212)754-8100
Fax: (212)826-0280

Siguler Guff & Company
630 Fifth Ave., 16th Fl.
New York, NY 10111
(212)332-5100
Fax: (212)332-5120

Spencer Trask Ventures Inc.
535 Madison Ave.
New York, NY 10022
(212)355-5565
Fax: (212)751-3362
Website: http://www.spencertrask.com

Sprout Group (New York City)
277 Park Ave.
New York, NY 10172
(212)892-3600
Fax: (212)892-3444
E-mail: info@sproutgroup.com
Website: http://www.sproutgroup.com

US Trust Private Equity
114 W.47th St.
New York, NY 10036
(212)852-3949
Fax: (212)852-3759
Website: http://www.ustrust.com/
privateequity

Vencon Management Inc.
301 West 53rd St., Ste. 10F
New York, NY 10019
(212)581-8787
Fax: (212)397-4126
Website: http://www.venconinc.com

Venrock Associates
30 Rockefeller Plaza, Ste. 5508
New York, NY 10112
(212)649-5600
Fax: (212)649-5788
Website: http://www.venrock.com

Venture Capital Fund of America, Inc.
509 Madison Ave., Ste. 812
New York, NY 10022
(212)838-5577
Fax: (212)838-7614
E-mail: mail@vcfa.com
Website: http://www.vcfa.com

Venture Opportunities Corp.
150 E. 58th St.
New York, NY 10155
(212)832-3737
Fax: (212)980-6603

Warburg Pincus Ventures, Inc.
466 Lexington Ave., 11th Fl.
New York, NY 10017
(212)878-9309
Fax: (212)878-9200
Website: http://www.warburgpincus.com

Wasserstein, Perella & Co. Inc.
31 W. 52nd St., 27th Fl.
New York, NY 10019
(212)702-5691
Fax: (212)969-7879

Welsh, Carson, Anderson, & Stowe
320 Park Ave., Ste. 2500
New York, NY 10022-6815
(212)893-9500
Fax: (212)893-9575

Whitney and Co. (New York)
630 Fifth Ave. Ste. 3225
New York, NY 10111
(212)332-2400
Fax: (212)332-2422
Website: http://www.jhwitney.com

Winthrop Ventures
74 Trinity Place, Ste. 600
New York, NY 10006
(212)422-0100

The Pittsford Group
8 Lodge Pole Rd.
Pittsford, NY 14534
(716)223-3523

Genesee Funding
70 Linden Oaks, 3rd Fl.
Rochester, NY 14625
(716)383-5550
Fax: (716)383-5305

Gabelli Multimedia Partners
One Corporate Center
Rye, NY 10580
(914)921-5395
Fax: (914)921-5031

Stamford Financial
108 Main St.
Stamford, NY 12167
(607)652-3311
Fax: (607)652-6301
Website: http://www.stamfordfinancial
.com

Northwood Ventures LLC
485 Underhill Blvd., Ste. 205
Syosset, NY 11791
(516)364-5544
Fax: (516)364-0879
E-mail: northwood@northwood.com
Website: http://www.northwood
ventures.com

Exponential Business Development Co.
216 Walton St.
Syracuse, NY 13202-1227
(315)474-4500
Fax: (315)474-4682
E-mail: dirksonn@aol.com
Website: http://www.exponential-ny.com

Onondaga Venture Capital Fund Inc.
714 State Tower Bldg.
Syracuse, NY 13202
(315)478-0157
Fax: (315)478-0158

Bessemer Venture Partners (Westbury)
1400 Old Country Rd., Ste. 109
Westbury, NY 11590
(516)997-2300
Fax: (516)997-2371
E-mail: bob@bvpny.com
Website: http://www.bvp.com

Ovation Capital Partners
120 Bloomingdale Rd., 4th Fl.
White Plains, NY 10605
(914)258-0011
Fax: (914)684-0848
Website: http://www.ovationcapital.com

North Carolina

Carolinas Capital Investment Corp.
1408 Biltmore Dr.
Charlotte, NC 28207

(704)375-3888
Fax: (704)375-6226

First Union Capital Partners
1st Union Center, 12th Fl.
301 S. College St.
Charlotte, NC 28288-0732
(704)383-0000
Fax: (704)374-6711
Website: http://www.fucp.com

Frontier Capital LLC
525 North Tryon St., Ste. 1700
Charlotte, NC 28202
(704)414-2880
Fax: (704)414-2881
Website: http://www.frontierfunds.com

Kitty Hawk Capital
2700 Coltsgate Rd., Ste. 202
Charlotte, NC 28211
(704)362-3909
Fax: (704)362-2774
Website: http://www.kittyhawkcapital
.com

Piedmont Venture Partners
One Morrocroft Centre
6805 Morisson Blvd., Ste. 380
Charlotte, NC 28211
(704)731-5200
Fax: (704)365-9733
Website: http://www.piedmontvp.com

Ruddick Investment Co.
1800 Two First Union Center
Charlotte, NC 28282
(704)372-5404
Fax: (704)372-6409

The Shelton Companies Inc.
3600 One First Union Center
301 S. College St.
Charlotte, NC 28202
(704)348-2200
Fax: (704)348-2260

Wakefield Group
1110 E. Morehead St.
PO Box 36329
Charlotte, NC 28236
(704)372-0355
Fax: (704)372-8216
Website: http://www.wakefieldgroup
.com

Aurora Funds, Inc.
2525 Meridian Pkwy., Ste. 220
Durham, NC 27713
(919)484-0400
Fax: (919)484-0444
Website: http://www.aurora funds.com

Intersouth Partners
3211 Shannon Rd., Ste. 610
Durham, NC 27707
(919)493-6640
Fax: (919)493-6649
E-mail: info@intersouth.com
Website: http://www.intersouth.com

Geneva Merchant Banking Partners
PO Box 21962
Greensboro, NC 27420
(336)275-7002
Fax: (336)275-9155
Website: http://www.genevamerchant
bank.com

The North Carolina Enterprise Fund, L.P.
3600 Glenwood Ave., Ste. 107
Raleigh, NC 27612
(919)781-2691
Fax: (919)783-9195
Website: http://www.ncef.com

Ohio

Senmend Medical Ventures
4445 Lake Forest Dr., Ste. 600
Cincinnati, OH 45242
(513)563-3264
Fax: (513)563-3261

The Walnut Group
312 Walnut St., Ste. 1151
Cincinnati, OH 45202
(513)651-3300
Fax: (513)929-4441
Website: http://www.thewalnutgroup
.com

Brantley Venture Partners
20600 Chagrin Blvd., Ste. 1150
Cleveland, OH 44122
(216)283-4800
Fax: (216)283-5324

Clarion Capital Corp.
1801 E. 9th St., Ste. 1120
Cleveland, OH 44114
(216)687-1096
Fax: (216)694-3545

Crystal Internet Venture Fund, L.P.
1120 Chester Ave., Ste. 418
Cleveland, OH 44114
(216)263-5515
Fax: (216)263-5518
E-mail: jf@crystalventure.com
Website: http://www.crystalventure.com

Key Equity Capital Corp.
127 Public Sq., 28th Fl.
Cleveland, OH 44114

(216)689-3000
Fax: (216)689-3204
Website: http://www.keybank.com

Morgenthaler Ventures
Terminal Tower
50 Public Square, Ste. 2700
Cleveland, OH 44113
(216)416-7500
Fax: (216)416-7501
Website: http://www.morgenthaler.com

National City Equity Partners Inc.
1965 E. 6th St.
Cleveland, OH 44114
(216)575-2491
Fax: (216)575-9965
E-mail: nccap@aol.com
Website: http://www.nccapital.com

Primus Venture Partners, Inc.
5900 LanderBrook Dr., Ste. 2000
Cleveland, OH 44124-4020
(440)684-7300
Fax: (440)684-7342
E-mail: info@primusventure.com
Website: http://www.primusventure.com

Banc One Capital Partners (Columbus)
150 East Gay St., 24th Fl.
Columbus, OH 43215
(614)217-1100
Fax: (614)217-1217

Battelle Venture Partners
505 King Ave.
Columbus, OH 43201
(614)424-7005
Fax: (614)424-4874

Ohio Partners
62 E. Board St., 3rd Fl.
Columbus, OH 43215
(614)621-1210
Fax: (614)621-1240

Capital Technology Group, L.L.C.
400 Metro Place North, Ste. 300
Dublin, OH 43017
(614)792-6066
Fax: (614)792-6036
E-mail: info@capitaltech.com
Website: http://www.capitaltech.com

Northwest Ohio Venture Fund
4159 Holland-Sylvania R., Ste. 202
Toledo, OH 43623
(419)824-8144
Fax: (419)882-2035
E-mail: bwalsh@novf.com

Oklahoma

Moore & Associates
1000 W. Wilshire Blvd., Ste. 370
Oklahoma City, OK 73116
(405)842-3660
Fax: (405)842-3763

Chisholm Private Capital Partners
100 West 5th St., Ste. 805
Tulsa, OK 74103
(918)584-0440
Fax: (918)584-0441
Website: http://www.chisholmvc.com

Davis, Tuttle Venture Partners (Tulsa)
320 S. Boston, Ste. 1000
Tulsa, OK 74103-3703
(918)584-7272
Fax: (918)582-3404
Website: http://www.davistuttle.com

RBC Ventures
2627 E. 21st St.
Tulsa, OK 74114
(918)744-5607
Fax: (918)743-8630

Oregon

Utah Ventures II LP
10700 SW Beaverton-Hillsdale Hwy.,
Ste. 548
Beaverton, OR 97005
(503)574-4125
E-mail: adishlip@uven.com
Website: http://www.uven.com

Orien Ventures
14523 SW Westlake Dr.
Lake Oswego, OR 97035
(503)699-1680
Fax: (503)699-1681

OVP Venture Partners (Lake Oswego)
340 Oswego Pointe Dr., Ste. 200
Lake Oswego, OR 97034
(503)697-8766
Fax: (503)697-8863
E-mail: info@ovp.com
Website: http://www.ovp.com

Oregon Resource and Technology Development Fund
4370 NE Halsey St., Ste. 233
Portland, OR 97213-1566
(503)282-4462
Fax: (503)282-2976

Shaw Venture Partners
400 SW 6th Ave., Ste. 1100
Portland, OR 97204-1636
(503)228-4884

Fax: (503)227-2471
Website: http://www.shawventures.com

Pennsylvania

Mid-Atlantic Venture Funds
125 Goodman Dr.
Bethlehem, PA 18015
(610)865-6550
Fax: (610)865-6427
Website: http://www.mavf.com

Newspring Ventures
100 W. Elm St., Ste. 101
Conshohocken, PA 19428
(610)567-2380
Fax: (610)567-2388
Website: http://www.newsprint
ventures.com

Patricof & Co. Ventures, Inc.
455 S. Gulph Rd., Ste. 410
King of Prussia, PA 19406
(610)265-0286
Fax: (610)265-4959
Website: http://www.patricof.com

Loyalhanna Venture Fund
527 Cedar Way, Ste. 104
Oakmont, PA 15139
(412)820-7035
Fax: (412)820-7036

Innovest Group Inc.
2000 Market St., Ste. 1400
Philadelphia, PA 19103
(215)564-3960
Fax: (215)569-3272

Keystone Venture Capital Management Co.
1601 Market St., Ste. 2500
Philadelphia, PA 19103
(215)241-1200
Fax: (215)241-1211
Website: http://www.keystonevc.com

Liberty Venture Partners
2005 Market St., Ste. 200
Philadelphia, PA 19103
(215)282-4484
Fax: (215)282-4485
E-mail: info@libertyvp.com
Website: http://www.libertyvp.com

Penn Janney Fund, Inc.
1801 Market St., 11th Fl.
Philadelphia, PA 19103
(215)665-4447
Fax: (215)557-0820

Philadelphia Ventures, Inc.
The Bellevue
200 S. Broad St.

Philadelphia, PA 19102
(215)732-4445
Fax: (215)732-4644

Birchmere Ventures Inc.
2000 Technology Dr.
Pittsburgh, PA 15219-3109
(412)803-8000
Fax: (412)687-8139
Website: http://www.birchmerevc.com

CEO Venture Fund
2000 Technology Dr., Ste. 160
Pittsburgh, PA 15219-3109
(412)687-3451
Fax: (412)687-8139
E-mail: ceofund@aol.com
Website: http://www.ceoventurefund
.com

Innovation Works Inc.
2000 Technology Dr., Ste. 250
Pittsburgh, PA 15219
(412)681-1520
Fax: (412)681-2625
Website: http://www.innovation
works.org

Keystone Minority Capital Fund L.P.
1801 Centre Ave., Ste. 201
Williams Sq.
Pittsburgh, PA 15219
(412)338-2230
Fax: (412)338-2224

Mellon Ventures, Inc.
One Mellon Bank Ctr., Rm. 3500
Pittsburgh, PA 15258
(412)236-3594
Fax: (412)236-3593
Website: http://www.mellonventures
.com

Pennsylvania Growth Fund
5850 Ellsworth Ave., Ste. 303
Pittsburgh, PA 15232
(412)661-1000
Fax: (412)361-0676

Point Venture Partners
The Century Bldg.
130 Seventh St., 7th Fl.
Pittsburgh, PA 15222
(412)261-1966
Fax: (412)261-1718

Cross Atlantic Capital Partners
5 Radnor Corporate Center, Ste. 555
Radnor, PA 19087
(610)995-2650
Fax: (610)971-2062
Website: http://www.xacp.com

Meridian Venture Partners (Radnor)
The Radnor Court Bldg., Ste. 140
259 Radnor-Chester Rd.
Radnor, PA 19087
(610)254-2999
Fax: (610)254-2996
E-mail: mvpart@ix.netcom.com

TDH
919 Conestoga Rd., Bldg. 1, Ste. 301
Rosemont, PA 19010
(610)526-9970
Fax: (610)526-9971

Adams Capital Management
500 Blackburn Ave.
Sewickley, PA 15143
(412)749-9454
Fax: (412)749-9459
Website: http://www.acm.com

S.R. One, Ltd.
Four Tower Bridge
200 Barr Harbor Dr., Ste. 250
W. Conshohocken, PA 19428
(610)567-1000
Fax: (610)567-1039

Greater Philadelphia Venture Capital Corp.
351 East Conestoga Rd.
Wayne, PA 19087
(610)688-6829
Fax: (610)254-8958

PA Early Stage
435 Devon Park Dr., Bldg. 500, Ste. 510
Wayne, PA 19087
(610)293-4075
Fax: (610)254-4240
Website: http://www.paearlystage.com

The Sandhurst Venture Fund, L.P.
351 E. Constoga Rd.
Wayne, PA 19087
(610)254-8900
Fax: (610)254-8958

TL Ventures
700 Bldg.
435 Devon Park Dr.
Wayne, PA 19087-1990
(610)975-3765
Fax: (610)254-4210
Website: http://www.tlventures.com

Rockhill Ventures, Inc.
100 Front St., Ste. 1350
West Conshohocken, PA 19428
(610)940-0300
Fax: (610)940-0301

Puerto Rico

Advent-Morro Equity Partners
Banco Popular Bldg.
206 Tetuan St., Ste. 903
San Juan, PR 00902
(787)725-5285
Fax: (787)721-1735

North America Investment Corp.
Mercantil Plaza, Ste. 813
PO Box 191831
San Juan, PR 00919
(787)754-6178
Fax: (787)754-6181

Rhode Island

Manchester Humphreys, Inc.
40 Westminster St., Ste. 900
Providence, RI 02903
(401)454-0400
Fax: (401)454-0403

Navis Partners
50 Kennedy Plaza, 12th Fl.
Providence, RI 02903
(401)278-6770
Fax: (401)278-6387
Website: http://www.navispartners.com

South Carolina

Capital Insights, L.L.C.
PO Box 27162
Greenville, SC 29616-2162
(864)242-6832
Fax: (864)242-6755
E-mail: jwarner@capitalinsights.com
Website: http://www.capitalinsights.com

Transamerica Mezzanine Financing
7 N. Laurens St., Ste. 603
Greenville, SC 29601
(864)232-6198
Fax: (864)241-4444

Tennessee

Valley Capital Corp.
Krystal Bldg.
100 W. Martin Luther King Blvd.,
Ste. 212
Chattanooga, TN 37402
(423)265-1557
Fax: (423)265-1588

Coleman Swenson Booth Inc.
237 2nd Ave. S
Franklin, TN 37064-2649
(615)791-9462
Fax: (615)791-9636
Website: http://www.colemanswenson
.com

Capital Services & Resources, Inc.
5159 Wheelis Dr., Ste. 106
Memphis, TN 38117
(901)761-2156
Fax: (907)767-0060

Paradigm Capital Partners LLC
6410 Poplar Ave., Ste. 395
Memphis, TN 38119
(901)682-6060
Fax: (901)328-3061

SSM Ventures
845 Crossover Ln., Ste. 140
Memphis, TN 38117
(901)767-1131
Fax: (901)767-1135
Website: http://www.ssm ventures.com

Capital Across America L.P.
501 Union St., Ste. 201
Nashville, TN 37219
(615)254-1414
Fax: (615)254-1856
Website: http://www.capitalacross
america.com

Equitas L.P.
2000 Glen Echo Rd., Ste. 101
PO Box 158838
Nashville, TN 37215-8838
(615)383-8673
Fax: (615)383-8693

Massey Burch Capital Corp.
One Burton Hills Blvd., Ste. 350
Nashville, TN 37215
(615)665-3221
Fax: (615)665-3240
E-mail: tcalton@masseyburch.com
Website: http://www.masseyburch.com

Nelson Capital Corp.
3401 West End Ave., Ste. 300
Nashville, TN 37203
(615)292-8787
Fax: (615)385-3150

Texas

Phillips-Smith Specialty Retail Group
5080 Spectrum Dr., Ste. 805 W
Addison, TX 75001
(972)387-0725
Fax: (972)458-2560
E-mail: pssrg@aol.com
Website: http://www.phillips-smith.com

Austin Ventures, L.P.
701 Brazos St., Ste. 1400
Austin, TX 78701
(512)485-1900
Fax: (512)476-3952

E-mail: info@ausven.com
Website: http://www.austinventures.com

The Capital Network
3925 West Braker Lane, Ste. 406
Austin, TX 78759-5321
(512)305-0826
Fax: (512)305-0836

Techxas Ventures LLC
5000 Plaza on the Lake
Austin, TX 78746
(512)343-0118
Fax: (512)343-1879
E-mail: bruce@techxas.com
Website: http://www.techxas.com

Alliance Financial of Houston
218 Heather Ln.
Conroe, TX 77385-9013
(936)447-3300
Fax: (936)447-4222

Amerimark Capital Corp.
1111 W. Mockingbird, Ste. 1111
Dallas, TX 75247
(214)638-7878
Fax: (214)638-7612
E-mail: amerimark@amcapital.com
Website: http://www.amcapital.com

AMT Venture Partners / AMT Capital Ltd.
5220 Spring Valley Rd., Ste. 600
Dallas, TX 75240
(214)905-9757
Fax: (214)905-9761
Website: http://www.amtcapital.com

Arkoma Venture Partners
5950 Berkshire Lane, Ste. 1400
Dallas, TX 75225
(214)739-3515
Fax: (214)739-3572
E-mail: joelf@arkomavp.com

Capital Southwest Corp.
12900 Preston Rd., Ste. 700
Dallas, TX 75230
(972)233-8242
Fax: (972)233-7362
Website: http://www.capitalsouthwest
.com

Dali, Hook Partners
One Lincoln Center, Ste. 1550
5400 LBJ Freeway
Dallas, TX 75240
(972)991-5457
Fax: (972)991-5458
E-mail: dhook@hookpartners.com
Website: http://www.hookpartners.com

HO2 Partners
Two Galleria Tower
13455 Noel Rd., Ste. 1670
Dallas, TX 75240
(972)702-1144
Fax: (972)702-8234
Website: http://www.ho2.com

Interwest Partners (Dallas)
2 Galleria Tower
13455 Noel Rd., Ste. 1670
Dallas, TX 75240
(972)392-7279
Fax: (972)490-6348
Website: http://www.interwest.com

Kahala Investments, Inc.
8214 Westchester Dr., Ste. 715
Dallas, TX 75225
(214)987-0077
Fax: (214)987-2332

MESBIC Ventures Holding Co.
2435 North Central Expressway, Ste. 200
Dallas, TX 75080
(972)991-1597
Fax: (972)991-4770
Website: http://www.mvhc.com

North Texas MESBIC, Inc.
9500 Forest Lane, Ste. 430
Dallas, TX 75243
(214)221-3565
Fax: (214)221-3566

Richard Jaffe & Company, Inc,
7318 Royal Cir.
Dallas, TX 75230
(214)265-9397
Fax: (214)739-1845

Sevin Rosen Management Co.
13455 Noel Rd., Ste. 1670
Dallas, TX 75240
(972)702-1100
Fax: (972)702-1103
E-mail: info@srfunds.com
Website: http://www.srfunds.com

Stratford Capital Partners, L.P.
300 Crescent Ct., Ste. 500
Dallas, TX 75201
(214)740-7377
Fax: (214)720-7393
E-mail: stratcap@hmtf.com

Sunwestern Investment Group
12221 Merit Dr., Ste. 935
Dallas, TX 75251
(972)239-5650
Fax: (972)701-0024

Wingate Partners
750 N. St. Paul St., Ste. 1200
Dallas, TX 75201
(214)720-1313
Fax: (214)871-8799

Buena Venture Associates
201 Main St., 32nd Fl.
Fort Worth, TX 76102
(817)339-7400
Fax: (817)390-8408
Website: http://www.buenaventure.com

The Catalyst Group
3 Riverway, Ste. 770
Houston, TX 77056
(713)623-8133
Fax: (713)623-0473
E-mail: herman@thecatalystgroup.net
Website: http://www.thecatalyst
group.net

Cureton & Co., Inc.
1100 Louisiana, Ste. 3250
Houston, TX 77002
(713)658-9806
Fax: (713)658-0476

Davis, Tuttle Venture Partners (Dallas)
8 Greenway Plaza, Ste. 1020
Houston, TX 77046
(713)993-0440
Fax: (713)621-2297
Website: http://www.davistuttle.com

Houston Partners
401 Louisiana, 8th Fl.
Houston, TX 77002
(713)222-8600
Fax: (713)222-8932

Southwest Venture Group
10878 Westheimer, Ste. 178
Houston, TX 77042
(713)827-8947
(713)461-1470

AM Fund
4600 Post Oak Place, Ste. 100
Houston, TX 77027
(713)627-9111
Fax: (713)627-9119

Ventex Management, Inc.
3417 Milam St.
Houston, TX 77002-9531
(713)659-7870
Fax: (713)659-7855

MBA Venture Group
1004 Olde Town Rd., Ste. 102
Irving, TX 75061
(972)986-6703

First Capital Group Management Co.
750 East Mulberry St., Ste. 305
PO Box 15616
San Antonio, TX 78212
(210)736-4233
Fax: (210)736-5449

The Southwest Venture Partnerships
16414 San Pedro, Ste. 345
San Antonio, TX 78232
(210)402-1200
Fax: (210)402-1221
E-mail: swvp@aol.com

Medtech International Inc.
1742 Carriageway
Sugarland, TX 77478
(713)980-8474
Fax: (713)980-6343

Utah

First Security Business Investment Corp.
15 East 100 South, Ste. 100
Salt Lake City, UT 84111
(801)246-5737
Fax: (801)246-5740

Utah Ventures II, L.P.
423 Wakara Way, Ste. 206
Salt Lake City, UT 84108
(801)583-5922
Fax: (801)583-4105
Website: http://www.uven.com

Wasatch Venture Corp.
1 S. Main St., Ste. 1400
Salt Lake City, UT 84133
(801)524-8939
Fax: (801)524-8941
E-mail: mail@wasatchvc.com

Vermont

North Atlantic Capital Corp.
76 Saint Paul St., Ste. 600
Burlington, VT 05401
(802)658-7820
Fax: (802)658-5757
Website: http://www.northatlantic
capital.com

Green Mountain Advisors Inc.
PO Box 1230
Quechee, VT 05059
(802)296-7800
Fax: (802)296-6012
Website: http://www.gmtcap.com

Virginia

Oxford Financial Services Corp.
Alexandria, VA 22314
(703)519-4900
Fax: (703)519-4910
E-mail: oxford133@aol.com

Continental SBIC
4141 N. Henderson Rd.
Arlington, VA 22203
(703)527-5200
Fax: (703)527-3700

Novak Biddle Venture Partners
1750 Tysons Blvd., Ste. 1190
McLean, VA 22102
(703)847-3770
Fax: (703)847-3771
E-mail: roger@novakbiddle.com
Website: http://www.novakbiddle.com

Spacevest
11911 Freedom Dr., Ste. 500
Reston, VA 20190
(703)904-9800
Fax: (703)904-0571
E-mail: spacevest@spacevest.com
Website: http://www.spacevest.com

Virginia Capital
1801 Libbie Ave., Ste. 201
Richmond, VA 23226
(804)648-4802
Fax: (804)648-4809
E-mail: webmaster@vacapital.com
Website: http://www.vacapital.com

Calvert Social Venture Partners
402 Maple Ave. W
Vienna, VA 22180
(703)255-4930
Fax: (703)255-4931
E-mail: calven2000@aol.com

Fairfax Partners
8000 Towers Crescent Dr., Ste. 940
Vienna, VA 22182
(703)847-9486
Fax: (703)847-0911

Global Internet Ventures
8150 Leesburg Pike, Ste. 1210
Vienna, VA 22182
(703)442-3300
Fax: (703)442-3388
Website: http://www.givinc.com

Walnut Capital Corp. (Vienna)
8000 Towers Crescent Dr., Ste. 1070
Vienna, VA 22182
(703)448-3771
Fax: (703)448-7751

Washington

Encompass Ventures

777 108th Ave. NE, Ste. 2300
Bellevue, WA 98004
(425)486-3900
Fax: (425)486-3901
E-mail: info@evpartners.com
Website: http://www.encompass
ventures.com

Fluke Venture Partners

11400 SE Sixth St., Ste. 230
Bellevue, WA 98004
(425)453-4590
Fax: (425)453-4675
E-mail: gabelein@flukeventures.com
Website: http://www.flukeventures.com

Pacific Northwest Partners
SBIC, L.P.

15352 SE 53rd St.
Bellevue, WA 98006
(425)455-9967
Fax: (425)455-9404

Materia Venture Associates, L.P.

3435 Carillon Pointe
Kirkland, WA 98033-7354
(425)822-4100
Fax: (425)827-4086

OVP Venture Partners (Kirkland)

2420 Carillon Pt.
Kirkland, WA 98033
(425)889-9192
Fax: (425)889-0152
E-mail: info@ovp.com
Website: http://www.ovp.com

Digital Partners

999 3rd Ave., Ste. 1610
Seattle, WA 98104
(206)405-3607
Fax: (206)405-3617
Website: http://www.digitalpartners.com

Frazier & Company

601 Union St., Ste. 3300
Seattle, WA 98101
(206)621-7200
Fax: (206)621-1848
E-mail: jon@frazierco.com

Kirlan Venture Capital, Inc.

221 First Ave. W, Ste. 108
Seattle, WA 98119-4223
(206)281-8610
Fax: (206)285-3451
Website: http://www.kirlanventure.com

Phoenix Partners

1000 2nd Ave., Ste. 3600
Seattle, WA 98104
(206)624-8968
Fax: (206)624-1907

Voyager Capital

800 5th St., Ste. 4100
Seattle, WA 98103
(206)470-1180
Fax: (206)470-1185
E-mail: info@voyagercap.com
Website: http://www.voyagercap.com

Northwest Venture Associates

221 N. Wall St., Ste. 628
Spokane, WA 99201
(509)747-0728
Fax: (509)747-0758
Website: http://www.nwva.com

Wisconsin

Venture Investors
Management, L.L.C.

University Research Park
505 S. Rosa Rd.
Madison, WI 53719
(608)441-2700
Fax: (608)441-2727
E-mail: roger@ventureinvestors.com
Website: http://www.ventureinvesters
.com

Capital Investments, Inc.

1009 West Glen Oaks Lane, Ste. 103
Mequon, WI 53092
(414)241-0303
Fax: (414)241-8451
Website: http://www.capitalinvestment
sinc.com

Future Value Venture, Inc.

2745 N. Martin Luther King Dr., Ste. 204
Milwaukee, WI 53212-2300
(414)264-2252
Fax: (414)264-2253
E-mail: fvventures@aol.com
William Beckett, President

Lubar and Co., Inc.

700 N. Water St., Ste. 1200
Milwaukee, WI 53202
(414)291-9000
Fax: (414)291-9061

GCI

20875 Crossroads Cir., Ste. 100
Waukesha, WI 53186
(262)798-5080
Fax: (262)798-5087

Glossary of Small Business Terms

Absolute liability
Liability that is incurred due to product defects or negligent actions. Manufacturers or retail establishments are held responsible, even though the defect or action may not have been intentional or negligent.

ACE
See Active Corps of Executives

Accident and health benefits
Benefits offered to employees and their families in order to offset the costs associated with accidental death, accidental injury, or sickness.

Account statement
A record of transactions, including payments, new debt, and deposits, incurred during a defined period of time.

Accounting system
System capturing the costs of all employees and/or machinery included in business expenses.

Accounts payable
See Trade credit

Accounts receivable
Unpaid accounts which arise from unsettled claims and transactions from the sale of a company's products or services to its customers.

Active Corps of Executives (ACE)
A group of volunteers for a management assistance program of the U.S. Small Business Administration; volunteers provide one-on-one counseling and teach workshops and seminars for small firms.

ADA
See Americans with Disabilities Act

Adaptation
The process whereby an invention is modified to meet the needs of users.

Adaptive engineering
The process whereby an invention is modified to meet the manufacturing and commercial requirements of a targeted market.

Adverse selection
The tendency for higher-risk individuals to purchase health care and more comprehensive plans, resulting in increased costs.

Advertising
A marketing tool used to capture public attention and influence purchasing decisions for a product or service. Utilizes various forms of media to generate consumer response, such as flyers, magazines, newspapers, radio, and television.

Age discrimination
The denial of the rights and privileges of employment based solely on the age of an individual.

Agency costs
Costs incurred to insure that the lender or investor maintains control over assets while allowing the borrower or entrepreneur to use them. Monitoring and information costs are the two major types of agency costs.

Agribusiness
The production and sale of commodities and products from the commercial farming industry.

Americans with Disabilities Act (ADA)
Law designed to ensure equal access and opportunity to handicapped persons.

Annual report
Yearly financial report prepared by a business that adheres to the requirements set forth by the Securities and Exchange Commission (SEC).

Antitrust immunity

Exemption from prosecution under antitrust laws. In the transportation industry, firms with antitrust immunity are permitted under certain conditions to set schedules and sometimes prices for the public benefit.

Applied research

Scientific study targeted for use in a product or process.

Assets

Anything of value owned by a company.

Audit

The verification of accounting records and business procedures conducted by an outside accounting service.

Average cost

Total production costs divided by the quantity produced.

Balance Sheet

A financial statement listing the total assets and liabilities of a company at a given time.

Bankruptcy

The condition in which a business cannot meet its debt obligations and petitions a federal district court either for reorganization of its debts (Chapter 11) or for liquidation of its assets (Chapter 7).

Basket clause

A provision specifying the amount of public pension funds that may be placed in investments not included on a state's legal list (see separate citation).

BDC

See Business development corporation

Benefit

Various services, such as health care, flextime, day care, insurance, and vacation, offered to employees as part of a hiring package. Typically subsidized in whole or in part by the business.

BIDCO

See Business and industrial development company

Billing cycle

A system designed to evenly distribute customer billing throughout the month, preventing clerical backlogs.

Blue chip security

A low-risk, low-yield security representing an interest in a very stable company.

Blue sky laws

A general term that denotes various states' laws regulating securities.

Bond

A written instrument executed by a bidder or contractor (the principal) and a second party (the surety or sureties) to assure fulfillment of the principal's obligations to a third party (the obligee or government) identified in the bond. If the principal's obligations are not met, the bond assures payment to the extent stipulated of any loss sustained by the obligee.

Bonding requirements

Terms contained in a bond (see separate citation).

Bonus

An amount of money paid to an employee as a reward for achieving certain business goals or objectives.

Brainstorming

A group session where employees contribute their ideas for solving a problem or meeting a company objective without fear of retribution or ridicule.

Brand name

The part of a brand, trademark, or service mark that can be spoken. It can be a word, letter, or group of words or letters.

Bridge financing

A short-term loan made in expectation of intermediateterm or long-term financing. Can be used when a company plans to go public in the near future.

Broker

One who matches resources available for innovation with those who need them.

Budget

An estimate of the spending necessary to complete a project or offer a service in comparison to cash-on-hand and expected earnings for the coming year, with an emphasis on cost control.

Business and industrial development company (BIDCO)
A private, for-profit financing corporation chartered by the state to provide both equity and long-term debt capital to small business owners (see separate citations for equity and debt capital).

Business birth
The formation of a new establishment or enterprise. The appearance of a new establishment or enterprise in the Small Business Data Base (see separate citation).

Business conditions
Outside factors that can affect the financial performance of a business.

Business contractions
The number of establishments that have decreased in employment during a specified time.

Business cycle
A period of economic recession and recovery. These cycles vary in duration.

Business death
The voluntary or involuntary closure of a firm or establishment. The disappearance of an establishment or enterprise from the Small Business Data Base (see separate citation).

Business development corporation (BDC)
A business financing agency, usually composed of the financial institutions in an area or state, organized to assist in financing businesses unable to obtain assistance through normal channels; the risk is spread among various members of the business development corporation, and interest rates may vary somewhat from those charged by member institutions. A venture capital firm in which shares of ownership are publicly held and to which the Investment Act of 1940 applies.

Business dissolution
For enumeration purposes, the absence of a business that was present in the prior time period from any current record.

Business entry
See Business birth

Business ethics
Moral values and principles espoused by members of the business community as a guide to fair and honest business practices.

Business exit
See Business death

Business expansions
The number of establishments that added employees during a specified time.

Business failure
Closure of a business causing a loss to at least one creditor.

Business format franchising
The purchase of the name, trademark, and an ongoing business plan of the parent corporation or franchisor by the franchisee.

Business license
A legal authorization issued by municipal and state governments and required for business operations.

Business name
Enterprises must register their business names with local governments usually on a "doing business as" (DBA) form. (This name is sometimes referred to as a "fictional name.") The procedure is part of the business licensing process and prevents any other business from using that same name for a similar business in the same locality.

Business norms
See Financial ratios

Business permit
See Business license

Business plan
A document that spells out a company's expected course of action for a specified period, usually including a detailed listing and analysis of risks and uncertainties. For the small business, it should examine the proposed products, the market, the industry, the management policies, the marketing policies, production needs, and financial needs. Frequently, it is used as a prospectus for potential investors and lenders.

Business proposal
See Business plan

Business service firm
An establishment primarily engaged in rendering services to other business organizations on a fee or contract basis.

Business start
For enumeration purposes, a business with a name or similar designation that did not exist in a prior time period.

Cafeteria plan
See Flexible benefit plan

Capacity
Level of a firm's, industry's, or nation's output corresponding to full practical utilization of available resources.

Capital
Assets less liabilities, representing the ownership interest in a business. A stock of accumulated goods, especially at a specified time and in contrast to income received during a specified time period. Accumulated goods devoted to production. Accumulated possessions calculated to bring income.

Capital expenditure
Expenses incurred by a business for improvements that will depreciate over time.

Capital gain
The monetary difference between the purchase price and the selling price of capital. Capital gains are taxed at a rate of 28% by the federal government.

Capital intensity
The relative importance of capital in the production process, usually expressed as the ratio of capital to labor but also sometimes as the ratio of capital to output.

Capital resource
The equipment, facilities and labor used to create products and services.

Catastrophic care
Medical and other services for acute and long-term illnesses that cost more than insurance coverage limits or that cost the amount most families may be expected to pay with their own resources.

CDC
See Certified development corporation

Certified development corporation (CDC)
A local area or statewide corporation or authority (for profit or nonprofit) that packages U.S. Small Business Administration (SBA), bank, state, and/or private money into financial assistance for existing business capital improvements. The SBA holds the second lien on its maximum share of 40 percent involvement. Each state has at least one certified development corporation. This program is called the SBA 504 Program.

Certified lenders
Banks that participate in the SBA guaranteed loan program (see separate citation). Such banks must have a good track record with the U.S. Small Business Administration (SBA) and must agree to certain conditions set forth by the agency. In return, the SBA agrees to process any guaranteed loan application within three business days.

Channel of distribution
The means used to transport merchandise from the manufacturer to the consumer.

Chapter 7 of the 1978 Bankruptcy Act
Provides for a court-appointed trustee who is responsible for liquidating a company's assets in order to settle outstanding debts.

Chapter 11 of the 1978 Bankruptcy Act
Allows the business owners to retain control of the company while working with their creditors to reorganize their finances and establish better business practices to prevent liquidation of assets.

Closely held corporation
A corporation in which the shares are held by a few persons, usually officers, employees, or others close to the management; these shares are rarely offered to the public.

Code of Federal Regulations
Codification of general and permanent rules of the federal government published in the Federal Register.

Code sharing
See Computer code sharing

Coinsurance
Upon meeting the deductible payment, health insurance participants may be required to make additional health care cost-sharing payments. Coinsurance is a payment of a fixed percentage of the cost of each service; copayment is usually a fixed amount to be paid with each service.

Collateral
Securities, evidence of deposit, or other property pledged by a borrower to secure repayment of a loan.

Collective ratemaking
The establishment of uniform charges for services by a group of businesses in the same industry.

Commercial insurance plan
See Underwriting

Commercial loans
Short-term renewable loans used to finance specific capital needs of a business.

Commercialization
The final stage of the innovation process, including production and distribution.

Common stock
The most frequently used instrument for purchasing ownership in private or public companies. Common stock generally carries the right to vote on certain corporate actions and may pay dividends, although it rarely does in venture investments. In liquidation, common stockholders are the last to share in the proceeds from the sale of a corporation's assets; bondholders and preferred shareholders have priority. Common stock is often used in firstround start-up financing.

Community development corporation
A corporation established to develop economic programs for a community and, in most cases, to provide financial support for such development.

Competitor
A business whose product or service is marketed for the same purpose/use and to the same consumer group as the product or service of another.

Consignment
A merchandising agreement, usually referring to secondhand shops, where the dealer pays the owner of an item a percentage of the profit when the item is sold.

Consortium
A coalition of organizations such as banks and corporations for ventures requiring large capital resources.

Consultant
An individual that is paid by a business to provide advice and expertise in a particular area.

Consumer price index
A measure of the fluctuation in prices between two points in time.

Consumer research
Research conducted by a business to obtain information about existing or potential consumer markets.

Continuation coverage
Health coverage offered for a specified period of time to employees who leave their jobs and to their widows, divorced spouses, or dependents.

Contractions
See Business contractions

Convertible preferred stock
A class of stock that pays a reasonable dividend and is convertible into common stock (see separate citation). Generally the convertible feature may only be exercised after being held for a stated period of time. This arrangement is usually considered second-round financing when a company needs equity to maintain its cash flow.

Convertible securities
A feature of certain bonds, debentures, or preferred stocks that allows them to be exchanged by the owner for another class of securities at a future date and in accordance with any other terms of the issue.

Copayment
See Coinsurance

Copyright
A legal form of protection available to creators and authors to safeguard their works from unlawful use or

Glossary

claim of ownership by others. Copyrights may be acquired for works of art, sculpture, music, and published or unpublished manuscripts. All copyrights should be registered at the Copyright Office of the Library of Congress.

Corporate financial ratios
The relationship between key figures found in a company's financial statement expressed as a numeric value. Used to evaluate risk and company performance. Also known as Financial averages, Operating ratios, and Business ratios.

Corporation
A legal entity, chartered by a state or the federal government, recognized as a separate entity having its own rights, privileges, and liabilities distinct from those of its members.

Cost containment
Actions taken by employers and insurers to curtail rising health care costs; for example, increasing employee cost sharing (see separate citation), requiring second opinions, or preadmission screening.

Cost sharing
The requirement that health care consumers contribute to their own medical care costs through deductibles and coinsurance (see separate citations). Cost sharing does not include the amounts paid in premiums. It is used to control utilization of services; for example, requiring a fixed amount to be paid with each health care service.

Cottage industry
Businesses based in the home in which the family members are the labor force and family-owned equipment is used to process the goods.

Credit Rating
A letter or number calculated by an organization (such as Dun & Bradstreet) to represent the ability and disposition of a business to meet its financial obligations.

Customer service
Various techniques used to ensure the satisfaction of a customer.

Cyclical peak
The upper turning point in a business cycle.

Cyclical trough
The lower turning point in a business cycle.

DBA (Doing business as)
See Business name

Death
See Business death

Debenture
A certificate given as acknowledgment of a debt (see separate citation) secured by the general credit of the issuing corporation. A bond, usually without security, issued by a corporation and sometimes convertible to common stock.

Debt
Something owed by one person to another. Financing in which a company receives capital that must be repaid; no ownership is transferred.

Debt capital
Business financing that normally requires periodic interest payments and repayment of the principal within a specified time.

Debt financing
See Debt capital

Debt securities
Loans such as bonds and notes that provide a specified rate of return for a specified period of time.

Deductible
A set amount that an individual must pay before any benefits are received.

Demand shock absorbers
A term used to describe the role that some small firms play by expanding their output levels to accommodate a transient surge in demand.

Demographics
Statistics on various markets, including age, income, and education, used to target specific products or services to appropriate consumer groups.

Demonstration
Showing that a product or process has been modified sufficiently to meet the needs of users.

Deregulation
The lifting of government restrictions; for example, the lifting of government restrictions on the entry of new businesses, the expansion of services, and the setting of prices in particular industries.

Disaster loans
Various types of physical and economic assistance available to individuals and businesses through the U.S. Small Business Administration (SBA). This is the only SBA loan program available for residential purposes.

Discrimination
The denial of the rights and privileges of employment based on factors such as age, race, religion, or gender.

Diseconomies of scale
The condition in which the costs of production increase faster than the volume of production.

Dissolution
See Business dissolution

Distribution
Delivering a product or process to the user.

Distributor
One who delivers merchandise to the user.

Diversified company
A company whose products and services are used by several different markets.

Doing business as (DBA)
See Business name

Dow Jones
An information services company that publishes the Wall Street Journal and other sources of financial information.

Dow Jones Industrial Average
An indicator of stock market performance.

Earned income
A tax term that refers to wages and salaries earned by the recipient, as opposed to monies earned through interest and dividends.

Economic efficiency
The use of productive resources to the fullest practical extent in the provision of the set of goods and services that is most preferred by purchasers in the economy.

Economic indicators
Statistics used to express the state of the economy. These include the length of the average work week, the rate of unemployment, and stock prices.

Economically disadvantaged
See Socially and economically disadvantaged

Economies of scale
See Scale economies

EEOC
See Equal Employment Opportunity Commission

8(a) Program
A program authorized by the Small Business Act that directs federal contracts to small businesses owned and operated by socially and economically disadvantaged individuals.

Electronic mail (e-mail)
The electronic transmission of mail via phone lines.

E-mail
See Electronic mail

Employee leasing
A contract by which employers arrange to have their workers hired by a leasing company and then leased back to them for a management fee. The leasing company typically assumes the administrative burden of payroll and provides a benefit package to the workers.

Employee tenure
The length of time an employee works for a particular employer.

Employer identification number
The business equivalent of a social security number. Assigned by the U.S. Internal Revenue Service.

Enterprise
An aggregation of all establishments owned by a parent company. An enterprise may consist of a single, independent establishment or include subsidiaries and other branches under the same ownership and control.

Enterprise zone
A designated area, usually found in inner cities and other areas with significant unemployment, where businesses receive tax credits and other incentives to entice them to establish operations there.

Entrepreneur
A person who takes the risk of organizing and operating a new business venture.

Entry
See Business entry

Equal Employment Opportunity Commission (EEOC)
A federal agency that ensures nondiscrimination in the hiring and firing practices of a business.

Equal opportunity employer
An employer who adheres to the standards set by the Equal Employment Opportunity Commission (see separate citation).

Equity
The ownership interest. Financing in which partial or total ownership of a company is surrendered in exchange for capital. An investor's financial return comes from dividend payments and from growth in the net worth of the business.

Equity capital
See Equity; Equity midrisk venture capital

Equity financing
See Equity; Equity midrisk venture capital

Equity midrisk venture capital
An unsecured investment in a company. Usually a purchase of ownership interest in a company that occurs in the later stages of a company's development.

Equity partnership
A limited partnership arrangement for providing start-up and seed capital to businesses.

Equity securities
See Equity

Equity-type
Debt financing subordinated to conventional debt.

Establishment
A single-location business unit that may be independent (a single-establishment enterprise) or owned by a parent enterprise.

Establishment and Enterprise Microdata File
See U.S. Establishment and Enterprise Microdata File

Establishment birth
See Business birth

Establishment Longitudinal Microdata File
See U.S. Establishment Longitudinal Microdata File

Ethics
See Business ethics

Evaluation
Determining the potential success of translating an invention into a product or process.

Exit
See Business exit

Experience rating
See Underwriting

Export
A product sold outside of the country.

Export license
A general or specific license granted by the U.S. Department of Commerce required of anyone wishing to export goods. Some restricted articles need approval from the U.S. Departments of State, Defense, or Energy.

Failure
See Business failure

Fair share agreement
An agreement reached between a franchisor and a minority business organization to extend business ownership to minorities by either reducing the amount of capital required or by setting aside certain marketing areas for minority business owners.

Feasibility study
A study to determine the likelihood that a proposed product or development will fulfill the objectives of a particular investor.

Federal Trade Commission (FTC)
Federal agency that promotes free enterprise and competition within the U.S.

Federal Trade Mark Act of 1946
See Lanham Act

Fictional name
See Business name

Fiduciary
An individual or group that hold assets in trust for a beneficiary.

Financial analysis
The techniques used to determine money needs in a business. Techniques include ratio analysis, calculation of return on investment, guides for measuring profitability, and break-even analysis to determine ultimate success.

Financial intermediary
A financial institution that acts as the intermediary between borrowers and lenders. Banks, savings and loan associations, finance companies, and venture capital companies are major financial intermediaries in the United States.

Financial ratios
See Corporate financial ratios; Industry financial ratios

Financial statement
A written record of business finances, including balance sheets and profit and loss statements.

Financing
See First-stage financing; Second-stage financing; Thirdstage financing

First-stage financing
Financing provided to companies that have expended their initial capital, and require funds to start full-scale manufacturing and sales. Also known as First-round financing.

Fiscal year
Any twelve-month period used by businesses for accounting purposes.

504 Program
See Certified development corporation

Flexible benefit plan
A plan that offers a choice among cash and/or qualified benefits such as group term life insurance,

accident and health insurance, group legal services, dependent care assistance, and vacations.

FOB
See Free on board

Format franchising
See Business format franchising; Franchising

401(k) plan
A financial plan where employees contribute a percentage of their earnings to a fund that is invested in stocks, bonds, or money markets for the purpose of saving money for retirement.

Four Ps
Marketing terms referring to Product, Price, Place, and Promotion.

Franchising
A form of licensing by which the owner-the franchisor- distributes or markets a product, method, or service through affiliated dealers called franchisees. The product, method, or service being marketed is identified by a brand name, and the franchisor maintains control over the marketing methods employed. The franchisee is often given exclusive access to a defined geographic area.

Free on board (FOB)
A pricing term indicating that the quoted price includes the cost of loading goods into transport vessels at a specified place.

Frictional unemployment
See Unemployment

FTC
See Federal Trade Commission

Fulfillment
The systems necessary for accurate delivery of an ordered item, including subscriptions and direct marketing.

Full-time workers
Generally, those who work a regular schedule of more than 35 hours per week.

Garment registration number
A number that must appear on every garment sold in the U.S. to indicate the manufacturer of the garment,

which may or may not be the same as the label under which the garment is sold. The U.S. Federal Trade Commission assigns and regulates garment registration numbers.

Gatekeeper
A key contact point for entry into a network.

GDP
See Gross domestic product

General obligation bond
A municipal bond secured by the taxing power of the municipality. The Tax Reform Act of 1986 limits the purposes for which such bonds may be issued and establishes volume limits on the extent of their issuance.

GNP
See Gross national product

Good Housekeeping Seal
Seal appearing on products that signifies the fulfillment of the standards set by the Good Housekeeping Institute to protect consumer interests.

Goods sector
All businesses producing tangible goods, including agriculture, mining, construction, and manufacturing businesses.

GPO
See Gross product originating

Gross domestic product (GDP)
The part of the nation's gross national product (see separate citation) generated by private business using resources from within the country.

Gross national product (GNP)
The most comprehensive single measure of aggregate economic output. Represents the market value of the total output of goods and services produced by a nation's economy.

Gross product originating (GPO)
A measure of business output estimated from the income or production side using employee compensation, profit income, net interest, capital consumption, and indirect business taxes.

HAL
See Handicapped assistance loan program

Handicapped assistance loan program (HAL)
Low-interest direct loan program through the U.S. Small Business Administration (SBA) for handicapped persons. The SBA requires that these persons demonstrate that their disability is such that it is impossible for them to secure employment, thus making it necessary to go into their own business to make a living.

Health maintenance organization (HMO)
Organization of physicians and other health care professionals that provides health services to subscribers and their dependents on a prepaid basis.

Health provider
An individual or institution that gives medical care. Under Medicare, an institutional provider is a hospital, skilled nursing facility, home health agency, or provider of certain physical therapy services.

Hispanic
A person of Cuban, Mexican, Puerto Rican, Latin American (Central or South American), European Spanish, or other Spanish-speaking origin or ancestry.

HMO
See Health maintenance organization

Home-based business
A business with an operating address that is also a residential address (usually the residential address of the proprietor).

Hub-and-spoke system
A system in which flights of an airline from many different cities (the spokes) converge at a single airport (the hub). After allowing passengers sufficient time to make connections, planes then depart for different cities.

Human Resources Management
A business program designed to oversee recruiting, pay, benefits, and other issues related to the company's work force, including planning to determine the optimal use of labor to increase production, thereby increasing profit.

Idea
An original concept for a new product or process.

Import
Products produced outside the country in which they are consumed.

Income
Money or its equivalent, earned or accrued, resulting from the sale of goods and services.

Income statement
A financial statement that lists the profits and losses of a company at a given time.

Incorporation
The filing of a certificate of incorporation with a state's secretary of state, thereby limiting the business owner's liability.

Incubator
A facility designed to encourage entrepreneurship and minimize obstacles to new business formation and growth, particularly for high-technology firms, by housing a number of fledgling enterprises that share an array of services, such as meeting areas, secretarial services, accounting, research library, on-site financial and management counseling, and word processing facilities.

Independent contractor
An individual considered self-employed (see separate citation) and responsible for paying Social Security taxes and income taxes on earnings.

Indirect health coverage
Health insurance obtained through another individual's health care plan; for example, a spouse's employersponsored plan.

Industrial development authority
The financial arm of a state or other political subdivision established for the purpose of financing economic development in an area, usually through loans to nonprofit organizations, which in turn provide facilities for manufacturing and other industrial operations.

Industry financial ratios
Corporate financial ratios averaged for a specified industry. These are used for comparison purposes and reveal industry trends and identify differences between the performance of a specific company and the performance of its industry. Also known as Industrial averages, Industry ratios, Financial averages, and Business or Industrial norms.

Inflation
Increases in volume of currency and credit, generally resulting in a sharp and continuing rise in price levels.

Informal capital
Financing from informal, unorganized sources; includes informal debt capital such as trade credit or loans from friends and relatives and equity capital from informal investors.

Initial public offering (IPO)
A corporation's first offering of stock to the public.

Innovation
The introduction of a new idea into the marketplace in the form of a new product or service or an improvement in organization or process.

Intellectual property
Any idea or work that can be considered proprietary in nature and is thus protected from infringement by others.

Internal capital
Debt or equity financing obtained from the owner or through retained business earnings.

Internet
A government-designed computer network that contains large amounts of information and is accessible through various vendors for a fee.

Intrapreneurship
The state of employing entrepreneurial principles to nonentrepreneurial situations.

Invention
The tangible form of a technological idea, which could include a laboratory prototype, drawings, formulas, etc.

IPO
See Initial public offering

Job description
The duties and responsibilities required in a particular position.

Job tenure
A period of time during which an individual is continuously employed in the same job.

Joint marketing agreements
Agreements between regional and major airlines, often involving the coordination of flight schedules, fares, and baggage transfer. These agreements help regional carriers operate at lower cost.

Joint venture
Venture in which two or more people combine efforts in a particular business enterprise, usually a single transaction or a limited activity, and agree to share the profits and losses jointly or in proportion to their contributions.

Keogh plan
Designed for self-employed persons and unincorporated businesses as a tax-deferred pension account.

Labor force
Civilians considered eligible for employment who are also willing and able to work.

Labor force participation rate
The civilian labor force as a percentage of the civilian population.

Labor intensity
The relative importance of labor in the production process, usually measured as the capital-labor ratio; i.e., the ratio of units of capital (typically, dollars of tangible assets) to the number of employees. The higher the capital-labor ratio exhibited by a firm or industry, the lower the capital intensity of that firm or industry is said to be.

Labor surplus area
An area in which there exists a high unemployment rate. In procurement (see separate citation), extra points are given to firms in counties that are designated a labor surplus area; this information is requested on procurement bid sheets.

Labor union
An organization of similarly-skilled workers who collectively bargain with management over the conditions of employment.

Laboratory prototype
See Prototype

LAN
See Local Area Network

Lanham Act
Refers to the Federal Trade Mark Act of 1946. Protects registered trademarks, trade names, and other service marks used in commerce.

Large business-dominated industry
Industry in which a minimum of 60 percent of employment or sales is in firms with more than 500 workers.

LBO
See Leveraged buy-out

Leader pricing
A reduction in the price of a good or service in order to generate more sales of that good or service.

Legal list
A list of securities selected by a state in which certain institutions and fiduciaries (such as pension funds, insurance companies, and banks) may invest. Securities not on the list are not eligible for investment. Legal lists typically restrict investments to high quality securities meeting certain specifications. Generally, investment is limited to U.S. securities and investment-grade blue chip securities (see separate citation).

Leveraged buy-out (LBO)
The purchase of a business or a division of a corporation through a highly leveraged financing package.

Liability
An obligation or duty to perform a service or an act. Also defined as money owed.

License
A legal agreement granting to another the right to use a technological innovation.

Limited Liability Company
A hybrid type of legal structure that provides the limited liability features of a corporation and the tax efficiencies and operational flexibility of a partnership. Depending on the state, the members can consist of a single individual (one owner), two or more individuals, corporations or other LLCs.

Limited liability partnerships
A business organization that allows limited partners to enjoy limited personal liability while general partners have unlimited personal liability

Liquidity
The ability to convert a security into cash promptly.

Loans
See Commercial loans; Disaster loans; SBA direct loans; SBA guaranteed loans; SBA special lending institution categories Local Area Network (LAN) Computer networks contained within a single building or small area; used to facilitate the sharing of information.

Local development corporation
An organization, usually made up of local citizens of a community, designed to improve the economy of the area by inducing business and industry to locate and expand there. A local development corporation establishes a capability to finance local growth.

Long-haul rates
Rates charged by a transporter in which the distance traveled is more than 800 miles.

Long-term debt
An obligation that matures in a period that exceeds five years.

Low-grade bond
A corporate bond that is rated below investment grade by the major rating agencies (Standard and Poor's, Moody's).

Macro-efficiency
Efficiency as it pertains to the operation of markets and market systems.

Managed care
A cost-effective health care program initiated by employers whereby low-cost health care is made available to the employees in return for exclusive patronage to program doctors.

Management Assistance Programs
See SBA Management Assistance Programs

Management and technical assistance
A term used by many programs to mean business (as opposed to technological) assistance.

Mandated benefits
Specific treatments, providers, or individuals required by law to be included in commercial health plans.

Market evaluation
The use of market information to determine the sales potential of a specific product or process.

Market failure
The situation in which the workings of a competitive market do not produce the best results from the point of view of the entire society.

Market information
Data of any type that can be used for market evaluation, which could include demographic data, technology forecasting, regulatory changes, etc.

Market research
A systematic collection, analysis, and reporting of data about the market and its preferences, opinions, trends, and plans; used for corporate decision-making.

Market share
In a particular market, the percentage of sales of a specific product.

Marketing
Promotion of goods or services through various media.

Master Establishment List (MEL)
A list of firms in the United States developed by the U.S. Small Business Administration; firms can be selected by industry, region, state, standard metropolitan statistical area (see separate citation), county, and zip code.

Maturity
The date upon which the principal or stated value of a bond or other indebtedness becomes due and payable.

Medicaid (Title XIX)
A federally aided, state-operated and administered program that provides medical benefits for certain low income persons in need of health and medical care who are eligible for one of the government's welfare cash payment programs, including the aged, the blind, the disabled, and members of families with dependent children where one parent is absent, incapacitated, or unemployed.

Medicare (Title XVIII)
A nationwide health insurance program for disabled and aged persons. Health insurance is available to insured persons without regard to income. Monies from payroll taxes cover hospital insurance and monies from general revenues and beneficiary premiums pay for supplementary medical insurance.

MEL
See Master Establishment List

Merchant Status
The relationship between a company and a bank or credit card company allowing the company to accept credit card payments

MESBIC
See Minority enterprise small business investment corporation

MET
See Multiple employer trust

Metropolitan statistical area (MSA)
A means used by the government to define large population centers that may transverse different governmental jurisdictions. For example, the Washington, D.C. MSA includes the District of Columbia and contiguous parts of Maryland and Virginia because all of these geopolitical areas comprise one population and economic operating unit.

Mezzanine financing
See Third-stage financing

Micro-efficiency
Efficiency as it pertains to the operation of individual firms.

Microdata
Information on the characteristics of an individual business firm.

Microloan
An SBA loan program that helps entrepreneurs obtain loans from less than $100 to $25,000.

Mid-term debt
An obligation that matures within one to five years.

Midrisk venture capital
See Equity midrisk venture capital

Minimum premium plan
A combination approach to funding an insurance plan aimed primarily at premium tax savings. The employer self-funds a fixed percentage of estimated monthly claims and the insurance company insures the excess.

Minimum wage
The lowest hourly wage allowed by the federal government.

Minority Business Development Agency
Contracts with private firms throughout the nation to sponsor Minority Business Development Centers which provide minority firms with advice and technical assistance on a fee basis.

Minority Enterprise Small Business Investment Corporation (MESBIC)
A federally funded private venture capital firm licensed by the U.S. Small Business Administration to provide capital to minority-owned businesses (see separate citation).

Minority-owned business
Businesses owned by those who are socially or economically disadvantaged (see separate citation).

Mission statement
A short statement describing a company's function, markets and competitive advantages.

Mom and Pop business
A small store or enterprise having limited capital, principally employing family members.

Multi-employer plan
A health plan to which more than one employer is required to contribute and that may be maintained through a collective bargaining agreement and required to meet standards prescribed by the U.S. Department of Labor.

Multi-level marketing
A system of selling in which you sign up other people to assist you and they, in turn, recruit others to help them. Some entrepreneurs have built successful companies on this concept because the main focus of their activities is their product and product sales.

Multiple employer trust (MET)
A self-funded benefit plan generally geared toward small employers sharing a common interest.

NASDAQ
See National Association of Securities Dealers Automated Quotations

National Association of Securities Dealers Automated Quotations
Provides price quotes on over-the-counter securities as well as securities listed on the New York Stock Exchange.

National income
Aggregate earnings of labor and property arising from the production of goods and services in a nation's economy.

Net assets
See Net worth

Net income
The amount remaining from earnings and profits after all expenses and costs have been met or deducted. Also known as Net earnings.

Net profit
Money earned after production and overhead expenses (see separate citations) have been deducted.

Net worth
The difference between a company's total assets and its total liabilities.

Network
A chain of interconnected individuals or organizations sharing information and/or services.

New York Stock Exchange (NYSE)
The oldest stock exchange in the U.S. Allows for trading in stocks, bonds, warrants, options, and rights that meet listing requirements.

Niche
A career or business for which a person is well-suited. Also, a product which fulfills one need of a particular market segment, often with little or no competition.

Nodes
One workstation in a network, either local area or wide area (see separate citations).

Nonbank bank
A bank that either accepts deposits or makes loans, but not both. Used to create many new branch banks.

Noncompetitive awards
A method of contracting whereby the federal government negotiates with only one contractor to supply a product or service.

Nonmember bank
A state-regulated bank that does not belong to the federal bank system.

Nonprofit
An organization that has no shareholders, does not distribute profits, and is without federal and state tax liabilities.

Norms
See Financial ratios

North American Free Trade Agreement (NAFTA)
Passed in 1993, NAFTA eliminates trade barriers among businesses in the U.S., Canada, and Mexico.

NYSE
See New York Stock Exchange

Occupational Safety & Health Administration (OSHA)
Federal agency that regulates health and safety standards within the workplace.

Operating Expenses
Business expenditures not directly associated with the production of goods or services.

Optimal firm size
The business size at which the production cost per unit of output (average cost) is, in the long run, at its minimum.

Organizational chart
A hierarchical chart tracking the chain of command within an organization.

OSHA
See Occupational Safety & Health Administration

Overhead
Expenses, such as employee benefits and building utilities, incurred by a business that are unrelated to the actual product or service sold.

Owner's capital
Debt or equity funds provided by the owner(s) of a business; sources of owner's capital are personal savings, sales of assets, or loans from financial institutions.

P & L
See Profit and loss statement

Part-time workers
Normally, those who work less than 35 hours per week. The Tax Reform Act indicated that part-time workers who work less than 17.5 hours per week may be excluded from health plans for purposes of complying with federal nondiscrimination rules.

Part-year workers
Those who work less than 50 weeks per year.

Partnership
Two or more parties who enter into a legal relationship to conduct business for profit. Defined by the U.S. Internal Revenue Code as joint ventures, syndicates, groups, pools, and other associations of two or more persons organized for profit that are not specifically classified in the IRS code as corporations or proprietorships.

Patent
A grant made by the government assuring an inventor the sole right to make, use, and sell an invention for a period of 17 years.

PC
See Professional corporation

Peak
See Cyclical peak

Pension
A series of payments made monthly, semiannually, annually, or at other specified intervals during the lifetime of the pensioner for distribution upon retirement. The term is sometimes used to denote the portion of the retirement allowance financed by the employer's contributions.

Pension fund
A fund established to provide for the payment of pension benefits; the collective contributions made by all of the parties to the pension plan.

Performance appraisal
An established set of objective criteria, based on job description and requirements, that is used to evaluate the performance of an employee in a specific job.

Permit
See Business license

Plan
See Business plan

Pooling
An arrangement for employers to achieve efficiencies and lower health costs by joining together to purchase group health insurance or self-insurance.

PPO
See Preferred provider organization

Preferred lenders program
See SBA special lending institution categories

Preferred provider organization (PPO)
A contractual arrangement with a health care services organization that agrees to discount its health care rates in return for faster payment and/or a patient base.

Premiums
The amount of money paid to an insurer for health insurance under a policy. The premium is generally paid periodically (e.g., monthly), and often is split between the employer and the employee. Unlike deductibles and coinsurance or copayments, premiums are paid for coverage whether or not benefits are actually used.

Prime-age workers
Employees 25 to 54 years of age.

Prime contract
A contract awarded directly by the U.S. Federal Government.

Private company
See Closely held corporation

Private placement
A method of raising capital by offering for sale an investment or business to a small group of investors (generally avoiding registration with the Securities and Exchange Commission or state securities registration agencies). Also known as Private financing or Private offering.

Pro forma
The use of hypothetical figures in financial statements to represent future expenditures, debts, and other potential financial expenses.

Proactive
Taking the initiative to solve problems and anticipate future events before they happen, instead of reacting to an already existing problem or waiting for a difficult situation to occur.

Procurement
A contract from an agency of the federal government for goods or services from a small business.

Product development
The stage of the innovation process where research is translated into a product or process through evaluation, adaptation, and demonstration.

Product franchising
An arrangement for a franchisee to use the name and to produce the product line of the franchisor or parent corporation.

Production
The manufacture of a product.

Production prototype
See Prototype

Productivity
A measurement of the number of goods produced during a specific amount of time.

Professional corporation (PC)
Organized by members of a profession such as medicine, dentistry, or law for the purpose of conducting their professional activities as a corporation. Liability of a member or shareholder is limited in the same manner as in a business corporation.

Profit and loss statement (P & L)
The summary of the incomes (total revenues) and costs of a company's operation during a specific period of time. Also known as Income and expense statement.

Proposal
See Business plan

Proprietorship
The most common legal form of business ownership; about 85 percent of all small businesses are proprietorships. The liability of the owner is unlimited in this form of ownership.

Prospective payment system
A cost-containment measure included in the Social Security Amendments of 1983 whereby Medicare payments to hospitals are based on established prices, rather than on cost reimbursement.

Prototype
A model that demonstrates the validity of the concept of an invention (laboratory prototype); a model that meets the needs of the manufacturing process and the user (production prototype).

Prudent investor rule or standard
A legal doctrine that requires fiduciaries to make investments using the prudence, diligence, and intelligence that would be used by a prudent person in making similar investments. Because fiduciaries make investments on behalf of third-party beneficiaries, the standard results in very conservative investments. Until recently, most state regulations required the fiduciary to apply this standard to each investment. Newer, more progressive regulations permit fiduciaries to apply this standard to the portfolio taken as a whole, thereby allowing a fiduciary to balance a portfolio with higher-yield, higher-risk investments. In states with more progressive regulations, practically every type of security is eligible for inclusion in the portfolio of investments made by a fiduciary, provided that the portfolio investments, in their totality, are those of a prudent person.

Public equity markets
Organized markets for trading in equity shares such as common stocks, preferred stocks, and warrants. Includes markets for both regularly traded and nonregularly traded securities.

Public offering
General solicitation for participation in an investment opportunity. Interstate public offerings are supervised by the U.S. Securities and Exchange Commission (see separate citation).

Quality control
The process by which a product is checked and tested to ensure consistent standards of high quality.

Rate of return
The yield obtained on a security or other investment based on its purchase price or its current market price. The total rate of return is current income plus or minus capital appreciation or depreciation.

Real property
Includes the land and all that is contained on it.

Realignment
See Resource realignment

Recession
Contraction of economic activity occurring between the peak and trough (see separate citations) of a business cycle.

Regulated market
A market in which the government controls the forces of supply and demand, such as who may enter and what price may be charged.

Regulation D
A vehicle by which small businesses make small offerings and private placements of securities with limited disclosure requirements. It was designed to ease the burdens imposed on small businesses utilizing this method of capital formation.

Regulatory Flexibility Act
An act requiring federal agencies to evaluate the impact of their regulations on small businesses before the regulations are issued and to consider less burdensome alternatives.

Research
The initial stage of the innovation process, which includes idea generation and invention.

Research and development financing
A tax-advantaged partnership set up to finance product development for start-ups as well as more mature companies.

Resource mobility
The ease with which labor and capital move from firm to firm or from industry to industry.

Resource realignment
The adjustment of productive resources to interindustry changes in demand.

Resources
The sources of support or help in the innovation process, including sources of financing, technical evaluation, market evaluation, management and business assistance, etc.

Retained business earnings
Business profits that are retained by the business rather than being distributed to the shareholders as dividends.

Return on investment
A profitability measure that evaluates the performance of a business by dividing net profit by net worth.

Revolving credit
An agreement with a lending institution for an amount of money, which cannot exceed a set maximum, over a specified period of time. Each time the borrower repays a portion of the loan, the amount of the repayment may be borrowed yet again.

Risk capital
See Venture capital

Risk management
The act of identifying potential sources of financial loss and taking action to minimize their negative impact.

Routing
The sequence of steps necessary to complete a product during production.

S corporations
See Sub chapter S corporations

SBA
See Small Business Administration

SBA direct loans
Loans made directly by the U.S. Small Business Administration (SBA); monies come from funds appropriated specifically for this purpose. In general, SBA direct loans carry interest rates slightly lower than those in the private financial markets and are available only to applicants unable to secure private financing or an SBA guaranteed loan.

SBA 504 Program
See Certified development corporation

SBA guaranteed loans
Loans made by lending institutions in which the U.S. Small Business Administration (SBA) will pay a prior agreed-upon percentage of the outstanding principal in the event the borrower of the loan defaults. The terms of the loan and the interest rate are negotiated between theborrower and the lending institution, within set parameters.

SBA loans
See Disaster loans; SBA direct loans; SBA guaranteed loans; SBA special lending institution categories

SBA Management Assistance Programs
Classes, workshops, counseling, and publications offered by the U.S. Small Business Administration.

SBA special lending institution categories
U.S. Small Business Administration (SBA) loan program in which the SBA promises certified banks a 72-hour turnaround period in giving its approval for a loan, and in which preferred lenders in a pilot program are allowed to write SBA loans without seeking prior SBA approval.

SBDB
See Small Business Data Base

SBDC
See Small business development centers

SBI
See Small business institutes program

SBIC
See Small business investment corporation

SBIR Program
See Small Business Innovation Development Act of 1982

Scale economies
The decline of the production cost per unit of output (average cost) as the volume of output increases.

Scale efficiency
The reduction in unit cost available to a firm when producing at a higher output volume.

SCORE
See Service Corps of Retired Executives

SEC
See Securities and Exchange Commission

SECA
See Self-Employment Contributions Act

Second-stage financing
Working capital for the initial expansion of a company that is producing, shipping, and has growing accounts receivable and inventories. Also known as Second-round financing.

Secondary market
A market established for the purchase and sale of outstanding securities following their initial distribution.

Secondary worker
Any worker in a family other than the person who is the primary source of income for the family.

Secondhand capital
Previously used and subsequently resold capital equipment (e.g., buildings and machinery).

Securities and Exchange Commission (SEC)
Federal agency charged with regulating the trade of securities to prevent unethical practices in the investor market.

Securitized debt
A marketing technique that converts long-term loans to marketable securities.

Seed capital
Venture financing provided in the early stages of the innovation process, usually during product development.

Self-employed person
One who works for a profit or fees in his or her own business, profession, or trade, or who operates a farm.

Self-Employment Contributions Act (SECA)
Federal law that governs the self-employment tax (see separate citation).

Self-employment income
Income covered by Social Security if a business earns a net income of at least $400.00 during the year. Taxes are paid on earnings that exceed $400.00.

Self-employment retirement plan
See Keogh plan

Self-employment tax
Required tax imposed on self-employed individuals for the provision of Social Security and Medicare. The tax must be paid quarterly with estimated income tax statements.

Self-funding
A health benefit plan in which a firm uses its own funds to pay claims, rather than transferring the financial risks of paying claims to an outside insurer in exchange for premium payments.

Service Corps of Retired Executives (SCORE)
Volunteers for the SBA Management Assistance Program who provide one-on-one counseling and teach workshops and seminars for small firms.

Service firm
See Business service firm

Service sector
Broadly defined, all U.S. industries that produce intangibles, including the five major industry divisions of transportation, communications, and utilities; wholesale trade; retail trade; finance, insurance, and real estate; and services.

Set asides
See Small business set asides

Short-haul service
A type of transportation service in which the transporter supplies service between cities where the maximum distance is no more than 200 miles.

Short-term debt
An obligation that matures in one year.

SIC codes
See Standard Industrial Classification codes

Single-establishment enterprise
See Establishment

Small business
An enterprise that is independently owned and operated, is not dominant in its field, and employs fewer than 500 people. For SBA purposes, the U.S. Small Business Administration (SBA) considers various other factors (such as gross annual sales) in determining size of a business.

Small Business Administration (SBA)
An independent federal agency that provides assistance with loans, management, and advocating interests before other federal agencies.

Small Business Data Base
A collection of microdata (see separate citation) files on individual firms developed and maintained by the U.S. Small Business Administration.

Small business development centers (SBDC)
Centers that provide support services to small businesses, such as individual counseling, SBA advice, seminars and conferences, and other learning center activities. Most services are free of charge, or available at minimal cost.

Small business development corporation
See Certified development corporation

Small business-dominated industry
Industry in which a minimum of 60 percent of employment or sales is in firms with fewer than 500 employees.

Small Business Innovation Development Act of 1982
Federal statute requiring federal agencies with large extramural research and development budgets to allocate a certain percentage of these funds to small research and development firms. The program, called the Small Business Innovation Research (SBIR) Program, is designed to stimulate technological innovation and make greater use of small businesses in meeting national innovation needs.

Small business institutes (SBI) program
Cooperative arrangements made by U.S. Small Business Administration district offices and local colleges and universities to provide small business firms with graduate students to counsel them without charge.

Small business investment corporation (SBIC)
A privately owned company licensed and funded through the U.S. Small Business Administration and private sector sources to provide equity or debt capital to small businesses.

Small business set asides
Procurement (see separate citation) opportunities required by law to be on all contracts under $10,000 or a certain percentage of an agency's total procurement expenditure.

Smaller firms
For U.S. Department of Commerce purposes, those firms not included in the Fortune 1000.

SMSA
See Metropolitan statistical area

Socially and economically disadvantaged
Individuals who have been subjected to racial or ethnic prejudice or cultural bias without regard to their qualities as individuals, and whose abilities to compete are impaired because of diminished opportunities to obtain capital and credit.

Sole proprietorship
An unincorporated, one-owner business, farm, or professional practice.

Special lending institution categories
See SBA special lending institution categories

Standard Industrial Classification (SIC) codes
Four-digit codes established by the U.S. Federal Government to categorize businesses by type of economic activity; the first two digits correspond to major groups such as construction and manufacturing, while the last two digits correspond to subgroups such as home construction or highway construction.

Start-up
A new business, at the earliest stages of development and financing.

Start-up costs
Costs incurred before a business can commence operations.

Start-up financing
Financing provided to companies that have either completed product development and initial marketing or have been in business for less than one year but have not yet sold their product commercially.

Stock
A certificate of equity ownership in a business.

Stop-loss coverage
Insurance for a self-insured plan that reimburses the company for any losses it might incur in its health claims beyond a specified amount.

Strategic planning
Projected growth and development of a business to establish a guiding direction for the future. Also used to determine which market segments to explore for optimal sales of products or services.

Structural unemployment
See Unemployment

Sub chapter S corporations
Corporations that are considered noncorporate for tax purposes but legally remain corporations.

Subcontract
A contract between a prime contractor and a subcontractor, or between subcontractors, to furnish supplies or services for performance of a prime contract (see separate citation) or a subcontract.

Surety bonds
Bonds providing reimbursement to an individual, company, or the government if a firm fails to complete a contract. The U.S. Small Business Administration guarantees surety bonds in a program much like the SBA guaranteed loan program (see separate citation).

Swing loan
See Bridge financing

Target market
The clients or customers sought for a business' product or service.

Targeted Jobs Tax Credit
Federal legislation enacted in 1978 that provides a tax credit to an employer who hires structurally unemployed individuals.

Tax number
A number assigned to a business by a state revenue department that enables the business to buy goods without paying sales tax.

Taxable bonds
An interest-bearing certificate of public or private indebtedness. Bonds are issued by public agencies to finance economic development.

Glossary

Technical assistance
See Management and technical assistance

Technical evaluation
Assessment of technological feasibility.

Technology
The method in which a firm combines and utilizes labor and capital resources to produce goods or services; the application of science for commercial or industrial purposes.

Technology transfer
The movement of information about a technology or intellectual property from one party to another for use.

Tenure
See Employee tenure

Term
The length of time for which a loan is made.

Terms of a note
The conditions or limits of a note; includes the interest rate per annum, the due date, and transferability and convertibility features, if any.

Third-party administrator
An outside company responsible for handling claims and performing administrative tasks associated with health insurance plan maintenance.

Third-stage financing
Financing provided for the major expansion of a company whose sales volume is increasing and that is breaking even or profitable. These funds are used for further plant expansion, marketing, working capital, or development of an improved product. Also known as Third-round or Mezzanine financing.

Time management
Skills and scheduling techniques used to maximize productivity.

Trade credit
Credit extended by suppliers of raw materials or finished products. In an accounting statement, trade credit is referred to as "accounts payable."

Trade name
The name under which a company conducts business, or by which its business, goods, or services are identified. It may or may not be registered as a trademark.

Trade periodical
A publication with a specific focus on one or more aspects of business and industry.

Trade secret
Competitive advantage gained by a business through the use of a unique manufacturing process or formula.

Trade show
An exhibition of goods or services used in a particular industry. Typically held in exhibition centers where exhibitors rent space to display their merchandise.

Trademark
A graphic symbol, device, or slogan that identifies a business. A business has property rights to its trademark from the inception of its use, but it is still prudent to register all trademarks with the Trademark Office of the U.S. Department of Commerce.

Trend
A statistical measurement used to track changes that occur over time.

Trough
See Cyclical trough

UCC
See Uniform Commercial Code

UL
See Underwriters Laboratories

Underwriters Laboratories (UL)
One of several private firms that tests products and processes to determine their safety. Although various firms can provide this kind of testing service, many local and insurance codes specify UL certification.

Underwriting
A process by which an insurer determines whether or not and on what basis it will accept an application for insurance. In an experience-rated plan, premiums are based on a firm's or group's past claims; factors other than prior claims are used for community-rated or manually rated plans.

Unfair competition

Refers to business practices, usually unethical, such as using unlicensed products, pirating merchandise, or misleading the public through false advertising, which give the offending business an unequitable advantage over others.

Unfunded accrued liability

The excess of total liabilities, both present and prospective, over present and prospective assets.

Unemployment

The joblessness of individuals who are willing to work, who are legally and physically able to work, and who are seeking work. Unemployment may represent the temporary joblessness of a worker between jobs (frictional unemployment) or the joblessness of a worker whose skills are not suitable for jobs available in the labor market (structural unemployment).

Uniform Commercial Code (UCC)

A code of laws governing commercial transactions across the U.S., except Louisiana. Their purpose is to bring uniformity to financial transactions.

Uniform product code (UPC symbol)

A computer-readable label comprised of ten digits and stripes that encodes what a product is and how much it costs. The first five digits are assigned by the Uniform Product Code Council, and the last five digits by the individual manufacturer.

Unit cost

See Average cost

UPC symbol

See Uniform product code

U.S. Establishment and Enterprise Microdata (USEEM) File

A cross-sectional database containing information on employment, sales, and location for individual enterprises and establishments with employees that have a Dun & Bradstreet credit rating.

U.S. Establishment Longitudinal Microdata (USELM) File

A database containing longitudinally linked sample microdata on establishments drawn from the U.S.

Establishment and Enterprise Microdata file (see separate citation).

U.S. Small Business Administration 504 Program

See Certified development corporation

USEEM

See U.S. Establishment and Enterprise Microdata File

USELM

See U.S. Establishment Longitudinal Microdata File

VCN

See Venture capital network

Venture capital

Money used to support new or unusual business ventures that exhibit above-average growth rates, significant potential for market expansion, and are in need of additional financing to sustain growth or further research and development; equity or equity-type financing traditionally provided at the commercialization stage, increasingly available prior to commercialization.

Venture capital company

A company organized to provide seed capital to a business in its formation stage, or in its first or second stage of expansion. Funding is obtained through public or private pension funds, commercial banks and bank holding companies, small business investment corporations licensed by the U.S. Small Business Administration, private venture capital firms, insurance companies, investment management companies, bank trust departments, industrial companies seeking to diversify their investment, and investment bankers acting as intermediaries for other investors or directly investing on their own behalf.

Venture capital limited partnerships

Designed for business development, these partnerships are an institutional mechanism for providing capital for young, technology-oriented businesses. The investors' money is pooled and invested in money market assets until venture investments have been selected. The general partners are experienced investment managers who select and invest the equity and debt securities of firms with high growth potential and the ability to go public in the near future.

Venture capital network (VCN)
A computer database that matches investors with entrepreneurs.

WAN
See Wide Area Network

Wide Area Network (WAN)
Computer networks linking systems throughout a state or around the world in order to facilitate the sharing of information.

Withholding
Federal, state, social security, and unemployment taxes withheld by the employer from employees' wages; employers are liable for these taxes and the corporate umbrella and bankruptcy will not exonerate an employer from paying back payroll withholding. Employers should escrow these funds in a separate account and disperse them quarterly to withholding authorities.

Workers' compensation
A state-mandated form of insurance covering workers injured in job-related accidents. In some states, the state is the insurer; in other states, insurance must be acquired from commercial insurance firms. Insurance rates are based on a number of factors, including salaries, firm history, and risk of occupation.

Working capital
Refers to a firm's short-term investment of current assets, including cash, short-term securities, accounts receivable, and inventories.

Yield
The rate of income returned on an investment, expressed as a percentage. Income yield is obtained by dividing the current dollar income by the current market price of the security. Net yield or yield to maturity is the current income yield minus any premium above par or plus any discount from par in purchase price, with the adjustment spread over the period from the date of purchase to the date of maturity.

Index

Listings in this index are arranged alphabetically by business plan type, then alphabetically by business plan name. Users are provided with the volume number in which the plan appears.

Index